Spirit of Himalaya

the story of a Truth seeker

Swami Amar Jyoti

8 Full Color Plates

Book designed by the author

Library of Congress Catalog Card Number: 78-73995

Published by:
        Truth Consciousness Inc.
        3403 Sweetwater Drive
        Tucson, Arizona 85705
        602-743-0384

Manufactured in the United States of America

ISBN 0-933572-00-X

This book .....

... is neither a biography of any *particular* seeker or master, nor the author's autobiography. The characters, episodes and locations, isolated or as a whole, are not necessarily correlated with any of the above ...

... But again, the story is really everyone's, at least in the sense that the life we see here can be a future life for any of us; the steps taken here and the attachments purged away might be anyone's, or everyone's.

The truth contained herein has been rendered in story form to interest the multitude in metaphysics—also, because life is a story and not only a philosophy.

The author's purpose is to present the Spirit of Himālaya, symbolic of the Eternal Wisdom and the beauty of Mother Nature, in such a way as to help unfold the Spirit of Man in accordance with the Eternal Cosmic Reality. There is an ancient saying:

God sleeps in the mineral
dreams in the plant
stirs in the animal
and awakes in man.

Although the story is told through one tradition and culture, this is but a vehicle. The message is universal and eternal, neither rejecting nor advocating any one path, religion or culture, but the completion of all religious and spiritual aspirations of man.

the author

5

Dedicated to
those countless souls
who are seeking Perfection

Throughout this book, the Himālayās have been referred to as Himālaya, the correct Indian name of the mountains.

DESIRES
(summer)

Once upon a time,
far, far away . . . . .

... on the banks of the river Saraswati, near the village of Sonar Linga, lived a sage. In this far-off region of north central Himalaya, amidst snow-peaked mountains, the sage gazed down across the Saraswati at this last outpost of the Himalayan route. Perched high on the slopes at about 8000 feet, Sonar Village appeared as nothing more than a few brown huts clustered together. A villager or two cut wood in the tall pine forest, a few birds chirped here and there. Meadows dotted with pines rolled over the slopes, silent, lush and lovely. Gray boulders of various sizes lay all around the valley. Saraswati Kund, the source of the Saraswati river, was only one day's hike away. The weather was cold, wet, fresh and invigorating.

Dawn vanished into the rising sun on the eastern peaks of the ranges. The sage emerged from his wooden hut carrying a begging bowl in his hand and proceeded to the river. He walked erect with a bearing worthy only of a sage. He stood tall, with a broad forehead and matted hair flowing down to his waist; only scanty clothing covered his lean body. His serene but pleasant countenance dispersed all doubts with its unspeakable peace and radiant joy. It was difficult to guess his age, but judging by his physical appearance, one could surmise that he was about sixty.

After finishing his bath in the cold river, the sage returned to the hut and put the water-filled bowl inside. As he came out of the door, a young man descended the slopes at the back of the hut. In a short while, the stranger reverently approached the holy man, and with awe touched his forehead to the sage's bare feet. From his closed lips the holy man uttered a simple *hnu*—a sort of relaxed acknowledgement. The young man stood up, this time his face beaming, eyes shining and a sweet smile dancing on his lips. In no time his fatigue, seemingly from a long journey on foot, vanished. With a little impatience he waited for the next move from the holy man.

The sage sat down on a nearly flat stone and bade the stranger to sit on the one opposite.

"So you have come, Satyakam," asserted the sage with satisfaction.

"How do you know my name, sir? You seemed to know I was coming, didn't you?"

Without replying directly to the questions, as if taking them for granted, the sage continued: "After you take a bath, eat and rest for today. Tomorrow you'll receive your first lessons on the spiritual path."

"But sir, I wanted to say so much about my search, my difficulties, your whereabouts, my aspirations . . . "

Cutting him off in mid-sentence, the seer said abruptly with a firm and measured tone, "There needn't be any formalities or introduction between a disciple and a guru of birth to birth acquaintance."

"So you are my guru from birth to birth!" Saying this with astonishment and satisfaction, he became choked with emotion. His eyes brimmed with tears. He closed his eyes slowly with unspeakable joy, and tears rolled down his cheeks as his hands involuntarily folded in the manner of respectful greeting. His forehead bent down a little, but he could not hold himself further and fell spontaneously at the feet of the Master.

The Master touched Satyakam's head with his right hand and slowly left the place.

·　·　·　·　·　·　·

The day moved on, rhythmic in ageless splendor; the sky was clear blue, snow glimmered on the peaks, a crow or two flew from one end of the valley to the other. Water rushed in the river, making the only sound in the valley. The lure and enchantment of the unspoiled waters beckoned Satyakam to relax and absorb the natural beauty.

Smoothly and methodically, Satyakam went on finishing his chores, respectfully taking, on occasion, necessary instructions from his mentor, till the day ended in peaceful dusk.

Calling him with a little indifference, the holy man said, "I'll see you tomorrow morning. You may retire to your hut now," pointing a little farther south.

Next morning a few patches of cloud filled the sky, but sunshine broke through—a blessing in this region of snow. The rainy season was still two months away. The two solitary figures silently ascended the mountainside behind the Master's hut where Satyakam had appeared the day before. A short while after, on fairly level ground on the slope, the Master sat down facing the river. On slightly lower ground sat Satyakam, looking at his Master and waiting anxiously.

Satyakam was of average build, relatively fair skinned and in his early twenties. An uneven scanty beard had grown on his face, giving him the look of an aspirant; his hair had nearly grown to the back of his neck, but was not quite flowing yet. He had more or less a round face, and on it one could easily read his transparent sincerity, devotion and self-control. Truth was ready on his lips anytime. Even though he was fatigued and somewhat undernourished, he appeared rather healthy.

The guru looked at him and said, "Satyakam, we'll start where we ended in the previous birth."

"But I don't remember my last birth, sir!" responded Satyakam innocently.

"You'll come to know it as the days go by. There is no use in just telling you and satisfying only your curiosity. Better that you *know* it rather than simply be *informed*. Suffice it to say that it won't take you long to *see* your previous incarnation. Your present balance of mind and merit are what really matter. And you have these sufficiently—truthfulness, self-control and sincerity.

"From today onward forget calculating time measurements of days, months and years or even births. Just watch the sun rising and setting. Let each day be simply a day and each night a night. Let the day flow with your living. By this, a newness—ever newness will be present with you. Past, present and future will mingle into one, and you'll float into indescribable joy—light, relaxed and free."

"Sir, I have a question," replied Satyakam reverently. "How much time will it take to achieve this?"

"You are again counting time! Unless you have stopped this, you cannot grow into freedom. A habit, isn't it?" The sage had a twinkle in his eyes and a smile on his lips.

"But doesn't it take time to demolish habits, *Maharaj?*"* inquired the disciple innocently.

"Certainly," continued the sage lovingly, "but is your time so limited as to worry about its exhaustion? Isn't it sufficient that you are living *now* and that you just be *aware* of it? Dirt can be accumulated and dirt can be removed. In between you call it time. But all the while, you are either forming a habit or removing one. Is it not enough to acknowledge that time is eternal for you to do whatever you want to do? To calculate it is to prolong a habit! Form no habit that you cannot easily break."

"But what if thoughts continue hovering in the brain? I mean, what method should I employ in order to overcome habits already formed?" the seeker inquired uneasily.

The holy man looked lovingly at Satyakam, greatly soothing him so that his uneasiness vanished. Before he could speak further, the seer replied, "See the thoughts, watch them and be a witness ... and wait ... patiently ... till obstructions are over and consciousness flows smoothly and freely. Call it a method if you will."

Maharaj—lit. great king; a customary address to holy men

Satyakam placed his face fully on the ground bowing toward his guru. He wished that he could exclaim "What a grace!" but that, too, was a thought! Thereupon peace, almost solid and tangible, reigned supreme in the atmosphere.

Together they walked quietly down the mountain. Satyakam was unaware of any heartbeat. Even pulsations and bodily actions seemed nonexistent; he felt very light—as if floating in the air! Was all this happening as a result of questions and answers merely, or something else beyond? Satyakam wondered in awe. He even forgot to bid farewell to his Master. Nearing his hut, he entered unobtrusively and plunged face down onto the one blanket. Tears swelled in his eyes. He couldn't contain the surging love in his heart. In uncontrollable gratitude, he could only utter from the depths of his heart, "Thank you, Lord."

. . . .

Time moved on timelessly and so, too, the search of Satyakam. The more he tried to forget about time and tried to transcend it, the more it thickened. Past memories, habits—both hard and soft—and internal dialogue went on hovering in his mind. The three qualities of mind—dullness, activity and equilibrium—kept revolving and rotating around his ego. As much as he wished to follow his guru's instructions, he would be pulled away by established tendencies of his conscious as well as subconscious mind and, who knows, by those from his past births too!

This internal battle, however, did not disturb the daily duties performed for his Master and himself. From sunrise to sunset and through the night, discipline and cleanliness mingled harmoniously with his practices. The Master seemed pleased with him, although he seldom expressed it. Whenever necessary, they would speak; otherwise each one kept to himself. Bathing in the cold river, sweeping the area, cooking and cleaning the utensils, bringing water from the river, washing clothes and cutting firewood in the forest— these duties and others were carried on around the clock and culminated in rubbing the feet of the Master before retiring to bed.

Occasionally Satyakam put questions to his guru to clarify his mind. Like a ray of light, the sage would disperse the clouds of his doubts, fears or dullness. For the first time in his present life, Satyakam saw visibly the significance of the guru: the dispeller of the darkness of ignorance. Repeatedly his ego went on humbling itself as his understanding grew in the sunshine of his Master's love, through a graceful glance or a helpful rebuke. Involuntarily, his fourth *chakra** began opening and he often felt blessed beyond words.

Whenever a need arose for food, he would beg alms in the village Sonar, on the other bank of the Saraswati. Crossing a rustic wooden bridge made of pine logs placed over stone platforms, he would climb about five hundred feet up the mountain to enter the village. Sonar was primitive, with dirt and stone streets winding up and down. Cow dung lay here and there. The houses consisted mostly of dirt and stones held together by wooden frames and covered by roofs made of straw and dead tree branches. Occasionally the villagers bowed down halfway to Satyakam as they passed by. He would respond by a slight smile or a nod of his head as was customary in such situations. From the open courtyards and verandahs of some houses, children seeing him would exclaim "Maharaj!" and make childlike gestures of greeting. Ladies often brought uncooked food to put in his cloth bag. Rice, wheat flour, potatoes and pulses were the normal offerings. But on special festival days, the ladies arrived in new colorful costumes bedecked with jewelry and carried extra

---

*chakra—one of the seven plexuses; the fourth is the heart chakra (See Glossary)

16

"...the holy man said, 'I'll see you tomorrow morning. You may retire to your hut now,' pointing a little farther south." (P. 13)

"Whenever a need arose for food, he would beg alms in the village Sonar, on the other bank of the Saraswati." (P. 16)

things such as sweets and buttermilk. With joy and honor they filled his bag. Before and after each offering he would utter with devotion, "Nārāyan ... Nārāyan*." Sometimes those who were more understanding offered tea packets and molasses or even a piece of coarse cloth. As soon as his cloth bag and begging bowl were full, he retraced his steps down the slope. Any further voluntary offers he politely declined. If by chance someone not knowing his vows offered cooked food, he would softly reply, "We eat food cooked only by our own hands." An increasing respectfulness grew in the eyes of the offerer since such a vow by a mendicant was considered to be an act of austerity. Sometimes a solitary voice called, "Come again, Maharaj," and his face would involuntarily turn to that direction. Then, slightly pulled by the sight of a mountain belle smiling with heavenly beauty, he would quickly bend his blushing face downward. At such moments, he frequently remembered the line heard elsewhere in his pilgrimages, "Trapped—if you respond to a smile!" The same episode occurred on almost each occasion that he went to the village for begging alms. Without responding in any way and with bent head, he would walk away.

Was he weak in such tendencies? Was his subconscious mind storing something of the kind which gave rise to shyness on the surface? Did he really feel attracted? Was he not suppressing something he did not analyze and reflect upon? Could he not just be normal and reciprocate the innocent flow of love from the simple girl of the mountains? Was it an escape?

He did not want to think about all this, but would go on repeating his mantra inside to overlap such thoughts and feelings. These waves then receded into the background of his mind as he slowly walked down to the bridge, crossed the river and returned to his hut. It seemed he never felt bothered

---

*Nārāyan—name of God

by this occurrence and memories of it never persisted after he left the village. His discipline, meditations, service and nearness to his Master kept him too busy to indulge in the luxury of romance. If ever there were such thoughts underneath, he was not aware of them, or possibly he did not wish to be aware of them!

Sometimes Satyakam and his Master took silent walks over the meadows or through the pine forests, occasionally pausing for a word of wisdom. His mind slowly began to settle and merge in tune with his Master and the heavenly surroundings. Intermittently, though imperceptibly for the most part, his mind would have outbursts and explosions. But the healing art of the Master would calm it without fail.

One day the Master called Satyakam and said, "Let us go to Saraswati Kund. We'll be back on the third day. You may take your blanket and bowl. As there are no more villages on this route for begging alms, you may tie up some food. Prepare soon, as we have to arrive at the Kund before darkness descends."

Satyakam did as he was told and soon they were seen walking quietly on the trail towards higher altitudes and glaciers.

About noon, they sat down at a comfortable spot on the high mountain trail. Satyakam felt tired as well as hungry. Such steep climbs and cold! But fortunately the sky was fairly clear and he could warm himself slightly in the sun. The Master seemed exempt from fatigue, hunger and cold. However, with a gesture of his finger, he indicated to Satyakam that he should start eating. The dry unleavened bread, molasses and boiled potatoes tasted heavenly at such a moment.

Soon after he finished eating, he went to a nearby stream, washed his cloth bag, drank water and quietly came and sat down at his place. The Master, serene as Himalaya, was lost in his reverie. Against the fathomless blue sky, the white snow peaks seemed to crest just a hand's stretch away. Through the clear and crisp cold, the pale golden sun seemed devoid of warmth. A mild sweet breeze blew almost imperceptibly as a stream of crystal clear water flowed down with a rhythmic, sonorous strain. No wonder Satyakam was soon lost in Nature's hypnotic spell. He didn't know when, but upon opening his eyes, he found his Master looking at him expectantly. Presumably he had caught his inner mind and whatever was going on there. With a sweet, full and rich voice the Master spoke:

"Aren't you thinking of creation, its mysteries and purpose?" And without waiting for an answer, which was evidently unnecessary, the sage went on, "All this creation is merely a play. It is not only a subject-object relationship, but deeper than that. Something started something else, and, as one thing led to another, form and name thereby became apparent. This is called creation. The theory of phenomenal appearance is to be distinguished from the theory of transformation."

Suddenly he caught hold of Satyakam's hand and said, "Just see. I extended my hand to you, and you may extend your other hand to a third person and so on. After a while this line of extension forms a circle, a triangle, or a square, or whatever, and lo, we have dimension. This movement goes on eternally in a variety of forms and colors."

Letting go his hand, the holy man continued in his inimitable style, "Tell me Satyakam, what is the purpose of all this extension? Is it not merely a play, a cause and effect sequence, karma? This whole creation is a garland of which karmas are the flowers strung with a mysterious force called Law."

Still under a partial spell, Satyakam posed a question for the first time on this journey. "But sir, who willed or created this force in the first place, and what was the wisdom thereof?"

"Will. Will of God? Will of the unknown? Self-will? Whatever you call It, It is beyond form and name, something inherent in the totality of consciousness. Call It omnipotence. The Will is supreme. And as It willed, It became, and went on forming innumerable patterns. The witness thereof, the basic consciousness, by virtue of Its being the substance, was omniscient, and transmitted wisdom through Its becoming. This incessant dynamic becoming produced the cosmic dance of the Lord. The rhythm of the flow of energy has never ceased. This ever-changing phenomenon is destructible and indestructible at the same time—particles and waves of omnipresent energy colliding and thus breaking apart, but ever giving rise to innumerable other particles of the same quality. All the time the energy manifests in unspeakable and unpredictable designs, holding vast stretches of space in between. All calculations and measurements of time and space become fictitious at these atomic and subatomic levels of existence."

The sage closed his eyes and went into deep meditation again. Satyakam, already in semiconsciousness and lost in his guru's communication, fell into meditation too. All of a sudden, like a flash, something dawned on Satyakam and he inquired, "Sir, may I ask you a question?"

"Am I not Veda Vyās*?" the sage interjected. "But I have no one identity that I could relate to," he continued. "From age to age I have assumed so many forms that I can hardly specify what I was or am. To me, all the series of lives are but one continuous life supported by awareness. Seeming variations are simply different patterns interwoven by energy and motion." The Master would have continued, who knows how long! But they had to reach Saraswati Kund before darkness. Like one awakened from a dream, Satyakam followed the

---

*Veda Vyās—author of the Vedās

20

footsteps of the Master, and both headed for still higher altitudes. Satyakam's mind began asking many more questions, but seeing his Master striding briskly, he hurried behind to finish the day's journey.

The sun had gone down behind the western ranges, silhouetting the violet slopes patched with snow. The great mountains stretched in endless diversity of form and color. Sometimes the trail passed through exquisite flora and fauna of multitudinous variety which only Himalaya could produce—the thrills of Mother Nature's handiwork were present at every turn of the trail—and at other times the trail passed over glaciers, entering a space which was quiet, austere and cold. Satyakam felt much quieted too, but not without melancholy. He couldn't understand why. Suddenly it crossed his mind that someone was transmitting thought patterns to him to show him how comfortable, warm and cozy he would have been in his home in the plains! Feeling guilty, he looked at the back of his Master, who turned around and glanced at him. Satyakam saw clearly the radiant and joyful countenance of the sage. Like a miracle, his melancholy mood vanished and joy danced upon his face in tune with his Master's. He again looked toward the upward stretched arms of Himalaya and saw the holiness, beauty and splendor of the heavenly abode. His soul leapt in ecstasy.

This was the third day of the month, and a crescent moon appeared in the east. A hardly perceptible dim moonlight spread over the silvery mountains. The sky was crystal clear.

The Master broke the silence:

"In a short while we'll reach the Kund." By now the river had considerably reduced in breadth and depth. The nectarlike water softly murmured an unknown song, sending a tingling vibration of joy through Satyakam's spine. A sign of life?

The last climb was quite steep. Stayakam felt no fatigue this time, but was fresh, light and full of energy. His soul too was quietly singing an unknown tune. His inner world was in perfect tune with this golden region of Himalaya, canopied by the fathomless sky. On the way, he had seen wild flowers of riotous colors stretched over the meadows, and the memory still lingered in his heart.

As they climbed to the top of the steep slope, a breath-taking view captivated Satyakam. A fantastic lake, surrounded on three sides by still higher mountains, spread over a large area. From the near end, the river Saraswati flowed silently and smoothly. As the sun set behind the high ranges, the lake darkened with the mountainous shadows reflected in it.

The holy man looked around and proceeded to a spot which he seemed to know already. A big, flat rock jutted like a cantilever out of the side of the mountain, and underneath was a flat space that looked like an unwalled open room—just sufficient for one person to lie down. At the farther end of it lay a log, cut semicircular and giving the impression that it could be used as a pillow. Something clicked in Satyakam and he exclaimed, "It occurs to me that I have seen this spot before! I seem to feel that I have visited this place sometime . . . !"

But his Master, interrupting his strange feelings, said hurriedly, "Satyakam, you rest here tonight and I'll see you tomorrow morning."

Satyakam didn't feel the need of asking where his Master would stay, as by now he knew his capacities well enough.

Soon the sage vanished in the darkness of the approaching night. Satyakam spread his blanket on the stone floor, with one end of it overlapping the semicircular log. The bed was complete. He did all this so naturally that it seemed as if he had been doing it every night!

He looked around, but all he could see was a very dim blue sky with twinkling stars, a soothing rippling of water in the lake, and the tall snow-peaked sentinels—the eternal Himalaya. Quiet enveloped Satyakam with a motherly caress. He felt at home and gradually began to relax. He wasn't very sleepy, so he sat in lotus posture on the blanket facing the lake. The heat generated by climbing up the trail was slowly subsiding and he began to feel chilly. He pulled his thick woolen shawl around his shoulders and covered his whole torso. Gazing timelessly at the waters, his eyes closed like petals of a lotus and he was lost in meditation.

Much later, in the dead of night, in his half drowsiness, he lay back on the blanket. His head rested on the blanket-covered log, the thick shawl stretched over his whole body. The mysterious lullaby produced by the sweet rippling water drew Satyakam into slumber.

His first night of sleep in this heavenly 13,000 foot high abode of Himalaya—the fortune of only a few lucky souls— gradually transformed into a gray dawn. Once again, like lotus petals, his eyelids opened slowly. He couldn't believe where he was! But soon the recollection came back to him and he arose. Sitting in a comfortable pose, Satyakam folded his hands and bowed down—to whom? Water? Mountains? Sky? Perhaps to all creation, to his almighty God!

He got up, took his bowl and advanced toward the lake. Filling the bowl with water, he went behind the big boulders a fair distance from the lake. After finishing his morning wash-ing, just as he was remembering his Master, the first rays of the golden sun fell on him. He felt the warm welcome. Facing the east, he bowed down to the sun, and in loving obeisance remained in the bent pose for quite a while.

The water in the lake was very bright this morning as the sunshine lay over it. The images of the triple mountains did not make dark shadows as they had last evening, for now the sun faced them. Except for intermittent snow on the banks, fresh green grass lay like a carpet all over. Many wild flowers of exquisite color and variety adorned the soft verdant grass. The shining snow peaks looked, to Satyakam, like messengers, and behind them lay a limitless blue void. He might have lost himself in that white, blue and gold, when suddenly and unbelievably he saw two fleecy white bodies at a far distance, lightly floating on the surface of the water like white lotuses, moving slowly toward him. As they approached he clearly saw that these were swans! They were bigger than usual with an otherworldly look in their eyes. Pinkish red rims circled their eyes, giving them a divine look, an embodiment of purity and serenity. Their eyes hardly winked as if they were continually open. Their very sight transported Satyakam in amazement and rapture. These swans belonged not to this world, as Satyakam would like to believe. Their sage-like bearing, their eyes open but with an inward gaze and their smooth sailing radiated peace and joy all around. Satyakam was about to lose himself in ecstasy when he heard soft footsteps nearby. He looked to his right. His Master was standing there looking at him with love and an unknown new hope. Satyakam remained in nearly total awe.

The sage spoke softly like quiet morning music, "There has been a legend around here since time immemorial that those two swans are the embodiment of Shiva and His eternal consort Durga. They roam about all over Himalaya and appear and disappear in various lakes. Only a few fortunate souls have been blessed with their vision, and you are one of those, Satyakam."

Satyakam again turned his face to behold the divine pair. He just couldn't take in the perfection which emanated from their halos in the form of dreamlike beauty, purity and fullness. Although it seemed shallow, he bowed down traditionally on the ground facing the eternal couple, uttering, with a trembling voice, "Shiva ... Shiva ... Durga ... Durga ... " In humble admiration he bathed in nature's magnificent spectacle.

24

After a short while he arose on bended knees and then got to his feet. Once again he looked, with more intimacy, love and reverence, at the rare sight. Their feathers were like snowflakes and white like fleecy clouds. Their long slender necks gently held the radiantly haloed heads. The great birds turned back and sailed smoothly away and away, until, all at once, they vanished. Satyakam was stunned. It seemed a dream. No longer could he hold on. With utmost surrender, he lay his head on his guru's feet. Thereupon he lost all external consciousness. While he was still upon his Master's feet, an unexpected dreamlike scene appeared to his inner eye. An ochre-robed monk, with shaven head and bare feet, holding a bamboo staff in his right hand, was standing upright. He recognized his previous birth and simultaneously heard *hnu* overhead from his guru, as a confirmation of what he was seeing. Also "That's right," which he couldn't miss. The name of the monk followed immediately and he couldn't have thought otherwise. His fifth chakra opened this day.

As he raised himself slowly and faced his Master quite closely, he saw a pleasant smile on his face. Like a movie, all the connected scenes and memories passed before him in quick succession. The lake, the small open cave where he had slept last night: these surroundings seemed very familiar to him, as if yesterday's occurrence. Yes, he had lived here, meditated and done various austerities in his previous incarnation!

His face burned with the sweet warmth and brilliance of newborn radiance. His eyes were shining like clear crystals and joy unspeakable filled his whole face, nay, his whole body. This was his initiation in the present birth, linking him with where he had left off in his last birth. The bond was set.

The holy man spoke as if in a murmur, quite in tune with the rest of the happenings, "We'll stay here for today and tonight; we shall leave for Sonar Linga tomorrow morning. Whenever you feel hungry you may eat, but only once and not after sunset. If need be, I'll come to see you; otherwise I'll meet you tomorrow morning before departure.''

Satyakam had never seen such a benevolent look on his Master's face—and what love! He wished to clasp the whole body of his guru, but etiquette prevented him from doing so. The ageless one approved of this control of emotion with satisfaction, and bade him good-bye. Satyakam watched him going, but lo! he too, like the swans, vanished suddenly in thin air. He had believed all along that his guru could do all this, but this was the first time he actually saw him doing it! The quick succession of the two vanishings jolted him to the core of his spine, waking him fully. Soon he settled into the new dimensions of his opening consciousness.

As he aimlessly turned back to walk on the grassy bank of the lake, he felt that his feet were not touching the ground! Curiosity compelled him to look down, but he couldn't bend his neck. He felt his body subject to a certain vibratory phenomenon where he could only stir the pupils of his eyes. From the corners of his eyes he visualized that his feet were a few inches above the ground. He was walking as usual, but on air! His whole body seemed light, in an unusual state of cheerfulness and inspiration. It simply floated as he walked more and more. Soon he came to the southeast corner of the lake where the mountain started towards the north. His eyes spontaneously looked up to the peak and a subconscious drive to reach there arose. All of a sudden his body flew up and, in the speed of a thought, he was standing on the peak! He became afraid and felt uncertain as he stood there, not knowing how to get down! Soon he gazed down on the northeast corner of the lake and saw his Master standing and looking up at him with amusement! Satyakam felt a vibratory pull, a sort of controlling computer, and, as if on wings, he descended slowly toward where his Master was standing. As he landed nearby, he felt secure. A teasing smile crossed the lips of his Master. Satyakam seemed neither ashamed nor mindful. He had enough self-control at his command. Each lesson that his guru had imparted to him, whether through words, example or actual happening, was grasped by him intelligently. He immediately knew how to descend from the mountaintop. He was becoming more and more in tune with his Master, and that kept him receptive to the finer suggestions and subtle indications from him. As an advanced yogi, he could hardly miss the finer points as a novice or a less experienced disciple might have.

Watching him closely, the holy man said, "So much for today," and vanished away again.

It was now noon and the sun shone brightly at its zenith. The day was passing quietly. The white of the snow was extraordinarily milky against the dazzling blue Himalayan sky, where not even a streak of clouds cast a blemish. The mountains, with whites and greens, seemed more alive and the lake was more serene. With no breeze blowing, a solid silence pervaded the latent dynamism in the atmosphere, compelling one to be contemplative and go within.

Satyakam roamed about the beautiful surroundings much of the day. Occasionally he would sit here, then there, and go on musing. The occult achievements unfolded in him by his Master, the heavenly sight of the divine swans and a new understanding of his Master went on one by one passing alternatively through his mind. He didn't feel hungry today, nor tired, nor melancholy. Just natural in his new-found peace!

As the sun moved towards the west, the panorama began to change in Himalaya: sweet cold, lonely beauty, and grace indescribable! Satyakam moved toward the open cave—his home for the time being. Looking around once more, he sat quietly on the blanket in lotus posture, facing the waters. Suddenly the stones, water, snow, the green grass and everything else began to vibrate with shimmering light, gradually losing their identity and outlines. The material distinction gave way to intermingling of light waves, and soon it became a great sea of vibratory light, throbbing and pulsating with incessant activity, ever changing but all the same, indivisible and imperishable. The all-pervasiveness of energy was too much for Satyakam's eyes to remain open and he was lost to the distinction of the observer and the observed. Bliss reigned supreme throughout the night and he neither slept nor remembered anything else.

It seemed as if ages had passed before he opened his eyes to the approaching dawn. Light shot through his eyes as he slowly moved his gaze on Divine Nature. His whole body felt free and his nervous system seemed entirely open, energetic and elastic. The flow of life force was full and within control. No longer did the cold bother him, nor were morning chores in his memory.

He might have sat like this for millenia to come, but something touched his left shoulder and shook him gently. Slowly, he moved his heavy face, as if it were a mountain, and saw the Master standing by him. Not only was benign love on his face, but a mark of respect and divine indifference too.

Satyakam's body quivered a little, his legs began to loosen and his hands came apart. In a few moments he got up from the seat and touched the feet of his Master with his fingers, feeling a new relationship between the two of them.

The holy man quietly said, as if in a whisper, "Let's go back to Sonar Linga. Today we'll go by another route which is a short cut. It would have been very steep and hazardous had we come up this way."

Slowly they descended toward the east and then to the south, Satyakam following his Master. They spoke hardly a word on the way, nor did they feel any need to eat. By early afternoon they reached their huts and quietly entered.

· · · · · · ·

Days and nights continued as usual, and so too did Satyakam's meditations. External duties were greatly reduced as he ate only once a day, sometimes not even that. He went to the village less often as his needs diminished. Also, the villagers would sometimes bring the necessities to them, knowing that Satyakam was too busy with his daily practices.

One day as they sat outside the Master's hut, the Master said, "Satyakam, something is gnawing at your mind, it seems."

"Yes, Maharaj," spoke Satyakam with visible agony. "For a few days now one question has been haunting me ... "

Interrupted the sage, " ... What prevented you from finishing the journey in your last birth, and what do you still have to accomplish in this birth, as far as the life on this planet is concerned?"

Satyakam looked reverently at his Master but spoke no word.

The Master continued, "Ordinarily it would seem that very little karma had remained in your previous incarnation and that you could have easily finished then. But your sub-conscious mind retained some desires which I have tried to dissolve in you. Those were quite strong, like carvings in a stone, deep rooted perhaps from a few births. Then I sup-pressed those in you, in order to help you do some necessary preparations so you could sustain the effects to be accrued by the exhaustion of those desires later on. By the time you accomplished the required preparations, it was too late to exhaust your karmas." The Master took a brief pause and added, "Because it was your time to leave your physical body.

While at Saraswati Kund, at the time of initiation, you re-member my having told you that the previous birth's practices were linked now to the present one. Due to your rigorous austerities in the last life, you could accomplish very advanced yogic insights so soon in this birth.

"But as of now, I am afraid, that period of your life is approaching which has been left unfinished, the cause for not finishing so far the entire journey toward Full Enlightenment. It does seem ridiculous that even after such advanced realiza-tions and grace, karmas or desires could not be nullified! But such is the way of cosmic laws, that without letting go of ego-identity, all desires don't burn away."

Satyakam was listening quietly without being disturbed or agitated. He had no difficulty in accepting all this. But still, his agony would not leave him; he somehow wished to be free from desires without working on them!

The Master read his mind. With utmost sympathy and tenderness he restated, "Satyakam, fortunately you are still young in the present life. Thus you can afford to spend some time and energy in the exhaustion of your remaining hard-core desires. It is imperative now that you finish your karmas in this life. Don't forget that the fulfillment of karma is not the direct means to release; it is to be regarded as an auxiliary."

"But what if it takes a long time or even a lifetime to be free from such desires, in which case I am nowhere again!" Sadness arose in his words.

The Master consoled him, saying, "I am aware of all this. It won't be a lifetime before you resume your last lap of the journey. I assure you that I'll be with you to guide you safely ashore."

Satyakam relaxed a little, but he still had a last question. "Sir, can you tell me which desires are still pending to be worked out?"

The all-knowing sage slowly got up from his seat. Without looking at his face he declared, "You'll know this in a short time," and walked away.

Satyakam was left deep in thought but couldn't see clearly what he wanted to know. Releasing a deep sigh, he got up and muttered, "God knows best!"

• • • • • • •

After the last conversation with his Master, Satyakam's mind was mostly occupied with the subject of desires and karmas. His concentration gradually began to suffer and he couldn't sit in meditation as before. Often he would be restless without any apparent reason, leading him to commit minor mistakes in daily duties. He would be sorry for them but could hardly blame himself, since he now took it for granted that to err was human! Vigilant discipline, which he had believed would lead him to Perfection, began to falter. But he didn't lament anymore. Perhaps in the secret recesses of his heart he even enjoyed such human frailties! Although he didn't mean to be, he was less and less aware of his Master's presence and more occupied with his new and indefinable tingling. He would rather enjoy the fresh meadows of unexplored flatlands below than climb again the rugged and harsh pinnacles of knowledge!

Days lingered on slowly and heavily. Carefree sleep at night became less frequent. Satyakam often came out of his hut at midnight and sat outside for nothing! Sometimes his eyes would lift up toward the opposite bank and way up to Sonar. Soft oil lamps of village huts and farm houses seemed to enchant him.

On moonlit nights, the luminous sky began to give him some unknown message which he couldn't figure out. Somewhere in his life complex he felt a deep pressure tearing at him. He felt no need to consult with his Master. Something was blocking him from doing so.

Miles and miles of sky no longer inspired him to vastness. Rather, he preferred to tread on the earth, to see and meet with immediate exigencies. In a few days' span, Satyakam looked like a small boy, as if he knew nothing. He wondered why he was there at all! The heavenly Himalayan surroundings no longer inspired him to ecstasy as they had before. On the contrary, they seemed dry, forlorn and desolate. His heart became heavy. Wasn't the earth so big and fascinating as to inspire one to wander on it and to read it as an open book of life?

Early one morning he heard a knock on his door. Although this was unusual, he felt a hidden sense of relief. Quite restlessly he got up from his blanket and opened the door. The Master was standing outside. Satyakam came out and touched his feet. The holy man seemed more tender than usual, and unexpectedly entered Satyakam's hut, inviting him to sit with him on the blanket. This was the first time that Satyakam didn't feel any hesitation to sit on the same level and same seat with his Master. He began to feel like a son before this holy man. For a short while he was at home with his father, who spoke lovingly:

"Satyakam, I am aware of your feelings," and without going into unnecessary words, he continued, "It is time that you embark on wanderings and find out for yourself what you want."

Satyakam didn't feel like questioning the holy man's wisdom, to say nothing of rejecting it! He hung his head and tears began to fall from his eyes. He didn't understand why, but he had no words either.

The sage inquired softly, "Do you have any more questions before you enter today the next chapter of your life?"

"As they climbed to the top of the steep slope, a breathtaking view captivated Satyakam.
A fantastic lake, surrounded on three sides by still higher mountains..." (P. 22)

Still with head down, Satyakam asked shyly, "Can you guide me please? Where should I go or what should I do? I don't know what I want!"

He seemed to have no objection to leaving Himalaya though. The benevolent sage replied, "As you descend into the lower valleys and into the plains, you'll go on getting what you need. Your needs will be provided for you."

Hesitatingly, Satyakam lifted up his tear-streaked face and asked, almost helplessly, "Shall I ever see you again?" There was a plea in his voice.

With dignity and kindness, the sage assured him with his closing words, "At the right time and right place, when you will need me, I'll be present again."

Rains fell
throughout the
whole day....

... Monsoons had started in full swing from the south-east, from the side of the Bay of Bengal. This was the season of rice cultivation in the south and east of India. Vast stretches of the rural fields of Bengal were partially flooded with water. Tiny green paddy shoots were just raising their heads above the flooded fields.

Farmers relaxed in their mud houses after many days of strenuous labor in the fields. They were known for their honesty, self-respect and willing endurance. Sometimes a late returning villager would be seen tarrying homeward through muddy paths, barefooted, sandals in one hand and loose lower clothing held high above the knees in the other. Passing by a familiar home, he would call out hello, get a response from inside the house—a word or two more—and then carry on the last lap of his homeward journey. Outer activities were otherwise hardly noticeable.

In the nights, from far-off distances, Bengali devotional and folk songs were faintly audible with their rhythmic drum beats instilling a mystifying and enchanting mood.

·   ·   ·   ·   ·   ·   ·

Village Kadambini was about four miles from the last railway station on the narrow gauge line. A dusty road led from the station to the village, fit only for pedestrians and bullock carts. At the outskirts of the village was a well-known Kali temple, a great center for Tantra practices. Nearby at the cremation ground, Tantrics lived and practiced their crude techniques night after night.

Common people often shunned visiting the place after dark. Many stories of dreadful episodes made people some-what fearful. But not everyone kept away. Some adherents of occult sects came daily after darkness descended. Some would enter the cremation ground and start their practices, while others sat in the vicinity of the Kali temple. Before dawn they would leave, one by one, for their homes.

But the story changed one day when a young Bhairavī* arrived in the temple and occupied a corner of the verandah. She always remained in silence. No one saw her eating any food. She hardly slept. Most of the time her eyes remained closed in deep reverence. She seemed unaware of outer surroundings. When news of her arrival spread throughout the nearby villages, throngs of people began pouring in day and night to see her. Rarely would she open her eyes to look at the people standing nearby; her head seldom raised beyond this point. Gradually people began to bring various gifts. After bowing down to her and placing the offerings at her feet, they waited for her blessings. Her silence was eloquent; her occasional glance pacified visitors. Some would then go away, but others kept waiting for hours.

Not long after that, stories began circulating about healings, problems being solved, and successes attained. Even larger crowds arrived, blocking the way so that it was sometimes even difficult to see her face. A few self-appointed volunteers started managing the crowd so visitors could stand in line and, one by one, see her. They often addressed her as Devījī.**

Rains didn't seem to bother most of the people. The temple's spacious open grounds accommodated hundreds. They even forgot their dread of the cremation ground and the Tantrics, believing that the Deviji was near them!

The Bhairavi seemed about 22 years of age, fairly tall and slim, with skin a bit dark. Her face was long and well chiseled and her limbs well proportioned. Usually her black hair was tied up at the back of her head, but when untied, it fell down to her slender waist. When she opened her big eyes, visitors would be reminded, chiefly by her prominent eyelashes, of

---

*Bhairavī—a female Tantric
**Devījī—lit. goddess; respectful address to holy women

the eyes of a musk deer. Deviji never seemed to notice anyone in particular, but her quiet, calm and powerful bearing made everyone feel at home in her presence.

A few months after Deviji's arrival at the temple, a young holy man was seen standing in the line. He was drenched by the monsoon rains and the volunteers made way for him, helping him reach the Bhairavi by giving him preference.

In the hustle and bustle, Devi's eyes opened and fell upon the holy man. After a brief and barely noticeable hesitation, a very faint smile—hardly a smile—appeared on her face. The unfamiliar holy man responded involuntarily with a shy smile. He waited for some time, and while he waited her eyes didn't close. This was perhaps the first time that she was seen watching someone in particular! But soon the holy man moved farther in the line and the usual beholding continued.

Every day, as soon as the holy man arrived, volunteers would usher him near the Bhairavi. Gradually and quite naturally his stay grew longer and longer, sometimes extending through the whole day, and rarely, even up to late night.

Now Devi sometimes spoke a word or two. Once she asked his name. "Satyakam," he replied in a simple tone.

•   •   •   •   •   •   •

After spending three years in Himalaya with his Master and wandering for a year in search of Tantric education all over north and central India, Satyakam arrived in Bengal with a fully grown beard. At twenty-five, he was thinner than before, but still radiant in his face—as if not of this world!

While wandering in Calcutta, Satyakam had met an old man with a flowing silvery beard and shining eyes, who directed him to Kadambini for Tantra training. Upon reaching the Kali temple, he was guided toward the cremation ground.

There he met *Kapālak**—middle aged and robust, with only a loin cloth on his body. He was sitting in a hut made of mud and roofed with hay. His seat was built on five skulls and before him a log fire was smoldering.

Kapalak greeted Satyakam in a challenging way. But remaining poised, Satyakam saluted him in a detached manner and sat down opposite the fire.

Kapalak inquired fiercely, "What do you want?" Fire emanated from his eyes.

"I want to learn Tantra," replied Satyakam quietly.

"Who told you about this place?" Kapalak's tone was the same.

Satyakam politely narrated the story of the old man in Calcutta. Then suddenly a smile shone forth from Kapalak's lips and Satyakam couldn't believe what he saw! Kapalak's fierce face turned extremely sweet, dazzling with gentleness, so different from what he had just observed. Two such contrary moods!

"Do you know who that old man was?" inquired Kapalak in a cordial manner.

"I am not sure, but just now it occurred to me in a flash that it could be my Master!" Satyakam seemed surprised but pleased.

"You're right, and he is my Master too." Kapalak's heart was full of devotion. "You and I," he continued, "are co-disciples."

Satyakam seemed bewildered as he irresistably asked, "But your path and mine are, at least up to this point, so different!"

"He knows all the paths, not only the current ones, but also various ancient ones which seem to be obsolete now. He

---

Kapālak—kapāl lit. means skull; a Tantric who sits on a seat of skulls and practices Tantric rites says that no path is obsolete: only the number of adherents increases and decreases according to the influence of a particular evolution. We call a path obsolete or otherwise only in relation to the number adhering to it."

Satyakam jerked a little, adjusted his sitting position and spoke softly, "Do you know who our Master is?"

"I wish I could tell you! It is a mystery to me," Kapalak confessed, "It is enough for me to know that he is guiding me and I am pleased with it."

There was silence for a long time. Satyakam's eyes were closed.

Some time later, upon a stir at the log fire, Satyakam's eyes opened.

"I forgot to ask your name."

"Satyakam."

"Would you like to have tea?" Kapalak stirred the firewood and blew on it.

"No thanks. I don't drink tea," replied Satyakam politely.

"I'll have some." Kapalak arranged the kettle which was all black from smoke. It seemed never to have been washed since it was bought or given to him.

While sipping tea from an old and somewhat broken mug, Kapalak said, "Satyakam, Adi Ganga flows at the edge of this cremation ground, about two hundred yards from here. Go and have a good bath there. Tonight I'll start some preliminary lessons in Tantra with you. But bear in mind that I am not your guru, but an elder brother, a senior brother disciple. It is my honor to teach you Tantra because it'll be a service to my Master. You are already an advanced soul and have brought quite a credit balance from your previous births."

"May I ask you a question, sir?"

"Don't say 'sir' to me. 'Kapalak' will do. Go ahead."

"When I first approached you today, you looked so fierce and wild. Can you explain to me why?"

"First, this shields me from laymen or uninitiates who might disturb me; second, I was testing your stamina, patience and reactions before I could take on teaching you Tantra." He paused momentarily and then said, "You passed the test successfully and with a good degree of maturity."

Satyakam bowed down half way, got up slowly and headed toward the rivulet.

. . . .

That night was the new moon. Pitch dark. A mild breeze rustled the leaves. The frequent barking of a dog in some corner of the cremation ground interrupted the awesome silence of the lonely night.

Amidst a grove of thick trees lay Satyakam's mud and straw hut, engulfed in the dark shade. On the mud floor a small wood fire was burning, and on opposite sides of it sat Kapalak and Satyakam facing each other. Wearing only loin cloths, they had smeared the rest of their bodies with wood ashes; both sat motionless.

Kapalak began, "Whatever I teach you is the blessing of our Master. I am simply an instrument, a flame, kindled by the Master, and in turn kindling other instruments. I am particularly glad you are already an advanced yogi so I can directly impart advanced courses to you.

"But before I start the first technique, I would like to feel sure that you understand the faith required. The greater the faith, the better the results. Faith instills courage, which is especially required in Tantra for practicing the so-called supernatural techniques. Supernatural, because they are different than ordinary, natural dimensions. Thus the need of faith in an unknown phenomenon."

"Would you call faith a flight of imagination?" inquired Satyakam.

"Even if we call it imagination, it requires a certain amount of concentration to objectify it. And concentration cannot develop without a correspondingly sufficient faith in the reality of an object. It is only a semantic problem. Perhaps the only difference may seem that faith involves devotion, whereas imagination does not. But this is only a superficial view. As you scrutinize imagination more and more, you'll clearly see that inherent in it is an attitude of devotion, though it may be only very faintly perceptible. In short, what you call imagination, I call faith."

Satyakam, approving of the explanation, waited for the technique.

Kapalak seemed satisfied and continued, "We'll start with *Nāda Yoga**. It is one of the paths of concentration through sounds. These sounds ring inside and as you go deep, the gross sounds go on terminating into subtle and more subtle sounds, till the concentration culminates into the last one which is transcendental.

"There are seven major sounds, of which the first two are the short and long sounds of a cricket. The other five are: those of drum beats, the rumbling of dark clouds, conch shell, bell and flute. At times these sounds will seem as if they are coming from outside you, but if you'll open your eyes the sounds will be gone.

"As you are already well advanced in concentration, it won't take you a long time to accomplish it. First, concentrate on the sounds of the cricket. Just keep on that and you will find that gradually one sound will lead to another as your concentration deepens."

Satyakam inquired, "What is Nāda?"

Kapalak explained, "Nada or sound is the intrinsic quality of space or Silence. It expands into space as waves do in an ocean. Sound has three stages: verbal, subtle and causal.

---

*Nāda Yoga—the Yoga of sound

"Subtle sound, or Nada, can be heard, but not necessarily. The syllable vanishes with the sound. Causal sound is without vibration and is sometimes called Silent Sound.

"The will that is inherent in nature creates vibrations called Nada or sound. Nada contains all possibilities of becoming. Everything from the subtle to the gross is a manifestation of various combinations of vibrations.

"Nada is the nucleus of concentrated energy, which provides the source of causal sound in the echo aspect. The point, through the will, expands into a wave in the dynamic aspect.

"There is no vacuum anywhere. The universe is a continuum of vibratory phenomena. At the audible level, sound manifests different vibrations that create light, heat, dimensions, and so forth." Kapalak paused briefly. Satyakam was listening intently.

Kapalak continued, "I'll leave you here tonight to practice the technique. But before I leave I would like to see if you are hearing the first sound. So close your eyes and see if you are hearing anything."

Satyakam calmly closed his eyes and waited. After a while, he couldn't make heads or tails of it.

"It'll happen if you wait patiently. The first short range sound—that of a cricket—rings all the time in anyone. It is a matter of training your inner ear to catch it and then of prolonged linking with it . . . "

As Kapalak was still talking softly, Satyakam was lost within—the continuous, soothing, pacifying sound of the cricket. His face assumed a more settled expression of peace and he seemed unaware anymore of outer surroundings.

Kapalak quietly arose from his seat and left the hut.

·   ·   ·   ·   ·   ·   ·

Days passed on steadily and Satyakam spent more and more time in his hut. During the nights he immersed himself in his spiritual practices and part of the days he rested and bathed in Adi Ganga. He ate only once a day—a light meal—and remained silent practically all the time. He and Kapalak saw each other when needed and sometimes spoke on Nada Yoga. Satyakam didn't seem to have much difficulty with the technique, reaching the fifth sound in the course of about three months.

The world around Satyakam merged into oblivion. Even the customary greetings with Kapalak oftentimes went unobserved. The Nada-Yoga practices would have carried Satyakam to the end, but for the news of the advent of Bhairavi. Her story was no longer obscure.

One day as Kapalak began describing some facets of Bhairavi, Satyakam seemed highly interested and wanted to know more about her. What attracted him the most was her accomplishment in Tantra at such an early age! He felt eager to see her as soon as Kapalak threw a hint.

· · · · · · ·

Talks between Satyakam and Kapalak now lingered mostly on Bhairavi. As soon as Satyakam returned from seeing her, Kapalak would ask him about his experience. Satyakam grew enthusiastic as he talked less about Nada Yoga and more about his dialogues with Bhairavi. Kapalak hardly chastened him, as if this were bound to happen and his training with Satyakam had thus ended.

The attraction between Satyakam and Bhairavi no longer remained a secret. Many pondered the right and wrong of it. However, none had the courage to object to it openly or to pry into it further. The whole drama seemed the product of a divine decree, and slowly people began to take it quite easily and naturally, regarding the couple as a part of their company. Some people, of course, came to resent all this, but those who did, gossiped a lot and kept away. The overall rush of people to visit Bhairavi remained more or less the same.

Often Bhairavi and Satyakam would be seated together when the people paid their respects and gave offerings. Since they sought blessings from both of them, Satyakam did not hesitate to touch their heads with his benign hands.

The year ended with the great Durga Puja festival. Then came Kali Puja, most auspicious for Tantrics. Throngs of people poured into the temple day and night, enjoying a double feast this year—Kali Puja as well as a holy couple in human form.

But with increased worship by the people and the warmth and love between the two, there grew in Satyakam a lingering apprehension about all this. He began to question its legitimacy.

Kapalak, who couldn't help noticing this, invited him for a dialogue one day. Seated on the bank of Adi Ganga, Satyakam expressed his confusion over this man-woman relationship versus his spiritual practices. His love for Bhairavi was full, but he couldn't hide his traditional doubts. He knew the power of temptations. Kapalak heard him with cool patience and loving care. For a long while there was silence. Confused and disheartened, Satyakam became deeply sad for the second time. He remembered the first time he had become sad, when his Master had entered his hut for the last time in Himalaya.

The muddy water of Adi Ganga flowed slowly and quietly. Without lifting his face, Kapalak began to speak in a rich, heavy voice.

"Satyakam, you have been sent here for this purpose. An inclination for learning Tantra was simply an excuse, though not altogether a hollow one. Precisely speaking, you were to go through Tantra education so as to know and fully appreciate the relationship between man and woman, not in the way people generally understand it, but on a much higher level: as the mystical phenomenon of creation.

"Be mindful, Satyakam, that each male has a portion of female in him and each female has a male portion in her. According to Tantric teachings, a man has four elements of male and three of female in him, and a woman has four elements of female and three of male in her. This difference of one element makes a man and a woman. Otherwise there is no essential difference between the two. Both have been created in this way so as to make creation possible. Woman is an embodiment of nature, which is part of man.

"Barring one elemental difference, both have the same characteristics: birth-death, love-hatred, toleration-anger, lust-belligerence, thirst-hunger, fear-courage, passion, will to live, the search for happiness, and so forth. Together they make a complete combination of the seven elements and thus make union possible."

Heaving a deep sigh, Kapalak looked at Satyakam, who was listening intently. Kapalak continued, "Whatever perfection you may achieve in yourself will always remain incomplete without knowing the corresponding relationship with nature, of which woman is an embodiment—for man. Universal Nature, often called the Divine Mother, pervades not only you but a woman too! Traditional ways of dealing with a woman are no longer practical for a man who wants to achieve perfection. Temptation is another word for fear.

"I do not mean to emphasize the relationship as such, but rather your knowing the secret of that relationship. Once you realize that woman is in you, as man is in woman too, you'll hardly find a struggle necessary to have or not have a relationship."

"Do you mean that once a man knows his nature fully within him, including the female aspect, then the need for a woman, or the absence of this need, is immaterial, and the same holds true for a woman, too?"

"Exactly," Kapalak continued, "In other words, man and woman no longer remain a temptation to each other, but are complimentary. When you know your nature within fully, the outer world, including the opposite sex, merely presents a reflection of it. In short, whatever weakness or strength lies within your mental fabric, the corresponding temptations or mastery will follow without. Greatest of all is the knowledge which releases you from temptation and weakness and makes you *see* the Truth. Consequently, having a relationship or not loses its distinction and thus frees you from temptations or avoidance."

Satyakam turned his gaze on Kapalak's face, asking sharply, "Why did you prefer not to have a consort since you have known the secret of the man-woman relationship?"

Kapalak smiled and raised his head. Majestically, he turned his whole torso toward Satyakam and with utmost command he replied, "Who told you I didn't have one in this or the previous birth? And didn't I say that after you know the mystical secret of your nature you are no longer in need of or without need of such a relationship?"

Kapalak looked triumphantly at Satyakam and released the last missile, "I have avoided having a consort with me, if that is what you mean, not to avoid temptation or downfall, but because I no longer feel a craving for one. I feel so full inside because, having known and mastered my nature, I hardly need a companion outside. This does not mean either

"...you'll encounter some dreadful voices and perhaps ugly sights...Remind yourself again and again that you are upheld by the power that dwells within you." (P. 51)

that if I had one it would make any difference in my behavior. Perhaps you may take it that within and without have lost any meaning for me, and this is the way I am in this incarnation."

Satyakam became sober and with his head bent down, like a defeated target, he humbly asked, "Then why do you encourage me to have a consort, when the possibility of deriving full knowledge and perfection lies in my knowing my own nature independently?"

Benignly, Kapalak spoke, "Your karmas at present are different from mine. Perhaps at one point I had the same need as you have now. One has to follow the path according to one's requirements and not by mechanically imitating someone else.

"Also, you must bear in mind that each one's mission on this earth is one's own, and thus different from another's. In one respect you are very lucky, Satyakam, in that you won't have to struggle much with this man-woman problem, because both you and Bhairavi are already advanced souls. You will be pleasantly surprised one day when you'll find that the thing that perhaps bothered you so much, that brought you down from Himalaya, was not really a temptation or a downfall. Rather, it was a fulfillment and completion of your understanding, a mission for you to bridge a gap in your understanding of man in general and of the whole relationship between man and woman."

Satyakam released a long breath and looked at Kapalak with thankfulness and amusement.

Kapalak suddenly jumped up and quietly began walking away from the river. Satyakam, half dazed, followed after him.

Nearing the hut, Kapalak abruptly turned back and announced, "On the day of the new moon, at midnight, meet me at the same spot on the riverbank where we were just sitting. I'll start some more Tantric techniques with you." Saying this, he entered his hut and closed the door behind him. Satyakam was beginning to see a hitherto unknown facet of Kapalak.

• • • • • • •

Adi Ganga was flowing unruffled. In the pitch dark, hardly a hand could be seen. Satyakam waited under a tree on the bank where, five days before, Kapalak had solved his baffled despair. He was now much at ease. Suddenly he heard footsteps. Kapalak brought his lips near Satyakam's ear and quietly whispered, "Tonight I'll teach you how to achieve fearlessness from the Tantric point of view, and also to commune with spirits. In a little while, a woman's corpse will float by. You have to enter the waters slowly, catch hold of it, and bring it toward the bank. I'll help you pull it out."

"But how do you know it's coming?" asked Satyakam in alarm. His heart beat faster and he became filled with dread.

"This is not the time to discuss all this. Just go on doing as I tell you," commanded Kapalak. Satyakam felt he was a helpless instrument.

The leaves of the trees remained motionless. To Satyakam the whole atmosphere seemed frightfully hushed. Suddenly Kapalak announced, "Here it comes."

Satyakam was bold by nature. Only rarely in his life had he submitted to fear. But this time proved too much. Indeed, all along he had believed that he was fearless. So when Kapalak told him that he would be taught fearlessness that night, he took it too lightly. But now he could see the merit in Kapalak's utterance. He had yet to encounter his subtle ego.

Satyakam hesitated briefly but could not resist entering the water on Kapalak's command. The water was not deep. He could walk through it, his feet sinking into the muddy bottom. The job was not pleasant, especially since he was under the spell of fear. Numbly, he grabbed the floating body and began moving backward. The stench was suffocating. He reached the bank quickly; then Kapalak bent down and grabbed the legs of the corpse. While still holding its shoulders, Satyakam came out of the water and together they pulled the body out.

Both sat down quietly near the body which lay on the bank. Physically Satyakam was not quite exhausted, but mentally he was dazed. He couldn't comprehend all this. Before long, Kapalak broke the silence.

"We should now shift the body to the nearby grove and start your training."

Cautiously, they got up and removed the corpse to where Kapalak directed. To Satyakam's surprise, he found a dim oil lamp burning in the dark grove. Nearby lay a bowl of grain and a glass of liquid. The corpse lay upon fairly level ground. The brown-skinned body was difficult to judge in age—maybe about thirty. The death probably occurred earlier in the day. Satyakam stood like a stone, while Kapalak acted as if this was his normal business, showing no fear, no astonishment, no clouds of unknowing around him. He hastened, "Now I'll initiate you into the fold of Kapalaks with an appropriate mantra, which recalls the spirits back into the dead bodies. Be aware that you have to get rid of fear altogether. If you succumb to fear at any time during the night, you may harm yourself."

Kapalak paused and then resumed, "You have to take off all your clothes and sit on the dead body in a meditative pose. While you'll be repeating the mantra inside, at one point, the dead body will open its mouth. Here is some grain and a glass of wine. When the mouth opens, put some of the grain and a little wine into it, and then it'll close again. At times, the corpse may utter words. Reply or question as best you can." Kapalak paused again and then continued, "Satyakam, you'll encounter some dreadful voices and perhaps ugly sights. But remember, don't fear; hold on to your strength. Remind yourself again and again that you are upheld by the power that dwells within you. Any slip may cause you some damage. But if you come out successfully, which I don't doubt, you'll be quite a different person by early morning."

By now, Satyakam felt half dead. Kapalak moved near him. He was an embodiment of courage; his vibrations helped Satyakam somewhat. Satyakam could see that what was happening was a fact and not a dream. A slight boldness entered him contagiously. He began to undress himself. Then Kapalak brought his lips near his left ear and uttered the infallible mantra three times. The mantra infused an electric current throughout his body and he was no longer fearful, but alive and prepared to do what he was supposed to do. He carefully assumed a posture on the dead body facing toward its head. Folding his palms together near his chest, he bowed to Kapalak from a distance and then lowered his hands, resting them on his knees. Kapalak came forward and touched the point between his eyebrows. As Satyakam closed his eyes, Kapalak walked quietly away into the darkness.

Hardly one phase of the night was over when Satyakam felt a slight movement in the underlying corpse. Opening his eyes, he saw its mouth move as if asking for something. He put some grain and wine into it. Then the mouth closed again. Meanwhile he kept repeating the mantra. This process continued until the second phase of the night was over.

All of a sudden sharp shrieks and wild screams became audible from all sides. At first Satyakam tried to be unmoved and continued repeating the mantra. But the howling noises and threatening challenges grew too nightmarish for him. No longer could he keep his eyes closed. For the first few moments what he saw curdled his blood. Various ugly and fierce-looking creatures were ready to attack and devour him. These creatures looked hideous and demonic. But soon

Satyakam heard Kapalak saying: "You are upheld by the power which dwells within you." Instantly his fear subsided. With renewed courage he closed his eyes and continued the mantra. The dreadful voices and hellish sights persisted for some time, but no longer did they disturb him. Gradually they subsided, then silenced altogether. Now the third phase of the night was over.

Quiet reigned once again. Deep in his mantra, Satyakam felt the night of the new moon, calm and free. But as before, something caught his attention. From the corpse came a thick wailing sound, as if it were dreaming. She sounded as if she were in pain. Her body quivered slightly. Satyakam maintained his posture. The agonizing sound became louder and louder. He burst out quite involuntarily, "Who are you?"

Very faintly and in a quavering voice it spoke, "Re..l..e..a..se m..ee." The voice was thick and heavy. For a moment Satyakam became alarmed. But soon he gathered his consciousness and asked again, "Who are you?"

"Yo..u..r ma..a...y...a..a,*" spoke the same voice, and then her whole body became dead as before.

Satyakam waited for some time to see if anything further would happen. But there was no more movement. Even the mouth seemed still. He then closed his eyes and again concentrated on the mantra. His whole attutide became that of compassion toward the spirits—of the corpse as well as the other demonic ones he had encountered earlier in the night. An utter purity filled his heart, the sublimity of which he had never experienced before. His heart opened wide in gratitude to that indwelling power which upheld him throughout.

The last phase of the night passed peacefully. Satyakam felt relieved and lost in deep absorption.

---

*māyā —illusory appearance

Dawn approached imperceptibly. As if by divine alarm, he opened his eyes and saw Kapalak standing nearby, smiling broadly. Satisfaction filled his face.

"Now get up and we'll immerse the body in the river," said Kapalak, who helped Satyakam lift the body ever so reverently, as if it were a holy, consecrated thing. Then they brought it to the Adi Ganga and tenderly let it flow with the waters. For some time they kept looking at the floating body, as if it were their own kith and kin, until it disappeared. Then Kapalak turned to Satyakam and said, "Wash your body thoroughly in the river before you dress and then come to my hut."

The morning sun's first rays fell upon the ground as Satyakam entered Kapalak's hut. The world seemed quite different to him that day. He couldn't believe he was the same person who existed yesterday. Hardly a trace of the old self remained. He felt transposed to a dimension where he could see only with his third eye. He had no particular questions for Kapalak, who seemed totally different to him. The memory of his Master in Himalaya arose spontaneously and his understanding of him grew larger than ever before. For a while he was lost in loving remembrance of him.

"You accomplished not only a great task last night but also a benevolent one, Satyakam."

Satyakam looked questioningly at Kapalak. Kapalak continued, "You not only got released from fear but you released her spirit too. Many Tantrics recall the spirit back into the dead body and make it work for their selfish and nefarious motives. Under the spell of power, the spirit obeys the command of the Tantric, accomplishing tasks of vengeance as well as horrifying and dark deeds. When the spirit comes into bondage, there is a growing degradation of the Tantric himself until he reaches his terrible end. It is because they often abused the power of Tantra that Tantra fell into disrepute. Rightly taken, it not only fulfills the earthly life but bestows salvation.

"Because you had no selfish motive, nor intended to acquire powers, you achieved fearlessness and simultaneously finished some karmas of that soul. With the power of the mantra you directed the soul of the dead person, although without your knowing, to higher realms. This was apparent from her pathetic plea for release, not only from her body but also from her lower self. And because you responded to it honestly and selflessly you too found relief. This led to calm absorption and the transformation of your personality."

There was a pause. Then Satyakam quietly asked, "You said that I directed her soul without my knowledge. Can you throw more light on this?"

Kapalak stirred the firewood and the sparks flew up like a hundred fireflies. Then he blew on the coals and flames burst forth. Raising himself up, he replied, "The mantra with which I initiated you is the seed mantra. It contains the potentiality of a full doctrine. With repetition, it creates a cerebral vibration which generates the power that in turn can be activated at will. Being harmless and pure hearted by nature, you subconsciously responded to the request of the soul and activated the power of the mantra to release her. It simply worked. Be mindful that no master, however capable, can help a disciple unless that disciple helps himself by his own willingness and efforts. If you were simply a blind follower, you could not have accomplished all this. The task of a seeker is not merely to acquire the mechanics of various techniques, but *to be*. The correct psychological disposition is achieved only after you grow out of a sense of selfishness."

Satyakam inquired further, "What do you mean by a mantra containing the full potentiality of a doctrine?"

"A doctrine may contain hundreds of aphorisms. These can be condensed into some stanzas which may be reduced to a few statements. These, in turn, can be crystallized into a seed mantra which will potentially contain the full power of the doctrine."

Satyakam asked further, "Can you now tell me how you knew the exact time and day of the dead body's coming?"

"When a Tantric becomes much advanced and knows the science of time, he can foresee both birth and death, including the time and mode of disposal of the dead body. That day when I was talking to you on the bank of Adi Ganga, I was clearly seeing a dead body floating by that spot on the day and at the time I mentioned to you later. After some time it won't be difficult for you to know all this."

Day after day they met either at Kapalak's hut or in the grove-hut where Satyakam had once practiced Nada Yoga. Kapalak imparted Tantric techniques, including raising of the Kundalini, and paused only for deep discussions on abstruse mystical subjects. This, however, did not stop or reduce Satyakam's visits to Bhairavi. On the contrary, she became more meaningful and comprehensible to him. Often he would tell her all that he was undergoing. She would simply smile in an understanding way.

Once, as Satyakam was narrating the latest technique to her, she opened her mouth to speak for the first time about her past. "My guru, whom we call *Mātājī**, taught me this technique too, and many more."

With slight surprise, Satyakam asked, "Where was your guru?"

"In Vindhyāchal near Benares. I lived with Mataji for four years, after which she sent me here to finish my karmas."

"Here!"

"With you," politely replied Bhairavi.

---

*Mātājī—respected mother

"Did you know this when you first saw me standing in the line to see you?"

"Not immediately. But it didn't take long to recognize the link." There was peace on her face.

Satyakam's head bent down and he seemed to be lost in deep thought—or revelation.

With the same peaceful disposition, Bhairavi continued, "At the time of parting, Mataji told me, 'You have to make a path for yourself. You yourself are the path,' and blessed me."

Jarred out of his reverie, Satyakam could not help but ask, "Tell me more about Mataji. I mean, what relationship you felt toward her."

"Mataji was not only my guru but also Divine Mother to me. I would have never left her had she not asked me to do so. I had never even imagined that I could ever stay without her!" Bhairavi paused for a moment and then continued, "I could never imagine a different Divine Mother than her. She is the embodiment of sweetness, beauty, and power—what grace and benevolence emanated from her whole body all the time!" Tears appeared in her eyes, and she slowly lowered her forehead.

"Do you miss her?" There was sympathy in Satyakam's words.

"She is hardly away from me." Satyakam could feel the presence of Mataji as Bhairavi uttered this. Both remained silent for a while.

Bhairavi spoke again, "Mataji is an embodiment of Durga—at least that is what we believe. In the sanctuary, when she would come and sit on the dais, we could hardly look straight at her face. Such dazzling power and radiance! What an accomplishment of Tantra in her! Her beauty and perfection provided an easy communion."

•   •   •   •   •   •   •

As Kapalak and Satyakam were sitting one day around the fire, talking about the practices, the conversation once again turned to the topic of *Shakti**.

Satyakam asked, "What is the difference between Shakti and an ordinary woman?"

"Shakti is a personification of a goddess," replied Kapalak in his characteristic manner, "a transubstantiation of an ordinary woman into an embodiment of the divine. By visualizing the essence of his Shakti, the practitioner gains the vision of reality. Only through divine vision can the practitioner apprehend the innate divine qualities of the physical woman. The female plays the role of the divine energy and the body is merely an instrument used in the quest for transformation. Vital energy is seen as divine in itself, thereby acting with transforming force on the mind and spiritualizing it."

"Through Bhairavi I have begun to see this," responded Satyakam. "This interplay of male and female is simply a compliment of thoughts and feelings which relates more completely to one's inner self." Satyakam paused for a moment and exclaimed, "But one thing I can't understand: why is there desire for union on the biological level, apart from procreation or physical gratification—I mean, from the Tantric point of view?"

Kapalak smiled amusedly and spoke, "The cosmic drama is represented in the human body. According to Tantra, individual and universal are the same. Both male and female play roles and they move together toward the fulfillment of unity. In essence, the physical and biological ritual of union is an experience of *feelings* and not one of *explanations*.

"Biological needs aren't moral, indulgent or permissive; they're simply a way of realization. The ritual of union is

---

Shakti—lit., energy or power; in Tantra, used for the female consort of a seeker

58

devoid of emotions and sentimental impulses. One has to recognize the spiritual values of sex. By manipulating this energy, revitalizing and sublimating it, the Kundalini, which is dormant in the human body, rises to the brain center to unite with cosmic consciousness. Ultimately this energy evokes creative powers to ascend to the transcendental union of *Shiva-Shakti* for the realization of bliss."

Kapalak looked intently at Satyakam and continued, "Satyakam, starting tonight I'll impart to you the final secret stages of Tantra which will give you the fulfillment of union and thus prepare you for the mission you are to carry out."

Satyakam was quiet and seemed relieved. On his face were the signs of a fatigued traveller who is nearing his destination.

Kapalak seemed at his best that day. In an inspiring mood, he went on, "Before we part today, I would like to give you my farewell message, Satyakam.

"The spirit of man is immortal; its growth and splendor have no limits. The divine principle which gives life dwells within and without us and is eternally beneficent. Each man is his own lawgiver, the dispenser of glory and doom to himself.

"In the final sacrifice, a man turns for liberation to the redeeming Spirit within and achieves exaltation to divine glory."

After a pause he ended, "Satyakam, one day you'll shed a blessing on mankind."

3

DREAMS WITHIN DREAMS
(autumn)

Trees began to change colors. . . .

... Marriages, so it is said, are made in heaven. The inevitable happened. On an auspicious day Satyakam and Bhairavi were married through Tantric rites under Kapalak's personal supervision. Hundreds of people attended the ceremony. All day long, streams of devotees flowed in and out of the temple grounds. Clouds of dust rose in the air, and music sung to Lord Shiva and Mother Kali rang sonorously. Those who entered the precincts were greeted by the constantly chiming temple bells. Satyakam and Bhairavi beamed with an inexplicable joy and a glow surrounded their bodies. With silent gestures they welcomed the people who had come from various surrounding villages. Many said the couple was an incarnation of Shiva and Durga.

Soon the ceremony ended, followed by a constant rush to touch their feet. The clamor was so great that people could hardly hear one another above it all. The couple patiently accepted the obeisance. Afterwards Satyakam and Bhairavi rose, turned toward the shrine, and bowed together before the imagine of Kali. As they stood up, Kapalak came near. Both touched his feet. This was Kapalak's first appearance before such a large crowd.

"How do you feel about all this tumult?" asked Kapalak humorously.

Satyakam replied with a sober smile, "It is the spirit that I love."

Kapalak commented, "You shall teach the Truth as taught by the ancient seers and leave it in the hearts of the people."

Volunteers distributed consecrated food among the visitors and gradually people began leaving for their homes.

Dusk came and, except for a few nearest devotees, all were gone. Once again, silence pervaded the temple courtyard.

The story of Satyakam and Bhairavi would have been

like any other householder couple had it not been for their extraordinary spiritual achievement. This marked difference was sharpened by Satyakam's proficiency in many sublimation techniques of Tantra which he shared with his advanced Bhairavi.

The specific physical requirements of an ideal couple, according to Tantra, were not lacking in them. Both were healthy figures. He was manly as much as she was lovely, with her slender waist, full breasts, soft skin and lotus eyes.

In the temple's solitary compound, free from noise and pollution, they occupied the priest quarters. Because their feelings and actions were harmonious, they were well suited for perfect expression. The devout Bhairavi played the role of the divine energy and became a perennial source of joy to her lord.

People addressed them as "Maharaj" and "Deviji" respectively. Deviji diligently looked after arrangements for worship in the temple with meticulous care and Maharaj gave *Satsangs** daily in the afternoon. He often talked on devotion to Mother Divine. Singing groups visited from time to time and the attendance at the temple functions grew larger and larger. This was the first time in the history of the temple that Satsangs were being held in it.

After two years had passed, a son was born. Many devotees brought presents for the special feast. Rohit was brown colored, healthy, and grew happily in this atmosphere of love, power and harmony. When he was about two years old, a second son was born. Again, there was a big festival and the child was named Pūran.

Puran was more fair skinned and delicate than Rohit, with an aura of shining light around him. He seemed more sweet, quiet and intelligent than his brother, but nonetheless,

---

*Satsang—association with Truth or holy people; spiritual discourse

they grew side by side with judicious treatment and care. Rohit, in features, resembled his mother and was most fond of her, whereas Puran took after his father. The divine family lived in joy, peace and abundance, while Puran grew to be one year old.

But nature is changeful and no state of affairs remains constant. One autumn afternoon when Deviji got up from a short nap, she discovered Rohit missing. Casually, she looked here and there and then grew secretly apprehensive. As she searched further, their housemaid came running and weeping, "Deviji, Rohit drowned in the pond!" Stunned, Deviji ran towards the temple's pond. The housemaid ran after her screaming, "I went to the pond to bathe and as I entered the water, something struck my feet. I lowered my hands with fear and caught hold of the body and brought it out ... " She was gasping for breath.

Upon reaching the pond, they found Rohit's body lying at the water's edge. Quiet tears filled Deviji's eyes as she collapsed to the ground like a lump of flesh. Taking Rohit's head, she gently placed it on her thigh. In the meanwhile, a number of people accompanying Maharaj came hurriedly as the news spread. As if a dam had burst, Deviji exploded in a poignant wail, falling on Maharaj's feet. With tears flowing profusely, she pleaded to him, "Please revive him. I know you can recall the spirit in a dead body." No one had seen Deviji in such a condition of helplessness. There were tears in everyone's eyes and some people were even sobbing. All faces were turned toward Maharaj with expectant eyes.

Maharaj serenely sat down near Deviji, touched the forehead of Rohit and uttered softly, "What had to happen has happened. There is no use going against the will of Divine Mother who knows best." Deviji was suddenly quiet for a moment, but with a heavy sadness she pleaded deeply, "Won't you save him, lord?"

"I would have if Mother had wanted that." Satyakam bowed his head and remained silent. Lifting his hand from Rohit's forehead, he placed it on Deviji's shoulder and resumed, "This is a test for us and an opportunity as well to know human feelings and attachments. One of the lessons for which Mataji sent you here is to outgrow attachments and clinging by *experiencing* and not merely by *conceptualizing*."

Deviji looked at Rohit. A thrust of sobbing rose again in her full breast and then she looked at Maharaj. Like a dying deer she spoke, "You don't feel any sadness and loss?" A tinge of sad envy marked her words.

"Death," replied Maharaj, "is the same as birth. Both are simply two sides of the same phenomenon. Without birth there is no death and vice versa. The span of life in between is but a fragment of the total life, which is never lost nor dead.

"Rohit was somewhere else before he came to us and they must have lost him before he came here. So we too must lose him before others get him on his onward journey to Perfection. Who are we to determine a soul's life span?"

After proper rituals and ceremonies were done at home, Rohit's body was taken for burial on the bank of Adi Ganga. The priest was summoned to perform the final rituals. The body was then lowered into the pit which was filled in with earth. Others brought water from the river and sprinkled it over the grave. All were quiet.

On the way back someone asked, "How did he drown?" One lady replied, "At one point he was seen playing near the pond, but no one knew when he might have gotten in or slipped into the water." Another said, "Poor boy! Destiny!" There was a heavy silence all around.

Upon entering the house Deviji, in a relatively more composed attitude, looking intently at Maharaj said, "You are very cruel!" With a dry smile he replied, "The serenity of knowledge and the stonelike quality of cruelty may seem the same from the outside. But what a difference! You understand that."

That night Bhairavi could hardly sleep. Puran was sound asleep at her left. She turned restlessly in her bed a few times and then got up. Approaching Satyakam's bedside, she whispered, "Are you awake?"

Satyakam was lying on his back in a restful pose. He slowly sat up and said, "You couldn't sleep?"

"I am not as miserable now, although it is hard to forget about Rohit. I hope by tomorrow I'll be much better, by Mataji's grace."

As Satyakam put his right hand on her left shoulder to comfort her, she continued, "Can I ask you a question?" He gave consent by his silence.

"Did you know that Rohit would die this way? Couldn't you have prevented it?"

"Yes, I knew his destiny and could have prevented it, but Mother didn't want it. The whole scene was arranged by Her in order to make you free from attachment. It reminds me of Kapalak's training to make me free from fear, although at that time I felt I didn't need it and that fear was not in me. But when I went through the dreadful practice in the night, I could then understand that it is one thing to *believe* but quite another to *realize*. The next morning I could clearly *see* how the ghost of fear had gone out of me."

He heaved a deep sigh and continued in a deep, resonant voice, "When you first came to this place and people used to stand in line to see you, who could have believed that you had even a trace of attachment in you! Perhaps you and even I would have rejected the notion right off. But now you can easily see that, at least for a while, you could hardly avoid being a mother. A test is given not only to show an imperfection to you, but also to make you come out of it. This was one of the reasons why Mataji sent you here. A mother's attachment to her offspring is the hardest for her to let go of. This was your biggest hurdle."

"But what guarantee is there," asked Bhairavi, "that after only this one experience I will be free from attachment for all times to come, especially when I have Puran to care for!"

Satyakam moved closer to her and with utmost love replied, "Because you are already an advanced soul on the spiritual path, this one experience is enough to pull you out of earthly clinging. Also this is not your first lifetime to experience attachment. In a series of births you have had various such experiences, and in your last birth you had just arrived at completing your attachment but somehow fell short of release. So now the death of Rohit gave the finishing touches to this attachment."

He paused and then said, "The price of evolution to a superhuman stage is the renunciation of some existing human values, both likeable and dislikeable.

"Puran will not be pulling you down, but quite the opposite ... " Suddenly Satyakam checked himself and then resumed, "but that'll be sometime later."

Bhairavi hesitated for a while before asking politely, "And what was the cause of your being sent here?"

"You," replied Satyakam, "to teach me the Truth of life as well as the fulfillment of its mission. Divine Mother in you is my worshipful deity and my *Shakti*."

Bhairavi calmly put her head on his feet and returned to her bed.

Early next morning, on hearing of the child's death, people slowly came by to offer their condolences to Maharaj and Deviji. Many were sad and distraught, but quite a few waiting outside the house became critical. "Such high souls to have such a tragedy!" They proclaimed, "What is the difference between them and common people like us? Couldn't they save their own child?" Others assumed to be part-time teachers: "Sinner or virtuous, all are subject to karmas. All have died, laymen and saints and prophets. This is the law of Nature, what else?" Discussion—or was it criticism?—carried on. "But I have heard, I don't know though, that unless one is a sinner, one does not lose younger ones first." Another quickly replied after a sigh of impatience, "It is the Iron Age now, sir. What you say was true only in the Golden Age." And the discussion continued. They seemed much wiser after the experience, though at another's expense. Others waiting there merely kept quiet and silently shed tears.

At one point Maharaj and Deviji came out to greet the visitors. Both seemed nearly normal. But few could understand their inner stage of consciousness.

•   •   •   •   •   •   •

Day followed after day, and month after month. Bhairavi carried on her temple duties as lovingly as before. No trace remained of the loss of Rohit. She was an embodiment of devotion, joy and power, which magnetically attracted people to her. They would wait on and on to see her. And each day Satyakam's Satsang became fuller and fuller. People from various walks of life filled the temple compound in the afternoons. Maharaj was a picture of serenity, love and compassion.

Often in Satsang people posed questions to Maharaj ranging from spiritual or social to human or even political problems. Whatever the topic, it would invariably be turned to the spiritual by Maharaj's masterful touch. People listened in rapt attention.

One day, as oftentimes occurred, a person who seemed to be a humanist asked, "Isn't it unfair to preach about God to those thousands who are worried about their basic physical needs?"

Maharaj replied, "Certainly those who are occupied

with the problem of food cannot remember God much. They should be helped by food and employment; but one should not extend this philosophy as an excuse for all those who are able to maintain their basic needs. The evolution of man, individually or collectively, is not uniform for everyone. Consequently, each one has to grow on his or her own according to the Law of Karma. Thus the only question remains, who should serve whom in what way? This is established according to the Law which determines temperament and capacity. Each reformer, preacher or leader has different functions to perform according to his tendencies and mission.

"One common factor which is a must is selflessness. If one is selfless and sincere, the help becomes genuine and the people receive the required benefit. For this there is no need to change one's choice of duties, which may have been determined by temperament."

"Don't you think, Maharaj, that if persons like yourself entered politics, then politics would be purified and people would receive much needed justice and welfare?" asked a devotee.

Satyakam lowered his head slightly and replied unassumingly, "Perhaps yes, if such be the need. But according to the Spiritual Laws, holy people should only guide and help other sections of society and not get directly involved in politics. This is necessary to keep spirituality above corruption, favoritism and gratification—to maintain it as a reservoir of unselfish power. Also, by this method, people can work out their own karmas, increase their understanding and arrive at maturity to grasp their responsibility.

"To get the full benefit from such a reservoir, people have to listen to and follow holy men and not expect them to do everything for them. There is no need for holy people to become politicians, but to guide politicians and leaders in other fields and help them purify their motives. This cannot be accomplished without the active cooperation of the leaders concerned. In other words, the integration of spirituality with other facets of human society can only be achieved by the willing cooperation of the leaders and the people.

"But there are special occasions in the history of man, when selfishness runs rampant, and social reformers, politicians and various leaders fail to deliver the goods; when the Divine by His own will enters into these fields—as a Krishna, a Moses, a Buddha or a Jesus—to purify and to establish righteousness. The decision in such epochs is done from above by divine will, depending as well upon the call and readiness of the people."

After a night of heavy rain, while the temple grounds were still wet, people began pouring in for the customary afternoon Satsang. That day Satyakam seemed more tender and gentle than usual, yet powerful.

Scattered all around the grounds were fallen branches and autumn leaves from the previous night's heavy storm. By early afternoon the gray overcast sky began to clear. Preeminent master of the critical moment, Satyakam had a fine sense of timing. He called the people to collect the scattered refuse and clean the grounds. Some of them plunged into the work immediately, while others held back.

Soon the grounds were clean, although still damp. Most people didn't mind sitting down. That day a few scholarly pundits from a nearby town had come to hear Maharaj for the first time. All the while the temple grounds were being cleaned they had waited in a corner. Now they approached the dais upon which Satyakam was sitting and sat in front of the audience. They seemed tough and experienced.

One of them suddenly asked, "What is the merit of such works—I mean, the cleaning of the grounds by the devotees, when it could have been done by servants?" A tinge of superiority colored his words.

In his usual soft voice Satyakam replied, "Selfless works purify the heart. Without a purified heart, knowledge is hollow and arrogant. The seed of evil doesn't get uprooted until true humility and devotion are born. An impure heart cannot have devotion. The sense of high and low, spiritual and menial, cannot make a seeker qualified to receive enlightenment. The high does not contradict the low but conserves what is of value in it and sublimates it . . . "

Another pundit interrupted, "What is evil, Maharaj?"

"Evil is an unstable state, being opposed to the true nature of things," replied Satyakam. "It is a principle of death, while good is a principle of life."

"Is evil real?" inquired a third learned pundit.

"Evil is real and unreal both. It is real to the extent that it requires effort to transform its nature. It is unreal in the sense that it is bound to be transmuted into good."

"But sometimes it is so painful to do that!" one commented.

"Yes, the good and the pleasant are not always conjoined. In such cases one should choose the good always. The pleasant, where it is opposed to the good, misses the goal."

"What is the goal, sir?"

"Realization of the Spirit," answered Satyakam serenely.

"But then, why are there so many trials and tribulations on the path of spiritual seeking?" shouted a lady from the audience, as if in agony.

Satyakam looked up at the woman with utmost compassion and replied, "The realization of Spirit is not an uninterrupted advance. Suffering and pain cannot be abolished as long as the spiritual life has to be lived under human conditions. Until one's whole integrated being is offered with devotion to the Divine, the process of gradual upliftment through tests and suffering cannot cease. When devotion matures and becomes complete, one has the vision of God."

After a deep sigh he continued, "Pleasures seem to lie in the satisfaction of impulses, but the good requires the taming of the lower tendencies. Conscious actions tend to become unconscious habits.

"The illusions of life are to vanish and our cherished dreams are to disperse before the life divine can be realized."

And another afternoon, while the temple grounds blazed beneath the autumn sun, devotees without fail began coming in to listen to the marvelous sermon of Maharaj. It was not so much the words that attracted the people, although they undoubtedly did, but what he was: an embodiment of holiness and wisdom, detached to the core of his being from all clingings.

That day a number of university students were present among the multitude. Satyakam, relaxed in his seat, looked at them questioningly. One student raised his hand. Maharaj nodded consent.

"What is true education, Maharaj?" There was a keen desire in the student to know.

"True education is what liberates, liberates the spirit of man. Knowledge must be one with truth because truth gives freedom—not the freedom of unrestrained flood water, but that of water flowing freely within the banks of relativity."

"Then all this secular and academic education is untrue and useless?" another student asked in slight agitation.

Maharaj smiled and in a restrained manner said, "Secular knowledge is untrue in the sense that it fails to give wings to the soul of man. But it is true and useful in its own sphere of the dualistic play of observer and observed."

The first student politely resumed, "Is the true knowledge of which you are kindly speaking capable of knowing everything, including the sciences, arts and various humanities?"

"In principle, yes," Satyakam lovingly and emphatically replied. "By realizing your Spirit you know everything creatively and blissfully. But in the process of knowing, on the way, one encounters the urges and impulses to know and have mundane knowledge, a tiny reflection of that great aspiration to be omniscient.

"Thus, secular knowledge is called indirect, whereas spiritual knowledge is direct."

A third student asked, "Should one then renounce an academic career to pursue spiritual knowledge?"

"Not necessarily," replied Satyakam understandingly, "it all depends on what you want and where your aspiration lies. Ultimately, the aim of all knowledge—secular or otherwise—is to know the true Self or Spirit. Science may call it the Ultimate Essence. The most telling difference between these two is that the secular never imparts full satisfaction whereas knowledge of the Spirit does."

Another student asked meekly, "Is there any chance of reconciliation between direct and indirect knowledge, Maharaj?"

Satyakam released a deep sigh and said, "Yes, and rightly so. By knowing your true Self you attain immortality of Spirit and thereby live in perpetual awareness and joy. On the other hand, secular knowledge imparts to you the capacity to live in and maintain the relative world.

"But without spiritual awareness, secular subjects are hollow and incomplete, mere intellectual gymnastics. So unless the Spirit shines through the intellect, making life and body an integrated whole, the clash between the two will not cease. Fulfillment of the mundane is possible only when the Divine penetrates through it and removes the darkness of ignorance.

"After all, what is the purpose of education if not to get freedom from ignorance and attain light?"

·   ·   ·   ·   ·   ·   ·

About two years had passed since Rohit's death. Puran was now about three years old. He was a very bright boy with something otherworldly about him. His face glowed like that of an angel, and it wasn't necessary to tell him a thing twice to make him understand. His keen grasp of things made others careful when talking to him. Often he would remain unusually quiet, more so than other children of his age.

His most usual pastimes were intently watching his mother perform the rituals in the Kali temple, and sitting near his father in Satsang. Often he would try to do as his mother did in the temple. During Satsang he would watch the audience in such a way as to feel their response to his father!

People were all praise for Puran, wanting to love and fondle him, but as soon as they approached he would run away. Neither proud nor shy, Puran was too mature inside to need outside care or attention. A transparent wisdom shone in his eyes. As he sat crosslegged with his mother in the temple or with his father in Satsang, his body remained amazingly motionless. Devotees of Maharaj and Deviji revered him as a born yogi.

On the occasion of the festival of Shāradā pūjā, people turned out in great numbers. As the central figure, Bhairavi wore a white silk saree with a wide blood-red border. Golden ornaments sparkled about her neck, arms and hands, and upon her broad forehead a large red powder mark sanctified her, making her face shine in divine beauty. Standing in front of the temple image to perform the ceremony, Bhairavi appeared as a manifestation of the Universal Mother that day. Her back was to the audience. Facing the deity sat Satyakam and Puran, on her right and left. On the far right, facing halfway between the deity and the audience, sat Kapalak, who had been specially invited to honor the occasion.

At an appointed moment the ritual commenced with Bhairavi slowly performing worship in a systematic and rhythmic way. The drum beats and ringing temple bells joined with Bhairavi's rhythmic movements, enhancing a hypnotic spell throughout. Occasionally the sound of the conch shell was heard, awakening the sleeping souls. The charged atmosphere, elevated with Divine Mother's vibrations, absorbed the people in the awesome scene.

Gradually, Bhairavi's body began waving slightly, keeping tune with the rhythm of the worship rituals and drum beats. As the worship was climaxing in a crescendo of ecstasy, the lights and incense fell from her hands and she became oblivious to everything around her. The ladies' section of the audience simultaneously began making a special invocation as the force of Divine Mother descended into Bhairavi. The men's side was repeating "Mā ... Mā* ... " with joyful tears in their eyes.

Before her body could fall, two ladies caught hold of her and gently laid her divine body on the floor over the seat. Her body seemed lifeless, a soft bundle of flesh and bones with eyes partially closed and gaze drawn inward. An indescribable luster shone on her face.

No trace of restlessness stirred the people. Occasionally some of them arose to behold her, but otherwise all were serene and oblivious to the world outside. The bells, drums and conch shell continued their rhythmic spell in time with the ladies' invocation.

All this time, Puran sat spellbound, looking quietly at his mother. But now he could no longer hold himself. He

---

*Mā—Mother

began to cry loudly. His father, who had remained soaked in the divine atmosphere, lifted Puran into his lap and pressed him against his bosom. Puran soon grew quiet. Kapalak too seemed in high ecstasy.

Some time later, the eyes of Bhairavi slowly began to open and her body showed signs of life. She moved her open eyes around, but they still did not seem focused on this world. Torrents of tears began flowing from her unusually large and reddened eyes. What immense love and purity filled them!

Taking up the ritual material, some ladies began waving lights and incense in front of Bhairavi. Jubilance once again filled the audience when she sat up. Slowly she turned her body and faced the people who, with folded hands, began bowing down to her from wherever they were sitting. Bhairavi's very appearance would melt away evil propensities. The hands of the devotees remained folded in adoration for a long time.

· · · · · · ·

When Puran reached his fourth year, Satyakam began educating him. On the first day before the lessons commenced, Satyakam held a small ceremony in worship of Saraswati, the goddess of learning. Puran looked like a small angel, dressed in a simple white cloth, with a sacred thread round his bare torso. His head was shaven completely except for a hair tail on the back of his head. A small mark of sandalwood paste was on his forehead and his feet were bare. His face, nay his whole body, shone in purity and glory. At the conclusion of the ceremony, when he bowed down before the goddess, one could not help but be sobered by his devotion.

Satyakam started teaching him the Sanskrit alphabet, sentences and small rhymes. Hungry for education, Puran went on gulping down the lessons quickly and with good appetite. For one full year, with unabated enthusiasm, he continued digesting everything his father imparted to him. Occasionally he had his fun too, playing and running with other boys in the vicinity. Undoubtedly, he stood out far beyond his companions. People standing by watched him with greedy eyes, feasting on the extraordinary aura around him. Unlike other children, he was not fond of toys, except for a flute that he tried to play upon.

Afternoon Satsang remained the essence of each day. The variety of people grew enormously, now including even patriots and holy men, among others. Satyakam's fame traveled like wild fire and quite frequently there was not enough space on the temple ground to contain the multitude. However, the silence and attentiveness of the people remained unaffected, interrupted only by the occasional cry of a child.

One pleasant day a well-known patriot came to visit Maharaj. When everyone was seated he asked challengingly, "What is *Dharma**?"

"Whatever you are doing," came the pat reply from Maharaj. The stranger seemed caught unaware and was suddenly left unarmed. For a few surprised moments he couldn't find words to express himself. He soon gathered his courage and asked, "Don't we owe an obligation to our nation, our birthplace?"

"Undoubtedly yes," replied Satyakam, "but where do you draw the boundaries of your birthplace?—village, state, nation, good earth, this solar system or even the universe? Where you owe the obligation depends on where your consciousness is, doesn't it? 'The whole world is my family,' as the saying goes. So it depends on which is your world—there your Dharma lies!"

---

*Dharma—Law, duty; that which holds together

"Does that mean that each individual has a different Dharma?" asked the patriot, in a subdued tone.

"Not only individually, but also collectively, we have different Dharma according to our temperament and stage of evolution."

"I am glad that you include collective Dharma as well, because should we not then collectively respond to the national needs as the present evolution demands, and work accordingly?"

"I have already given a reply to this, unless you mean that all and sundry should jump into the same boat—which would mean that all have, necessarily, the same karmas! Also, one point which is equally important is that serving our Motherland may be done through various fields, unless you mean that there is only one field which is the most important, and that is the one *you* have been interested in!"

The patriot smiled, as if caught red-handed, and confessed, "You have hit the nail on the head, Maharaj," and then kept quiet.

One holy man asked, "What is the mystery behind life and death, and can we overcome death and decay?"

Maharaj replied, "Mother Nature has a mysterious way of continually keeping herself renewed, recreated and rejuvenated. Although change is the inherent quality of nature, life is in perpetual identity with it. So change, which is symbolized in birth and death, helps nature to continue in an unending vigorous flow of life, interrupted, of course, by the junctions of birth and death.

"If life were to be maintained in its static and pure existence, there would be no need for relative change, and thus there would be no relative life as we know it. So the phenomenon of birth and death is a necessary consequence of the kind of life we have chosen. To avoid death, and therefore birth, is to finish the whole drama of dualistic life and arrive at perennial pure existence.

"Birth and death have been exemplified in various ways—as new and old garments, as the two gates of entrance and exit—and rightly so. Thus, philosophically speaking, one way to avoid death and decay is to avoid birth and regeneration. But there is another way of actually existing in the relative world without decay and death of the physical body. This state is attained by knowing the inner mystery of nature and then being motivated by one's will power. All this requires rigorous practice of yogic techniques learned from an adept master.

"Energy pervades the cosmos. One only has to know how to tap this force and recharge and renew one's metabolism. This regeneration of the cells is not necessarily done from outside one's own body, but from inside too. After all, outside and inside are just two sides of the same coin. Thus in replenishing the energy, the source lies within and without. After prolonged practices one discovers the mystery of nature, which is actually simple and common knowledge."

Another holy man questioned, "What makes this common knowledge so difficult to discover?"

In his usual manner, Satyakam explained, "Habits. We are so very preoccupied with our desires and unconscious actions that these form a pattern of habits, the mass of which builds up an individual or collective personality, which in turn obscures the common secret of Mother Nature. These habits build up a shell, as it were, around true nature and thus make it difficult to know.

"So, to rediscover this natural knowledge, one has to employ certain techniques with will and devotion as a counter-effect to these previous habits. This is hard to do without the help and grace of a qualified master."

•　•　•　•　•　•　•

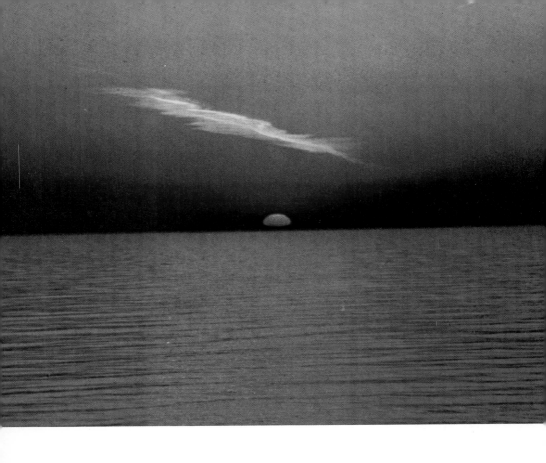

"At sunset time, the sun grew into a big red ball of fire before sinking into the horizon on the opposite bank of Ganga. A mystical quiet pervaded." (P. 90)

Puran had progressed a lot by now and he was in his fifth year. In this one year he had heard many heroic and spiritual stories from epics at the feet of his father and in the lap of his mother. Philosophical questions much beyond his age poured out of him, to which his present mentors gave cautious and well informed answers. His reading and writing were superb. Bhairavi was often amazed at his knowledge, which she no doubt attributed to his previous birth. Frequently he would say something very deep and enlightening, throwing her into deep thought, admiration and secret joy.

Satyakam described Puran as a fallen yogi who had taken a birth through parents whose environment would, from childhood, provide an adequate outlet for his karmas and thereby allow him to proceed towards the fulfillment of his aim properly. Birth in such a family is so rare and so blessed! Such a soul either becomes a realized one or a monarch.

Days lingered on and Puran continued studying Vedic mathematics, epics and light philosophy, and in this way he reached his seventh year. He was a blissful child. More devoted than attached, Bhairavi displayed a noticeable reverence for him. She began to recognize an extraordinary greatness in him and held a secret wish for guidance from him!

Coming events cast their shadows before them. Satyakam was feeling clearly that the time had come for him to be alone again, in order to finish the remainder of his journey toward the Highest. His family and professional karmas seemed to be over and he felt relieved of such obligations, however good and noble they were. Each stage in life has its own limited purpose, and as soon as it is served, that particular stage comes to an end. To cling to it beyond this point would be to prolong an unnecessary attachment and thus make it simply a stagnant rut. Satyakam was wise enough to recognize this juncture in his great and eventful life.

His loving thoughts went to his Master, whom he had never forgotten or even felt distant from. He wished he could see and meet with him just then! He remembered the promise of his Master that he would appear whenever need arose.

Next morning, Satyakam wished to see Kapalak. As he approached his hut, he saw Kapalak returning from Adi Ganga. There was a blessed smile on his lips. Without any formalities, Kapalak came near him and put his right hand on his left shoulder like a chum and spoke lovingly, "That's right. You'll meet our Master soon."

"And what about you?" inquired Satyakam mysteriously, with a twinkle in his eye.

"What about me? I am okay!" and both laughed heartily.

Day by day, Bhairavi began noticing a little change in Satyakam, but she was not perturbed. A slight sadness pricked her though, and a curiosity to know what was happening.

One midnight, while Puran slept, she rose from her bed and proceeded to Satyakam's, but he was not there. She felt a pang in her heart, but soon gathered her awareness and came out of the house. The moon shone brightly in the lonely sky and she saw Satyakam sitting in meditation near the pond. Slowly, with soundless steps, she approached him and sat down. He opened his eyes and turned his face toward her.

"What is happening to you nowadays?" asked Bhairavi in a slightly excited tone.

"My days are ended in this chapter of life ... "

Bhairavi interrupted, "So I have been observing!"

For a short while both remained quiet. Then Bhairavi resumed, "But what about me?"

Satyakam, with a distant look in his eyes, replied, "Your days with me are also over."

"But that's not the way I see it!" expressed Bhairavi, "And what about Puran?"

Satyakam looked at her with love and spoke softly, but with detached feelings, "Puran will grow remarkably under your care with the guidance of Mataji."

Bhairavi's head bowed down a little in Mataji's memory. Then she said, "Are you seeking only your salvation? What about my salvation?"

Satyakam touched her head with his right hand, showering her with blessings. This was the first time that he had blessed her as her elder. He replied, "Your salvation will come, ultimately, through Puran. He will achieve his goal in a relatively short period. With his help and grace, you will achieve spiritual absorption, and spend the last years of your life on the banks of the Narbadā River."

"Couldn't it be done through you?" Bhairavi asked sadly.

"Possibly. But my mission is different. I am leaving you, not because you are a burden on me, but because our being together has fulfilled its purpose."

"Didn't you say once that I am your Shakti?"

"Yes, but Shakti is all-pervading. Once Mother Divine came through you to help me fulfill my karmas in this particular way. Again She pervades the cosmos for me and beckons that I play accordingly."

"Can't both be reconciled in a twin play?" asked Bhairavi with sober understanding.

Satyakam resumed, "Yes, but I have to fulfill the purpose which Mother Nature has assigned for me."

"You no longer love me?" Bhairavi seemed human again after a long time.

"I don't feel our separation. So the question of not loving does not arise at all. It is simply a physical separation. Our souls are united and one and thus love is inherently present all the while. You are an acme of love and devotion and you'll be a model example of love for the people. In these physical pangs of separation, your love will remain sublimely enshrined."

That night Bhairavi saw Mataji in a dream. It was vividly real. Mataji was floating backward in the air with her hands stretched out, calling Bhairavi to her and saying, "Come to me ... come to me ... come ... come ... " until her figure receded into some unknown mountain ranges. Bhairavi got up joyfully shouting, "Mataji ... Mataji! ... "

Satyakam held her with both hands. Her face was beaming with full joy as she said, "I understand now. My time has come to join the Divine Mother," and then she asked, "And who was that child in her right hand? Puran, I guess!"

"Yes," replied Satyakam.

"Mataji knows everything," murmured Bhairavi.

•   •   •   •   •   •   •

Autumn was overlapping into winter. News spread throughout the area that Mataji had come—rare in her case— at the behest of her devotees, to meet them in Calcutta. Satyakam took Bhairavi and Puran to meet Mataji. Before leaving Kadambini, they also shared the news that they might not come back. Four miles away, at the small village railway station, surging crowds of people bade them farewell with tearful eyes and garlands of flowers. As far as the gaze could reach, innumerable tear-streaked faces glimmered in the morning sun. Sky rending voices shouted, "Victory to Maharaj! ... Victory to Deviji! ... " Somebody from the crowd shouted, "Victory to Puran!" Everyone was trying to get near the divine couple to touch their feet. Soon the stationmaster came near, touched their feet most reverently, and guided them to the first class compartment.

The steam engine of the narrow-gauge train gave a blast from its smokestack and began puffing and gasping for power. The train, at a snail's speed, started dragging with jerks. Other commuters leisurely began climbing aboard, as if they were entering a stationary train. Devotees moved alongside the train sobbing. Some of them held onto the side of the train, as if to hold it back if they could. Gradually the train picked up more speed and the people were left behind wailing. All the while Maharaj and Bhairavi, with garlands around their necks, leaned out of the window smiling divinely and waving their hands in blessings. In between them, Puran peeped out occasionally. He had also been garlanded profusely.

People remained gazing toward the vanishing train until, finally, it slipped out of sight.

4

SILENCE
(winter)

Mile after
flowing mile...

... from Himalaya through valleys, plains, towns and villages, Gangā* widens till she reaches Calcutta, the last city on her pilgrimage before she merges with the Bay of Bengal. On the way she accumulates dirt, filth and drainage. But when one stands quietly on her bank and glances over her breadth, what a mystical and healing aura she has! Feelings of devotion and spirituality well up inside, transcending the considerations of good and bad. After all, does she not absorb the dark sins of vast humanity, groping in the stark darkness of ignorance? Like a good mother, she provides for her children, helping and guiding them to their destiny. In the process, she becomes contaminated and old—but what a glorious sacrifice!

The sacrificial vapors of purification again rise higher into the sky, slowly traveling toward the fountainhead in Himalaya—the reservoir for thirsty mankind. Thus the cycle is completed under the guidance and with the help of the benevolent and dazzling sun. Where does it all start and where does it end? From perfection it rises and into perfection it merges.

At Kālīghāt in Calcutta, Satyakam, along with Bhairavi and Puran, met Mataji at the home of one of her devotees. She had been waiting for them! A special seat had been placed near Mataji's seat for Maharaj to occupy. The whole house was charged with high energy. It was such a delight to see the august presence of all those great souls in one place! Indeed, the devotee in whose house Mataji was staying must have been a thrice blessed soul.

Mataji and Maharaj exchanged customary greetings. Then Mataji called Bhairavi and her son to sit near her. Both bowed down to her. Mataji asked the boy, smilingly, "What's your name?"

---

*Gangā—the Ganges

"Pūran*," sweetly uttered the boy.

"What an appropriate name," Mataji spoke with great tenderness. "Pray you'll fulfill your name."

"He is your child, Mataji," replied Bhairavi devotedly.

Mataji, with a heavenly sweet smile on her face, looked at all three with much intimacy and blessing. Such a rare bond of Spirit!

Late in the afternoon many devotees of Mataji arrived. As Bhairavi and Puran sat before her, Satyakam slipped out of the house, hired a horse carriage, and headed toward the north of the city. In a lonely place some miles away, he got down from the carriage and started walking toward Ganga. The river here was wide—more than a mile. At a secluded spot on the bank he found some brick steps, and stood there motionless, gazing at the river. Then, closing his eyes, he touched his forehead with folded hands, and whispered tenderly, "Ganga, make me as pure as thou art. Thou art the sustainer and mother to all. Fulfill my destiny. As thou art perfect, bestow upon me thus."

Two tears ran down from his closed eyes. For some time he stood there feeling released and light. Upon straightening himself, he heard footsteps at his back. He looked around, but saw no one.

At sunset time, the sun grew into a big red ball of fire before sinking into the horizon on the opposite bank of Ganga. A mystical quiet pervaded. Satyakam sat down on the steps in a meditative pose. For about seven years this was the first time he had been really alone, but how full he felt! There was no trace of attachment or worry. Nothing, it seemed, existed between him and his goal except his Master, who was in his constant remembrance these days. Who would have even imagined that a few miles away his great wife and soon

---

*Pūran—lit., perfect; personal name

to be great son were staying? It all seemed ages apart, as if a story of another incarnation. But were they separate from him?

This was the time when winter mingled with autumn. Mild cold had set in, but the weather remained pleasant. Except for some red streaks at the horizon, the sun had completely set. The soft murmuring of the flowing Ganga, the quieting croaks of frogs somewhere nearby, the soft touch of the mild breeze—these were the only witnesses here at this hour of twilight.

Once again Satyakam heard footsteps behind him. Looking back, he saw the same white bearded old man who, seven years back, had directed him to the village Kadambini. He abruptly got up, placed his head on the old man's feet and shed tears of joy.

"Gurudev," cried Satyakam, "I can't mistake you anymore." After a pause, he asked, "Why couldn't I see you when I first heard your footsteps?"

The Master spoke graciously, "It seems you had lost some of your powers and consequently couldn't communicate with me beyond the audible sound. Then I waited until your level enhanced to higher perception and you could see me. It is all right now."

After a brief pause, the Master asked, "What do you intend to do now?"

"As you instruct me, I will do," replied Satyakam with utmost surrender.

"Take the train to the foothills of Eastern Himalaya at a place called Siliguri. I'll meet you there." So saying, the white robed sage vanished again.

Night was descending quietly. In the darkening sky, the stars gradually began to appear. Satyakam headed toward the Calcutta railway station.

•　•　•　•　•　•　•

Next morning, as Satyakam alighted from the train at Siliguri, an ochre robed middle-aged holy man approached to receive him. After customary greetings, the holy man said, "The Master has instructed me to guide you to the place where he'll meet you." Upon leaving the platform, they hired a horse carriage. After a few miles, they got down and started walking up a hilly path.

Immense tea gardens grew on both sides. Before them rose the first ranges of Eastern Himalaya. Satyakam and his companion remained mostly quiet. As he looked up at the majestic mountains, Satyakam's eyes brimmed crystal clear as he felt his homecoming well up inside. His face turned softer.

Leaving the common pathway, they turned eastward onto a less trodden footpath. The trail began to rise slowly. Lush green forest surrounded them. They walked for about three miles before reaching a delightful stream winding its way through the woods. It wasn't very wide and they crossed it in knee-deep water.

Feeling utterly quiet and cut off from the hustle and bustle of the town, they sat down to rest amidst the lonely surroundings. The magic of the season had transformed the mountains and valleys into a spectacular panorama of colors. They perspired lightly in the cool air. Satyakam felt slightly more tired than his companion, as it had been about seven years since he had climbed the mountains.

The holy man opened his cloth bag and brought out food. While they ate, the holy man said, "We still have to walk about two miles more to see our Master. It's a very secluded spot and even many holy men do not know about it. Hardly anyone goes there. The Master has found a nice cave there for you." Satyakam listened quietly but said nothing.

The next two miles were uneventful except for steep climbing. Both felt a little exhausted, but the ordeal did not last long. At the end of the journey soft meadows greeted them, beyond which rose the peaks of the earth.

On one end of the meadows, by the side of the mountain, a sweetwater stream trickled past a cave. Beside it the Master awaited them. He looked exactly the same, with the same clothing as he wore at Sonar Linga in North Central Himalaya seven years back. Not a trace of change could be seen.

Satyakam and his companion bowed down at the Master's feet. The sage seemed grave but merciful. "Satyakam," he said, "now starts your last lap of the journey. Be sure that you scale all the peaks of your mind and attain unspeakable silence."

Satyakam again bowed down at his Master's feet and, as he rose, he noticed the other holy man was missing. Although he was not surprised, the Master clarified, "That was another body of mine and it merged into this body again."

After a day's rest, Satyakam resumed his quest, or was it the end of all quests? Thus the Master spoke to him while sitting in the cave, "Get free from all desires, impositions and thoughts, and merge into the true Source, as the spider rolls back his cobweb into himself. Be aware that even the greatest occult powers are the product of that Substance and thus not greater than It. Magic is not necessarily the sign of spirituality.

"The Ultimate is not achievable. It is self-existent. Even the mind is a partial consciousness of It. Therefore the mind cannot concentrate objectively upon It, but can only merge back into the Whole, all-pervading Consciousness. So release yourself into the great Silence, as a drop merges into the ocean."

Satyakam said nothing. The sage resumed, "Desires are insatiable. Fortunately, you have fulfilled your pending desires to whatever extent possible. Beyond that point, the desires would only rotate and repeat, numbing the senses, both physically and astrally. A wise man learns this lesson and transcends the monotonous and habitual appetite of desires."

Satyakam listened in oneness with his Master, not saying a word.

"In this cave today," continued the sage, "I'll initiate you into the highest tradition of yogis, the pathless path toward the causal—the great rest in silence."

Winter had descended in fullness, clothing the high peaks in white garb. After bathing in the nearby stream, Satyakam threw away his clothing into the stream as his Master had told him. Then, wrapping himself in a blanket, he entered the cave.

At the appointed seat, he sat in perfect posture before his Master and closed his eyes. The sage uttered nothing but began communicating silently, grooming him for the great task that awaited him.

Slowly the mind of Satyakam began to relax and, one by one, thought waves started subsiding. Like the links of a chain, each self-imposed barrier was cut asunder and fell away. A newly felt purity surged through him. He became unaware of his Master, who left the cave quietly.

Intermittently, Satyakam would feel obsessed by upsurging thought vibrations. When a soul gets close to the final perfection, he once again reviews his every thought, feeling and idea—nay, even past births which have touched him. But he continues the process of relaxation day by day, in an attitude of supreme *letting go*. A fine sense of matured devotion, hitherto unattained, began to unfold in him and he felt more tender and withdrawn—a perfect inner renunciation. His sixth chakra had begun opening.

One year passed away. Winter had brought occasional snowfall in this lower region of Himalaya. Except for his Master, Satyakam did not meet anyone. Milk and fruit, somehow provided by his Master, were his only diet. Sometimes he stepped out of his cave for a dip in the stream and other ablutions. Occasionally he walked awhile in the soft meadows. Hardly any talk existed between him and the rarely seen sage. Mostly they communicated through silence.

At one point the sage told him to observe a vow—a last one—not to come out in the daylight for forty days. He could come out for any needs only during the hours when it was dark. Before Satyakam undertook this, his Master said, "I'll see you again after the forty days. If there is any need meanwhile, it'll be provided. Let Silence be your refuge."

Satyakam was lost for hours and sometimes for days in inner silence, oblivious of even sunrise and sunset. Many a time food seemed a bygone dream, and he lived only on air, water and subtle energy from the sun. And time came to a stop for Satyakam.

His lean body dazzled with ethereal energy, and more than before, a mysterious glow shone in his eyes. His dark beard ripened to fullness along with his brown matted hair, which flowed to the shoulders. After these days in darkness, his serene face glowed like a blazing sun. He hardly felt any cold.

The second winter was coming to an end with his forty days of not seeing daylight. It had seemed like a long night of dreamless sleep, severing him from all the world. He felt no need even of his physical body.

The first day after his vow had ended, he began ascending the mountains to unknown heights. His mission on earth, so it seemed, had ended there, and he wouldn't have minded his body dropping off anywhere, anytime, on the sacred Himalaya, like a worn-out shell.

It was very foggy at the higher altitudes and very, very cold. Satyakam was unmindful of the terrain he was walking on. At one spot he couldn't see any way out but to cross through the waterfall of a stream. This region was beyond the treeline and only green meadows extended in all directions. Most of the ground was still robed in white solitude. It had begun to drizzle. Crossing the waterfall, he reached the other side but his drenched body began trembling convulsively. Then, in utter cold and exhaustion, he lost control and fainted. In the late afternoon, Satyakam lay on the Himalaya, while above him stretched the vast canopy of foggy sky. In his fainting he was shaken all through his spine, yet through his third eye he saw somewhere a soothing space of light. With radar-like superintelligence, his Master appeared there and spoke, "Satyakam, you should not give up your physical body like this. You have yet to accomplish the greatest mission of helping mankind to the blessedness of unexcelled peace. Get up!"

Stayakam opened his eyes, and before him stood the sage in his ineffable glory. Calmly, Satyakam slowly got up.

The drizzle had stopped and it was less foggy now. Together they began their descent, reaching the cave by sunset.

"When he reached Benares, his fame had preceded him. On the ghats of Ganga..."
  (P. 103)

5

ENLIGHTENMENT
(spring)

As wintry cold
subsided ......

. . . the snow began melting from the towering mountain slopes. With the advent of spring, birds once again hopped through the green woods, singing the glory of their Creator. Patches of dry grass gradually began turning green, while the meadows provided a festive look of dancing joy as tiny, exquisite flowers shot forth everywhere. Streams roared down on their great mission to soothe the burning thirst of the multitude. Gray sky had turned to crystal clear blue. And the morning sun, shining in full glory, glistened brilliantly through countless dew drops perched upon the verdant grass.

Satyakam was silence incarnate. One could call him a conscious stone or solid silence. He seemed unaware of anything around him, but was he really? Now he was all the while in silent communication with his Master; nay, he found his Master residing in him permanently. He and his Master had become one.

In tune with the surrounding nature, Satyakam flowed in truth, beauty and goodness. Who was deciding? Who was performing? Who was responding?

After leaving the cave, he began climbing Himalaya. In the prime of spring, the pleasant climate invited more villagers and passers-by to climb the mountain paths. Often they greeted Satyakam with awe and deep reverence, but Satyakam was Satyakām*! He left them all behind to finish what he had begun.

After a day's journey, he reached a spot about ten miles away from Darjeeling. The spot was rugged and uninhabited, and no one ever passed by. Finding a small cave, he spread his blanket inside and came out.

To the east stood Mount Everest against the clear blue

---

*Satyakām—lit., seeker of Truth

sky, majestically covered with perennial snow. Its lofty head penetrated the heavens, haloed by ineffable purity and glory. Its challenging message: "Come ye who are heavy with bondage and find freedom in the abode of your True Self." And to this, the Kanchenjunga ranges to the west provided silent affirmation and inspiration.

Here, amidst one of the most rapturous landscapes of Mother Earth, Satyakam settled for a final assault.

·   ·   ·   ·   ·   ·   ·

Days passed on. He never left his seat even for a moment. One rare clear night brought the full moon out, as if to witness an unspeakable silent glory. The rest of the sky was not barren. Twinkling stars decorated the firmament up to the visible depths.

Satyakam sat on his seat looking toward serene Everest. His eyes closed. Was he meditating? Was he enthroned in the great Silence? Or was he waiting?

As he was sitting with eyes closed, a question, like a beam of light, pierced his silent screen of consciousness, "What is obstructing me still from full Enlightenment?"

"You," arose a silent answer from within him. "Enlightenment is absolute and not objective. Either ego or Enlightenment."

Another question from within him followed, "I have always believed in God's existence but have never seen Him! Does God exist?"

"Yes." And with that, there appeared in his consciousness the full vision of radiant form—more radiant than thousands of suns. His golden face, with a divine smile having no outline, permeated the limitless space, and the light grayish body spread over the whole universe. Satyakam beheld, in naked glory, God's universal form.

The last question arose in him, "What is your name?"

100

"Narayan. But many are My names. I appear in the form in which you worship Me."

Then the form disappeared, and so disappeared what was hitherto Satyakam, like the night which terminates with the rise of the sun. The seventh chakra became luminous. Satyakam plunged into *samādhī**.

The epic journey had ended. Satyakam became Satyānanda**. He sat there immersed in Light and Bliss. The mysteries and powers of the universe were spontaneously revealed to him one by one. He was no longer *having* knowledge, which does change, but *was* pure consciousness, which does not change. God, Satyananda and the vast universe had become one, and thus he realized the immutability of the Law of One. Satyananda was enlightened. The invisible angels appeared to behold the valiant fighter of the greatest victory—the victory in which no one else knew defeat. The angels showered ethereal flowers over this child of the virgin spirit of Himalaya. He bathed in transforming ecstasy.

He remained there, lost in superconsciousness, for who knows how many days. And then one day he arose and looked about. His eyes were shining with divine luster, the same as he had beheld long ago in the two swans on the lake. A halo of light surrounded his head. He looked majestic in his Lord's glory.

He glanced at Everest; the mountain seemed humble. Step by step, as a king of kings, he descended the slopes until he reached a trail. It had been a long time since he had seen human figures passing by. None could resist the pull and they spontaneously bowed down to him. Their faces also shone for a while as they beheld Satyananda's divine glow. Awestruck and humbled in his presence, they didn't know who he was, nor did they dare to ask.

---

*samādhī—oneness with Spirit, Lord; superconsciousness; egolessness
**Satyānanda—lit., blissful in Truth; personal name

The sun had set. Satyananda gently crossed the pathway and stood secluded on a cliff where no one could see him ... he opened his arms and looked to the sky like a great bird. A warmth and brilliance shone forth from his being and his physical body disappeared. He traveled astrally by the skyway till he reappeared on the ocean beach at Pūrī in the state of Orissa, in the East. He passed the night on the sands.

In the early morning, as the first rays of sun brightened the ocean waves, Satyananda headed toward the Jagannath Temple. As he walked through the streets, those who saw him kept looking at him, not knowing what to do or where to start! They had seen many holy men visiting this famous shrine, but the power and light emanating from him kept them at bay. They simply bowed down to him.

The priest saw him as he was entering the temple gate. He could not help but come forward to greet him and take him to the inner precincts of the sanctuary. Satyananda bowed down reverently before the Lord of the Universe. After a while he retraced his steps out of the temple and proceeded once again to the beach.

News spread fast and soon throngs of people were seen heading toward the rare holy man. Satyananda sat silently on the sand in a yogic posture. People bowed down before him, like iron to a magnet, and kept looking at him. He glanced over them but said nothing.

Finally one man folded his hands, and in a most reverential and humble manner asked, "May we have the acquaintance of thy revered self?"

"As it is difficult to draw a line marking the course a bird flies in the sky, so it is with the acquaintance of a sage, " spoke Satyananda softly.

"Where is thy residence, sir?" someone else wanted to know.

"The common home of all beings—the Supreme Self."

People continued staring at him. Someone brought fruit

and flowers, placing them before him. Silently he blessed these and returned them for distribution. More people brought fruit and flowers, and again these were blessed and distributed in the same way.

Soon, as was not unusual, people old and in pain came near him and prayed for their cure. Satyananda looked upon them with compassion, touching their bodies with his benign hands. Their pain left them and they began to feel recovery. People were amazed but silent.

The whole day the sands were covered with people, and many more kept arriving. In the late afternoon he entered the sea for a bath. All watched him. Two people waited on the beach with a set of new but simple clothes. Afterwards he ate some fruit and, when he proceeded to the temple where he was invited to rest, two men followed him and prayed to be his disciples. Satyananda readily initiated them and renamed them Upāsak and Shrīkānt.

Early next morning he left Puri by foot with his two disciples to begin their journey. From place to place wherever he went, people felt uplifted. Whenever someone would ask him questions, he would reply with persuasion and sweet reasonableness.

In this manner Satyananda continued on his earthly pilgrimage, healing wounds, showing people the path to spiritual sanity and health, revealing to them that disunity is the root cause which eats into the vitals of society, and that the knowledge of unity, the vision of nondualistic Spirit, is the only remedy for the ills of man and society.

When he reached Benares, his fame had preceded him. On the *ghats* of Ganga, many scholars and holy men came to see and converse with him. One learned holy man asked Satyananda, "What is the nature of the Absolute?"

He replied, "The nature of the Absolute cannot be defined in any one category. The Supreme Truth is nondualistic. There is nothing real beside It. To define a thing is to limit it."

"Then there is no God?" asked the same learned man pointedly.

"From our empirical standpoint, Absolute Spirit appears as God, the cause of the universe. But there is no real causation. The world is merely a transitory phenomenon, illusion—appearance on the Substance. Illusion has significance—not from the Absolute viewpoint—but from the relative viewpoint."

"What is illusion?" asked another pundit.

"Illusion is neither real nor unreal. It is real because it is perceptible to the senses, and unreal because it is not permanent.

"The purpose of any inquiry into illusion is not to make the idea comprehensible, but to enable one to transcend it."

Here also, among those who approached him to be his disciples, he accepted one learned man and initiated him as Vidyāpatī.

Gradually he and the disciples headed south and as usual encountered various sects and creeds.

At Madūrai, in the Meenakshi Temple, while he was surrounded by a multitude of people, a group of scholars came tearing through the crowd and sat near him. Satyananda looked at them. An attitude of fury marked their faces. One of them asked, "We have heard that your teachings are atheistic—is that true?"

With utmost gentleness, he replied, "Spirit is not a rival to the various sytems. Mere orthodoxy has nothing better to offer than atheism. As a body does not quarrel with its own limbs, Spirit has no dispute with any philosophy. It is embodied in all."

Still there was no peace in the hearts of these people. Satyananda touched their chests with his healing hands and instantly they felt released. Behind the manifest knowledge of

Satyananda, they could easily feel his love flooding their hearts.

Satyananda spoke again, "God is not an irrelevance, nor a concession to the masses. Devotion to God is a necessary step to spiritual realization and Oneness. Those who know the Supreme Godhead call It by various names and explain It in various ways.

"Rediscover the spirit of unity and wholeness. Avoid tumult and discord to restore the warring parts to their proper place in the whole."

Among them, one scholar was chosen by him and initiated as Bhaktīdev.

When Satyananda, with his four disciples, reached the midwest village of a *Kolī* tribe, a small group of village folk advanced toward him. A woman led them, weeping and wailing, and carrying her dead son in her arms. Dropping at his feet, she begged that he revive the child. Satyananda first hesitated, then asked the woman to lay the body on the ground. Touching the dead body on the top of the head, he closed his eyes and uttered something silently. Slowly, the child opened his eyes and came to life.

The head of the village, along with many others, came reverently to see him when they heard of this. Such a feat they had never witnessed. Yet there were still some doubtful learned ones. One of them said, although politely, "It is said that the use of occult powers is detrimental to spiritual growth. One should renounce it in order to reach the goal."

Spoke Satyananda, "It is of no use just theoretically to condemn occultism when, in practice, one is attached to the gross forms of power, greed, anger and selfishness. Occult powers, when used as weapons of aggression, are detrimental to the soul. But one can find in these the solace of life, if they are exercised selflessly with a pure motive. Power in any form, gross or occult, can be a block or a help, depending upon the potency and motive of the person using it."

Satyananda continued his wondrous mission, building a golden bridge over the ignorance of humankind's soul. His luminous heart helped others to climb the difficult ascent from darkness to light. Many a stubborn sorrow melted just by beholding the splendor of his beauty.

On the banks of the Narbadā river, at Sūkhdev, he met a group of yogis. News of him had already reached there and the people were waiting. Also, a more sensational reason drew people from the surrounding areas. Some time back, Bhairavi had attained *samādhī* there and had left her body consciously on the bank of the river. Puran, before entering the deep forests, had played a major role in helping his mother attain Transcendence.

The common people kept asking Satyananda questions. And while he was still replying, some could not help talking simultaneously, hardly listening to him. At one point he said, "It is better to open your ears and close your mouths instead of vice versa. Vanity frustrates the fulfillment of your will. Truth cannot be imparted to those who do not listen. To discover the vast unknown depths of God, silence is imperative. How else would you achieve the joy which you are consciously or unconsciously seeking?"

Quiet descended on the crowd like a dove. Satyananda stayed there for quite a number of days sharing intimate dialogue and communication with the yogis. He initiated two of them as his new disciples, renaming them Shradhāvān and Nishthāvān.

Thereafter, accompanied by his six disciples, he moved with courage and nobility from place to place until they reached Dwārkā on the west coast. While he was sitting on the temple verandah with his disciples on his right, some priests and pilgrims came forward and sat quietly around them.

One of the priests asked Satyananda, "Does the path of devotion to God lead to release or does only the path of knowledge—that is, self-inquiry—lead to it?"

Satyananda gave a pleasant smile and returned the question, "What do you mean by release?"

The priest fumbled and hesitated to find words. It seemed that he had never thought on his own what release meant—that he had perhaps been repeating the word all his life mechanically, like a parrot, because he had read or heard about it! Eventually, he came out with: "Freedom from sorrow, feeling peace and happiness, no worries or miseries, no poverty, and the rest."

Satyananda spoke, "Then do you think, even in your wildest imagination, that when you realize God through the path of devotion you will still retain sorrow, worries, miseries, and confusion?"

"No."

"Let us analyze it further. What is it that constitutes miseries or feelings of sorrow, and how does that make a difference once you realize God or True Self?"

Satyananda took a short breath and asked, "Who is feeling the sorrow and miseries?"

"A person; you, me and everyone," replied the priest.

"What is a person, you and me?" Satyananda asked again.

The priest got stuck, and before he could find an answer, another priest said in a rather loud tone, "Soul or individual consciousness?"

"In short, ego?" expressed Satyananda.

"Yes," came the reply from both priests.

"Then is it not clear that when you merge into God or

Spirit—meaning that ego no longer exists—you are released from sorrow and miseries? In other words, is not ego the sole basis of miseries, and does not release from sorrow mean release from ego?"

"Right," agreed the priests.

Satyananda continued, "Let us now come back to your original question. If ego dissolves in both the paths of devotion and self-inquiry, in terms of release, there is no essential difference between the two. Do you agree with me?"

"Yes," replied the priests.

"But the difference exists in approach only. That is: on the path of devotion, devotion is predominant and knowledge is born eventually, and on the path of knowledge, self-inquiry is predominant and devotion is born eventually. Both lead to self-surrender, which is the most effective means of release."

An atmosphere of quiet enveloped them. All at once, a beautiful peacock with closed plumes sailed serenely above them in the sky, like a boat moving gracefully upon the waters. An amazing feat! Down below the temple verandah, in the compound, a polio-stricken beggar was sitting on the dusty ground. He had been watching them all along but could not understand a word. His whole outer attention was on Satyananda, but his inner attention was on his polio. Finding all quiet now, he limped toward the verandah.

Touching his forehead to the edge of the marble floor, he spoke with utmost devotion in a halting and sad voice, "Please bless me so that I get rid of this dreadful disease."

Satyananda looked at the poor man benignly and came near the edge. He touched his palm somewhere on the ailing man's neck, and gently massaged his spine there for some time. The man's eyes slowly began to close, and soon he lost consciousness. Upasak and Bhaktidev rushed to hold him, slowly laying him on the ground. The man rested there, as if asleep, for some time. Then his body began to show signs of recovery and gradually he opened his eyes. Satyananda commanded him, "Get up." The man got up—cured and whole.

The whole audience acclaimed loudly in one voice, "Victory to Maharaj!"

The priests stepped forward, touched the feet of Satyananda, and with tender love in their eyes said, "We wish to be thy disciples if thou thinkest that we are worthy."

He picked up one of them and renamed him Pavītra. And thus the eight resumed their unending journey. People followed them to the outskirts of the town and the party headed toward Mount Abū.

On the way, a young fellow traveler who had long been wandering in search of a true master was magnetically attracted to Satyananda. The man, who seemed sincere and faithful, bowed down to him and asked reverently, "Have you seen God?"

"Yes," came the simple and direct answer.

"Can you bless me with His vision?" pleaded the man.

"Yes, provided you fulfill the prerequisites and get sufficiently purified to behold His vision," came the direct guidance from Satyananda.

The man spontaneously surrendered himself at the feet of Satyananda, who readily accepted him and initiated him as Sharandev.

Day by day Satyananda's following began to swell as hundreds of lay people were initiated as his devotees. Wherever he and his eight disciples went, crowds gathered to see and hear him. Healing was not rare. They never stayed at one place for long.

On their steady march, one afternoon the nine reached Kurukshetra in the North. The local people lodged them in the inn near the famous temple. In the evening a very large congregation gathered in the temple auditorium. During Sat-sang one youth asked, "Is the life of contemplation superior to the life of action? Is the renunciation of action necessary to obtain the sublime bliss?"

Satyananda replied, "These are simply two paths: that of wisdom and that of action. Simply by abandoning action, one does not get freedom from activity, for one's nature will compel one to act whether one wishes to or not.

"One who refuses to act, but all the while is thinking about sensuous objects, is deluded and a hypocrite. One does not reach perfection by merely refusing to act.

"Only those actions steady the straying intellect which are performed when the mind is concentrated on the Divine and has renounced attachment to the fruit of actions. This allows one to contemplate one object alone. Spirituality is the real art of living and implies equanimity.

"The path of wisdom is for one who meditates on God. Such a soul is content to serve Him. There remains nothing more for him to accomplish. Performance or nonperformance of action loses its distinction for him, for he has nothing to gain or lose anymore.

"Thus, sublime bliss is not dependent upon what you do but what your attitude and motives are.

"Those who act by consulting only their desires con-struct their own heaven or hell, secure their own pleasures and power, and the only result is rebirth. Guided by Pure Intelligence, the sages renounce the fruit of action and thus, freed from the chains of rebirth, reach the highest bliss. They have conquered themselves and their desires have vanished. By such renunciation, they have reached the summit of perfect freedom where action completes itself and leaves no seed."

At the end of Satsang, this youth came forward and

touched Satyananda's feet. With folded hands he said, "I have decided to follow the path of contemplation. May I be your disciple, sir?"

Satyananda imparted his benediction with a smile and changed his name to Arpan.

All ten moved toward the northeast. At one place they were invited by a wealthy merchant to his garden house. At the back of the house was a pleasant grove under which Satyananda, flanked by his disciples, gave an informal discourse to the family members and their friends. Shrikant and Vidyapati were in front of the house waiting to greet those who came.

While Satyananda was still speaking to the group, Shrikant came in and stood quietly with folded hands. After some time, Satyananda paused and looked at him. "Gurudev," said Shrikant, "a group of ladies is at the gate. They seek permission to come and talk to your revered self." Satyananda acceded.

One who seemed to speak for the ladies said politely, "It seems that only men are thy near disciples who are initiated for salvation. What about us?"

He replied, "Women are also entitled to salvation. But my life is that of a wanderer, so it is not practical for women to be with me wherever I go."

"That means we have no hope, even if we choose to follow you?" humbly inquired the same lady.

"Not necessarily. It is a matter of deciding the course by which it would be best to open and conduct your internal growth."

All were quiet and waited for further instructions. After a while Satyananda spoke again, "You can establish a center for women at Benares and you shall be guided. Name it Shaktīpeeth."

He initiated three of them and renamed them Shāradā, Vimalā, and Shodoshī. Thereafter, he gave them further instructions about their growth and the upkeep of Shaktipeeth.

* * * * * * *

Here, by his seventy-fifth year, ended Satyananda's mission on earth, but for his final teachings and benediction. Leaving the multitude far behind, he took his chosen nine and journeyed toward the region of Ladākh in the interior of North Himalaya. After many days' journey, they reached a very secluded spot which had a number of caves. Surrounded by tall pine forests and enriched by a sweetwater stream, the area gave an impression of having once been inhabited.

Everyone occupied a cave as indicated by their guru. The largest cave, which stood on the edge of the slope facing a vast quiet valley, was arranged for the Master. The stream touching the edge of this cave flowed downward in gorgeous waterfalls. The colorful hues of the lush foliage were reflected in the shimmering, irridescent water cascading down the steps of the falls. There could be no more perfect setting for the last project of Satyananda.

Each cave had a stone platform raised like a bed, carved out of the wall. The disciples spread their blankets—one underneath and one for covering the body. There was no other ventilation inside except the carved entrance which had no door as such. The only other belongings they had were water pots made from dried gourds, some loose leaves of paper for writing and two sets of simple clothes.

Gradually, they all settled there. After a few days, all nine disciples began meeting in their Master's cave, mornings and evenings, to drink the nectar of his immortal wisdom.

Upon the day of their first meeting, Satyananda sat on his deerskin-covered rock bed and recited,

"It is the Spirit
      which is within every being;
That which breathes by the breath
      is the Spirit
And that is within every being."

The disciples, sitting on their blankets facing him, re-cited after him. Their Master continued: "To realize Spiritual Love one has to renounce the sense of possession and belong to no particular creed, caste or country—but embrace the whole world. Be like a sun and freely course the infinite sky, illuminating the dark regions and lifting the veil of ignorance."

The nine listened in rapt attention. Satyananda cast his eyes from the cave's entrance to the vast sky and Himalayan peaks beyond. A vacant look fell upon his benign face as he continued, "According to your true nature, liberate your-selves from the bondage of impositions and be free eternally.

"All that is perceptible within time and space is subject to change and is thus mortal. The science of immortality is known by meditating on the all-pervading Eternal Light of Spirit, which is verily your true Self. You and your universe are essentially the same.

"But all this can never be known in its truest nature by mere conversation. Exclude all vain talk. With unflinching faith and unshakable concentration, meditate, meditate and meditate.

"Those who look back follow the shadow, but those who look toward the Sun of dazzling light leave the shadow behind."

Vidyapati then asked, "What attributes of the Self or Spirit should one meditate upon to grasp It as tangible?"

Satyananda replied, "Spirit is not tangible by the senses nor the intellect. As the very essence of everything, It is the source of all attributes. How can It be conceived and perceived by any attributes which are explained only in the realms of time and space!

"The nearest possible attributes of the Absolute, as far as language can go, are: Existence, Consciousness and Bliss.

"But unless you go beyond the spoken word and subtle thought waves, you cannot come face to face with Reality. Thus, while meditating, keep on transcending all kinds of mental modifications and philosophical outlooks. The higher you soar, the more the horizons broaden. Be assured that the highest Truth exists in Its own bosom, and that nothing else satisfies so fully as being one with that Sacred Truth, from the heart of which emanates deep and tangible love. In this way, one can almost envision particles of bliss breaking away and dancing throughout the universe."

Day by day, the disciples became more absorbed in meditation. At other times they collected firewood and cooked some light food. Their sleep was scanty. As they came daily to sit at their Master's feet and absorb his communication, nothing delighted them so much as a look from him who was one with the substratum of the Universal Truth. Slowly, occult powers began manifesting in some of them. But Satyananda insisted that they ignore these, not because they were evil in themselves, but because they would distract them from the Ultimate Goal. Once they had become sufficiently pure they could use the powers according to their inner guidance. Faithfully, all followed the indisputable instructions of their mentor. Some kept records of his sayings as well as their own commentaries.

On one such afternoon, Satyananda told them, "The supreme bliss of Self-Realization is the highest Goal, surpassing all other happiness derived from the physical body, wealth, name and fame, and scholarship, even the happiness of those who dwell in the astral world. People can be free from various afflictions of the body and mind if only they direct their search within, beyond reasoning, to bathe in the ocean of ambrosial bliss."

Arpan asked, "What if they have no faith and depend solely on rationality, believing that by it alone man has almost reached the acme of knowledge?"

His Master replied, "It is a pathetic reversion to rationalism, an old fear complex of the thinker and logician. The power of faith has never been explained by so-called scientific research. But still faith remains unchallengeable.

"Rationality has never explained the power of faith because it is outside the scope of its methodology. Intuition is the valid method of knowing Reality.

"The intellect itself is not capable of this realization of Spirit—how can a part know the whole?"

. . . .

It was about five years since they had come to stay in the caves. The day came when Satyananda announced his departure from the body. He summoned all his disciples to his cave and said, "This day I must leave the body to merge into the Absolute. The banner of the ancient wisdom of Immortality is in your hands now. Be free from death and remain ever revealed in your Self.

"The world is sorely in need of this unalloyed Truth that potentially everyone is divine. Everyone is seeking, consciously or unconsciously, the freedom of the soul, which is its inherent nature. Go and proclaim the Truth without fear or favor and reveal the Himalayan Spirit on earth."

So saying, Satyananda quietly lay down on the rock bed. A holy radiance emanated from his being as an aura of light enveloped his body. With serene countenance and a blissful smile on his lips, he merged into the Unknown. A mysterious glow filled the cave.

And outside the cave, in the blue sky, two radiant swans, with broad and powerful strokes, winged their way toward the heavens.

Often one
wonders...

... how to ever be capable of achieving what one wants to! The yardstick often employed assumes that present conditions are permanent. This fallacy—perhaps the only fallacy—makes it difficult to know the Truth. If only man could overcome this fallacy, it would not be difficult to know the unalloyed Truth. Man expects something to be achieved on the grounds of existing conditions, which is too much to ask from Mother Nature. This fallacy has been carried on from age to age and consequently man has found himself seemingly helpless, not because the conditions are hard, but because of his resistance to changing his consciousness and his stubborn clinging to old habits.

Perfection is not static. It is an endless conscious living from moment to moment. It implies dynamic changefulness which is the law of nature. Thus man is required, by his willingness, to keep open to change and remain conscious of his goal of Perfection.

GLOSSARY

Ādī—lit., the original; 'Adi Ganga' refers to a tributary of Ganges, the original course that the Ganges allegedly took ages back.

Arpan—lit., a dedicated one; personal name.

Bhairavī—a female Tantric.

Bhaktīdev—lit., angel of devotion; personal name.

Chakra—lit., circle; a plexus in the spinal column controlling a certain number of nerves. There are totally seven chakras according to Tantra.

Devī—lit., goddess; respectful address to special women.

Dharma—Law, that which holds together; used also to mean religion.

Dūrgā—lit., one who removes sins; goddess of power, consort of Lord Shiva; one of the incarnations of Divine Mother.

Gangā—Ganges.

Gurū—lit., dispeller of darkness (ignorance); a Master.

Himālaya—lit., the abode of snow; the Himalayas.

Jagannāth—Lord of the Universe.

jī—a suffix denoting respect.

Kālī—lit., goddess of time; consort of Lord Shiva; one of the incarnations of Divine Mother.

Kapālak—Kapāl means skull; a male Tantric who sits in meditation on a seat of five skulls.

Karma—action, also destiny; cause-effect sequence.

Kolī—a tribe on the southwest coast of India consisting mostly of fishermen.

Kūnd—lit., a pool; the mouth of a river.

Kūndalinī—lit., a coil; the sleeping coil of energy at the base of the spinal column.

Mā—Mother.

Mahārāj—lit., great king; a customary address to holy men.

Mantra—a mystical word or words, like OM, used for the awakening of latent powers.

Mātā—Mother.

Māyā—appearance, but not real; illusory perception.

Nāda—subtle sound.

Nārāyan—name of God.

Nishthāvān—lit., sincere; personal name.

Pavitra—lit., pure; personal name.

Pūjā—worship.

Pūran—lit., perfect; personal name.

Samādhī—oneness with Spirit, Lord; superconsciousness; egolessness.

Saraswatī—goddess of learning, music and art; consort of Brahmā, the creator aspect of the Trinity of God.

Satsang—association with Truth, holy men or holy books; spiritual discourse.

Shaktī—lit., energy or power; in Tantra, used for the female consort of a seeker.

Shaktīpeeth—a center or abode of power.

Shāradā—one of the incarnations of Divine Mother; personal name.

Sharandev—lit., one who has taken refuge; surrendered one; personal name.

Shiva—destroyer aspect of the Trinity of God.

Shodoshī—one of the incarnations of Divine Mother; personal name.

Shradhāvān—lit., faithful one; personal name.

Shrīkant—lit., the most auspicious one; personal name.

Tantrā—Yoga path dealing with the nervous system, to awaken the kundalini.

Upasak—lit., worshipper; personal name.

Veda Vyās—the illustrious author of the Vedas—the sacred books of knowledge.

Vidyāpatī—lit., husband or master of knowledge; personal name.

Vimalā—lit., taintless woman; pure; personal name.

Yogi—a male yoga practitioner or one who is perfected in Yoga.

ACKNOWLEDGEMENTS

The author is very thankful to those who have helped in bringing "Spirit of Himalaya" to its present form:

typing the manuscript again and again

corrections and suggestions to improve the language, diction and flow

publishing and printing duties, lay out, etc. etc.

For PHOTOGRAPHS, to:

Ron and Bonnie Reese of Boulder, Colorado,
cover jacket and facing pages 33 and 97.

Rishi Ashram (Himalayas), facing page 17.

Harley Koopman of Glenwood Springs, Colorado,
facing page 81.

For ARTWORK, to:

Joshi Arts, Poona (India) for the drawing on page 6 and the paintings facing pages 1, 49, 65 and 113.

PRAISE FOR *HEALTH CARE UNDER THE KNIFE*

"It takes courage to challenge core concepts that everyone around you accepts as a given. This book does exactly that. *Health Care Under the Knife* forces us to ask whether better health care and better health are possible within a capitalist system that prizes market-based solutions above all else. Reading this book pushed me to challenge my assumptions and ask fundamental questions that I probably should have asked a long time ago. I am grateful to the authors for putting this volume together and pushing me to think."
—**SANDRO GALEA**, Dean and Robert A Knox Professor, School of Public Health, Boston University

"Bravely calling out capitalism as a key obstacle to health equity in the U.S. and globally, this timely volume by Waitzkin and colleagues offers fresh insights into the multi-generational struggle for economic and political democracy, public accountability, and human rights, which together inextricably bind the ties between social justice and the people's health."
—**NANCY KRIEGER**, Professor of Social Epidemiology, Harvard T.H. Chan School of Public Health

"This analysis of health care in the U.S. gives a deep understanding of what is happening under neoliberal globalization. This book shows how medical care has turned into a privileged field of capital accumulation and super profits at the expense of our health. The urgent answer is to resist and struggle for the right to health."
—**ASA CRISTINA LAURELL**, Former Secretary of Health, Mexico City

"The health care system in the United States is an international scandal, with per capita costs far higher than comparable countries, relatively poor outcomes, and tens of thousands with no guaranteed health care at all. What is worse still, the current Republican wrecking-ball is aimed at ruining it even more. The core problem is the severe inefficiency of privatization and the immense political power of private capital, which repeatedly overrides popular will and legitimate needs. The incisive essays included here unravel the deep institutional roots and serious flaws of this failing system and indicate directions that can lead to establishing decent health care as a fundamental human right."
—**NOAM CHOMSKY**, Institute Professor Emeritus, Massachusetts Institute of Technology; Laureate Professor, University of Arizona

"Reflecting decades of scholarship and activism that have challenged both neoliberal and neoconservative policies, *Health Care under the Knife* pinpoints how contemporary contradictions of capitalism straightjacket health professionals as much as patients—as well as those struggling to access care. At a time when there often seems to be no escape from nightmares, this tour-de-force opens up space to forge new dreams."
—**CHARLES BRIGGS**, Alan Dundes Distinguished Professor of Anthropology, University of California, Berkeley; author, *Making Health Public*

"This volume of essays by critical health professionals, sociologists and public health policy scholars shows how neoliberal capitalism has produced massively dysfunctional health systems in the United States and some other countries. The authors provide a valuable vision of how health care could be reorganized to serve the needs of the people of the world. This timely book clarifies the structural roots of health inequalities and proposes solutions

requiring a major reorganization of power and institutions, which can only succeed if a capable and organized mass movement emerges to demand the needed changes."
—**CHRISTOPHER CHASE-DUNN**, Distinguished Professor of Sociology and Director, Institute for Research on World-Systems, Department of Sociology, University of California-Riverside

"Critical analysis of the highest order—and a radical cure for our failing, for-profit medical system. Howard Waitzkin and his team of progressive doctors and health-care experts dissect and expose the workings of big capital that dominate every element of medicine, nutrition, and health-care delivery, including the so-called 'nonprofit' philanthropic control of medical education and global aid programs through behemoths like the Gates Foundation. Their analysis is indispensable for understanding how we, participating in political and social networks at the grassroots level, can outflank the capitalists, whose grossly inefficient medical system is a gargantuan failure. The prescription of these good doctors and experts? Put the system out of its misery; create new, non-capitalist networks of good health, through community organizations and national programs that advocate free and comprehensive health care for all."
—**STEVE BROUWER**, author, *Revolutionary Doctors: How Venezuela and Cuba Are Changing the World's Conception of Health Care*

"This excellent and powerful book written by physicians and health professionals who have labored in hospitals, clinics, and related institutions, rests upon certain fundamental 'core principles,' including 'the right to health care . . . water and other components of a safe environment' and the 'reduction of illness-generating conditions such as inequality.' It is a must-read, given the capitalist assault on the public's health and well-being."
—**JOHN MARCIANO**, Professor Emeritus, SUNY Cortland; author, *The American War in Vietnam: Crime or Commemoration?*

"Waitzkin and colleagues provide a trenchant analysis of health care and population health under neoliberal capitalism. The breadth of coverage and the depth of analysis are excellent. The analysis is oriented towards action; not answers and blueprints but inspiration. It is a book to engage with: read, absorb, criticize, develop, and apply; from anguish to hope to action. A must-read for public health students and practitioners; a light bulb for health care workers looking for new directions."
—**DAVID G LEGGE**, People's Health Movement, Australia

"This is a book that needs to be read. It shows in a very clear and very convincing way what is ignored so frequently in the conventional wisdom. The current social class, race, gender, and international relations of dominance are the major obstacles for the achievement of health, quality of life, and well-being of populations. The evidence is overwhelming that putting the interests of capital over all other considerations leads to an authentic disaster, which is what is happening today. It is time for that to change. This book will help end the silence that has existed for too long."
—**VICENTE NAVARRO**, Professor, Johns Hopkins University School of Public Health and Johns Hopkins University-Pompeu Fabra University Health Policy Center

HEALTH CARE
under the KNIFE

Moving Beyond Capitalism for Our Health

by HOWARD WAITZKIN
and the Working Group on Health beyond Capitalism

MONTHLY REVIEW PRESS
New York

Library of Congress Cataloging-in-Publication Data:

Names: Waitzkin, Howard and the Working Group on Health Beyond
  Capitalism.
Title: Health care under the knife : moving beyond capitalism for our health
  / Howard Waitzkin and the Working Group on Health Beyond
  Capitalism.
Description: New York : Monthly Review Press, [2018] | Includes
  bibliographical references and index.
Identifiers: LCCN 2017058687 (print) | LCCN 2017059403 (ebook) | ISBN
  9781583676769 (trade) | ISBN 9781583676776 (institutional) | ISBN
  9781583676745 (pbk.) | ISBN 9781583676752 (hardcover)
Subjects: | MESH: Social Medicine | Delivery of Health Care—economics |
  Physician's Role | Capitalism | Health Care Reform | Social Determinants
  of Health | United States
Classification: LCC RA418 (ebook) | LCC RA418 (print) | NLM WA 31 | DDC
  362.1—dc23
LC record available at https://lccn.loc.gov/2017058687

Typeset in Minion Pro

MONTHLY REVIEW PRESS, NEW YORK
monthlyreview.org

5 4 3 2 1

Contents

HEALTH CARE UNDER THE KNIFE

To Asa Cristina Laurell and Vicente Navarro,
whose vision and leadership have guided us.

What We're Trying to Do Here and Why

Howard Waitzkin

"Of all the forms of inequality, injustice in health is the most shocking and inhuman." Martin Luther King, Jr., said these words in 1966, after more than half a century of failed efforts to achieve a national health program in the United States that provides universal access to services.[1] About half a century later, a reform occurred—Obamacare—that reduced the number of uninsured by about 40 percent, markedly increased the costs of care for many who previously held health insurance, shifted responsibility for health care costs increasingly to patients and away from insurance companies (leading to greater "underinsurance"), and additionally provided huge tax-generated public subsidies for the private insurance industry. Partly because the out-of-pocket costs for the average family under Obamacare were projected to equal half of the average family income within the next several years, this reform headed toward a very problematic future.[2]

This unsuccessful trajectory was occurring even before Donald Trump officially tried to repeal Obamacare. The Trump administration quickly failed in this quest and then renewed it, as the Republicans controlling the U.S. Senate and Congress made clear their intention to continue many components of Obamacare in any replacement for it. Skeptics have questioned whether the "failure" of repealing Obamacare and the apparently halfhearted attempt to enact a Trumpcare that retains key elements of Obamacare constituted another act of political theater and manipulation of political symbolism so typical in the age of Trump. Given the close linkages between congressional Republicans and the private insurance industry, which has enjoyed unprecedented profitability under Obamacare, doubt has arisen about whether the Trump administration and Congress really were trying to destroy the financial bonanza that Obamacare created. The theatrical failure to deliver on campaign promises despite superficially ardent attempts has characterized a spectrum of Trump policy initiatives, including promises to workers that he would punish corporations for exporting jobs and importing foreign parts, would renounce components of international trade agreements adversely affecting U.S. workers, and so forth. Due to its persistent contradiction of high costs with inadequate coverage, Obamacare morphing into Trumpcare continued its failing trajectory.

The capitalist system in which capitalist health care is situated has become more fragile, with deepening stagnation, recurrent crises of increasing severity, unemployment and underemployment, and inequality. Capital accumulation for the richest sector of the population (characterized by the Occupy Movement as the 1 percent) occurs mainly by financialization (lucrative and largely fictional financial instruments unlinked from the dwindling productive economy) and by "disaster capitalism" (the creation of disasters mainly through perpetual war, followed by profitable operations to rebuild). As Samir Amin and many others have noted, capitalism is slowly "imploding" due to its own inherent contradictions.[3] Meanwhile, capitalism is creating ecological threats to the survival of humanity and other species.[4]

In contrast, social movements worldwide are pressing for sustainable models of economic production and human services based on solidarity rather than commodification and profit. For instance, Latin America offers many examples of local communities supported by progressive governments that have constructed innovative programs in medicine and public health. These programs have attracted widespread support and already have improved measurable outcomes like mortality and morbidity rates. Despite continuing attempts by the United States to undermine these governments, struggles for reconstructed, public sector health programs often build upon struggles against prior neoliberal policies of public sector cutbacks and privatization. Further, organizing toward improved health care systems usually links with efforts to protect access to clean water supplies, the rights of "Mother Earth," and the construction of non-capitalist economic systems.

In this context, several questions require answers based on a deeper understanding of changing structural conditions, especially those linking capitalism, health care, and health. This book grew from a recognition that such linkages deserve closer study and that this will assist in real-world struggles for change. Several of us felt a need to strengthen our work at the interface of health and political economy. For that reason, during 2013 Matt Anderson and I approached members of the *Monthly Review* editorial committee to explore ways we could collaborate. Conversations with John Bellamy Foster, Michael Yates, and Brett Clark revealed their hopes of extending their own efforts to the challenges that we face in common during this scary and exciting period of history.

We wrote much of the book before the election of November 2016 but then updated it to take into account the era of Trump. Despite what seemed like a drastic change in national governance, we found that we actually needed to change relatively little in the analysis, which focused, before and after Trump's election, more on the relationships between capitalism and health care than on the superficially shifting panorama of elected elites. Capitalist health care became further entrenched under Obama, has persisted under Trump, and would have differed little under Clinton.

The authors of this book all work as activists and scholars in the United States and other countries. We came together partly because we all recognize a need for clearer knowledge and analysis so that our activism becomes more effective. In this collaboration, we hope that our diverse backgrounds and experiences will help us answer a range of questions that we could not address adequately as individuals. As the initiator of the project, I started by asking colleagues and comrades to help me formulate the key questions that need answers during our current period of history. After clarifying the questions, we decided who would take the lead in trying to answer them.

Part One of the book examines social class and medical work, especially how the social-class positions of health workers have changed during recent decades as medicine has become more corporatized, privatized, and financialized. In Part One, we ask:

- How have the social-class positions of health workers, both professional and non-professional, changed along with changes in the capitalist global economy?
- How has the process of health work transformed as control over the means of production and conditions of the workplace has shifted from professionals to corporations?

I take the liberty of beginning with an account of my own experience as a physician, making the decision to disobey an administrative order because I decided it did not contribute positively to patient care. The repressive response that I received for a seemingly minor act of insubordination shows how medical professionals have become proletarianized, and how our changing social-class position opens a potential for broader organizing to transform the current corporatized system.

Based partly on his own background as a practitioner and teacher of family medicine, as well as a scholar, journal editor, and activist in social medicine, Matt Anderson follows with an account of the changing social-class position among medical professionals, which involves loss of autonomy and control over the labor process, wages, and benefits. He analyzes the "sorry state of U.S. primary care" and critically examines such recent misleading innovations as the "patient-centered medical home," "pay for performance," the electronic medical record, quantified metrics to measure quality including patient satisfaction ("we strive for five"), and conflicts of interest as professional associations and medical schools receive increasing financial support from for-profit corporations ("sleeping with the enemy").

Gordy Schiff and Sarah Winch's chapter focuses on the changing characteristics of medical work, including the degradation of medical labor and the shifting meaning of quality in health care. As clinicians and researchers on quality of care, Gordy and Sarah take their bearings partly from the seminal work of Harry Braverman on labor and monopoly capital.[5] Alienation in work becomes not just a matter of "burnout," as it is commonly viewed, but rather is a response to loss of control over the means of production in medical work. They also examine the frustrating impact of information technology in the medical workplace and show how the struggle toward improved quality in health care depends on more fundamental changes in the overall political economy.

David Himmelstein and Steffie Woolhandler conclude Part One by responding to a series of questions that I posed to them about the changing nature of medical work and how that relates to the struggle for a non-capitalist model of a national health program. As primary care practitioners, leading researchers on health policy, and people who played important roles in organizing and maintaining Physicians for a National Health Program (PNHP)—the organization of more than 20,000 health professionals who advocate a single-payer program for the United States and other countries—David and Steffie comment on the commodification of health care, the transformation that has occurred during the current stage of capitalism, the changing class position of health professionals, and the impact of computerization and electronic medical records. They also describe some of the key strategic directions that PNHP has taken over the years, discuss the organization's strengths and weaknesses, and make some recommendations about where to head from here, which they develop further in a later chapter.

We tackle several questions in Part Two, which focuses on the medical industrial complex in the age of financialization:

- What are the characteristics of the current "medical industrial complex," and how have these changed under financialization and deepening monopolization?

Corollary questions:

- Are such traditional categories as the private insurance industry and pharmaceutical industry separable from the financial sector?

• How do the current operations of those industries reflect increasing financialization and investment practices?

To begin, Matt Anderson collaborates with Robb Burlage, a political economist and activist who coined the term "medical industrial complex" (MIC) decades ago with colleagues at the Health Policy Advisory Center (Health PAC) in New York. Matt and Robb show how the MIC has expanded and shifted during recent decades, focusing on some striking examples such as the Columbia University Medical Center and Weill Cornell Medical School in New York, as well as the National Academy of Medicine. They analyze the growing similarities and overlaps between the for-profit and so-called not-for-profit sectors in health care, considering especially the conversion of previously not-for-profit corporations such as Blue Cross and Blue Shield to for-profit status. The increasingly monopolistic character of medical institutions receives critical attention, illustrated by the consolidation of multiple large academic medical centers connected with Harvard Medical School in Boston. Matt and Robb then focus on financialization, a fundamental shift in the process of capital accumulation in health care, as in the general economy. The interlocking investment networks of Columbia University's medical empire and the financialization of drug production in such corporations as Valeant Pharmaceuticals provide illuminating case studies. The chapter concludes with some implications of the changing MIC for organization, resistance, and strategies of transformation.

The pharmaceutical industry continues to flourish as an exploitative and very lucrative component of capitalist health care. Joel Lexchin, an emergency care physician and health policy researcher based in Canada, analyzes monopoly capital and the pharmaceutical industry from an international perspective. His chapter concretizes the tremendous profitability that the industry enjoys and demystifies claims about the costs and risks of pharmaceutical research and development. Additionally, Joel analyzes the growing crises that the industry currently faces, which he links to financialization and the shift from real capital investment to the buying and selling of financial instruments as the major route to capital accumulation. To cope with this crisis, he shows, the industry has shifted its strategy from "blockbuster" to "niche-buster" drugs, with a focus on the marketing of extremely profitable drugs that target rare rather than common medical conditions. Other strategies include trade agreements that strengthen intellectual property rights while making it more difficult for people to obtain needed medications, as well as techniques to restrict information about the benefits and harms of pharmaceutical products through corrupt regulatory processes for the approval of medications and through control of the conduct and publication of research. The chapter concludes with an argument that "a better world is possible," drawing attention to progressive struggles in several countries to combat the exploitative behavior of the pharmaceutical industry.

Part Three examines the relationships among neoliberalism, health care, and health. The questions are:

• What is the impact of neoliberalism on health reforms, in the United States and in other countries?

Corollary questions:

• What are the ideological assumptions of health reform proposals, and how are they transmitted?
• What are the effects of economic austerity policies on health reform and what are the eventual impacts on health outcomes?

In the United States, the Affordable Care Act (ACA, also known as Obamacare) sometimes appears as a reform that sprang into motion during the presidency of Barack Obama, but its origins actually date to the beginnings of neoliberalism during the 1980s and even earlier. Ida Hellander, a leading health policy researcher and activist, and I trace this history to policies initially developed by economists in the military sector during the Vietnam War, which were first imported into health reform debates during the Nixon administration. International financial institutions, especially the World Bank, promoted a boilerplate for neoliberal health care reforms, which focused mainly on privatization of services previously based in the public sector and on shifting public sector trust funds to private for-profit insurance corporations. This model became the basis for Colombia's health reform of 1994, Hillary Clinton's unsuccessful proposal for the United States during the same year, Mitt Romney's health plan that he spearheaded in Massachusetts during 2006, and eventually Obamacare in 2010. The chapter clarifies the ideological underpinnings of the neoliberal model and shows that the model has failed to improve access and control costs, although it has succeeded in enhancing the profitability of an increasingly financialized private insurance industry.

Closely linked to neoliberalism, economic austerity policies have led to drastic cutbacks in health services and public health infrastructure in many countries. They also have affected health outcomes adversely through increased unemployment, food insecurity, unreliable water supplies, and reduced educational opportunities. Adam Gaffney, a physician specializing in pulmonary and critical care medicine who writes widely on health policy and is a leader in the struggle toward a single-payer national health program in the United States, and Carles Muntaner, whose research, teaching, and international activism focus on social epidemiology, especially the impacts of economic policies on health and mental health outcomes, document the devastating impacts of austerity policies in Europe. Focusing on Greece, Spain, and England, they analyze four dimensions of austerity: 1) constriction of the public sector health system, 2) retreat from universalism, 3) increased cost sharing, and 4) health system privatization. Adam and Carles clarify the dialectic processes by which struggles against neoliberal austerity policies open a path toward post-capitalist alternative systems in these countries. They also show, however, that the achievement of universalism in health systems, as occurred previously in Europe, remains vulnerable to rollbacks as political and economic elites fight to preserve or to restore their own dominance.

Neoliberalism actually constitutes one historical phase in the broader rise and decline of imperialism. In Part Four, we trace the connections between health and imperialism historically and as part of the crises we currently face.

• What are the connections among health care, public health, and imperialism, and how have these connections changed as resistance to imperialism has grown in the Global South?[6]

Rebeca Jasso-Aguilar, an activist and sociologist originally from Mexico who has studied and taken part in struggles to combat neoliberal policies and construct alternatives in several Latin American countries, and I collaborate to analyze "imperialism's health component." We begin by summarizing the historical relationships between imperialism and health, including the contribution of public health interventions and health services in enhancing the productivity of labor, the creation of new markets for drugs and medical equipment, and an exploitative "brain drain" of health professionals from the Global South to economically dominant countries in the Global North. We go on to analyze the institutions that have mediated the connections among imperialism, public health, and health services: 1) philanthropic foundations, such as the Carnegie philanthropies, Rockefeller Foundation, and Gates Foundation; 2) international financial institutions and trade agreements, focusing on the World Bank, the International Monetary Fund, and the trade organizations and agreements that have impacted health and health care; and 3) international health organizations, especially the World Health Organization (WHO) and Pan American Health Organization (PAHO), which, increasingly, receive funding from the World Bank and Gates Foundation and implement policies that weaken public health standards and favor private corporations.

Reacting to the widening impact of foundations, especially the Gates Foundation, in shaping health policies worldwide, the following chapter in Part Four examines "philanthrocapitalism" in greater depth. Anne-Emanuelle Birn and Judith Richter, who are public health activists and scholars based in Canada and Czechoslovakia, analyze the startling parallels between the Rockefeller and Gates

Foundations, including a vertical, top-down, highly technological approach that sponsors new drugs or technologies, with agenda setting by a small group of international elites. These foundations' policies do not encourage development of a broad, locally decided public sector infrastructure to enhance health services and prevention. After describing the ideological struggles that affected WHO during the Cold War, Anne-Emanuelle and Judith analyze WHO's chronic financial crisis after the Reagan administration led other countries to withdraw financial support from WHO, necessitating a shift to outside donors. The Gates Foundation ultimately emerged as the key player in this scenario, and this foundation currently spends more money on global health than any government except the United States. As the authors show, the reductionist approach fostered by Gates has profoundly influenced international health organizations; programs to combat HIV, Ebola, and other emerging infections; and so-called private-public partnerships. Other problematic features of philanthrocapitalism, as the authors clarify, include tax advantages for philanthropic donors, with the resulting loss of important tax revenues to the public sector; conflicts of interest involving Gates's and colleagues' earnings from intellectual property rights, investments in the pharmaceutical industry, and sales of information technology; and the perpetuation of policy making by a small elite of rich people, mostly men, based in the Global North.

Part Five focuses on the road ahead—the contours of change that we foresee and the concrete actions that can contribute to a progressive transformation of capitalist health care and capitalist society.

- What examples provide inspiration about resistance to neoliberalism and construction of positive alternative models in the Global South?
- Because improvements in health do not necessarily follow from improvements in health care, how do we achieve change in the social and environmental determinants of health?
- How does progressive health and mental health reform address the ambiguous role of the state?

- What is to be done as Obamacare and its successor or lack of successor under Trump fail in the United States?

To envision transitions toward a better world, while not discounting recent struggles in the United States, we need to grapple with efforts in other countries that already have been moving along such a road. To begin, Rebeca Jasso-Aguilar and I analyze a series of popular struggles in which we have participated during the past decade as researchers and activists. These accounts focus on resistance against the privatization of health services in El Salvador and of water in Bolivia, as well as an ongoing struggle to expand public sector health services in Mexico. Such scenarios portray an image of diminishing tolerance among the world's peoples for the imperial public health policies of the Global North and a forceful demand for public health systems grounded in solidarity rather than profit. These cases also show how popular struggles concerning health can expand popular participation in policy decisions previously controlled by political and economic elites.

In the United States, the road ahead will involve intensified organizing to achieve the single-payer model of a national health program, a model that aims to provide universal access to care and to control costs by drastically reducing or eliminating administrative waste, profiteering, and corporate control. Adam Gaffney, David Himmelstein, and Steffie Woolhander in the next chapter present the most recent revision of the single-payer proposal developed by Physicians for a National Health Program during the late 1980s and most recently published during May 2016 in the *American Journal of Public Health*. Versions of this proposal have been introduced into the Senate by Bernie Sanders and the House of Representatives by John Conyers, with more than a hundred congressional co-sponsors. Adam, David, and Steffie, lead authors of the revised PNHP proposal, first analyze the three main ways that the interests of capital have encroached on U.S. health care during the decades since the original PNHP proposal: 1) the rise of for-profit managed care organizations (MCOs), 2) the emergence of high-deductible ("consumer-directed") health insurance, and 3) the entrenchment of corporate ownership.

They offer a critique of Obamacare, explaining and demystifying such innovations as Accountable Care Organizations, the consolidation and integration of health systems, and increasing share of costs for patients. The authors then summarize the key elements of the revised single-payer proposal, including its provisions about coverage, financing, and transition from the current corporatized and financialized arrangements, and comment on shifts in needed strategy during the era of Trump.

Improved medical care for physical illnesses remains an incomplete goal if it does not encompass a holistic vision of health that includes improved mental health as well. But what are the prospects for mental health during this waning phase of the world capitalist system? Updating and refining a perspective previously developed by Erich Fromm, Carl Ratner, a cultural psychologist and activist who has written widely on mental health under capitalism, mental health innovations in other countries, and cooperatives as an incompletely realized model for progressive organizational change, argues that mental health under capitalism entails "pathological normalcy." Seen through this lens, the day-to-day economic insecurities, violence, and lack of social solidarity experienced in capitalist society generate a kind of false consciousness, in which disordered mental processes become a necessary facet of survival, and emotional health becomes a deviant and marginalized condition. Carl dissects the well-known crises of our age in terms of the pathologies that have become seen as normal conditions of life: a normally polluted natural environment, a normally corrupt political system, a normally unequal hierarchy of social stratification, a normally unjust criminal justice system, normally violent living conditions due to the marketing of guns, normally dangerous working conditions, and so forth. Thus "pathologically normal economic practices—the daily manipulation, cheating, speculation, de-skilling, outsourcing, tax code revisions, and exploitation—are more destructive than the criminal thief." Reckoning the implications for the road ahead, Carl argues that the struggle for improved mental health conditions cannot limit itself to reforms in the delivery of services but must entail a struggle to change the economic, political, and social underpinnings of pathological normalcy.

Despite our own and others' efforts to improve access to health and mental health services, we recognize that such services are not the main determinants of health and mental health outcomes. As Carles Muntaner and evolutionary biologist Rob Wallace, who has done extensive research focusing on the impact of capitalist agriculture on infections, especially epidemics such as influenza, Ebola, and Zika, show in their chapter, social and environmental conditions have become more important determinants of health than access to care, and such broader conditions explain the greatest part of the variation in health outcomes. Concerning social determinants, Carles in prior work has focused on social class and has considered differing conceptualizations of class. He has shown the advantage of a theoretical and empirical definition of social class rooted in relations of economic production, as opposed to the more commonly used demographic indicators of inequality such as income, education, and prestige. The latter indicators impede clarity of understanding about the conditions that separate the 1 percent from the 99 percent; they also mystify needed directions of political change through the notion that adjusting "disparities" in income can produce more favorable health and mental health outcomes. The authors emphasize struggles that directly confront social determinants through changes in broad societal policies. They also analyze some of the key environmental determinants of health, including unsafe water (citing the egregious example of Flint, Michigan), capitalist agribusiness practices, and deforestation in addition to climate change. They refer especially to the impact of these environmental determinants on emergent and re-emergent infectious diseases like Ebola, Zika, and yellow fever.

To conclude the book, Adam Gaffney and I try to tackle the inevitable question of "what is to be done." First, let me express my delight to collaborate with Adam. While I and several other authors of this book are closer to the end of our work lives than the beginning, Adam is much closer to the beginning. As a physician, historian, and activist (among other things), Adam is one of an emerging cadre of young people who will carry forth this struggle in future years, and their brilliance and audacity in doing so give us much hope. In our conclusion, we recognize at the outset that we hold no corner on strategic truth, given the complexities and challenges of current realities. Still, we see four main priorities for action in the United States and in other countries still affected by the neoliberal, corporatized, and commodified model of health care during the era of Trump: 1) a sustained, broad-based movement for a single-payer national health program that assures universal access to care and drastically reduces the role of corporations and private profit; 2) an activated labor movement that this time includes a well-organized sub-movement of health professionals such as physicians, whose deteriorated social-class position and proletarianized conditions of medical practice have made them ripe for activism and change; 3) more emphasis on local and regional organizing at the level of communal organizations as envisioned by István Mészáros and attempted in multiple countries as a central component in the revolutionary process of moving "beyond capital";[7] and 4) carefully confronting the role of political parties while recognizing the importance of labor or otherwise leftist parties in every country that has constructed a national health program, and understanding that the importance of party building goes far beyond electoral campaigns to more fundamental social transformation. All these priorities emphasize the urgency of creating bridges that link health activism with social movements that focus on social-class oppression, including poverty and inequality, racism, sexism, environmental degradation, militarism and imperialism, and the dominant ideologies that lead women and men to accept pathological social conditions as normal.

With these contributions by leading scholars and activists based in several countries, our book tries to answer key and previously unresolved questions and to offer some guidance on strategy and political action in the years ahead. Through this work, we aim to inform future struggles for the transformation of capitalist societies, as well as the progressive reconstruction of health services and public health systems in the post-capitalist world.

At roughly the same stage in my work life as Adam's now, I asked (with a colleague), "Is a humane health care system possible in a capitalist society?" My focus then, as it remains today, involved "the exploitation of illness in capitalist society" and the "forms of social organization which foster this exploitation."[8] As the contradictions and weaknesses of global capitalism grow more profound and as the need for revolutionary transformation becomes clearer and more urgent, a non-exploitative health care system has entered the realm of the imaginable and the possible. The road leading to that place, for all its challenges, must become the road that travels "beyond capital" and beyond capitalism.

PART ONE

Social Class and Medical Work

1—Disobedience: Doctor Workers, Unite!

Howard Waitzkin

> A person can become free through acts of disobedience by learning to say no to power. . . . At this point in history the capacity to doubt, to criticize and to disobey may be all that stands between a future for mankind and the end of civilization.
> —ERICH FROMM, "ON DISOBEDIENCE"

I confess: I am a disobedient doctor.[1]

After a career in academic medicine and public health, I decided to work part-time in a rural health program. There I began to understand the loss of control over the conditions of medical practice that has affected so many doctors. Administrative demands multiplied and constrained my ability to care for my patients in the ways I thought best.

So I decided to disobey. A seemingly minor training requirement, the International Classification of Diseases, 10th edition (ICD-10), which Medicare and other insurers started to require for medical billing as of October 1, 2015, became yet another administrative demand that pushed me over the line to disobedience. But the struggle might have involved many other arenas of clinical medicine, where the requirements of employers infringe on a doctor's freedom to practice according to his or her professional judgment.

PROLETARIANIZATION

Intrinsically I have nothing against being a proletarian. Everyone in my immediate family was one, and I supported much of my education by working as a wage laborer in, for instance, a tire factory, where I learned firsthand about life as a worker in our capitalist society. Throughout my medical career, I have befriended secretaries, nursing assistants, janitors, and other "non-professional" health workers— wonderful people whose services on behalf of patients and doctors usually go underappreciated. Such people spend most of their waking lives doing tasks assigned by supervisors, and they enjoy little or no control over the conditions and rhythm of their work.

Medicine, I thought, would provide a way to seize control of my own work process and creativity by organizing at least a large part of the work week as I preferred. A position in academic medicine actually did allow me that liberty, despite the challenges of university bureaucracies, budget cuts, fund raising, and academic politics. Even in academia, the ability to control my activities started to erode, usually linked to financial shortfalls and measures of productivity.

However, entering the world of a non-academic medical employee revealed the awesome scope of proletarianization, a sharp change in a doctor's previous social-class position.[2] Until the 1980s, doctors for the most part owned and/or controlled their means of production and conditions of practice. Although their work often was challenging, they could decide their hours of work, the staff members who worked with them, how much time to spend with patients, what to write about their visits in medical records, and how much to charge for their services.

Now, the corporations for which doctors work as employees usually control those decisions. Loss of control over the conditions of work has caused much unhappiness and burnout in the profession. Early on, an esteemed clinician and mentor described medical proletarianization when it was first emerging as "working on the factory floor."[3] Most doctors have become employees of hospital and health system corporations,[4] and around half of doctors report feeling burned out due to the stresses of their work as employees.[5, 6] Due to the mystique of professionalism and relatively high salaries, doctors often do not realize that their discontent reflects in large part their changing social-class position.

DECIDING TO DISOBEY

As a doctor worker, I got into trouble by expressing concerns about the training that our health network (hereafter, OHN) was requiring for all practitioners before the implementation of ICD-10. Until then, I had not received significant adverse feedback from the administration, had received multiple expressions of praise and gratitude, and recently had obtained reappointment to the active medical staff.

OHN had contracted with a corporation (hereafter, "$Corp") to help cope with the transition to ICD-10. This corporation was one of hundreds that have emerged to sell consulting services to health care organizations facing the challenges of information technology (IT) required by the private insurance industry, Medicare, Medicaid, and various certifying and regulatory agencies. Such challenges include electronic medical records (EMRs), meaningful use, quality assurance, accountable care, medical homes, and similar arenas. These arenas all involve "metrics" that try to make quality quantifiable, a goal that has generated wide skepticism, debate, and worry in the medical profession, as well as the broader society (for instance, in the debate about standardized testing in schools).

$Corp's training for ICD-10 took multiple hours of unpaid time observing narrated slide shows and taking proficiency tests, and I decided to disobey the requirement. One reason involved a close friend who was dying from metastatic gastroesophageal cancer. His dying process and my desire to spend time with him had made me even more aware that each moment of life is too precious to waste, especially on activities whose purpose isn't clear.

After I previewed the $Corp training, I concluded that its educational quality was abysmal, conflicts of interest were not disclosed, most recommendations were not evidence based, and the narrator's comments implicitly encouraged "up-coding" diagnoses to higher levels of severity and more comorbid conditions, so billing codes could generate more payments for OHN. The federal government's prohibitions against up-coding were not mentioned. The training also didn't explain how to use ICD-10 on our particular EMR software. Brief discussions with other practitioners confirmed universal contempt for the training, as well as universal compliance with it because people felt they had no choice. I compared time wasted on the training program to time spent with my dying friend and decided to protest the training.

WORK REQUIREMENTS AND THE SLIPPERY SLOPE TO FASCISM

My subsequent interactions with OHN administrators surprised me, despite my knowledge about physicians' changing social class position. The Chief Medical Information Officer (CMIO) at OHN wrote that "practitioners with incomplete ICD-10 coursework at midnight on 10/7/15 will be suspended until the coursework is completed." In response, I sent an email message asking him to explain the rationale for the training requirement. Copying the Chief Executive Officer (CEO), the CMIO pasted his responses in the text of my original message:

1. Please provide evidence that additional training in ICD-10 . . . improves any measurable patient outcomes, costs, or collections.
   • Not a debatable point. This is a requirement by OHN, so, sorry to say, whether you agree with it or not, it must be done.
2. Please provide the costs to OHN for the training.
   • Not relevant, as this is a requirement.
3. Please provide quantitative estimates of the financial benefits of the training for OHN.
   • Not relevant, as this is a requirement.
4. Please give a concrete description of the process by which you concluded that "completion of this training allows us to achieve both appropriate care and remain fiscally responsible—part of OHN stewardship."
   • Not relevant, as this is a requirement.

This response pressed one of my alarm buttons, which I might call the fascism button. I responded that my dear grandfather, who was a farmer and then a housepainter after he lost the farm, taught me not to comply with requirements when I didn't understand the reasons for them. Doctors, I wrote, are complying with an ever-increasing burden of unjustified requirements that take the joy out of practice and cause many of us to leave medicine prematurely. Citing Arendt's classic book on Adolf Eichmann,[7] I explained the slippery slope to fascism, when people do what they are ordered in their jobs without understanding why. Such unjustified requirements, I argued, deserve our conscientious questioning and sometimes non-compliance—a very modest act of "civil disobedience."

Unimpressed, the CMIO replied: "Everyone must complete the training. We all make choices and I hope you will make the right one for you and your patients."

STANDARDIZATION

If an argument about incipient fascism in the workplace didn't work, I thought, maybe I could appeal to practicality. I proposed coming to the office, unpaid, and practicing ICD-10 within our EMR program, supervised by an IT staff person who then could attest to my competence. But the CMIO did not budge: "OHN's Transformation is a movement to ensure process consistency and standardization. . . . Therefore, your request for an 'exception' is outside the organization's expectation."

Again, the CMIO's reply pressed an alarm button, in this case the Henry Fordism button. Not only must I as a doctor worker accept orders without questioning them, but I also must behave at work like an automaton in a medical assembly line governed by "process consistency and standardization."[8] Without space for individual variation and creativity, the organization's "transformation" became what my mentor foresaw: "working on the factory floor."

I then requested details about what my forthcoming suspension would entail; the contractual authority for the suspension; a plan of coverage for my patients; an external review of OHN's interference with my professional judgment; and recognition of my rights under whistle-blower laws and regulations. I repeated my concerns about authoritarianism in the medical workplace and commented on the extensive evidence that standardization actually may reduce quality, creativity, and productivity. I also reiterated a request for a face-to-face meeting.

PUNISHMENT

My moral predicament deteriorated quickly. On the next morning, the CEO sent an email providing none of the information I had requested and asking for my resignation effective within one week, despite packed schedules including many unstable patients. Then, five days before the deadline for suspension, I received a letter by overnight mail from the CEO stating that I was in breach of contract. A second letter stated that the meeting I had requested had been canceled, and my office hours with patients also had been canceled until further notice. Because I needed to respond to lab results and urgent messages about patients from nurses, I tried to connect with the EMR system but found that I had been cut off. I also could not connect to email or even to the ICD-10 training.

I now faced the apparent abandonment of hundreds of my patients, who had not received any alternative plan of care. I knew and previously had taught medical students and residents that medical abandonment is unethical according to the AMA Code of Ethics[9] and other sources, and also is illegal in many states. For that reason, I contacted the chief of the medical staff and the chair of the physicians' council, who intervened with the CEO to get me reconnected to the EMR system, so I could manage acute problems for my unstable patients.

Because I was not willing to abandon my patients, I also persuaded an administrator to get me reconnected to the ICD-10 training, which I completed under protest late the next night, after spending time with my dying friend. On the following morning, a Sunday, I received an email from the CEO thanking me for completing the training and stating that my breach of contract had been "cured."

The nursing staff reconstructed my canceled schedule for the next day so I could see most of the patients. Nurses said patients had approached them in supermarkets and called them at home, asking what was going to happen now that I was gone. One patient asked if I had died.

REDEMPTION

As a doctor worker, I faced a challenging ethical situation that included loss of professional autonomy, authoritarian practices in the workplace, and apparent abandonment of patients. My first suspension in over forty years of practice also raised concerns: Would a report about the suspension from OHN to the National Practitioner Data Bank lead to effects on my medical licenses or ability to practice in other settings? Was it my responsibility to blow the whistle on OHN's practices to licensing, accreditation, and insurance agencies?

My small act of conscientious disobedience eventually led to some unexpected responses. My contract and state law required that OHN convene an external review based on my claim of interference with my professional judgment. The coordinator of the state agency that licenses health facilities expressed willingness to investigate this issue and the abandonment of patients. Facing the probability of external review, the CEO finally agreed to meet with me. At the meeting, I proposed a formal mediation process. Instead, the CEO composed a document that included an apology, a statement that information about breach of contract would be removed from my personnel file, a commitment to consider individual physicians' preferences in meeting future training requirements, and a promise to meet individually with a physician when a suspension is considered so patient care would not be disrupted.

Where is the path toward a non-corporatized vision of what we know medicine can be at its best? I don't think that path involves our continuing acquiescence. I confess that I have decided to approach these problems through personal acts of disobedience. For me, closer to the end of my medical career than the beginning, such acts don't risk much. For others, overcoming the risk will require a more organized approach to disobedience.[10] Dare I encourage disobedience in unison? To paraphrase someone else: Doctor workers of the world, unite![11]

2—Becoming Employees:
The Deprofessionalization and Emerging Social-Class Position of Health Professionals

Matthew Anderson

"No," said the priest, "it is not necessary to accept everything as true, one must only accept it as necessary."

"A melancholy conclusion," said K. "It turns lying into a universal principle."

—FRANZ KAFKA, THE TRIAL

During the early twenty-first century, control over the conditions of medical work and the means of production in medicine has become a key focus of contention, in both the United States and other countries.[1] The struggle for control involves the daily activities of the physicians and other licensed health care professionals who are legally sanctioned to make clinical decisions about patient care. Executives usually frame their attempts to achieve control over the work practices of clinicians as efforts to produce greater value (to improve efficiency and quality of care), while bringing "market discipline" to an overly expensive, irrational, and inefficient system.

I propose that such concepts—value, efficiency, quality, and market discipline—are part of an ideology designed to justify corporate control over the work of physicians and other workers providing health services. In describing the "deprofessionalization" of health care

workers, I keep in mind Marx's concept of alienation, the separation of the worker from the control and the product of his or her
labor, as a useful way of thinking about the clinician of the future,
who must learn what it means to become an employee. In the words
of Marx: "The object which labor produces—labor's product—con-
fronts it as *something alien*, as a *power independent* of the producer. ...
Realization of labor appears as *loss of realization* for the workers;
objectification as *loss of the object and bondage to it*; appropriation
as *estrangement*, as *alienation*."[2]

In this chapter, I clarify how the corporate model of medicine is
degrading the culture of clinical care and the work of clinicians. We
will see what happens when the corporate model enshrines the centrality of health care as a commodity and self-interest as a motivator:
the mission of the profit margin overtakes the mission of healing.

THE SORRY STATE OF PRIMARY CARE IN THE UNITED STATES

There is strong evidence to suggest that primary care improves the
health of populations and, unlike specialty care, it helps reduce
inequalities in health outcomes.[3] Primary care is also cheaper than
specialty care. There is even some evidence from the United States
suggesting that an overabundance of specialists can be bad for community health.[4] Yet, despite the demonstrated benefits of primary
care, only 12 percent of U.S. doctors work in it. The majority of our
doctors (over 85 percent) are specialists.[5] In Europe, by contrast, primary care doctors more typically make up about 70 percent of the
physician workforce.

The reasons for the specialist-heavy U.S. system are complex,
but they bring us back to the technology- and profit-driven character of the U.S. health care system.[6] It rewards new physicians for
choosing high-tech, expensive procedural-based specialties (such
as orthopedics and cardiology) rather than the more cognitive and
relationship-based specialties of internal medicine, family medicine,
and pediatrics. Medical students quickly learn to see primary care
as bringing low prestige and low pay. There is no particularly good
reason why primary care work should be undervalued. The essence

of this problem is a political one: specialists run our academic medical centers, have close financial ties to industry, and have been able to define medicine and healing as the use of expensive wonder drugs and high technology.

The Patient-Centered Medical Home: Neither Patient-Centered Nor a Home

In the past decade a new model of primary care, the "patient-centered medical home" (PCMH), has been promoted to solve the problems of primary care. The term "medical home" appeared initially in 1967 in the pediatric literature. It was designed to describe a place, a "single source," where a child's medical records would be kept.[7] In the 1990s the idea of the medical home was elaborated within the primary care community—by the American Academy of Pediatrics in 1992 and 2004, the American Academy of Family Physicians in 2004, and the American College of Physicians (internal medicine) in 2006. These efforts culminated in a joint statement issued by five primary care organizations in 2007. By 2008 a National Committee for Quality Assurance had promulgated standards for a PCMH, adherence to which guaranteed extra reimbursement for providers.

It is difficult to define exactly what a PCMH is because various organizations have promoted different conceptualizations.[8] But some of the components include better integration of health care, usually accomplished through electronic medical records (EMRs); the creation of health teams, as opposed to solo practices; improved access to care; a personal physician for each patient; and efforts to improve the quality of care as measured by standardized targets. To address pay disparities, primary care physicians are promised increased income when they meet certain quality standards, which is known as "Pay-for-Performance" (P4P).

While these initiatives are not necessarily detrimental, they address symptoms of the problem, not the problem itself. The flow of resources into (expensive) specialty care continues, as does the underfunding of primary care. If population health is the goal of the system, this approach makes little sense. However, if we understand the imperatives of profit, such initiatives appear both logical and inevitable.

The PCMH is a vehicle for the delivery of health services organized through a competitive, private insurance market. Purchasers of health insurance, whether individuals or organizations, are expected to make a yearly decision regarding which plan is most advantageous in terms of price and benefits. Adopting the "home" metaphor, it's a bit like getting the opportunity to move once a year and find new family members. Even if patients want to stay "home" with their current doctor, there is no guarantee that their doctor will be on the company-offered plan next year. Let us be clear: this is a business model, not a home. For that matter, the development of the PCMH was not really "patient-centered." Professional societies and large corporations developed and promoted the model. Patients have not been centrally involved in its conceptualization or in its elaboration. The PCMH is "patient-centered" only in the sense that McDonald's is "customer-centered." Ironically, the hype and fanfare surrounding the development of the PCMH model seem to arise from the demise of personalized health care rather than the dawn of a new era in primary care.

It is important to remember what the PCMH cannot address and what options it does not explore. There will continue to be tremendous class and racial biases in the system; these impact quality and access to care as well as access to careers in medicine. In addition, a system that is highly incentivized to hit quality targets may want to avoid poorer (or sicker) patients, whose outcomes are likely to be worse than those of patients with more social and financial resources.

Many models of clinical care have sought to make the health center an integral part of the local community, leveraging the ability of the clinic to participate in community development. There are clinical benefits gained by understanding local context. This is the basis for the very successful community health center program started by Dr. Jack Geiger in the 1960s.[9] But there is no room in the PCMH for the local community voice. Although the PCMH retains the paternalistic ethos of medicine, now the "father" of the medical home is the corporate bureaucracy. And how could the involvement of a clinic in health problems of the local community be incentivized, within a system of individually based private insurance?

PAY FOR PERFORMANCE (P4P)

One pillar of the PCMH is the P4P program, in which doctors receive monetary rewards for hitting specific, quantitative, clinical goals, for example, the percentage of patients who receive flu shots. Studies of P4P have shown widely differing effects of individual P4P programs on quality measurements.[10] In simple English, we don't really know if it works. If P4P were a pill, this lack of evidence would have prevented its approval or use. But the business world is different; the ideological imperative to turn health care workers into employees is powerful.

P4P's lack of success may result from the direct undermining of what has always been considered the central concern of the physician: the welfare of the patient. When patients ask me whether they should have flu shots, they are asking me for a disinterested answer based on my professional opinion and my knowledge of them. How would they feel if, as honesty demands, I told them I was receiving some amount of money (no matter how small) every time they got a flu shot? That admission would undermine the very trust that should be the foundation of our relationship.

Such measurement programs can also be faulted on more practical grounds. Usually they rely on easily measured goals: number of shots given, blood pressure, cholesterol measurements, patient-satisfaction surveys, and so on. But many of us believe that the heart of primary care involves relationships with families that are created over time; these relationships cannot be reduced to a number on a scale. When I visit my patients in the hospital—a familiar face in a frightening and strange environment—I provide a type of caring that is central to the role of a healer but is invisible to the highly technical world of "hard" targets. Patients remember these visits and thank me for them years later, when I perhaps have forgotten them.

In addition, clinical targets are notoriously fickle. Clinical medicine evolves rapidly, and what is good today will be seen as substandard in a few years. Goals for blood pressure, cholesterol, and diabetic control have undergone major revision in the past several years in ways that P4P programs either can't capture or don't. And, as more and more clinicians work in larger institutions, the attribution of clinical outcomes to any individual clinician becomes increasingly problematic.

Truly "patient-centered" medical care would require great flexibility in terms of clinical outcomes. Not all patients want all treatments. The externally generated quality targets may not reflect the real problems facing the patient, the clinic, or the community.

ENTER THE ELECTRONIC MEDICAL RECORD

The George W. Bush administration initiated a large federal initiative to promote the use of health technology and, specifically, electronic medical records (EMRs). This initiative received further impetus during the first year of the Obama administration, when medical practices were given incentives to purchase EMR systems under the American Recovery and Reinvestment Act, the 2009 stimulus package.[11] EMRs became a new, federally subsidized profit center, and dozens of vendors came forth to sell their EMR software to clinicians.

The result, ironically, is that health information has become even more fragmented. Now we have a bewildering variety of EMR systems, none of which talks to each other; within individual institutions there are often several different types of EMRs. Sorting out this chaos, created in the logic of a marketplace, may take decades. Who knows how many people will need to get extra vaccines or extra tests because their records are lost in some obsolete and inaccessible software? The "medical home" seems to have been colonized by various unruly families, none of whom speaks the same language.

There are other troubling features of EMRs. Most were designed to capture billing and quality information, not to facilitate clinical care. As a result, clinicians, rather than looking at their patients, sit hunched over their computers clicking little boxes indicating they have advised their patients not to smoke or that they need a colonoscopy, a true example of alienated labor. As one frustrated patient told me: "I used to talk to my doctor; now I just see the back of his head."[12] There is no particular rhyme or reason behind the flow of the clinical interview, since it now follows computer-generated prompts. As one works one's way through the required screens with the required answers, one might as well be standing behind a Burger King counter and noting if the customer wants fries or onion rings.

Not only is the voice of the doctor gone in many EMRs but, more crucially, so is the voice of the patient. In a menu-driven EMR, clinical histories are reduced to a random collection of facts taken out of context: *left abdominal pain / quality: crampy / duration: 2–4 days/ relieved by: defecation*. This is almost anti-medicine, because it perverts the essential task of understanding the patient's experience, to assist in diagnosis and treatment.

"We Strive for Five": Manufactured Satisfaction

One of the most pernicious aspects of the PCMH is the focus on massaging data to meet targets, a corruption of the very knowledge that should be the lifeblood of improvement. This is seen in the approach to satisfaction surveys, such as Press Ganey's *Improving Healthcare* "product."[13] Press Ganey, the leading for-profit corporation in the business of measuring patient satisfaction, sends surveys on quality of care to a sample of patients after visits. Mid-level managers are put under intense pressure to get and maintain good survey scores. In order to boost their numbers, a message that "We Strive for Five" (5 being the highest possible score) is often presented to patients either on posters, on appointment cards, or verbally by staff. If this does not work, Press Ganey can be contracted to advise the institution on how to improve scores, an interesting side-business for an agency that is supposed to provide impartial ratings.

Letting patients know that their doctor or clinic wants a "five" rating introduces a not-so-subtle bias into their answers. It is exactly the kind of condition we would scrupulously avoid in clinical research. A principal investigator who chewed out his or her research nurse because the blood pressure results were not as expected might be fired or at least censured for fraudulent research practices. A mid-level manager who does the same is rewarded.

This situation illustrates a dictum coined by American sociologist

Donald T. Campbell, which has come to be known as Campbell's Law: "The more any quantitative social indicator (sometimes even a qualitative indicator) is used for social decision-making, the more subject it will be to corruption pressures and the more apt it will be to distort and corrupt the social processes it is intended to monitor."[14] The massaged results of the satisfaction survey impede real attempts to improve systems. Of course, system improvement may be irrelevant, as long as money is being made.

SLEEPING WITH THE ENEMY, PART ONE: PROFESSIONAL ASSOCIATIONS

The corporate conquest of primary care has occurred with the complicity of physicians who head the professional organizations of primary care and whose leadership has been compromised by commercial interests. Following are three examples among many.

The American Academy of Family Physicians (AAFP) has chosen Coca-Cola as a corporate partner; a visitor to the AAFP page on sugar substitutes is advised: "*This content was developed with general underwriting support from the Coca-Cola Company.*"[15]

The American Academy of Pediatrics (AAP) endorses breastfeeding as the optimal form of infant nutrition, yet Nestlé, one of the leading makers of breast milk substitutes, is considered a valid corporate sponsor.[16] For years the AAP logo was prominently displayed in periodicals advertising baby formula. Advertising of breast milk substitutes is illegal in most countries.

Even the National Institutes of Health has corporate partners, which have included both Pepsi and Coca-Cola.[17] Consider a patient who must make sense of the fact that her doctor and her government, both charged with protecting health, are proud partners of Coca-Cola. Coke can't be all that bad, can it?

SLEEPING WITH THE ENEMY, PART TWO: ACADEMIC MEDICAL CENTERS

Academic medical centers train the physician workforce and mold its professional values. They conduct much of the research that fuels technical advances in medicine. And they promote specific social constructs (such as a genetic or racial basis for disease and social problems) that create social consensus. The academics who run this system are highly rewarded. In many large universities, the highest-paid officials are the basketball coach and the head of the teaching hospital.

This problem is typically conceptualized in terms of "conflicts of interest," which need to be disclosed and regulated. But industry is so interpenetrated with academia that their relationship is best described as symbiotic. For example, in 2007 Eric Campbell and his colleagues at Harvard Medical School published a survey of department chairs at U.S. medical schools. Of the 688 chairs surveyed, they received a response from 459 (67 percent). They found that two-thirds of the department chairs had a direct personal tie to industry. These ties came in a variety of forms, with the most common being consultancy (27 percent) but extended to direct roles in the corporation either as officer (7 percent), founder (9 percent), or director (11 percent). Over two-thirds reported that these relationships had "no effect on their professional activities."[18] This is a fascinating finding. What types of "non-professional" activities do department chairs undertake with corporations?

On the other hand, medical students have often contributed as activists in promoting change. Harvard Medical School is an interesting case in point. In 2008 a variety of high-profile conflict-of-interest cases came to light at Harvard. Medical school students formed a group to protest the fact that so many of their professors had undisclosed industry ties.[19] On a more national scale, the American Medical Students Association (AMSA) has played an important role as an advocate for change. AMSA was created by medical students in 1950 as a progressive alternative to the AMA-sponsored medical student organization. Former AMSA members were central to the creation in 2005 of the National Physicians Alliance, which was conceived as a progressive alternative to the AMA. AMSA regularly surveys medical schools regarding their involvement with pharmaceutical corporations and hands out grades ranging from A to F.[20]

Is "Evidence" Irrelevant?

Medicine has struggled over the past several decades to move away from care based on expert opinion toward "evidence-based" practice. But the corporate model's practices rarely are evidence-based. PCMH, P4P, and similar approaches have been introduced and implemented without thorough testing; usually they have provided further frontiers for corporate capital accumulation. It is striking that the for-profit corporation, whose scientific basis has been severely questioned,[21] is now running the show.

When individual clinicians object that they are being forced to do things that make no clinical sense or are even bad for patients, they are told that these things are necessary for the purposes of their employers. When family doctors protested to the American Academy of Family Physicians about its partnership with Coca-Cola, we were told that this too was necessary. In short, we have arrived at the land described by Kafka, where lying has become a universal principle.

3—The Degradation of Medical Labor and the Meaning of Quality in Health Care

Gordon D. Schiff and Sarah Winch

Health care quality matters. Confronting contemporary health care in the United States, we surprise ourselves by feeling the need to state this simple truism. Sick people want to trust that that their care meets good standards and will not result in harm. At times people may become so desperate for high quality care that they spend unaffordable sums of money or travel long distances to seek care. Because quality matters to everyone, a standard assumption is that it should not be apportioned by income or geography. Unfortunately, there are many times, places, and circumstances in which quality is suboptimal and results in error, mistreatment, and injury. Here are examples of ways that quality fails patients:

1. Failure to receive an accurate or timely diagnosis
2. Prescriptions of inappropriate, harmful medication(s) with errors in ordering or failure to monitor properly
3. Unnecessary tests and treatment
4. Rushed, rude, uncaring treatment, a lack of compassionate, personalized attention
5. Multifaceted communication failures, ranging from inability to reach practitioners to receive sensitive, understandable (in familiar language) explanations to learning about test results, etc.
6. Hospital-acquired infections or other iatrogenic (medically caused) complications

7. Lack of transparency, candor, or meaningful follow-up in response to concerns and/or adverse events
8. Unequal treatment based on ability to pay, race/ethnicity, geographic isolation, and stigmatized conditions like mental illness

"Quality" has taken on new meanings as health care has become more corporatized. In its reorientation and reduction to a set of metrics, quality also has become a focus of tension among health care workers, managers, and patients. Those seeing patients on the front lines have increasingly expressed frustration, burnout, and cynicism. Those practitioners concerned about quality feel constrained by the work conditions under which they are practicing, compounded by the failed promises of quality-improvement initiatives to which they have been subjected.[1]

To understand what is happening with "quality"—failures to improve, failures to engage health workers, unproductive and even counterproductive initiatives, frustrations with health information technology (IT) implemented to improve quality, and improvements that prove unsustainable—we view quality and its improvement through a historical and contextual lens. Our view is critical of the market-oriented thinking that has come to dominate quality improvement.

Such a lens helps us focus on contradictions inherent in how quality is being addressed. A critical lens also helps us understand, for example, the widespread imposition of numeric quality metrics, endeavors to implement "lean" quality-improvement methods, efforts to convert fee-for-service payment to "quality-based" remuneration, proliferation of problematic IT, and implementation of various pay for performance schemes.

This perspective helps us recognize that problems of quality are symptoms of deeper structural problems. For that reason, we look beyond the more superficial issues that dominate much of the quality literature, such as poor communication, organizational inertia, workers lacking empathy or sufficient training, variations and failure to standardize work processes, and insufficient patient education. Instead, we argue that quality problems reflect underlying contradictions that must be better understood and addressed.

Alienation in Health Work

As health care workers become burned out and disengaged from their work and their patients, Karl Marx's words capture much of their experience:

> The alienated character of work for the worker appears in fact that it is not his work but work for someone else, that in the work he does not belong to himself but to another person. . . . Alienation thus shows itself not merely in the results but also in the process, production, of the productive activity itself.[2]

Marx's descriptions of how workers become alienated from their work—from the product of their work, from the act of producing, from other workers, and even from themselves—is recognizable to many physicians, nurses, and other health care professionals today. For them, work that was intrinsically satisfying previously has become exhausting, unrewarding, and alienating.

More recently, Harry Braverman critiqued the ways workers were disrespected and stripped of meaningful contributions to the production process, with detrimental effects for workers and for the quality of the products produced.[3] Braverman linked this degradation on the factory and service sector floor to the increasingly intrusive "commoditization of all aspects of life" under the "universal market." He emphasized that these trends interfered with what made work fundamentally human and satisfying.[4]

Those of us who work in health care, as well as our patients, understand that care is fundamentally about relationships—healing, caring, empathetic, long-term, and personal relationships.[5] When Marx described what made humans special and therefore different from all other species, he wrote that it was our special instinctive need—"species need" as opposed to "natural need" shared by all animals for food or oxygen—to create, to transform the natural world by creative labor. In his view, undermining workers' creative connections with what they produce, stemming from the transformation of products created by workers' labor into commodities alien to them, causes alienation.

The manifestations of alienation are ubiquitous in health care today. It is impossible to open a newspaper or medical journal without reading a story about staff burnout, with rates as high as 60 percent and more than 20 percent reporting extreme or severe burnout.[6] Professionals are quitting due to frustration caused by the lack of joy and meaning in their work, computer screens and box-checking that displace meaningful human interactions, turnover of colleagues with resulting disruptions in continuity, production pressures to see more patients faster, encounters too rushed to either listen or answer questions, discontinuities of care and turnovers of patients via required handoffs to other practitioners,[7] proliferation of and increased time spent on complying with meaningless regulatory rules and requirements, and dominance of hospitals and clinics by managers and consultants with only a vague idea about how medicine is practiced.[8]

Seeing these problems as separate, disconnected issues rather than manifestations of deeper alienation from work would be a mistake. The work of caring for patients has become alien not because we don't have caring people, insightful managers, smarter metrics, or even enough time (although all of these would certainly help). Rather, alienation in health work has expanded to affect most health workers because we have lost control of the purpose, content, design, and products that we generate in our work. Previously, when professionals held more control, professional dominance did cause problems in patient care. But the more recent alienation of health professionals has transformed medical work.[9]

Policy experts often speak about these problems as unintended side effects of well-intended efforts to improve "value" or quality, as well as attempts to balance inherent or inevitable tradeoffs, arguing that we simply need to strike a better balance. Thus we hear much talk about finding the "sweet spot" between, for example, standardized versus flexible work, rigid versus customized metrics, privatized versus publicly run services, more versus less delegation, and autonomy versus accountability. However, we see these problems as *effects* rather than side effects, consequences of upstream structural determinants of how health care is organized within the political-economic system of capitalism. Seen through this lens, the more fundamental problems concern ownership of the means of medical production, control over the conditions of work, a work process marked by a loss of creative accomplishment, and the alienation experienced by health workers as a result.

To explain why quality is failing and quality-improvement efforts are falling short, we now examine contradictions that characterize several trends and paradigms in quality improvement: lean production, quality metrics and measurement, and health IT.

LEANING INTO QUALITY

It is hard to be opposed to the quality-improvement goals that "lean production" claims to champion: continuously improving quality by minimizing waste, fine-tuning work processes, addressing problems as soon as they emerge (even if it means "stopping the line"), closely matching capacity with demand, assessing problems with facts rather than opinions, getting to the root causes of problems in systems rather than blaming individuals for errors, and empowering workers with tools to measure and improve quality.[10]

As clinicians and practitioners of quality improvement, we candidly admit both our awe and ambivalence related to lean and related continuous improvement approaches to quality.[11] We have seen significant benefits from application of these approaches to a host of problems that plague health care and have observed what a difference they sometimes make in addressing the prevalent and often serious quality problems listed at the opening of this chapter.

However, there are profound and insufficiently acknowledged problems and contradictions with these "lean" methods with which anyone who genuinely wants to address quality issues must grapple. Many of the critiques are well-known concerns about lean production but are often dismissed as failures of technique, deficiencies in understanding and implementation, or lack of information about the true tenets and application of lean methods.[12] Such dismissals fail to heed warning signs that all is not so keen with lean.

- *Superficial commitment to quality and to workers.* "Quality" often poses as a proxy for deeper commitment to cutting costs. When push comes to shove, as it often does, organizations' rhetorical commitment to quality takes a back seat to the bottom line. Manifestations of this contradiction of rhetoric versus reality can range from more subtle variants such as lapses or distractions from quality aims, to not sustaining quality initiatives beyond short-term bursts of interest and excitement, to more serious violations of promises made to workers about respecting their input, avoiding layoffs, or outsourcing jobs. How often are workers' voices heard, and their experiences and concerns taken seriously? Evidence suggests far less often than claimed.

• *Failures to differentiate "waste" from healthier work rhythms.* The latter include adequate time with patients, beneficial time for breaks or rest, and avoidance of stress. The complexities of health care (and many other forms of work) mandate a respect for workers and work rhythms. To say, as Frederick Winslow Taylor—leader of the Efficiency Movement and developer of "scientific management" during early twentieth century capitalism in the United States—did, that workers often are "soldiering" (more pejoratively termed "loafing" or "malingering") and therefore need the discipline of more structured and monitored work, demonstrates both a disrespect for staff and an uninformed understanding of work.[13] In health care an industrial approach imposes ever more external production pressures on clinicians' work processes. Having one "easy" ten-minute patient in a fifteen-minute slot might allow a busy primary care physician running behind from serial forty-five-minute encounters booked for these fifteen-minute slots to catch up and catch our breath. But to a manager concerned with optimizing productivity, an easy patient might represent "wasteful slack" that could be seen by a less highly trained person, or even an avoidable visit.

• *Incremental improvements in comparison to systemic transformations.* The best intentions to improve quality are hardly a match for the powerful forces shaping health care today.[14] Mergers, acquisitions, corporate restructuring, leveraged buyouts of office practices and hospitals, and waves of privatizing previously public services make a mockery of quality-guru W. E. Deming's first principle, in which he called for "constancy of purpose toward improvement of product and service, with the aim to stay in business, and to provide jobs over the longer haul."[15] Workers are rightly skeptical and at times cynical about waves of new managers and management styles dictating their work. And changes enacted often pale in comparison to larger changes needed to transform work in a positive way, as lean and continuous quality improvement (CQI) focuses on smaller, incremental changes.

• *Lack of sustained commitment and gains.* Although this problem overlaps with several of the above concerns, the frequent failure of organizations and projects to follow through and sustain their lean investments and activities warrants attention. Improvements, particularly in the ways people work, often are barely detectable when revisited just a few years later. We have no hard data about the percentages of lean health care initiatives that are sustained over time versus those that fall by the wayside, but our experience suggests that sustained commitments are the exception rather than the rule.[16]

• *Failing to link wasteful medical processes with broader environmental waste.* The current system for production of goods and services in our society faces multiple environmental crises (global warming, air and water pollution, waste disposal, natural resource depletion, and deforestation). Though it is obviously unfair to hold lean production methods responsible for all the planet's environmental problems, given lean's rhetoric about reducing waste and its touted role in streamlining current production and consumption activities, failure to challenge and impact the broader problem of "waste" represents a profound contradiction.[17]

• *Biases distorting a fair assessment of lean's successes and failures.* There is a proliferation of books, cases studies, web testimonials, and consultants' claims about the value and virtues of lean. Though some pronouncements embody the well-known phenomenon of publication bias (more interest in publishing a positive than a negative study), there seems to be a particular conflict of interest in this domain. Hospitals eager to brand their high quality of service, consultants trying to sell their services, and even enthusiastic members of projects and teams (the authors included) are often eager to tell the world about their dedicated efforts and various successes. All of this tends to create an unbalanced picture of lean's virtues.

• *One big team versus "every man for himself."* Despite infusing lean-type efforts with the symbolic language of team, teamwork, and collaboration, competition often trumps cooperation. Our society and the ideology of the market are suffused with the language and behaviors of competition. We see this in myriad ways: using report card scores of quality to select the best doctors or hospitals; focusing on and rewarding smaller work units whose attention is narrowly directed on their own performance, often at the expense of interactions with the larger and more complex whole (a reductionist process aptly termed "sub-optimization"); rewarding individual performance ratings, thereby distracting from if not undermining teamwork; nonsharable health procedures and especially proprietary IT software; and opposition to public standards and even regulation that could encourage sharing.

• *Advantaging the already advantaged; punishing the under-resourced poor.* Poorer hospitals and clinics serve disadvantaged patients whose neglected illnesses and social problems make them harder to care for. These institutions, especially, need to be redesigned for delivering the highest-quality care. However, the reality, at least in the United States, is that the rich get richer, and Tudor Hart's Inverse Care Law—"The availability of good medical care tends to vary inversely with the need for it in the population served"—ends up applying not just to patients but to health care organizations.[18] Since institutions serving the poor lack the resources to invest in consultants, dedicate staff time to work on improvement projects, or simply play the game of polishing up their care appearances, they often fall further behind.[19] Organizations that favor rewarding performance (so-called Pay for Performance, P4P) admit that serving the disadvantaged remains an Achilles' heel, despite their best efforts at "risk adjustment" and metric tweaking (as we discuss further below).

• *Unequal benefits in organizations.* Here we are talking not simply about bonuses and high executive salaries (often shockingly unfair compared to what their workers receive—a hospital CEO often earns more than a thousand times the janitor's salary) but also about how workers who do the hard work on the front lines of health care and are tasked to work on quality-improvement efforts are poorly recognized or rewarded. Both the joys and frustrations of such hard work often remain unrecognized as managers and leaders take credit for accomplishments. Despite occasional kudos, health workers often see through the insincerity and say they resent the quality-improvement efforts they are asked to make on behalf of the organization.

Hit by Hit (Health Information Technology)

Another key area in which the promises of quality improvement confront the contradictions of contemporary capitalism involves IT. Historically, the emphasis was on health care computerization for billing purposes. However, it became evident to decision makers that while that was important for revenue generation and the bottom line, the costs and complexities of care delivery represented an even more important target ripe for electronic automation.

From reporting and managing laboratory test results, ordering medications and tests, and doing electronic clinical documentation, computerized health systems have come to dominate health care work. Multiple other functions have been layered atop these basic functions, such as decision support (to assist medication and test ordering), communication/messaging functions, patient portals (to allow patients to access portions of their own records online), population management tools (to aggregate and analyze data across patients, and to track patients needing preventive health screens), and reporting functions (to capture and report various care metrics to third parties such as health insurers and regulators).

Much of the desire for and design of early IT systems aimed at making clinicians' work easier. Focusing on repetitive tasks or documentation that had to be manually performed, IT was an attempt to streamline work. Pioneers working with early systems, often clinicians trying to make their own work easier or smarter, developed homegrown solutions. Another goal of these innovating developers was to decrease errors by standardizing and automating error-prone repetitive processes. Many of the initial successful reports of improvements in quality, safety, and efficiency came from individuals and institutions who were building such homegrown solutions.[20]

HIT systems sold by large commercial vendors are, however, replacing virtually all homegrown systems. The paradigm shift is from HIT tools aimed at making work easier to systems designed to control and standardize work. In theory this shift might be beneficial on multiple levels to help ensure less unwarranted variation, fewer errors, and more accountability. As currently implemented, frustrations among users, inefficiencies, and safety issues plague the corporatized HIT systems. These shortcomings have emerged despite massive investment totaling tens of billions of public dollars or euros, particularly in the United States and the United Kingdom, with derailed promises of HIT's lowering health care costs and helping clinicians deliver higher quality care.

Users' complaints, supported by research data, include a) that their work, especially note writing, now takes much more time; b) that they are pulled away from talking or even looking at their patients; c) that notes follow templates without a coherent story about lived experience (in the words of one clinician, "lacking life"); d) that EMRs are filled with less relevant or even accurate information; e) that EMR systems don't "talk to each other," leading to unsafe or ineffective care for patients receiving services at multiple sites; f) that confusing and poorly designed interfaces make it difficult to order medications and tests efficiently, g) that a profusion of irrelevant, false positive, and unhelpful alerts may lead to overlooking important warnings; and h) that billing requirements have become more cumbersome and expensive.[21]

Metrics: Tape Measures, Rulers, and the Ruled

When patients and health care workers complain that "they are being reduced to a number," they are describing a real phenomenon, whose depth they may not appreciate. "Metrics" measuring clinical performance and outcomes have come to dominate health care and quality-improvement activities. While leaders in HIT may express discomfort or even criticism about misapplications of lean and health IT in ways that can prove detrimental to patients and workers, such quibbles do not detract from an unabashed romance with measurement as a vehicle to better quality. "You can't improve something you can't measure" is an accepted truth, and there can be no room for doubting the central importance of numbers, lest one be labeled as unscientific and downright ignorant of the need to measure quality and quantify the results of interventions to improve quality. But like lean and HIT, neutral-sounding constructs like metrics come loaded with ideological assumptions and frameworks that can distort, misrepresent, ignore, distract from, and even deter true quality.

Foucault theorized, and demonstrated across many arenas of social life, that analytics resonate powerfully with contemporary methods of disciplining, normalizing, and governing medical conduct.[22] By ranking health workers and quantifying their work on graphs, the work can be targeted for discipline. Foucault termed this process "normalization." The ability to monitor from a distance enables governing from a distance with resulting loss of local control, with frontline workers progressively losing control of the work process, including decisions about its content and direction.[23] Governance by metrics gives the appearance that the metrics are actually doing the governing, masking realities about true power relationships and choices made remotely.

Ironically, physicians have long tended to reduce patients to numbers; for instance, by paying more attention to a patient's "objective" lab test results than to patients' actual experience, that is, their "subjective" symptoms. Now this process has become inverted, as the bureaucratic gaze has been turned on medicine with physicians increasingly finding themselves on the receiving end of such objectification.

To unpack the baggage that accompanies the current obsession with and unbalanced application of narrow metrics, we need to examine measurement activities from several angles:

- *Value judgments.* Choice of what to measure represents a value judgment, often reflecting the needs of those who hold power in health care. This needn't imply any type of sinister plot. Decision-making tools seize particular metrics, based on how conveniently they can be quantified to measure and compare the performance of health practitioners. Hemoglobin A1C measurement in diabetes, which estimates blood sugar control during several preceding months, illustrates such a metric. Health insurers, managers, and quality improvers have seized upon this magic A1C number as the defining measure of physicians' quality, particularly primary care physicians who manage most diabetes patients. This administrative decision puts pressure on physicians who in turn put pressure on patients to lower their A1C number to pre-specified goals, although there is some disagreement about how low to set this goal and how or whether to make allowances for patients' age and other variables. Strict blood sugar control may be associated with fewer diabetes complications, although even this finding applies more to children and adolescents with insulin-dependent Type 1 diabetes than to adults with non-insulin-dependent Type 2 diabetes. We have also seen much harm, such as complications of low blood sugar, from aggressively pushing drugs (pills and insulin) to treat the A1C, without considering the whole patient and the broader social context of care. As one leading spokesperson for quality and safety aptly said, "We're hitting the targets, but missing the point."[24]

• *Narrow and distorted definitions.* In some management circles, quality has been defined as defect-free quantity produced at the lowest possible price. Though this definition might apply to manufacturing, health care involves multiple complex variables and social interactions that often create a fundamental tension between production and protection of the patient.[25] Definitions and metrics of quality usually fail to measure key interpersonal and qualitative aspects of what is good care, overlooking the care that health workers spend most of their time delivering, such as diagnosis quality, something critically important but absent from current metrics. While Antonio Gramsci's notion of quality as art or beauty also may be unattainable, ideas about excellence of care, autonomy in practice, and focus on the patient seem less valued in the production of a health care that stresses speed and efficiency.[26] Narrow views of quality often overlook the more complicated story beneath quality-improvement work and outcomes.

• *Who should judge quality?* Co-workers and patients are usually the best judges. They understand quality more accurately than a numeric rating or an artificial report card. Those seeking to "drive quality" by harnessing market forces have been repeatedly disappointed at the failure of such strategies. We instead need to understand health workers' intrinsic commitments to quality rather than hoping the market will somehow magically induce good quality.

• *Measurement burden.* Measurement now places a huge and unacceptable burden on those working in the system.[27] One recent study estimated that the average U.S. physician practice spends more than $40,000 per year on reporting quality measures, with each physician spending roughly 2.6 hours each week, the equivalent of about nine patient visits, on such activities.[28] In the words of Don Berwick, former head of the Centers for Medicare and Medicaid Services (CMS):

> Overall, the enterprise of performance measurement has become a relative free-for-all, with numerous agencies and stakeholders exercising their prerogatives to demand metrics in the form they want them, when they want them, and from whom they want them. Reconciliation, harmonization, parsimony, and utility are often discussed, but progress has been slow, and the resulting burden on those who give health care has become not just onerous but, frankly, silly. The costs of measurement have become huge.[29]

• *Gaming the system; mindlessly following rules.* Quality metrics lead to a focus on "scoring" points in quality games rather than serious efforts to uncover and learn from mistakes. Innovation, experimentation, and taking risks to connect with difficult patients are not the way the game is played or won. Players learn the rules of the game. In a study of how gaming works in contemporary medicine, Himmelstein and Woolhandler showed that improvement in Medicare patients' readmission rates are driven largely by ploys on the part of hospitals to stretch the definition of readmissions by classifying them as "observation stays" in the emergency department. They concluded, "Become good at cheating and you never need to become good at anything else."[30]

• *Part of the problem, not the solution.* Finally, we must ask whether such distracting, burdensome quality measurement not only is failing to lead us toward better quality practice, but also is actually getting in the way of better quality—by blocking moral connection, altruism, and relationships that drive actual quality. As the metric mentality becomes internalized and thus becomes the compass for moral and ethical behavior, caregivers become increasingly burned out and cynical. According to Robert Wachter, "These businesslike efforts to measure and improve quality are now blocking the altruism and love that motivates people to enter the helping professions."[31]

Conclusion: Quality and a National Health Program

Health workers and patients care deeply about quality. For quality to flourish, certain prerequisites are needed, and these are currently lacking in the U.S .health system. All persons need access to care, and services must be organized and provided in a fair and affordable way that is based on community, continuity relationships, and primary care, supported by specialty services where needed. These simple concepts require a universal and unified health insurance system to provide access and to pool the resources required for organizing and supporting needed services. As shown in later chapters of this book, such a universal and unified system can only be achieved by a public, single-payer national health program.[32]

Quality depends on achievement of such a basic framework to deliver quality care, as well as a recognition that liberating our collective desires for quality can help build, drive, and nurture such a shared universal system. Only in such a system can the values of public service rather than those of the market be unleashed to construct a system that values quality over profitability.[33]

4—The Political Economy of Health Reform

David Himmelstein and Steffie Woolhandler

NOTE FROM HOWARD WAITZKIN: This chapter takes the form of an interview, in which the authors respond to a series of questions I submitted to them about the political economy of health reform.

HW: *What is the commodification of health care?*
DH–SW: Health care was for millennia a deeply personal interaction between a patient and caregiver, a relationship between people. Of course, reality often fell short of this idealized version of the past. Doctors sometimes acted in venal, self-interested ways, and the ruling class often decreed that care for working people should encompass only the things needed to maintain their productivity. (Of course, many working people—for example, serfs and slaves—received little or no medical care.) But care was provided mostly by individual doctors and nurses who formed personal relationships with patients.

Over the past fifty years in the United States, health care has been transformed into an impersonal economic relationship between a patient, who is viewed as a buyer of care, and a large-scale corporate seller. Health care is a thing, or commodity, that is bought and sold. This transformation required a redefinition of care. Instead of a doctor who offers to "take care of you when you are sick or need help," corporate care providers offer a defined set of services for sale. Instead of turning to a particular human being for care, patients are supposed to relate to a corporate institution, where doctors and nurses are interchangeable parts.

HW: *How have health services been transformed in the current stage of capitalism? How has the social-class position of physicians and other health professionals changed?*

DH–SW: Until recently, the vast majority of doctors were self-employed, worked in solo practices or small groups, and were paid either directly by their patients or (starting mostly after the Second World War) by the patients' insurers. In these arrangements doctors had a great deal of control over their work and work environment. They also had great influence over how hospitals were run, and hospitals exercised little control of doctors.

Over the past decade it has become virtually impossible for small-scale, independent practices to survive economically. Insurers either refuse to contract with such practices or demand impossibly low fees—demands that huge corporate providers can resist because they control vital services such as hospitals providing specialized care, which insurers have to include in their networks. Moreover, many insurers now insist on paying a single annual fee, called "capitation," to cover all of a patient's care including hospitalizations, medications, and specialized services. The care of one severely ill patient can cost a million dollars, which would bankrupt a small practice but can be easily absorbed by a huge organization that receives capitation fees for hundreds of thousands of patients, most of whom are healthy and require little care.

As most doctors have been driven out of small-scale practices, they have become employees of large corporate health care organizations, such as hospitals, managed care organizations, or group practices with thousands of doctors. In those organizations, corporate executives and managers largely dictate where and when doctors work, how many patients they see, how much patients are charged for care, and, increasingly, the details of the care doctors are allowed to give.

Doctors who are unprofitable or uncooperative with management risk being fired and face a rapidly shrinking number of other options for practice. Hence, doctors are becoming proletarianized in terms of their relationship to management, although they remain a very highly paid group and are likely to remain so for the foreseeable future.

HW: *Has Obamacare contributed to corporate control of health care?*

DH–SW: Obamacare strengthened health care firms in several ways. First, it mandated that most people in the United States purchase private insurance, guaranteeing insurers' market. In addition, the new subsidies for private coverage provided a huge infusion of public money to the private insurance industry, nearly a trillion dollars over ten years. Obamacare also incorporated a deal with drug firms that omitted any restraint on drug prices. As a result, drug costs and drug company profits have soared since the passage of the Affordable Care Act (ACA) in early 2010. Finally, the law required Medicare to move to capitated payments for care. As we've described above, this is making small-scale practices non-viable and has greatly accelerated the shift to large-scale, corporate-owned practices.

HW: *How have electronic medical records affected this process?*

DH–SW: As long as doctor-patient interactions remained private (and hence largely opaque to management) it was difficult to implement corporate control of medical practice and to fully integrate doctors' work into corporate structures. Computerized medical records have been the key to "managing" doctors, allowing surveillance of how long they spend with each patient, their adherence to rigid care and billing protocols, and monitoring whether they are profitable for the corporation that employs them.

This focus on using computerization to manage doctors and to make health care a business has deformed electronic medical records (EMRs). Instead of realizing the great promise of computerization, the systems that have been widely adopted are essentially billing and management tools, with some patient care elements tacked on. In the past, doctors often wrote brief, informative, but sometimes illegible notes. Today, many electronic notes are little more than legible gibberish. Medical records are larded with pages of previously collected information of dubious quality that's auto-populated (or cut and pasted); documentation of extensive physical examinations and history-taking that justify billing for a lengthy visit and can be entered with a few keystrokes (whether or not the exams were actually done or the history taken); and myriad boxes checked to comply with orders from headquarters.

HW: *As co-founders of Physicians for a National Health Program (PNHP), please describe how PNHP was founded.*

DH–SW: Starting in 1982, we had worked with activists in Massachusetts advocating a single-payer reform. In 1986, those activists, led by the Massachusetts Gray Panthers, placed a resolution on the statewide ballot that would instruct the state's congresspersons to support such reform. We feared that the Massachusetts Medical Society would be a potent opponent of the referendum (although ultimately that group opted not to take a position on it), and thought that a pro-single-payer doctors' group could serve as a useful counterweight.

That summer, at a retreat in New Hampshire of physicians and other clinicians who cared for the poor, we proposed the formation of such a group. After considerable discussion the attendees decided to go forward with the project. That decision grew from the need to support the Massachusetts initiative and from frustration with previous efforts to defend the care of the poor, which mostly meant defending the Medicaid program—a poor program for poor people. Moreover, the health care system also poorly served many middle-class patients, and we were convinced that a movement that would upgrade coverage and care for both the poor and middle class had much more potential. A national health program could do just that, saving billions on health care bureaucracy that could be redirected to making universal, comprehensive coverage affordable.

HW: *How and why was the decision made to advocate a "Canadian-style" single-payer insurance program, rather than a national health service as Representative Ron Dellums and others had proposed?*

DH–SW: During the 1970s there had been a sharp division among progressive health care activists. Some, particularly in the labor movement, advocated for National Health Insurance (NHI) like Canada's that would pay for all care but not directly employ doctors and other health workers, nor nationalize hospitals and other health facilities. Others, often associated with the New Left and younger generation, pushed for a National Health Service (NHS) like England's, which had a publicly owned and operated system.

We decided to use the term "National Health Program" (NHP) to avoid sectarian fights between those two camps, and to express our support for a range of single-payer options, including both NHI and NHS models. Moreover, we thought that restricting the emergence of a parallel, private system—that is, mandating that everyone was in the same health care boat—was as important as the differences between NHS and NHI. In England, despite having an NHS, most wealthy people also have private insurance and can jump the queue for care. In contrast, Canada's NHI bans private insurance that duplicates the public coverage, so by and large the wealthy can't opt out or buy their way to better or quicker care.

When it came time to formulate a proposal for PNHP (which was published in the *New England Journal of Medicine* in 1989) we opted for the Canadian route, both because it was far easier to imagine a transition to that system and because we thought banning a parallel private sector for the wealthy was a priority. Recently, the emergence of huge integrated health systems incorporating multiple hospitals and thousands of physicians (so-called Accountable Care Organizations or ACOs), which dominate the care of entire regions, is causing us again to talk about NHS models. In the latest PNHP proposals we advocate that such dominant systems should be brought under direct public ownership.

HW: *Why did PNHP focus mainly on doctors as a target for organizing? In your answer, please feel free to address the social-class position of doctors and comment on their role in social change. Also feel free to comment on relationships with the labor movement and other organizations fighting for social change.*

DH–SW: The need for a physician group that could counter organized medicine's opposition to the 1986 single-payer ballot question in Massachusetts was a trigger for the formation of PNHP. It also seemed to us that in the longer term a group identified as presenting doctors' views could play an important role in reassuring the public that physicians were not uniformly opposed to an NHP, and that medical care would not be disrupted by such reform.

We also had in mind the practical question of what would be the best strategy to organize a large number of doctors to publicly support an NHP. We were convinced, based on surveys of doctors' opinions on NHI and our interactions with colleagues, that a substantial fraction of doctors favored such reform. In part, this reflected the threat that the incipient corporate takeover of medicine posed to doctors' privileged position. But while we thought we could gain substantial support, we also thought that relatively few colleagues would feel comfortable working closely in a political organization with non-physicians, especially working-class activists. As your question suggests, for many physicians, their social-class position and the cultural norms that arise from it present a barrier to their integration into a broader progressive movement.

Moreover, the social and professional structures of the medical community also favored organizing a specifically physicians' group. Medical journals offered a means to reach out to doctors that circumvented the virtual blackout on discussion of an NHP in the mainstream media. But while leading journals were open to progressive articles from a doctors' group, the bar was much higher for articles that came from outside the profession. In addition, doctors frequently gather for hospital grand rounds, department conferences, and meetings of regional and national specialty groups, which offer potential forums for discussion of health care reform and, again, are far more open to presentations on behalf of a physicians' group than from broader-based advocacy groups.

Finally, doctors have specific concerns and ideas about health care reform that need to be addressed if we are to gain their support. For instance, they're concerned about medical student debt, pay disparities among specialties, and medical malpractice laws. An organization of doctors facilitates engaging these issues, some of which carry little interest for non-doctors.

For all of these reasons, we thought it best to move ahead with a doctors' group, which we hoped would ally with nurses' groups, organized labor, and other elements of a progressive coalition. In fact, National Nurses United (a powerful union group) has been a key ally, and that organization's Executive Director serves as a Board Advisor for PNHP.

That said, PNHP welcomes non-physician members. Although only health professionals can vote in the organization, we virtually never actually vote on anything. We work on consensus, and several non-physicians have played important roles in the group.

HW: *How has PNHP addressed the contradictions of the capitalist state? Where would the single-payer system fit into the structure and political-economic processes of the capitalist state?*

DH–SW: PNHP has pushed for making health care a non-market good, one distributed based on medical need, not ability to pay. That's essentially an embodiment of the traditional slogan, "From each according to his [*sic*] ability, to each according to his need."

It's clear from the examples of several other capitalist countries that progress in this direction is possible, even without fundamentally restructuring the rest of the economy. But we also recognize the difficulties imposed by the context of a capitalist state. Though in our view government management of health care financing is preferable to management by private insurers, government largely reflects the interests of the corporate class. So, as in education, government is imposing damaging "pay-for-performance" incentives and computerization strategies that are part and parcel of making health care a commodity; is constantly seeking to channel public dollars to private health care investors; skews investments in new health care facilities toward the wealthy; and does little or nothing to address the most important determinants of health, namely, economic and racial inequality, global warming, toxic food environments, and public health issues like occupational hazards.

HW: *How has PNHP addressed the entrenched positions of for-profit insurance, pharmaceutical, and other corporations in the so-called medical-industrial complex? How would the single-payer proposal envision changes in these corporations' roles if the proposal passed at the state or federal level?*

DH–SW: We've been clear from the outset that private insurers should have no role in health care. There's no way to make a health care system that's reasonably fair and efficient if you allow them to persist. Of course, this means that insurers will wield their substantial financial and political power to oppose single-payer reform. Hillary Clinton once asked us how reformers could overcome this opposition. We suggested that the president should help lead a mass movement for change, a suggestion she dismissed out of hand. But it's clear that most Americans disdain insurance firms and favor single payer. Our challenge is to mobilize that sentiment. Some potential divisions with the corporate class also offer opportunities. For much of corporate America, health care represents a cost of production, one that shifts part of their profits to insurance firms. An NHP would lessen this drain.

We've also been clear that for-profit health care institutions like hospitals and nursing homes must be converted to nonprofit status. That's based on convincing evidence that for-profits provide inferior care at inflated prices and skew investments to gaining profit rather than meeting medical needs. Like insurers, such firms are powerful but not insurmountable foes. Some capitalist nations (for example, the Netherlands) ban them.

However, PNHP has not pushed to have pharmaceutical firms, which are much larger and more powerful than private insurance corporations, taken over by government or converted to nonprofits. The question for us is where to draw the line on our demands. Banning for-profits in every industry that supplies health care is tantamount to a demand for socialism. Though some members would favor that, there's not a consensus for it in PNHP. Hence, like the national health programs in other countries, PNHP would use the monopsony (one buyer) purchasing power of an NHP, along with much stricter regulation on drug pricing, to rein in profiteering by pharmaceutical corporations. Since the NHP would pay for virtually all prescription medications, it could use its market clout to force drug companies to accept lower prices.

HW: *What have been PNHP's strengths and weaknesses?*
DH–SW: PNHP has provided an important rallying point for progressives in medicine and has helped provide a focus for opposition to the corporate takeover of health care, as well as support for improving care of the oppressed.

We've been most successful in appealing to the generation of physicians who came of age during the 1960s and '70s. In recent years

PNHP has also done very useful organizing among medical students; we now have active chapters in nearly half of the schools in the country. But we've been less effective at involving the middle group, doctors who are now between thirty and forty-five. We've also not had sufficient outreach to African-American and Hispanic colleagues.

We think it's important that PNHP has remained an activist-led, rather than paid staff–led, organization for three decades. In many cases, progressive doctors' groups have become essentially a fundraising base that supports paid staff who do most of the organization's work. Though in the short term that sometimes facilitates getting the work done, since most doctors are busy with their day jobs, in the longer term it demobilizes and alienates the membership base. Moreover, the staff may be tempted to compromise a group's politics in order to raise the funds needed to keep getting paid. In PNHP's case, on several occasions we've been offered grants contingent on "softening" our "hard line" stance on reform, but we have been able to resist those temptations.

Of course, relying on busy members to do most of the group's work and serve as its public spokespeople also sometimes causes problems. Some things can't get done.

HW: *What have been the strengths and weaknesses of the single-payer movement in general?*
DH–SW: The narrow focus on reform of the health care system has been both a strength and a weakness. PNHP is a single-issue organization, as are many of the other groups working on health care reform. That's allowed the movement to reach out to many who are concerned about health care and prepared to support quite radical reforms, but not yet ready to engage a broader radical agenda. Yet realizing reform of the health care system will require a broad and powerful progressive movement that is able to challenge corporate power on many fronts. We think organizing for health care reform can be an important component of building such a broad movement, both because it builds in-depth understanding of an important sector of the economy and because it offers a concrete and obvious example of how the drive for profit interferes with rational solutions to major social problems.

Yet it remains unclear how single-payer efforts can be integrated effectively into the mass movement needed to address a multifaceted transformation of society. In other nations, national health insurance has almost always been implemented by a party with a clear socialist platform, or one that at least has close ties to a powerful labor movement. So a key question for our movement is how we can participate most effectively in building a broad and powerful progressive force.

HW: *If you could replay history, what would you have done differently?*
DH–SW: Too many things to enumerate. One that seems obvious is that we'd have learned more about how to use social media and other modern organizing techniques.

HW: *At this current critical moment of history, what strategies do you favor in moving forward? For instance, should doctors continue as a focus for political organizing as opposed to other groups?*
DH–SW: We don't view this as an either-or proposition. In the push for health care reform doctors have an important role to play, and substantial and vocal advocacy by physicians is important for mobilizing and supporting others. On the other hand, it's silly to think that doctors will be the main force for transforming health care, or society more generally.

We need activists from many walks of life, including doctors. Some of us can be most effective in rallying colleagues. A few might play leading roles in organizing the broader community, although we doubt that many physicians can or should assume such broad leadership.

HW: *Given the corporate transformation of medicine, the dominant role of finance capital, and the changing social-class position of physicians, is a single-payer strategy still what you favor? If not, what would you support?*
DH–SW: We continue to believe that a nonprofit, single-payer reform is both needed and possible, and remains an effective rallying point for organizing. For many years, we and others in PNHP have included an anti-corporate focus as a central aspect of our work. That's more important than ever. But ultimately, health care reform is about the

lives of our patients and the needless suffering they endure. And keeping that in the forefront is absolutely essential.

HW: *Please comment on examples and collaborations with activists in other countries.*
DH–SW: The corporate takeover of care in the United States is a model that the ruling class in many other nations aspires to achieve. Moreover, U.S. academics have served as the main purveyors of pro-market health policies that lead to privatization and exacerbate inequality. Hence, we have a special responsibility to help contain this spreading plague. For us personally that's mostly meant sounding the warning to colleagues in other countries by telling the truth about ours in international journals, meetings, and, occasionally, in speaking tours and media appearances. PNHP has collaborated with sister organizations in Canada and a few other nations, but such work has been logistically difficult and has not become a major focus.

HW: *Would you add anything else that you see as important to emphasize as the struggle continues?*
DH–SW: We've been heartened by the striking response to Bernie Sanders's candidacy, including the strong positive reaction to his proposal for single-payer reform. A recent Gallup poll found that 58 percent of Americans favor (and only 38 percent oppose) single payer, including 41 percent of Republicans. Although most politicians and much of the media have continued to insist that such reform, and the other measures that Sanders has championed, is impossible, his campaign has exposed the potential for mobilizing widespread support for radical change. It's demonstrated that there's fertile ground for organizing.

HW: *What if anything has changed in the era of Trump?*
DH–SW: The Trump regime is, of course, a major setback in the short term. But the mobilization of opposition to his policies promises better things ahead.

The Democrats created the opening for Trump by offering little for working families, and much for the wealthy, in health care as in other domains. Even though the ACA expanded coverage to about 20 million, it offered little or nothing to the other 300 million Americans, and in many respects it reinforced the corporate dominance of health care.

But when the Republicans tried to move back from the ACA, they generated a wave of opposition, and a surge of support for the single-payer reforms that would fix the ACA's defects. Tens of thousands have turned out for single-payer rallies. Dozens of congressional members have newly signed on to the single-payer bills. State-based efforts are burgeoning. And polls show strong and rising popular support for such reform—even among voters who label themselves "conservative."

So the period ahead holds undoubted dangers, but also real opportunity.

PART TWO

The Medical-Industrial Complex in the Age of Financialization

5—The Transformation of
the Medical-Industrial Complex:
Financialization, the Corporate Sector, and
Monopoly Capital

Robb Burlage and Matthew Anderson

The concept of U.S. health care as a medical-industrial complex was the product of Health/PAC (the Health Policy Advisory Center), an activist community that emerged in New York City in the late 1960s. The spark to form Health/PAC was an "exposé-analysis" written by Robb Burlage 1967.[1] Titled *New York City's Municipal Hospitals: A Policy Review,* this report documented how, beginning in the early 1960s, powerful New York City teaching hospitals had been granted lucrative affiliation contracts by the municipal government to provide teaching and funding for the city's beleaguered public hospitals. It offered a detailed critique about how academic centers were being lavishly subsidized by the municipal government to affiliate/manage the then twenty-one New York City public hospitals. Despite receiving this public largesse and regional institutional control, these centers were ignoring the public health of surrounding communities, particularly working-class communities and communities of color. Instead, the centers viewed these "populations" as research and teaching guinea pigs. Most institutions were also resisting staff unionization.

This was a period of intense community activism in New York City, much of it centered on health care institutions such as Lincoln

Hospital (built after the Civil War and known locally in the Bronx as "the butcher shop") and Harlem Hospital (then under the tutelage of Columbia University). In 1971 the Black Panthers and Young Lords staged a brief takeover of Lincoln Hospital, an event that led to immediate action to remedy some of the more pressing issues at Lincoln.

In order to document and understand these struggles, Robb Burlage and Maxine Kenny began publishing a monthly newsletter known as the *Health/PAC Bulletin*.[2] Within a year the *Bulletin* had ten full-time staff and "served as the strategic hub of a vibrant radical social movement around health care equality, one that paralleled (and sometimes conflicted with) more widely known liberal counterparts of the time."[3] By the end of 1970, Health/PAC would publish a popular book, titled *The American Health Empire*.[4]

Origins of the Term "Medical-Industrial Complex"

In the November 1969 issue, Health/PAC first described the U.S. health care system as a medical-industrial complex (MIC).[5] This term was adapted from President Eisenhower's farewell address in 1961, during which he warned the country of the dangers posed by the military-industrial complex: "In the councils of government, we must guard against the acquisition of unwarranted influence, whether sought or unsought, by the military-industrial complex. The potential for the disastrous rise of misplaced power exists and will persist."[6]

The MIC conceptualized the relationship between academic medical centers and local (usually poor) communities as a colonial one, in which the medical empires used poor communities for "teaching material" (patients on whom doctors-in-training could practice) and research subjects. The MIC reference was soon adopted by others and is now commonly used in mainstream discussions about health care. In contemporary mainstream discussions, however, the colonial implications of the term have been expunged.

This approach highlighted the complexity of U.S. health care, its connections with and support by the state, and its industrial, for-profit character. The analysis broke with traditional thinking about U.S. health care. Previous analyses explained the health care sector's recurrent crises by its being either a "non-system" or an overregulated industry not subject to market discipline. Health/PAC disagreed with both these mainstream views. The inefficiencies of the system, indeed its very evident disorganizations, were by-products of a system designed primarily to produce profits and only secondarily to improve health. Drawing again on the activist environment, Ehrenreich and Ehrenreich stated on behalf of Health/PAC: "Health is no more a priority of the American health system than safe, cheap, efficient, pollution-free transportation is a priority of the American automobile industry."[7]

Health/PAC began from the assumption that the top priority of the health care system was to produce profit. Additional functions of the MIC included research, training, and social control. An industrial and institutional system had come to dominate a system previously run by physicians and not-for-profit insurance companies (Blue Cross and Blue Shield). Health/PAC observed that "when it comes to making money, the health industry is an extraordinarily well-organized and efficient machine."[8]

ACADEMIC MEDICAL CENTERS, MEDICAL EMPIRES, AND THE MIC

In the 1960s Health/PAC saw the MIC primarily within a local context where academic medical centers used government funds to create local and regional systems. It identified and labeled these networks as medical empires. Most hospitals benefited from the federal government's creation of Medicare and Medicaid in 1965. Despite fierce opposition from the American Medical Association, Medicare proved very profitable for the medical community. As the number of seniors with health care insurance rose from about half in 1965 to nearly all by 1967, doctors' incomes began to soar. Between 1967 and 1993, Medicare payments to doctors rose at an annual rate of nearly 17 percent.[9] Hospitals benefited not only from the income generated taking care of the newly insured elderly, but also from the direct subsidization provided by Medicare for medical education. Essentially, Medicare assumed the cost of training specialist physicians, thus opening up yet another revenue stream for the academic centers.

Columbia University's College of Physicians and Surgeons exemplified what these arrangements looked like on the ground. The core of its operations involved three voluntary (that is, private) hospitals—Columbia-Presbyterian Medical Center, St. Luke's, and Roosevelt Hospital—and two affiliated public hospitals—Francis Delafeld and Harlem Hospital Center. Together these institutions contained over 4,500 hospital beds.

One might not begrudge Columbia such wealth and power if it were used for the betterment of community health. But members of the low-income community within which Columbia operated—the flash point of which was Harlem Hospital—felt that they were used by Columbia for research and teaching that did not help the residents of Harlem.[10] The *Health/PAC Bulletin* chronicled the efforts by community members and activists to oppose the medical empires. There were temporary victories, such as the construction of a new Lincoln Hospital after the takeover in 1971, but ultimately these efforts were not successful in giving the community a seat at the table when the key decisions were being made.

Sadly, we continue to fight these battles today. For instance, in October 2015, the chief executive officer (CEO) of New York–Presbyterian Hospital and the Dean of Columbia University College of Physicians and Surgeons decided to shut down the Columbia Family Medicine training program, which served a predominantly poor population from Washington Heights, the Bronx, Inwood, and Harlem.[11] This closing would have made it more difficult for these communities to access prenatal care. This occurred at a time when the hospital was expanding obstetric services in affluent Westchester County to the north of Manhattan. A group of well-organized students and residents came together to protest, and the school reversed this decision.[12]

AN ESTABLISHMENT CRITIQUE OF THE MIC

In 1980, Dr. Arnold Relman, editor of the *New England Journal of Medicine,* criticized the MIC in an article, "The New Medical-Industrial Complex."[13] Relman's concern was somewhat different from that of Health/PAC. Rather than focusing on the lack of attention to poor communities, Relman emphasized the "large and growing network of private corporations engaged in the business of supplying health services to patients for a profit—services heretofore provided by nonprofit institutions or individual practitioners." Relman analyzed several sectors within this new medical-industrial empire: for-profit hospitals (including multi-hospital networks run by large corporations often with overseas operations), for-profit nursing homes (whose growth was spurred by insurance policies covering long-term care), the home care industry, and corporations serving a variety of new "markets," including laboratory tests, hospital emergency rooms, and long-term hemodialysis. Relman noted that a growing, and profitable, medical sector fueled by private monies justified itself through the idea that free enterprise would control costs and improve quality through a competitive market.

Relman documented the ways in which health care did not fit the usual conditions of a marketplace. First, many consider health care a human right and a public good that should not be bought and sold like other goods and services. Second, patients don't directly pay the costs of health care; most of the money comes either from public sources (Medicaid and Medicare) or from private insurance. In practice, "the classic laws of supply and demand do not operate because health care consumers do not have the usual incentives to be prudent, discriminating purchasers." Finally, Relman referred to "derived demand," by which doctors influenced most decisions in health care through their recommendations to patients.

Relman's critique was that of a reformer. Unlike Health/PAC, he did not see the existing structure as essentially flawed. Rather, he advocated regulating what he considered "gross commercial exploitation." He also expressed concern over conflicts of interest when physicians invested in health care corporations. After his first article in 1980, Relman continued to trace the deepening challenges to clinical medicine raised by the growth of the MIC over time.[14]

MAKING CONFLICTS OF INTEREST ROUTINE

Relman's concerns about for-profit health care, and the erosive impact it would have on physicians' ethics and practice, became even more important since many physicians did not limit their involvement in profit-making activities and became collaborators with the MIC.[15] As a result a deeper alliance has developed between the medical community, particularly the medical elite, and for-profit corporations. This problem is typically conceptualized in terms of "conflicts of interest" that need to be disclosed and regulated. But industry has become so interpenetrated with academia that their relationship is best described as symbiotic. Two recent high-profile examples show the dimensions of conflicting interests among elites who bridge academia and the MIC.

Dr. Victor Dzau has served as president of the U.S. National Academy of Medicine (NAM). His academic career includes work as chairman of internal medicine at both Stanford University and Harvard Medical School's Brigham and Women's Hospital. Before joining NAM, he was president and CEO of Duke University Medical Center. During the process of his selection for the NAM presidency, students at Duke raised concerns about excessive compensation given to Dzau by the university. He had received over $2.2 million in 2009 at a time when the university was facing financial problems due to the international financial crisis.

Information later emerged that Dzau had served on the boards of directors of Medtronics, Alnylam Pharmaceutical, Genzyme—all health-related companies—as well as Pepsico's board. For his services in 2009, Dzau received an additional $1 million in compensation. These corporate ties, particularly his relationship with Pepsico, presented troubling conflicts of interest because as a board member he held a responsibility to protect the interest of Pepsico stockholders, presumably by not criticizing the detrimental public health effects of Pepsi products.[16] Dzau ultimately resigned from these corporate boards before working for NAM, but this action did not really resolve the question of his tangled loyalties. Was he an advocate for his patients? For Duke? For the health care corporations? Or for Pepsi? Can such relationships with industry be "managed"?

In 2011, Dr. Laurie H. Glimcher, a Harvard University immunologist, became dean of the Weill Cornell Medical School (WCMS). During the hiring process she revealed ties to two of the world's largest pharmaceutical companies: Merck and Bristol-Myers. She sat on the Bristol-Myers board, a position that paid her $244,500 in 2010 with an additional $1.4 million in deferred stock options. Officials of Cornell University resolved this problem by construing it as a good thing: "These outside jobs are crucial to advancing one of [the] long-term goals for WCMS: dramatically expanding its partnerships with industry."[17] This argument conveys an ideal MIC that seamlessly unites academia and corporations. Glimcher later returned to Harvard as President and CEO of the Dana Farber Cancer Institute, where she received criticism for declining to change a decision to hold a major fund-raising event during 2017 at Donald Trump's Mar-a-Lago Club in Palm Beach, Florida.[18]

These cases are high-profile but not unique. A study published in the *British Medical Journal* in 2015 examined 446 U.S. health care corporations that were traded on NASDAQ during 2013. Of these, 41 percent reported at least one director affiliated with academic medical and research institutions. These "dual" directors received a median compensation of $193,000 annually and owned a median of 50,699 shares of corporate stocks.[19]

THE GROWING SYMBIOSIS BETWEEN FOR-PROFIT, NOT-FOR-PROFIT, AND THE STATE

John Ehrenreich has described the modern-day MIC as an industry paradigmatic of "Third Wave Capitalism," characterized by interlocking relationships between business and government, blurring of the line between for-profit and not-for-profit status, and international financial operations.[20] Within this conceptualization, "not-for-profit" is just an alternative business model characterized by growth, creation of profits (understood as an excess of income over expenses), ownership or investment in for-profit subsidiaries (particularly in real estate), monetization of research through licensing and fraud, excessive pay for management, and purchasing goods and services from for-profit corporations. The conversion of not-for-profit health entities into profit-making enterprises has been going on since at least the early 1990s in health care.[21]

In most states charitable institutions that disband are required to turn their assets over to another, similar institution. None of the original value of the not-for-profit institution, which was supported by tax breaks and public funds, is supposed to remain with the original directors or executives. This principle reflects the idea that a not-for-profit institution serves the community rather than individuals.

But clever health care executives figured out ways to game this system. In late 1992, the California managed care organization (MCO) HealthNet won approval to convert to for-profit status. The new MCO was required to donate over $500 million to the California Wellness Foundation in compensation for the conversion.[22] As part of the deal, the company's executives were allowed to buy 20 percent of the new for-profit company's stocks for $1.5 million. Three years later those stocks were valued at $150 million. The CEO, Roger Greaves, turned his initial 2 percent investment in the company (some $300,000) into $24 million. Greaves remarked, "That the people who built this multimillion-dollar institution are compensated—that's America."[23] But this is a difficult argument to accept. The not-for-profit organization was subsidized with tax breaks and public funds to improve community health, not executive compensation.

THE FINANCIALIZATION OF THE BLUES

The history of Blue Cross and Blue Shield goes back to 1929 when they emerged as voluntary, not-for-profit, prepaid health plans. Though initially very successful, the Blues had difficulties over time competing with the growing for-profit insurance market. The Blues, unlike for-profit firms, would insure anyone who lived in their community, whereas the for-profit chains that so concerned Relman were able to select which patients they would cover. In essence they could "cherry-pick" the healthiest (and thus least expensive) people to insure.

By 1994 the Blue Cross and Blue Shield Association voted to allow its organizational members to become for-profit corporations with the hope that they could raise more capital on the stock market. As a result, many Blue plans converted to for-profit corporations. Despite some variability, large and aggressive for-profit insurance corporations replaced a voluntary, not-for-profit system dedicated to community health.[24] The conversions often resulted in fabulous economic benefits to the new for-profit corporations' executives.

THE VALUE OF BEING A MONOPOLY

The years since the 1980s have been a period of consolidation and mega-mergers within the health care industry. Hospitals, MCOs, and insurance companies merged in order to gain better bargaining power and become "too big to fail." In the ultimate move, some hospitals have started to become insurance companies.[25]

A prime example of this trend involved the 1994 merger between Massachusetts General Hospital and Brigham and Women's Hospital, two of Harvard's major teaching hospitals; their merger created a new entity called Partners HealthCare.[26] The hospitals merged in part to create a structure that would not allow the insurance companies to play one hospital off against the other. That is, they merged for anti-competitive reasons.

By 2008, Partners, still a not-for-profit organization, had become a powerhouse within the Massachusetts health care system. It was both the largest private employer and the largest health care provider in the state.[27] This meant it was able to demand higher prices from insurance companies and then use that extra money to expand and build a "war chest." Why on earth would a hospital build a war chest? To finance further acquisitions in the Boston suburbs. This was empire building on a grand scale.

A "private deal," unwritten and based on a handshake, between Massachusetts Blue Cross and Partners in 2000 accelerated the process. Blue Cross agreed to give large increases in payments to Partners' doctors as long as Partners got other insurance companies to pay similarly inflated prices. Indeed, Partners was able to get similar large increases in payments from the Tufts Health Plan and Harvard Pilgrim Health Care. The end result was that insurance premiums in Massachusetts increased by 78 percent between 2001 and 2009.[28]

Partners attributed these increases to general inflation in health care, but an extensive investigation by the Massachusetts Attorney

General's office reached different conclusions. It found variations in the prices that insurance companies paid to hospitals that could not be explained by quality, complexity of illness, status as an academic center, or the proportion of Medicare and Medicaid patients served. Price variations were, however, related to "market leverage as measured by the relative market position of the hospital or provider group." In addition, the Attorney General's investigation found that cost increases were a function of increasing prices, not increased utilization of health care services.[29]

In 2013 Partners asked for permission to acquire two additional hospitals. Even though a state commission estimated that this merger would increase medical spending by $15.5 million to $23 million per year, the Massachusetts Attorney General approved the acquisition.[30] In return, Partners agreed to restrict its growth and promised not to raise charges beyond the cost of general inflation for a period of ten years; after that there were to be no restrictions. The regulators felt this was the best possible deal short of breaking up Partners, which was considered impossible after two decades of expansion.

HEALTH CARE, FINANCE CAPITAL, INSURANCE, AND REAL ESTATE

To clarify the complex interactions among industry, academia, and health care, we now revisit Columbia University, the prototype medical empire in the 1960s. At the time of writing this chapter, twenty-four trustees, including the president of the university, Lee Bollinger, oversee Columbia. Who are the other twenty-three trustees? According to the Columbia University website we learn that sixteen (70 percent) are men. The largest group of trustees (thirteen, or 57 percent) comes from the finance and financial services sector; two work at Goldman Sachs. If we count all trustees associated with investing, 65 percent of the trustees are involved in finance. This total indicates the role that finance capital plays in one of our leading educational and scientific institutions. In addition to the financiers, two trustees are appellate judges, two are journalists, and the chair is a lawyer. There are three health-related trustees: a retired surgeon, a biotech entrepreneur, and the head of strategic partnerships at Memorial Sloan Kettering Hospital in New York.

The final trustee is Columbia's CEO, Marc Holliday. He is of particular interest since he is also the CEO of SL Green Realty Corporation, which the Columbia website describes as "New York City's largest owner of commercial office properties" and "a major investor in Manhattan retail properties [which] has also established itself as a market-leading investor in debt and preferred equity financing."[31]

The trustees illustrate the ongoing importance of both real estate and finance capital to the institution. Columbia has continued to expand into its surrounding area and is currently building a seventeen-acre Manhattanville Campus despite fierce community opposition; a 2010 New York State decision evoked "eminent domain" to negate local property owners' rights and turn the area over to Columbia. Columbia, in turn, negotiated a benefits agreement with the west Harlem community. Whether any amount of money can ever compensate for the destruction of a community is questionable.[32]

FINANCIALIZATION OF DRUG PRODUCTION

In the past few years we have seen dramatic increases in drug prices, based simply on the monopoly power given to drug companies by the patent system.[33] Valeant Pharmaceuticals International, Inc. (hereafter Valeant), exemplifies this trend.[34] Once the darling of Wall Street and later in financial trouble, Valeant originated in 1960 as ICN Pharmaceuticals. In 1994 it merged with two other drug companies, ultimately emerging as Valeant in 2003. The company did not do particularly well until February 2008, when Michael Pearson became CEO.

Pearson advocated a radical business strategy for the firm. He argued that money spent on research and development (R&D) would be better spent on acquiring pharmaceutical companies with successful drugs and then jacking up the prices of those drugs. In advocating this plan he was supported by "activist" investor Bill Ackman. Activist investors look for companies they think are mismanaged, invest in them heavily, and then force the company to change. Ackman agreed with Pearson that money spent on R&D would be better spent elsewhere and he soon acquired a seat on Valeant's board.

The model that evolved from this strategy involved three main components: acquisition, price gouging, and tax avoidance. First, Valeant would acquire a drug company that produced either a drug it was interested in or a drug that was competing with one of its own drugs. Costs at the acquired company were reduced by cutting funds spent on R&D and decreasing the sales staff. Valeant spent about 3 percent of sales on R&D compared with an industry average of 15 to 20 percent.

Secondly, prices of the pharmaceuticals owned by the acquired firm then dramatically increased. For example, after acquiring the drug Glumetza, used in diabetes, during the takeover of Salix Pharmaceuticals, the price of the drug increased from $519.92 a month to $4,643 a month.[35]

Thirdly, in an example of tax avoidance, Valeant executed an "inversion" with a Canadian firm, Biovall. In this "reverse merger" Biovall purchased a bit more than half of Valeant, making it the formal owner of the company. But the "new" entity kept the name Valeant, kept its base in the United States, and retained Pearson as CEO. These types of inversions allowed the company to avoid U.S. taxes. After Valeant officially became a Canadian company, it was taxed at Canadian corporate rates (between 3 and 5 percent; U.S. corporate rates are closer to 35 percent).[36] This ploy was not illegal, but Valeant became the first U.S. drug maker to avoid substantial taxation through such an inversion.

Pearson's strategy led to a series of acquisitions that made many executives rich, put Valeant heavily into debt, and fundamentally restructured the pharmaceutical industry. James Surowiecki summed up the Valeant story: "Valeant has been less like a drug company than like a super-aggressive hedge fund that just happened to specialize in pharmaceuticals. . . . It exemplified a corporate era in which financialization too often eclipsed production."[37]

Financialization and the MIC

The Valeant story actually displays some of the typical features of the increasingly financialized capitalist economy. Opportunities for income from real capital investments dwindle in late capitalism, so capital accumulation depends on imaginative financial manipulations rather than economic production.[38] The results include "more and more profits, fewer and fewer profitable investment opportunities, a recipe for slowing down capital accumulation and therefore economic growth which is powered by capital accumulation."[39] For Ackman and Pearson, capital accumulation came from acquisition, cost cutting, price gouging, and tax avoidance, all abetted by creative bookkeeping practices. None of this activity improved the public's health, nor did it result in improved pharmaceutical products. We don't really know how many people suffered harm because they could no longer afford their medications.

How has financialization specifically affected the MIC? Making a profit in the current environment relies less and less on actually producing goods and services and more and more on gaming the system or in extreme forms of debt-fueled speculation in high-risk and exotic financial instruments, an activity that has been called "Ponzi capitalism."[40] This was the case with Valeant, which exemplifies the divorce between the "real economy"—developing and producing pharmaceuticals—and the "financial economy," in which profits are generated through the manipulation of financial instruments.

Financialization of the MIC also relies on several interconnected economic strategies. One strategy, again illustrated by Valeant, involves cost cutting, usually by firing staff. We see this approach in hospital operations through various attempts to outsource operations, control and speed up staff, and replace union workers with non-union workers. It is often undocumented workers who do the cleaning work in elite institutions. Regarding professional employees, the United States continues to import large numbers of foreign health care workers, especially nurses and doctors, whose home countries have paid for their educations.

In addition, the MIC relies heavily on subsidization by the state for activities that allegedly serve the public, but which largely benefit for-profit institutions. We have seen this strategy in the changes of the Blue Cross–Blue Shield system. For-profit insurance corporations receive massive state support through Medicare and Medicaid programs, as well as more recently through the Affordable Care Act. The federal government also heavily subsidizes the development of biotech and information technology, either through direct grants or through tax exemptions.

Is There an Alternative to the MIC?

We have clarified several emerging directions of the MIC: expansion of academic medical centers into local communities, corporate capture of academic medicine and the medical elite, the gray line between for-profit and not-for-profit, the importance of monopoly power and real estate, and the dominance of finance capital. All these problems involve changing variations on Health/PAC's original theme: the MIC is about profit, not about health.

The concept of a MIC has held up across fifty years. If we see the primary function of the system as profit generation, all the ensuing "inefficiencies" begin to make sense. Constructing an alternative to the MIC will require a transformation that no longer permits the exploitation of illness for profit, and that transformation, as we will see in later chapters, will require fundamental changes in the capitalist economic system, within which the MIC occupies an important place.

6—The Pharmaceutical Industry in the Context of Contemporary Capitalism

Joel Lexchin

The pharmaceutical industry has remained near or at the top of the list for profitability during many decades.[1] The myth is that its profits come from producing and selling the many therapeutic advances that industry research has generated, but the reality is far different. In the first place, after tax deductions only about 1.3 percent of the money that the industry spends actually goes into basic research, the type of research that leads to new medications.[2] Second, most of the new medicines that come from the pharmaceutical corporations offer little to nothing in the way of new therapeutic options. For the decade 2005 to 2014, among 1,032 new drugs and new uses for old drugs introduced into the French market, for example, only sixty-six offered a significant advantage whereas more than half were rated as "nothing new," and 177 were judged "unacceptable" because they came with serious safety issues and no benefits.[3]

The industry also justifies its high level of profits with the claim that drug development is inherently risky. To this end, the pharmaceutical corporations maintain that only one in every 10,000 molecules actually results in a new drug. Though this may be true, most of the molecules that fall by the wayside do so in the very early stages of development when costs are minimal. The $2.6 billion figure that is now cited as the cost to bring a new drug to market[4] comes from data that are confidential, and the calculations are based on a set of assumptions that have been widely challenged.[5] Were drug development such a risky proposition, then one would expect that from time to time the fortunes of corporations would vary. On the contrary, since 1980, all the large corporations have done well financially. As Stanley Finkelstein, a physician, and Peter Temin, an economist, both based at the Massachusetts Institute of Technology, point out, "No matter how many times industry analysts warn that a patent expiration is going to make this or that company vanish, it hasn't happened."[6]

Despite the continuing impressive level of profit, the industry is undergoing a crisis from a trio of causes: patent expirations that were expected to lead to a loss of revenue in the range of $75 billion from 2010 to 2015, a poor pipeline of new drugs, and pressure on prices in many countries including, recently, the United States.[7] This crisis reflects the emergence of financialization, the shift in gravity of economic activity from production to finance as a key feature of modern capitalism. Pedro Cuatrecasas, from the Departments of Pharmacology and Medicine at the University of California, San Diego, argues, "Shareholders, investment bankers, and analysts, who know little about drug discovery, place intense pressures on CEOs and their boards for quick returns."[8]

To maintain its attractiveness to the financial community, the pharmaceutical industry has developed several strategies. With the blockbuster model of development drying up, corporations have shifted to a "nichebuster" model. With fewer potential products in the research and development (R&D) pipeline, it is even more critical to ensure that drugs being developed make it through the regulatory process intact, and to do that industry has deepened its relationship with regulatory agencies to circumvent or corrupt the intent of regulation, often with the collusion of government. Key to the industry's survival is its ability to extend the period during which it has a monopoly on the sale of products, and that translates into stronger intellectual property rights, both in the developed world and in the developing countries that represent the emerging sites of growth. With the threat of price controls looming, the other way of expanding revenue is to increase the volume of prescriptions for existing and new drugs. The approach to that goal is to control the knowledge about how and when drugs should be prescribed. An exploration of these four points informs the rest of this chapter: the development of nichebuster drugs, corrupting the regulatory process, strengthening intellectual property rights, and controlling knowledge about the benefits and harms of pharmaceutical products.

From Blockbuster to Nichebuster

Until a few years ago the pharmaceutical industry operated on what is known as a blockbuster model. The industry targeted drug development for chronic diseases that were common in developed countries, such as heart disease or diabetes, and then heavily marketed those drugs in the hope of reaching $1 billion annually in sales. Diseases that occurred predominantly or exclusively in developing countries were largely ignored because the people affected had no meaningful purchasing power. Of 850 new therapeutic products marketed between 2000 and 2011, only thirty-seven (4 percent) were indicated for those types of diseases.[9]

Recently, since all the easy targets are exhausted, there has been a shift away from the blockbuster model to the "nichebuster" model whereby corporations target small therapeutic markets with drugs that they can sell for hundreds of thousands of dollars per year per patient. In this sense, the challenges experienced by the pharmaceutical industry resemble those of others that operate in a capitalist economy. The exhaustion of markets is an intrinsic condition of capitalism that requires "product differentiation," in this case more and more expensive medications for narrower and narrower markets, assuring requisite growth. In the United States the cost of disease-modifying drugs for multiple sclerosis has gone from an average of $8,000 to $11,000 per year in the early to mid-1990s to $60,000 annually.[10] In 2013, 120 cancer specialists from more than fifteen countries came together to denounce prices for new oncology drugs that had reached $100,000 or more annually.[11] The idea that these prices were justified by the cost of R&D should be put to rest, as confirmed by the former CEO of Pfizer, Hank McKinnell, who said, "It's a fallacy to suggest that our industry, or any industry, prices a product to recapture the R&D budget."[12] Prices are based on what the market will bear. The more desperate patients become, the higher the price that they are willing to pay.

CORRUPTION OF THE DRUG REGULATORY PROCESS

Before corporations can start making money from the drugs they manufacture, those drugs need to be approved for marketing. This stipulation is merely pro forma in much of the developing world, however, where one-third of countries have no or very little drug regulatory capacity.[13] Even in countries like India, drug regulation is often a sham, as can be seen by a 2011–12 examination of fixed-dose combination (FDC) products, that is, products that contain two or more active ingredients. Research recently found that corporations took advantage of lax regulatory standards to sell "many millions of doses . . . of FDCs that included drugs restricted, banned, or never approved in other countries owing to their association with serious adverse events including fatality."[14]

Drug regulation in the United States and the European Union (EU) has been corrupted through the influence of the pharmaceutical industry. Courtney Davis and John Abraham, who teach pharmaceutical policy at King's College London, observe that "the last 30 years have seen a raft of deregulatory reforms, ostensibly to promote pharmaceutical innovation deemed to be simultaneously in the commercial interests of industry and the health interests of patients."[15] An explanation for why this is allowed to take place comes from corporate bias theory.[16] Abraham argues, "Corporate bias theory allows for the possibility of a relatively strong, pro-active state, which may encourage pro-business (de)regulation in collaboration with industry."[17] Abraham contends that industry can drive regulation by influencing not just the regulatory agencies but also the broader government directly through lobbying, financial donations, and other activities: for example, getting drug company representatives appointed to task forces that help form overall government policy. The ultimate result is that the state actively supports the broad regulatory goals of industry.

The clearest manifestation of corporate bias theory in pharmaceutical regulation is the widespread adoption of corporate-user fees to pay for the functions of drug regulatory authorities such as the U.S. Food and Drug Administration (FDA), the European Medicines Agency (EMA), and the Medicines and Healthcare Products Regulatory Agency in the United Kingdom (UK MHRA). Resource constraints on the FDA were the major driving force behind the implementation of user fees in the United States. The continuing reluctance of Congress to increase the FDA's budget ultimately led the FDA to abandon its previous position in opposition to user fees from the pharmaceutical industry. As part of the Prescription Drug User Fees Act (PDUFA) of 1992, the industry agreed to enter into an arrangement provided that the fees were supplemental to congressional appropriations and that the money was used exclusively to improve the efficiency and speed of new drug reviews for brand-name drugs. As a result, the majority of fee revenues went to hiring new drug reviewers. It was not until 2007 that the FDA was allowed to use any of this additional money to monitor the safety of the products that it had approved.

PDUFA subsequently has been reauthorized at five-year intervals, with the latest renewal in 2012. One of the key features of PDUFA is that it contains provisions committing the FDA to continual improvements in the percentage of new drug applications approved within set periods of time.[18] With limited patent life, the longer drugs are on the market the greater the return to the corporations marketing them. PDUFA, by getting drugs to the market faster, meant more profits for the corporations.

Prior to 1989, the Medicines Control Agency (the precursor of the MHRA) in the UK received 65 percent of its funding from user fees and 35 percent via taxes. At that point, funding moved to 100 percent from user fees, a reflection of the philosophy of the Thatcher Conservative government that science should be made "more responsive" to the needs of industry.[19] In the European Union as a whole, the philosophy of user fees seems to have been accepted from the inception of the Agency. The question then becomes whose priorities are being served, those of the public or those of the industry?

Evidence shows that user fees have had negative consequences for public safety. In the United States the standard review time for a new drug application is 300 days, and under PDUFA the FDA is required to complete 90 percent of applications within the timeline. If this goal is not achieved, renewal of user fees might be threatened, thereby depriving the agency of a substantial portion of its revenue. In practice, it appears that as the FDA is approaching its deadline for making a decision, it relaxes its standards for evaluating safety. As compared with drugs approved at other times, drugs approved in the two months before their deadlines were over five times more likely to be withdrawn for safety reasons and almost 4.5 times more likely to carry a subsequent black-box warning, the most serious safety warning that the FDA can require.[20]

In the EU, when a drug application is made to the EMA, the organization is responsible for choosing what is called the Rapporteur and Co-Rapporteur, that is, the national regulatory agencies that will do the actual evaluation of the new drug application. Since most of the regulatory agencies in EU countries are funded to a considerable extent by user fees, there is often intense competition among them for Rapporteur and Co-Rapporteur status to generate income.[21] This competition puts the national agencies under considerable pressure to conform to or to better the EU's 210-day timeline for drug approvals as corporations look for fast approval rates, one of their key criteria when recommending a Rapporteur and Co-Rapporteur. Out of fifteen German, Swedish, and UK regulatory personnel who were interviewed by Abraham and Graham Lewis from the University of York, five agreed that this timeline was a threat to public health, and an additional five thought that it possibly was.[22] In a similar vein, a British House of Commons Committee looking into the influence of the pharmaceutical industry concluded, "The MHRA, like many regulatory organisations, is entirely funded by fees from those it regulates. However, unlike many regulators, it competes with other European agencies for fee income. This situation has led to concerns that it may lose sight of the need to protect and promote public health above all else as it seeks to win fee income from the companies."[23]

Is Intellectual Property a "Right"?

Intellectual property rights (IPRs) are the key factor in driving revenue and profits for pharmaceutical corporations. In the contemporary pharmaceutical context, the primary IPRs are the patents over the products themselves and the data that the corporations generate when they conduct premarket clinical trials to evaluate the safety and efficacy of their products. The stronger a country's IPRs, the longer the corporations retain a monopoly on their products and the more money they can make from them. Therefore, it should not be any surprise that the pharmaceutical industry goes to great lengths not only to protect IPRs but to strengthen them.

One of the earliest manifestations of this obsession with IPRs was the industry lobbying that led the United States to insist that Canada dismantle its regime of compulsory licensing in return for getting the initial U.S.-Canadian Free Trade Agreement in 1987 and then the North American Free Trade Agreement (NAFTA) in 1994. At that time, compulsory licensing was cutting Canada's overall drug spending by about 15 percent.[24] (A compulsory license allows a generic manufacturer to produce a drug even if the patent on the product is still in effect.)

In the United States, the latest victory for stronger IPRs has been the twelve years of market exclusivity for biologic products, that is, those that are made from living cells. These twelve years come courtesy of four years of data protection and an additional eight years of exclusive use for biological products. This means that the FDA will not approve a "biosimilar," the equivalent of a generic product, during this eight-year period. In some ways, data protection can be even more important to corporations than patents since data protection cannot be challenged in the court system the same way that patents can. Although biologics represent fewer than 1 percent of prescriptions written in the United States, they account for 28 percent of drug spending, and that figure is only going to increase in the future.[25] For instance, Cerezyme, a treatment for Gaucher disease, a rare inherited enzyme deficiency, costs $200,000 a year per patient.

Internationally, the U.S. government, with strong backing from the pharmaceutical industry, pushed to make sure that an investor-state dispute settlement (ISDS) mechanism was included in international trade agreements. ISDS allows corporations to sue governments.[26] Eli Lilly has used the ISDS provisions in the North American Free Trade Agreement to demand $500 million from the Canadian government because Canadian courts invalidated patents on two of Lilly's drugs.[27] Although in developed countries the IPR provisions in trade agreements have a significant impact on drug access, causing delays in generics reaching the market, the consequences in developing countries are much more devastating. For instance, under current patent laws 68 percent of the HIV population in Vietnam receives antiretroviral medications, but under the failed Trans-Pacific Partnership that figure would have dropped to about 30 percent.[28]

The pharmaceutical industry has more than a three-decade history of successfully lobbying for stronger IPRs, beginning with the lead-up to the Uruguay Round of trade talks that ultimately resulted in the World Trade Organization (WTO). Pfizer and its then CEO Edmund Pratt played a key role in convincing the U.S. government to make IPRs a major issue in these talks.[29] The result, in 1994, was the Agreement on Trade-Related Aspects of Intellectual Property Rights (TRIPS), which required uniform patent standards for all WTO member countries, meaning product patents for pharmaceuticals of twenty years and limiting the use of compulsory licensing as a tool for accelerating the appearance of generic products. The pharmaceutical industry's goal was to have all countries adopt the same IPRs as those in the United States, regardless of their level of development or ability to deliver drug therapy to their populations at an affordable price. Many developed countries did not adopt full patent protection for pharmaceuticals until the 1970s or later when their gross domestic product (GDP) per capita was in the tens of thousands of dollars. The TRIPS Agreement required developing countries with a GDP in the hundreds or low thousands of dollars to have the equivalent standards.[30]

Due to the strengthening of IPRs, by 2000 many developing countries were confronting a situation where the price of triple therapy for HIV was greater than US$10,000 per person per year, and the ability to access low-cost generics was going to disappear in the near future.[31]

Faced with increasing rates of HIV infection and these prices for HIV treatment, the South African government in the late 1990s passed the Medicines and Related Substances Control Amendment Act, which allowed for generic substitution of off-patent medicines and the ability to import a non-counterfeit version of patented medicines from another country without the permission of the intellectual property owners. In response, during 1998 thirty-nine multinational pharmaceutical corporations, with the support of the U.S. government (under the Clinton administration) and the European Commission, took the South African government to court alleging that the legislation violated both the TRIPS Agreement and the country's constitution. Eventually, in the face of widespread public opposition, the U.S. government withdrew its support for the court case, and without the U.S. support the corporations dropped their lawsuit.[32]

Since then, the United States and the EU have used the TRIPS Agreement as a minimum for acceptable IPR standards and have tried to ratchet up their strength with each successive trade deal by incorporating newer and more stringent provisions. Some of the results can be seen in longer periods of patent extension (patents can be extended past twenty years) and in the elimination of objecting to patents before they are granted.[33] Like the consequences for HIV medication access in Vietnam, stronger IPR provisions in free trade agreements significantly decrease access to prescribed medicines.[34]

Thailand provides just one of many examples of how governments and the industry have used IPRs as a tool to bully developing countries. Citing high drug prices and its obligation to provide access to essential medicines, in 2006 Thailand issued a compulsory license for lopinavir/ritonavir, a drug combination used to treat HIV. The EU Trade Commissioner wrote to the Thai Minister of Commerce to complain about Thailand's move. Abbott, the maker of lopinavir/ritonavir, responded by withdrawing all new drug applications from the Thai Food and Drug Administration, including the much needed heat-stable version of lopinavir/ritonavir.[35]

When generic drugs are produced through compulsory licenses, brand-name corporations are quick to denounce this measure. Marijn Dekkers, CEO of Bayer, referred to compulsory licensing as "essentially theft," although it is perfectly legal under the TRIPS Agreement. In addition, when Dekkers was talking about his company's new and highly effective drug sobosbuvir (Sovaldi) for treating hepatitis C, he commented: "We did not develop this product for the Indian market, let's be honest. I mean, you know, we developed this product for Western patients who can afford this product, quite honestly."[36]

Controlling Knowledge

Clinical trials that fail to demonstrate effectiveness or that raise significant safety concerns can dramatically affect the sale of products. In July 2002 the results of a Women's Health Initiative clinical trial found that the estrogen/progestin combination of hormone replacement therapy (HRT) caused an increased risk of cardiovascular disease and breast cancer in postmenopausal women.[37] By June 2003 prescriptions for Prempro, the most widely sold estrogen/progestin combination, had declined by 66 percent in the United States.[38]

To avoid these scenarios and continue to expand revenue, corporations have evolved from controlling the development of new drugs to controlling the knowledge about those drugs, ensuring that their message is the one that reaches doctors and patients.[39] Pharmaceutical corporations fund almost all pre-market clinical trials, the ones used as the basis for approving a new drug or a new indication for an existing drug. These trials are the foundation of knowledge about a drug and as such their outcome is extremely important. As funders, corporations control all aspects of the trials from their initial design to the way that they are conducted and analyzed, how they are reported to drug regulatory agencies such as the FDA, whether and how they are published, and to a large extent how they are presented to doctors.

Pro-corporate bias starts with the trial design. When the new drug being tested is compared to another drug already on the market, inappropriately low or high doses of the comparator drug may be chosen to either minimize effectiveness or maximize side effects.[40] In the 1980s, the most common reason for terminating trials in the late stages of research, including treatments for cancer, cardiovascular disease, and neonatal sepsis, was financial consideration (43 percent), compared to efficacy (31 percent) and safety (21 percent).[41] The financial reasons included a limited commercial market, insufficient anticipated return on investment, and a change in research priorities following drug company mergers. However, termination solely on financial grounds can be viewed as a violation of Article 6 of the Declaration of Helsinki, the internationally recognized standard for the conduct of clinical research.[42] Article 6 states that "in medical research involving human subjects, the well-being of the individual research subject must take precedence over all other interests." Stopping trials before they are completed solely for financial reasons effectively means that the "quarterly business plans or the changing of chief executive officers" takes precedence over "the responsible conduct of medical research [that] involves a social duty and a moral responsibility that transcends quarterly business plans or the changing of chief executive officers."[43]

There is evidence that not all the data from clinical trials is made available to regulatory authorities and that it is presented in a misleading way. Merck failed to provide mortality data in a timely manner to the FDA from two trials involving the use of rofecoxib in patients with Alzheimer's or other cognitive impairment.[44] GlaxoSmithKline presented data to the FDA about its asthma drug, salmeterol, that produced an apparent decrease in the danger associated with the drug.[45]

One of the best-known examples of the way that corporations change the interpretation of trials between the time that they report results to the FDA and when the trials are actually published is the study that examined the effectiveness of celecoxib, a non-steroidal anti-inflammatory drug (NSAID) and pain reliever made by Pfizer. The published trial, based on six months of data, appeared to confirm the protective effect of celecoxib over traditional anti-inflammatories medications in reducing stomach bleeding. However, the two studies combined in the publication actually continued for twelve and sixteen months. At the 12–16-month time there was no difference in gastro-intestinal adverse effects between those patients who used celecoxib and those users of the traditional NSAID.[46]

Ghostwriting in the pharmaceutical industry refers to the practice whereby corporations, or someone working on their behalf, hire medical writers to write a journal article or letter based on company-owned data. The article is then taken to an academic researcher who agrees to sign it, usually for money or the prestige value of having a publication. When the article eventually appears in print, there is no acknowledgement of the role played by the ghostwriter in its production. Wyeth enlisted ghostwriters to defend the $2 billion in annual sales from Premarin and Prempro, its two HRT products, before and after the publication of the Women's Health Initiative, which showed that the risks from HRT drugs outweighed their benefits. Court documents show that ghostwriters played a major role in producing twenty-six scientific papers that backed the use of HRT. The articles did not disclose Wyeth's role in initiating and paying for the work.[47]

There are numerous examples of selective publication of industry trials with negative results. Out of thirty-seven studies on antidepressants that the FDA viewed as either negative or questionable, twenty-two were never published.[48] Failure to publish data can lead to overestimating the effectiveness of products and underestimating their harm. Published data overestimated the benefit of the antidepressant reboxetine versus placebo by up to 115 percent and also underestimated harm.[49]

Internal documents from GlaxoSmithKline were used to demonstrate differences between the actual results of a study that examined the safety and effectiveness of the antidepressant paroxetine in adolescents and the way the results were presented in published form.[50] The publication claimed that "paroxetine is generally well tolerated and effective for major depression in adolescents."[51] In contrast, based on the protocol-defined primary and secondary outcomes, "there was no significant efficacy difference between paroxetine and placebo on the two primary outcomes or six secondary outcomes," and paroxetine was associated with harm, including an increase in suicidal ideation.[52]

Finally, corporations recognize that there is a credibility gap when they directly present evidence about their products to doctors. To get around this problem they employ doctors and researchers known as "key opinion leaders" (KOLs). It's vital for the corporations to preserve the fiction that KOLs are independent sources of information in order to maintain the trust of doctors who hear the KOLs' presentations. However, it is precisely when KOLs start to act independently and deviate from the messages corporations are cultivating that their value to the corporations starts to be questioned.[53] One KOL wrote a series of case reports about a certain medication made by a company for which he often spoke that portrayed the product as less favorable than that of a drug made by a competitor. Once those case reports became public, his invitations to speak dropped from four to six times per month to essentially none.[54]

A BETTER WORLD IS POSSIBLE

In an unpublished paper the British economist Alan Maynard notes:

> Economic theory predicts that firms will invest in corruption of the evidence base wherever its benefits exceed its costs. If detection is costly for regulators, corruption of the evidence base can be expected to be extensive. Investment in biasing the evidence base, both clinical and economic, in pharmaceuticals is likely to be detailed and comprehensive, covering all aspects of the appraisal process. Such investment is likely to be extensive as the scientific and policy discourses are technical and esoteric, making detection difficult and expensive.[55]

Although the pharmaceutical industry seems like an invincible opponent, the crisis that it is facing also offers the opportunity to advocate for new ways of bringing drugs to the market that are affordable and meet real medical needs rather than maximization of profits. The Mario Negri Institute in Italy, in existence since the early 1960s, offers an alternative way for doing pharmacological research. It is willing to accept money from pharmaceutical corporations for research, but it insists on maintaining its independence by designing the trials, conducting them, collecting and analyzing the data, and writing up the results without any interference from the funding source. In addition, the Institute declines to take out any patents or to demand any other form of IPRs and makes all data freely available.

Finally, it rejects any funding when its scientists conclude that the results will not further the interest of public health.[56]

Though it is worth emulating the Mario Negri Institute model on a wider scale, this still leaves the choice of what drugs to focus on and their eventual price in the hands of the pharmaceutical corporations. To deal with these issues, there have been proposals circulating for over a decade to incentivize R&D into products that meet real medical needs rather than just enhancing profits and to base the revenue that corporations earn on the therapeutic value of products rather than their prices. U.S. Senator Bernie Sanders introduced and revised the Medical Innovation Prize Fund bill, which would de-link the incentives for R&D from high drug prices through innovation inducement prizes. "Incentives can target important goals such as products that . . . address research priorities from a health perspective".[57]

Going further, there is the "sequestration thesis" proposed by Arthur Schafer, Director of the Centre for Professional and Applied Ethics at the University of Manitoba.[58] Under this proposal, an organization such as the National Institutes of Health or its equivalent in other countries would organize and manage clinical trials and the data that come from them, with funding generated through taxes collected from the pharmaceutical industry and/or general tax revenue.[59] "Drug companies would no longer directly compensate scientists for evaluating their own products; instead, scientists would work for the testing agency."[60] Dean Baker, co-founder of the Center for Economic and Policy Research in Washington, D.C., goes even further in arguing for a system whereby all clinical trials would be publicly financed, with the cost of the trials in the United States being covered through lower drug prices under the Medicare drug program and other public health care programs.[61]

Some national health systems have experienced relative success in controlling overall drug expenditures through a variety of mechanisms. Canada sets a maximum introductory price for new patented medicines.[62] As a result, prices for brand-name drugs are, on average, about 50 percent lower than prices in the United States.[63] However, the benchmark that Canada uses is the median price in seven other countries, some with the highest prices in the world; this is one of the reasons why spending for medications in Canada is $713 per capita, fourth highest in the world.[64] Australia, with its Pharmaceutical Benefits Scheme that covers the entire population, negotiates prices at a national level. If drugs are not listed on its formulary, sales suffer significantly. Therefore, Australia is able to achieve prices for brand-name drugs that are about 9 to 10 percent lower than Canada's.[65] New Zealand is even more aggressive and uses competitive bidding for generic drugs and reference-based pricing for brand-name drugs. Reference-based pricing groups all drugs that are therapeutically equivalent for a particular problem, and the government then pays only for the lowest-priced drug in the group. Using these two approaches and a few others, instead of spending an expected NZ$2.34 billion in 2012, based on the rate of rise in drug spending in 2000, New Zealand paid out only NZ$777 million.[66]

However, despite successes in controlling overall spending, no developed countries have been willing to mount a challenge to the current intellectual property regime that grants monopolies for up to twenty years and keeps lower-priced generics off the market. All drug regulatory systems are funded to varying degrees by user fees, thereby embedding a system that makes regulators sensitive to the needs of the pharmaceutical industry when it comes to approving new products. Finally, clinical trials are still under control of pharmaceutical corporations worldwide. Promotion to both health care practitioners and consumers, even in countries like New Zealand, is poorly regulated, meaning that both prescribers' and patients' knowledge about medications remains limited.

Pharmaceutical corporations are extremely powerful due to their wealth. They achieve this power with the active collusion of regulatory authorities and the governments that oversee these authorities. The introduction of user fees has meant that commercial values are replacing public health as a priority for organizations such as the FDA. In the process, drugs are approved with increasingly weaker evidence, and the result is poor-quality therapy and more safety problems associated with the drugs that are marketed. Ratcheting up the strength of IPRs through international and bilateral trade deals helps protect the profits of the corporations but means that, globally, access to essential medicines is restricted, especially in developing countries.

Finally, the industry is able to manipulate knowledge about the value of pharmaceuticals not only to the detriment of what doctors know, but more important, to the detriment of people's health. At the same time as the industry is developing ways of coping with its internal crisis, a crisis that is inherent in the capitalist organization of pharmaceutical production, there are also serious proposals to curb its power and to ensure that drugs are developed and priced to meet real health needs and not the need for ever larger profits.[67]

PART THREE

Neoliberalism and Health Reform

7—Obamacare: The Neoliberal Model Comes Home to Roost in the United States —If We Let It

Howard Waitzkin and Ida Hellander

The Affordable Care Act (ACA, or Obamacare) has headed down a very bumpy road, and it is worthwhile asking where it came from and what comes next. Officially, Obamacare represents the latest in more than a century of efforts in the United States that have aimed to achieve universal access to health care. In reality, Obamacare has strengthened the for-profit insurance industry by transferring public, tax-generated revenues into the private sector. It has done and will do little to improve the problem of uninsurance in the United States and has already started to worsen the problem of underinsurance. Multiple projections show that Obamacare is financially unsustainable. Meanwhile, despite benefits for some of the richest corporations and executives, and adverse or mixed effects for the non-rich, a remarkable manipulation of political symbolism has conveyed the notion that Obamacare is a creation of the left, warranting strenuous opposition from the right. This symbolism reached a pinnacle when the Trump administration failed to repeal Obamacare, a failure that actually constituted a victory for the private insurance industry and its many Republican collaborators in Congress.

Abundant data substantiate that the failure of Obamacare has become nearly inevitable. Regarding access, Obamacare when fully implemented will still leave uninsured more than one-half of the previously uninsured population, at least 27 million people according to the non-partisan Congressional Budget Office, and at least twice that number underinsured.[1] Due to high deductibles (about $10,000 for a family bronze plan and $6,000 for silver) and co-payments, coverage under Obamacare has become unusable for many individuals and families, and employer-sponsored coverage is going in the same direction.[2] Private insurance generally shows administrative expenses about eight-fold higher than when plans are publicly administered. Administrative waste has increased even more under Obamacare and remains much higher than in other capitalist countries with national health programs.[3] Such administrative expenditures pay for activities like marketing, billing, denial of claims, processing co-payments and deductibles, exorbitant salaries and deferred income for executives (sometimes more than $30 million per year), profits, and dividends for corporate shareholders.[4] The overall costs of the health system under Obamacare are projected to rise from 17.4 percent of gross domestic produce (GDP) in 2013 to 19.6 percent in 2022.[5] A conservative projection shows that premiums and out-of-pocket expenditures for the average family will approach half of the average family income by 2019 and the full average family income itself by 2029.[6]

THE ORIGINS OF OBAMACARE

The overall structure of Obamacare is actually not new. Similar "reforms" have appeared in other countries over the last two decades. For instance, the year 1994 was a significant one for health reform worldwide. Colombia enacted a national program of "managed competition," which replaced its prior health system and was based largely in public-sector hospitals and clinics. The World Bank mandated and partly financed the reform. President César Gaviria and colleagues presented the reform to financial elites at the World Economic Forum and elsewhere. The same year, a similar proposal designed by the U.S. insurance industry and spearheaded by Hillary Clinton was advanced but ultimately abandoned. The right wing opposed the plan as a big-government boondoggle, while on the left, opposition centered on the massively increased, tax-subsidized role that the plan would create for the private insurance industry, especially a handful of the nation's largest companies.

During the 1990s, several European countries considered proposals for health reform that followed a similar model of privatization, called "managed competition," and increased access for the private insurance industry to public health care trust funds.[7] A few, like the Netherlands and the United Kingdom, implemented elements of the reform. But most European countries did not, because of opposition from left-oriented parties, labor unions, and civic organizations.

In Latin America, Asia, and some countries of Africa, for-profit multinational insurance corporations, mostly based in the United States, tried to expand their operations. Access to public-sector social security trust funds, previously designated to provide retirement and health care benefits, proved a primary motivation for this expansion.[8] Conferences and publications organized by the World Bank and insurance companies provided legitimacy for such efforts by recruiting progressive spokespersons like Desmond Tutu in South Africa.[9]

Then, in 2006, Republican governor Mitt Romney in Massachusetts implemented a reform that required all state residents to buy insurance through the state system if they did not already hold insurance coverage. Romney later disavowed the reform during his 2012 presidential campaign. But the same overall structure reemerged in Obamacare.

Though framed as programs to improve access for the poor and underserved, these initiatives facilitated the efforts of for-profit insurance corporations providing "managed care." The corporations could collect prepaid capitation fees or other premiums from government agencies administering trust funds, as well as from employers and patients, and could invest the reserves at high rates of return. Insurance corporations also profited by denying or delaying necessary care through strategies such as utilization review and preauthorization requirements; cost-sharing such as co-payments, deductibles, co-insurance, and pharmacy tiers; limiting access to only certain physicians; and frequent redesign of benefits.

Such proposals fostered neoliberalism. They promoted competing, for-profit, private insurance corporations. Programs and institutions previously based in the public sector were cut back and, if possible, privatized. Overall, government budgets for public-sector health care were cut. Private corporations gained access to public trust funds. Public hospitals and clinics entered into competition with private institutions, their budgets were determined by demand rather than supply, and prior global budgets for safety-net institutions were not guaranteed. Insurance executives made operational decisions about services, and their authority superseded that of physicians and other clinicians.

The Strange Career of Neoliberal Health Reform

The roots of the neoliberal model of health reform emerged from Cold War military policy. The economist Alain Enthoven provided much of the intellectual framework for these early efforts. Enthoven had worked as Assistant Secretary of Defense under Robert S. McNamara during the Kennedy and Johnson administrations, and while at the Pentagon between 1961 and 1969, he led a group of analysts who developed the "planning-programming-budgeting-system" (PPBS) and cost-benefit analysis, intended to promote more cost-effective spending decisions for military expenditures.[10] After leaving the military sector, Enthoven emerged as the principal architect of "managed competition," which became the prevailing model for the Clinton health care reform, Romney-care, Obamacare, and neoliberal health reform throughout the world. Decades later, he has remained a strong advocate for this model.[11]

After a brief excursion between 1969 and 1973 as vice president and then president of Litton Industries, a major military contractor, Enthoven joined the faculty at Stanford in 1973 as a professor of both management and health care economics. There his work on health policy incorporated several elements common to military and medical systems (Table 7.1): distrust of professionals, deference to managers, choice among competing alternatives, and cost-benefit analysis, but not necessarily cost reduction.[12]

TABLE 7.1: Complementary Themes in Military Planning-Programming-Budgeting System (PPBS) and Managed Competition in Health Care

Theme	Focus of Theme	
	PPBS	Managed Competition
Distrust of professionals	Military brass	Medical guild
Trust of managers	Independent analysts	Managers of organizational sponsors
Choice among competing alternatives	Weapon systems, military strategies	Organized health plans
Scientific method	Cost-benefit analysis in case studies	Cost-benefit analysis in case studies
"Tools" for managers	Cost-benefit analysis, 5-year defense plan, draft Presidential memos, development concept papers	Techniques to prevent "market failure": pricing, cost-benefit analysis, annual enrollment, quality assurance, subsidy management
Incrementalism with strains	Military officers, corporate contractors, members of Congress	Physicians, middle-class consumers, private insurance companies not equipped for managed care
Cost analysis but not necessarily cost reduction	No budget ceiling for military expenditures	No budget ceiling for health care expenditures

Sources: See note 11.

By 1977, only four years after leaving the defense sector, Enthoven offered the Carter administration his proposal for a Consumer Choice Health Plan. Although Carter rejected the plan, Enthoven soon published the proposal.[13] In this early work, Enthoven presented the basic concepts of most subsequent health reform proposals; Obamacare incorporates this same overall structure.

During the 1980s, Enthoven collaborated with managed care and insurance executives to refine the proposal. A new name, "managed competition," proved attractive to business leaders, who met regularly with Enthoven and Paul Ellwood in Jackson Hole, Wyoming.[14] The five largest insurance corporations funded this group, as well as Bill Clinton's presidential campaign and Clinton's Health Security Act.

Several conditions led to the creation of Obamacare as a reform that enhanced the fortunes of the private insurance industry. Campaign financing, as usual, played a major role. Obama, who as a state legislator in Illinois had favored a single-payer approach, drastically changed his position as a presidential candidate. For the 2008 campaign, Obama received the largest financial contributions in history from the insurance industry, more than three times the contributions received by his Republican rival, John McCain. With funding from the insurance industry and financial corporations linked to Wall Street, Obama became the first presidential candidate in history able to turn down government funds for his campaign.[15]

The Boilerplate Neoliberal Health Reform

The neoliberal health agenda, including Obamacare, emerged as one component of a worldwide agenda developed by the World Bank, International Monetary Fund, and other international financial institutions. This agenda to promote market-driven health care facilitated multinational corporations' access to public-sector health and social security trust funds. An underlying managerial ideology claimed, nearly always without evidence, that corporate executives could achieve superior quality and efficiency by "managing" medical services in the marketplace.[16] Enthoven and colleagues in academic health economics participated in this effort, refining terms and giving the enterprise a scholarly credibility.

Health reform proposals across different countries have resembled one another closely. The specific details of each plan appeared to conform to a cookie-cutter template, in which the names of national institutions and local actors have varied. Six broad features have characterized nearly all neoliberal health initiatives (see Table 7.2).

1. Organizations of providers. One element of neoliberal proposals involves large, privately controlled organizations of health care providers. These organizations operate under the direct control or strong influence of private insurance corporations, in collaboration with hospitals and health systems. The organizations may employ health care providers directly, or may contract with providers in a preferred network. In the Clinton proposal, these organizations were named Accountable Health Partnerships (AHPs). In Obamacare, they are called Accountable Care Organizations (ACOs). Technically, ACOs are supported only in Medicare, although Obamacare accelerated organizational consolidation in anticipation of broader implementation. The Colombian health reform labels them Provider Institutions of Health Services (Instituciones Prestadores de Servicios de Salud, or IPSSs).

TABLE 7.2: Structural Elements of Neoliberal Health Reform

Colombia Reform (1994)	Clinton Proposal (1994)	Obamacare (2010)
Large privately controlled organizations of health care providers		
"Provider Institutions of Health Services" (*Instituciones Prestadores de Servicios de Salud*, IPSSs)	"Accountable Health Partnerships" (AHPs)	Large organizations that include many physicians' practices, hospitals, and/or other health facilities; "Accountable Care Organizations" (ACOs) in Medicare
Large organizations of health care purchasers		
Corporations Promoting Health (*Empresas Promotoras de Salud*, EPSs)	Health Insurance Purchasing Cooperatives (HIPCs)	Large for-profit insurance corporations contract with networks of provider organizations for managed care coverage
Constriction of public hospitals and safety net providers		
Fiscal crisis of state and local public hospitals; many close	Predicted adverse effect on public hospitals and clinics	Fiscal crisis and closure of public hospitals; fiscal crisis of other safety-net providers
Tiered benefits packages		
Varying "health service packages"	"Uniform effective health benefits"	Designated by metals (bronze, silver, gold, platinum) in the "marketplaces"
Multi-payer and multi-payment financing		
• Capitation payments[†] • Copayments • Deductibles • Taxes	• Capitation payments[‡] • Copayments • Deductibles • Taxes	• Capitation payments[‡] • Copayments • Deductibles • Taxes
Changes in tax code		
• Increased payroll taxes for employees and employers	• Reduced tax deduction for "Cadillac" private plans that exceed minimum benefits standards • Tax incentive to buy less expensive coverage	• Excise tax on "Cadillac" private plans that exceed a specified cost limit. • Penalties through tax system for non-purchase of private sector health insurance

† Sources: patients, employers, public sector trust ("solidarity") funds (the latter being "contributory" for employed workers; and "subsidized" for low income and unemployed).

‡ Sources: patients, employers, public sector trust funds–Medicaid, Medicare.

In this model, for-profit managed care organizations (MCOs), usually subsidiaries of multinational insurance corporations, offer health plans competitively. In reality, competition is constrained by the small number of organizations large enough to meet the new laws' financial and infrastructure requirements, as well as by consolidation in the private insurance industry. The MCOs contract with or employ large numbers of health practitioners. This approach drastically reduces medical practice based on fee-for-service reimbursement. Instead, physicians and hospitals are largely absorbed into MCOs.

2. Organizations of purchasers. A second element of neoliberal proposals involves large organizations purchasing or facilitating the purchase of private health insurance, usually through MCOs. The Clinton proposal referred to these organizations as Health Insurance Purchasing Cooperatives (HPICs), even though they were not necessarily organized as member-owned or worker-owned cooperatives. Under Obamacare, the federal and state health insurance "exchanges"—later renamed "marketplaces" to reflect the reality of private, government-subsidized corporations—fulfill a similar role. The ACA does allow a small role for non-profit Consumer-Operated and Oriented Plans (COOPs), which so far have not achieved financial success.[17] In Colombia, the corresponding entities are called Corporations Promoting Health (Empresas Promotoras de Salud, or EPSs); some EPSs misleadingly include "cooperative" in their names (such as SALUDCOOP in Bogotá).[18]

Such organizations purchase or facilitate the purchase of health plans from private insurance corporations, which in turn contract with large, privately controlled organizations of health care providers, such as the AHPs, ACOs, or IPSSs described above. In the United States, the marketplaces serve the "non-group market," mainly people who previously paid for their own coverage or were uninsured. Private health plans in the marketplaces are heavily subsidized from general tax revenues, and public programs such as Medicaid and Medicare are rapidly becoming privatized. Instead of 1 to 2 percent overhead, as in the traditional Medicare program, private Medicare Advantage plans show overhead costs and profits of at least 14 percent.[19] In Colombia, purchasing organizations contract with provider organizations to deliver care for the previously uninsured, with funding provided by the federal government through national and local tax revenues and a payroll tax (termed the "subsidized regime"), and other purchasing organizations contract with companies that provide health insurance for workers and their families through the social security system (the "contributory regime").

3. Constriction of public hospitals and safety net providers. Public hospitals at the state, county, or municipal levels compete for patients covered under public programs like Medicaid or Medicare with

private, for-profit hospitals participating as subsidiaries or contractors of insurance corporations or MCOs. With less public-sector funding, public hospitals reduce services and programs, and many eventually close. Although community health centers (CHCs) sometimes see temporary improvements in funding, as in Obamacare, they increasingly serve as the providers of last resort for the remaining uninsured and underinsured. As a result, CHCs remain vulnerable to cutbacks and face an insecure future. Under Obamacare, multiple public hospitals have closed or have remained on the brink of closure.[20] In Colombia, public hospitals and clinics also have faced budget cuts and closures, and those that survive must confront the access barriers of the newly insured, such as high co-payments. Similar problems have occurred in Argentina, Mexico, Brazil, and other countries in Latin America.[21]

4. Tiered benefits packages. Neoliberal proposals define benefits packages in hierarchical tiers. The national reform provides a minimum package of benefits that experts view as essential, and individuals or their employers can buy additional coverage. Poor and near poor people in the U.S. Medicaid program are eligible for benefits that used to be free of cost-sharing, but since Obamacare passed, states increasingly have imposed premiums and co-payments.

With "minimum benefits packages," for instance, all women are entitled to Pap smears. But treatment of cervical cancer revealed by Pap-smear screening would not necessarily be covered, or might require cost sharing, leaving women vulnerable to different local government funding and policies. Benefits for treatment of cervical cancer for poor women with positive Pap smears have varied according to the financial resources and policies of different states or municipalities. This variability has occurred in Colombia, Mexico, and other countries that have adopted minimum benefits packages.

In the United States, neoliberal reforms also have included tiered benefits packages. The Clinton proposal aimed to create the "uniform effective health benefits" required under all health plans, but it also would have allowed the sale of additional benefits to patients or employers able to afford them. Under Obamacare, a package of minimum essential services may be only partially insured. Various metal names—bronze, silver, gold, platinum—identify the tiers of coverage, where bronze represents the lowest tier (covering 60 percent of in-network health care expenses) and platinum the highest (90 percent). Individual and family premiums cost the most under the most valuable metal, and out-of-pocket co-payments average the least. However, these percentages represent actuarial calculations of the insurance companies' financial payouts for services during a year among all beneficiaries in a specific tier. Therefore an individual or family expecting 60 percent coverage may pay much more in actual premiums, deductibles, and co-payments. Under Obamacare, the "value" of coverage in a tier is strictly a financial calculation, based on actuarial principles in accounting. Similar tiered benefit approaches to both services and medications have been instituted within managed care programs under Medicare (as well as Medicare Part D, for medications) and Medicaid.

5. Complex multi-payer and multi-payment financing. Financial flows under neoliberal health policies are complex (see Chart 7.1). The costs of administering these flows and other components of neoliberal policies are high (about 25 to 28 percent of total health care expenditures) and keep increasing. Under Obamacare, administrative overhead—also referred to as administrative waste, since the costs do not contribute to direct patient services—grew 10.6 percent in 2014, faster than any other component of health care except medications. Private insurance overhead is projected to increase by $273.6 billion from 2014 through 2022.[22]

Following are descriptions of the structure and sources of these various financial flows:

Outflow of payments: Each insured person is considered a "head," for whom a "capitation" must be paid to an insurance company or MCO. Capitated payments have been justified historically on the theory that organizations receiving the payments would encourage prevention, so their costs for providing expensive services would decrease, and their earnings increase. In practice, the prepaid capitation payments became a source of capital that MCOs could invest in the global financial marketplace, leading to an estimated return on equity of about 16 percent.[23]

CHART 7.1: Financial Flows under Neoliberal Health Reform

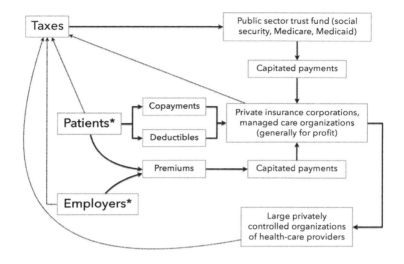

* Purchase of insurance policies for employers and patients mediated by large organizations of health care purchasers.

Inflow of funds: Funds for capitation payments come from several sources. One source involves premiums paid by workers and their families. Contributions from employers compose a second source. The proportion of premiums paid by workers and their families versus that paid by employers differs according to the benefit package selected by employers.

Public-sector trust funds provide a third source of capitated payments. Low-income individuals and families, the unemployed, and those without employer-provided health insurance are subjected to a "means test" requiring full documentation of their financial resources and expenses. Those with incomes below this means-tested limit, after other resources such as homes, cars, and prior savings are considered, receive a subsidy from a public-sector trust fund. Under the Clinton plan and Obamacare, the trust funds have involved Medicaid and Medicare. Medicaid trust funds include federal and state components that vary widely according to state-level decisions about using state revenues to improve eligibility and covered services under Medicaid. In the Colombian health program, the national social security system into which employees and employers contribute for health and retirement benefits became a public-sector trust fund (Fondo de Solidaridad y Garantía, or FOSYGA), used for capitated payments to private MCOs. Another trust fund, intended for the poor and uninsured, was created from the tax-generated budgets of the national Ministry of Health as well as the regional, state, and municipal health authorities (Fondo de Solidaridad del Régimen Subsidiado, Solidarity Fund of the Subsidized Regime).

Co-payments and deductibles constitute a fourth source of payments. Co-payments require out-of-pocket payments made at the time patients receive services. The rationale for co-payments rests on the largely untested assumption that people are less likely to use unneeded services if they must pay something when services are provided (the "point of delivery"). For the insured, the size of the co-payments usually decreases as premiums increase. Under Obamacare, for instance, those who pay higher premiums for the more precious metal plans usually pay lower co-payments at the point of delivery. The evidence that co-payments reduce unnecessary utilization for the non-poor is limited; for the poor, there is strong evidence that co-payments of any size reduce necessary care.[24] Deductibles are payments that patients must make at the beginning of each period of insurance coverage, before the insurance will begin to pay. In principle, deductibles are likewise intended to reduce unnecessary utilization, but like co-payments can actually become barriers to obtaining needed care. For instance, the least-precious metal tiers of Obamacare require deductibles as large as $6,000 per person per year, inhibiting patients from seeking anything other than catastrophic care.

Taxes are a fifth source for the inflow of capitated funds to insurance corporations. Workers pay such taxes as a deduction from their pay, and employers pay taxes as a proportion of their payrolls. In neoliberal programs, these payroll taxes shift to public-sector trust funds and then enter the flow of funds that MCOs receive for capitated services. But most neoliberal health programs also depend on additional taxes, usually general income taxes, to create and maintain the public-sector trust funds devoted to care for the poor. In the United States and Colombia, the income tax system remains regressive overall, as the rich pay a much smaller part of their income as taxes, exploiting the tax code's myriad loopholes and exemptions. As a result, the non-rich contribute proportionally more to neoliberal health programs through taxes, on top of their premiums, co-payments, and deductibles.

6. Changes in tax code. Partly because they increase administrative costs and profits, neoliberal reforms usually lead to higher taxes. In Colombia, payroll taxes for employers and employees have increased substantially, to approximately 11 percent.[25] Under the Clinton proposal, changes in the tax code would have restricted corporate and individual tax deductions for health care insurance, therefore providing incentives to purchase less expensive coverage overall. Obamacare reduces tax deductions and imposes a tax for so-called Cadillac insurance plans that go beyond the specified minimum coverage standards.

In addition, Obamacare calls for penalties, administered by the Internal Revenue Service, for those who do not purchase mandatory insurance coverage. One rationale for tax code changes usually involves claims that reduced tax deductions and tax penalties for non-adherence will lead to decreased overall costs for health care. However, the increased administrative costs of restructuring the tax code and then enforcing those changes generally go unrecognized. The changes in tax code will continue to evolve because the tax "reform" initiated by the Trump administration calls for elimination of the individual mandate to purchase health insurance.

APPRAISALS OF NEOLIBERAL HEALTH REFORMS

Those initiating neoliberal health reforms have produced evaluations that, as expected, indicate favorable results. For instance, the 2000 World Health Report of the World Health Organization (WHO), supported in part by the World Bank, ranked the world's health systems with a conceptual orientation and methodology that received criticism worldwide.[26] In the rankings, choice of insurance plan was a major criterion in evaluating health system performance. From this perspective, universal publicly delivered health systems that covered everyone but did not encourage choice among private insurers ranked lower than those that did. As a result, Colombia (ranked 22nd in the world and 1st in Latin America), Chile (33rd), Costa Rica (36th), and even the United States (37th) ranked higher than Cuba (39th), despite Cuba's much admired, accessible health system and outstanding health indicators. Brazil ranked very low, 125th, again due to its attempt to achieve a unified health system, codified in the Brazilian constitution of 1988.

The co-director of WHO's ranking project, Julio Frenk, later became an architect of neoliberal reform as Mexico's Minister of Health. He and his colleagues described Mexico's reform in *The Lancet*, again generating disapproval for their unsubstantiated claims of success.[27] Despite wide criticism of the WHO ranking project and of the reform in Mexico, Frenk and his co-workers became leading proponents of the neoliberal approach, which in recent years has taken on the misleading name "universal health coverage (UHC)," referring to insurance coverage.[28] UHC does not mean "health care for all"—a delivery system that provides equal services for the entire population regardless of an individual's or family's financial resources.[29]

As leaders of Latin American social medicine have pointed out, the UHC orientation has become "hegemonic" in global health policy circles.[30] Those limited studies that have analyzed UHC's outcomes in countries such as Colombia, Chile, and Mexico based on data rather than assertion of success have not confirmed ideological claims favoring managed care, competition in markets, efficiency, cost reduction, or quality. Under UHC, access barriers remain or worsen as costs and corporate profits expand.[31]

Such contrasts became clear in the Colombia health reform, which was considered pathbreaking by the neoliberal powers that be. The World Bank sponsored the reform and also evaluated it favorably, despite acknowledging weaknesses such as a lack of randomized data or ability to infer causality.[32] An ideological assumption underlying such evaluations, that the public sector interferes with the market, emerged from a study regarding Colombia released in 2009 by the

Inter-American Development Bank: "Achieving universal coverage faces several hurdles . . . because of the existence of safety-net providers that act as substitutes for insurance and provide incentives to ride the system for free. . . . The resistance of public hospitals to forgoing supply-side subsidies cannot be underestimated."[33]

By contrast, evaluations of the Colombia reform not tied to its sponsors have found mostly adverse effects. An influential study determined that in 2008 alone, Colombian citizens initiated approximately 143,000 lawsuits (tutelas) due to denial of treatment by private insurance companies, costs outstripped public funding, and inadequate "citizen consultation" in improving the program.[34] Other research showed that profit-seeking permeated the system, that insurance covered too few services, and that the system was unable to address the impact on health from poor living conditions.[35] An ethnographic study analyzed attempts to protect the system's market structure in the courts.[36] A prominent senator documented the system's monopolistic practices, delayed payments, corruption, high overhead, increasing legal actions due to denial of care, and illegal investment of health funds by for-profit insurance companies. Senator Jorge Robledo concluded: "Statute 100 does not work, because it is not a law intended for the health of Colombians, but rather a law intended to finance the business of the health of Colombians."[37]

Many countries have rejected the neoliberal model and instead have constructed health systems based on the goal of "health care for all" (HCA). Such countries strive to provide universal access to care without tiers of different benefit packages for rich and poor. For instance, Canada prohibits private insurance for services provided in its national health program. Because Canada's wealthy must participate in the publicly financed system, the presence of the entire population in a unitary system assures a high-quality national program. In Latin America, countries trying to advance the HCA model have included Bolivia, Brazil, Cuba, Ecuador, Uruguay, and Venezuela. The many failures of Obamacare may open a space, finally, for even the United States to pursue a national health program that does not follow the neoliberal model.

THE SINGLE-PAYER PROPOSAL

As a non-neoliberal model, a single-payer national health program (NHP) in the United States essentially would create "Improved Medicare for All." Under such a plan, the government collects payments from workers, employers, and Medicare recipients and then distributes funds to health care providers for the services that Medicare patients receive. Because it is such a simple system, the administrative costs under traditional Medicare average 1–2 percent.[38] The vast majority of Medicare expenditures pay for clinical services. Such a structure has achieved substantial savings by reducing administrative waste in Canada, Taiwan, and other countries.

The following features of a single-payer option come from the proposals of Physicians for a National Health Program (PNHP), which includes more than 20,000 members spanning all specialties, states, age groups, and practice settings.[39] (More information about the latest PNHP proposal can be found in chapter 12.) According to these proposals, coverage would be universal for all needed services, including medications and long-term care. There would be no out-of-pocket premiums, co-payments, or deductibles. Costs would be controlled by "monopsony" financing from a single, public source. The NHP would not permit competing private insurance and would eliminate multiple tiers of care for different income groups. Practitioners and clinics would be paid predetermined fees for services without any need for costly billing procedures. Hospitals would negotiate an annual global budget for all operating costs. For-profit, investor-owned facilities would be prohibited from participation. Most nonprofit hospitals would remain privately owned. To reduce overlapping and duplicative facilities, capital purchases and expansion would be budgeted separately, based on regional health-planning goals.

Funding sources would include current federal spending for Medicare and Medicaid, a payroll tax on private businesses less than what businesses currently pay for coverage, and an income tax on households, with a surtax on high incomes and capital gains. A small tax on stock transactions would be implemented, while state and local taxes for health care would be eliminated.[40] Under this financing plan, 95 percent of families would pay less for health care than they previously paid in insurance premiums, deductibles, co-payments, other out-of-pocket spending, and reduced wages.

From the corporate viewpoint, the insurance and financial sectors would lose a major source of capital accumulation. Other large and small businesses would experience a stabilization or reduction in health care costs. Companies that do not currently provide health insurance would pay more, but far less than the cost of buying private coverage.

National polls consistently have shown that about two-thirds of people in the United States favor the single-payer approach.[41] Within a month after the Trump administration failed to repeal Obamacare, more than a hundred members of Congress, led by Representative John Conyers and Senator Bernie Sanders, had co-sponsored single-payer legislation.[42] What, then, are the obstacles to a single-payer plan, and should such a program be the ultimate goal for the U.S. health system?

MOVING BEYOND SINGLE PAYER

The coming failure of Obamacare will become a moment of transformation in the United States, where neoliberalism has come home to roost. For that moment, those struggling for a just and accessible health system will need to address some profound changes that have emerged during the era of neoliberalism. These changes pertain to the shifting social class position of health professionals and to the increasingly oligopolistic and financialized character of the health insurance industry.

As described in Part One of this book, the social-class position of physicians and other health professionals has changed drastically. Previously most physicians worked in individual or group practices. Although some were employees receiving relatively high salaries and benefits, most were small entrepreneurs. In the "fee-for-service" system, they seldom accumulated capital on the scale of industrialists or financiers, but they still saw themselves and others saw them as members of an "upper class." Some Marxist-oriented theorists of class viewed them as members of a "professional managerial class."[43]

Physicians increasingly have become employees of hospitals or practices at least partially owned by large health systems. In a large 2015 survey, 63 percent of all physicians reported being employed, including 72 percent of women physicians.[44] These changes mainly reflect the increased costs of owning a private practice due to billing and other administrative requirements. In the average practice, annual overhead costs have reached about $83,000 per physician in the United States, compared to $22,000 in Canada.[45] As a result, doctors mostly have become employees of hospital and health system corporations, where relatively high salaries tend to mask the reality of employee status.

With loss of control over the work process and a reduced ability to generate very high incomes compared to other professional workers, the medical profession has become proletarianized.[46] Due to a mystique of professionalism and incomes that nonetheless remain high, physicians usually do not realize that their malaise reflects their changing social-class position. In a way, they have joined that highest stratum of workers to which V. I. Lenin and others referred as the "aristocracy of labor."[47] From Samir Amin's perspective of political economy, the current wave of "generalized proletarianization" has engulfed the medical profession: "A rapidly growing proportion of workers are no more than sellers of their labor power to capital . . . a reality that should not be obscured by the apparent autonomy conferred on them by their legal status."[48]

Beyond the changing class position of health professionals, the transition beyond Obamacare will need to address the oligopolistic character of the insurance industry, alongside the consolidation of large health systems. Obamacare has increased the flow of capitated public and private funds into the insurance industry. Through this process, Obamacare has extended the overall financialization of the global capitalist economy.[49]

In this context, it is important to reconsider the distinction between national health insurance (NHI) and a national health service (NHS). NHI involves socialization of payments for health services but usually leaves intact private ownership at the level of infrastructure. Except for a small proportion of institutions like public hospitals and clinics, the means of production in health care under NHI remains privately owned. Canada is the best-known model of NHI. The PNHP single-payer proposal, as well as the U.S. congressional legislation that embodies the singer-payer approach, is based on the Canadian model of NHI.

NHS, by comparison, involves socialization of both payment for health services and the infrastructure through which services are provided. Under NHS, the state generally owns and operates hospitals, clinics, and other health institutions, which become part of the public sector rather than remaining under private ownership and control. In the capitalist world, Scotland, Wales, and Sweden provide examples of NHS, where most health infrastructure exists within the public sector and most health professionals are employees of the state. The state apparatus includes elements that provide "welfare state" services like health care and other elements that protect the capitalist economic system. In the socialist world, Cuba offers the clearest remaining model of an NHS in which a private sector does not exist. The legislative proposal introduced in the United States during the 1970s and 1980s by Representative Ronald Dellums explicitly adopted the goals of an NHS.

The PNHP single-payer proposal emerged from a retreat in New Hampshire during 1986, where activists struggled with these distinctions. Although most participants at the retreat had worked hard for the Dellums NHS proposal, they reached a consensus—albeit with some ambivalence—to shift their work to an NHI proposal based on Canada. The rationale for this shift involved two main considerations. First, Canada's proximity and cultural similarity to the United States would make it more palatable for the U.S. population, and especially its congressional representatives. Secondly, a Canadian-style NHI proposal could be "doctor-friendly." Under the PNHP proposal, physicians could continue to work in private practice, clinics, or hospitals. The main difference for physicians was that payments would be socialized so that the physicians would not have to worry about billing and collecting their fees for services provided.

While PNHP has achieved great success in its research and policy work, these efforts, and those of many other organizations supporting single payer, have not yet generated a broad social movement in behalf of a Canadian-style NHI. Meanwhile, the neoliberal model with all its benefits for the ruling class and drawbacks for everyone else has gained hegemony. Partly as a result, physicians and other health professionals are becoming proletarianized employees of an increasingly consolidated, profit-driven, financialized health care system. And under Obamacare, the capitalist state has continued to prioritize protection of the capitalist economic system, in this case by overseeing huge subsidies for private insurance and pharmaceutical corporations.

Under these circumstances, it is no longer evident that socialization of payments for health services under a single-payer NHI is the only goal toward which progressive forces should struggle. PNHP calls for the removal of for-profit corporations from U.S. health care. But that change will not occur within the context of capitalism as we know it. As neoliberalism draws to a close and as Obamacare fails, a much more fundamental transformation needs to reshape not just health care, but also the capitalist state and capitalist society.

8—Austerity and Health Care

Adam Gaffney and Carles Muntaner

Events in the eurozone belie any naïve notion that movement toward universal health care progresses in a linear, unidirectional fashion.[1] Following the 2008 collapse of Wall Street (which, after a government bailout, soon rose again), a vortex of financial contagion spread throughout the world, dragging prolonged recession, soaring unemployment, and general misery in its wake.[2] Health and health systems were not immune from the consequences of these powerful currents.[3]

Still, as others have pointed out, the impact of economic recession on health is a complex phenomenon, one that is not always harmful[4] and sometimes beneficial, and is contingent on (or modified by) specific policy decisions made by the state.[5] The point of this chapter is not to synthesize or criticize the literature on the epidemiologic relationship between health and recession over time or over national boundaries. Instead, we focus on how, during the Great Recession and the austerity that accompanied it, political actors in the eurozone moved against public health care systems.[6] In all three countries that we examine in this chapter—Greece, Spain (with an eye to Catalonia), and the United Kingdom (mainly England)—the ultimate impact of these changes was to roll back the universal quality and strength of the systems.[7]

There are also important parallels among the changes in each nation. These changes fall under the umbrella of neoliberalism, which can be defined as an ideology and set of policies favoring a sharp "reduction of state interventions in economic and social activities and the deregulation of labor and financial markets, as well as of commerce and investments."[8] For each nation, we document movement along what we describe as the four axes of health system neoliberalism, namely: 1) health system austerity, 2) a retreat from universalism, 3) a rise in cost sharing, and 4) health system privatization.[9] Notably, and specifically in the case of the English National Health Service (NHS), such changes should be construed as part of a much longer historical process. We conclude with some thoughts about the ramifications of these developments for the United States. For those of us advocating a single-payer health reform, it is commonplace (and reasonable) to contrast the fragmented U.S. system with the universalism of other nations, including those of Europe. Yet, as we hope to demonstrate, that contrast is not always as stark as we may at times suggest. The reality is that a public system of universal health care is not a terminus. It is not constructed and then passively enjoyed forever after. A variety of political forces, aligned with health care corporations, frequently multinational in reach, have long sought its undoing.[10]

GREECE

Perhaps more than any other nation in the eurozone, Greece has suffered from the entwined, destructive processes of economic recession and fiscal austerity.[11] These processes have adversely affected the health of the nation and its health care system. Here, we first examine how a number of factors made Greece's health system especially vulnerable to austerity's onslaught. Second, we document how changes to its health system proceeded along the four neoliberal health policy axes. Third, we briefly discuss how recent political events in Greece color this still evolving picture.

To begin, it's worth emphasizing that Greece was, comparatively speaking, a latecomer in the development of a public health care system. As Vicente Navarro has noted, three out of four "PIGS" nations —Portugal, Ireland, Greece, and Spain—were ruled by right-wing dictatorships in the post–Second World War era. As with Spain and Portugal, this political context no doubt contributed to the weakness of the welfare state in Greece.[12]

Early reforms were mostly incremental steps toward a limited social insurance system. A 1934 law created an insurance scheme for some workers, and reforms in the 1950s and 1960s expanded this coverage to other groups. However, comprehensive health reform awaited the end of the dictatorship and the election in 1981 of the Socialist Party (PASOK). In 1983, PASOK passed Law 1397/83, which created Greece's National Health Service. The law was intended to establish a universal health care system that would provide equal care via public funding and provision, with private practice largely curtailed. In reality, key provisions of this legislation went unimplemented, however, so that a "comprehensive and universal health care system," as a 2010 review of Greece's health system put it, "has not yet been established."[13] Still, despite its shortcomings, Greece's public health system was a critical component of its safety net, providing health care to the great majority of its citizens.

The second factor to consider is Greece's vulnerable and subordinate political and economic position. As Yanis Varoufakis has emphasized, after joining the eurozone, Greece (like Spain) was flooded with euros from German and other European banks. This influx of capital created a bubble that, combined with low revenues from a regressive tax system, tax evasion, and fraud, later led to a fiscal disaster.[14] Greece was in an especially precarious position even compared to Spain: alone among eurozone nations, it had in fact been surreptitiously overspending relative to taxation in the years leading up to the recession, which Goldman Sachs helped it to conceal, a fact that came to light after the onset of the financial crisis.[15] These various factors contributed to the depth of Greece's recession and debt crisis.

The hammer of international capital fell hard and fast on Greece in the wake of the disaster on Wall Street. Greece's financial crisis helped bring to a close a brief period of a pro-Keynesian consensus (that is, expansionary fiscal and monetary policy), and its replacement by a punishing pro-austerity line pushed by Germany and the European Central Bank (ECB).[16] "The offensive against Keynesianism at the global level," as political economist Mark Blyth describes in *Austerity: The History of a Dangerous Idea*, "was married to the discovery of the Greek debt crisis and amplified via the threat of contagion to establish fiscal austerity as the new policy du jour."[17] This anti-Keynesian line, it is important to note, was subsumed within an already existing anti-welfare state agenda that the recession helped unleash.[18] Greece's health care system suffered under the assault, which unfolded along the four axes we have outlined.

We begin with axis 1, health-system austerity. Facing large deficits and no longer able to borrow on international markets, Greece was soon facing bankruptcy. It turned to the "Troika"— the decision-making group representing the ECB, the European Commission, and the International Monetary Fund (IMF)—for two bailouts totaling €240 billion (US$265 billion), and in the process agreed to a policy of severe economic austerity, with an estimated 90 percent of the funds used to bail out the government's creditors.[19] The first bailout, agreed to in May 2010, required a reduction in public health spending to 6 percent of gross domestic product (GDP). "Where that 6 percent target came from," note David Stuckler and Sanjay Basu in their book *The Body Economic: Why Austerity Kills*, "was never mentioned, but it was puzzling, since all other Western countries spend far more than that to maintain basic healthcare."[20]

The second bailout of €130 billion (US$172 billion), agreed to by the Greek government and European authorities during February 2012, called for further cuts.[21] These cuts had immediate ramifications for Greece's health system. In the first four years after the onset of the crisis, from 2009 to 2012, Greece experienced a 23.7 percent fall in total health spending, and a slightly greater 25.2 percent fall in public health spending.[22] The impact of such cuts could be discerned in media reports. "At public hospitals," noted the *New York Times*, "doctors report shortages of all kinds of supplies, from toilet paper to catheters to syringes. Computerized equipment has gone unrepaired and is no longer in use. Nurses are handling four times the patients they should, and wait times for operations—even cancer surgeries—have grown longer."[23] Additionally, some have linked particular program cuts to the emergence or reemergence of major epidemics. For instance, epidemics of West Nile virus and malaria occurred in the wake of cutbacks in insect control programs, and an

HIV epidemic followed reductions in funding to needle exchange and condom programs.[24]

Health-system austerity, however, was also accompanied by a "retreat from universalism," or axis 2. In 2011, Greece's seven social insurance organizations, which had previously provided coverage to almost all Greeks, were merged into a single fund, the National Health Services Organization (EOPYY).[25] Although this change might seem a welcome step away from fragmentation and toward universalism and unity, the new fund did little for the rising numbers of the uninsured.[26] EOPYY provided coverage for a maximum of two years following loss of employment, thereby leaving an estimated 2 million uninsured and without stable access to health care.[27] Additionally, the "common benefits package" of the EOPYY excluded many previously covered services: "A basic characteristic of the common package," notes a recent study, "is the reduction in benefits to which the insured are entitled. . . . Moreover, the introduction of a negative list for medicines [i.e., non-reimbursable drugs] in 2012 resulted in the withdrawal of reimbursement status of various drugs that had previously been reimbursed."[28]

This decline in health care access saw a concomitant rise in Greeks' use of charity clinics, run by organizations like Doctors Without Borders and Doctors of the World, that previously had been relied on mainly by undocumented immigrants.[29] As the result of the decline in health care access, an estimated 60,000 older adults reportedly went without needed care,[30] and an overall and significant rise in the likelihood of Greeks having "unmet medical needs" emerged in the early years of the crisis.[31]

There were also changes along the third axis of health care neoliberalism: cost sharing. Increases in co-payments for drugs, outpatient visits, and hospitalizations went into effect in 2011, albeit with exclusions for some groups.[32] Co-payments rose even more for specific conditions. For diabetes medications, for instance, co-payments increased from 0 percent to 10 percent, and those for coronary heart disease went up from 10 percent to 25 percent.[33]

Finally, efforts toward health system privatization (axis 4) accompanied these changes. In 2011, the Ministry of Health announced that at the same time it would reduce the number of beds in public hospitals, it would reserve hundreds of beds at public hospitals for patients with private health insurance.[34] The salaries of physicians serving the public health system were cut, while simultaneously these doctors were newly allowed to see private patients in public hospitals, a practice, some argue, that could encourage doctors to keep long public waiting lists so as to "syphon off public patients to their private practices."[35] Others have also noted that restrictions on the establishment of for-profit entities like health facilities and labs were lifted.[36]

Taken together, these policy changes created a substantial threat to the universalism of the Greek public health system.[37] There was, for instance, a 44 percent increase, from 2004 to 2011, in the proportion of Greeks who did not receive medical care for financial reasons; those with low income, low education, and no health insurance were especially likely to have such unmet needs.[38] And the gap in healthcare access between the well-off and the poor widened greatly over the course of the crisis.[39] In the longer term, it is possible that a combination of declining public resources and rising needs "could lead to a de facto two-tier health system where those who can afford to pay for private health services will be able to meet their health needs, while those without sufficient resources must attempt to access services from a severely strained public system."[40] And finally, there have been concerning trends not only in healthcare, but in health.[41] Austerity coincided with a rise in suicides.[42] There was an apparently adverse impact on mortality for certain conditions.[43] Meanwhile, Greeks' health—as they rated it—suffered.[44]

Yet the bludgeon of austerity has not been passively received. In the historic January 2015 elections, Greeks voted into power Syriza, a left-wing coalition with a strong anti-austerity platform, led by Alexis Tsipras. Syriza's platform included a plank to roll back the neoliberal assault on Greece's public health care system. The new government called for the provision of health care to the uninsured, the elimination of the new drug and outpatient co-payments, the hiring of more health workers, and an increase in the provision of primary care services.[45] Yet, although it was able to eliminate the €5 (US$5.9) hospital visit co-payment,[46] the ability of the new government to undo the damage inflicted by years of neoliberal attack was hampered by its subordinate economic and political position.[47] After months of tense negotiations and a referendum in favor of the government's anti-austerity stance, Tsipras and Syriza all but folded to Greece's international creditors. In the summer of 2015, Tsipras agreed to an €86 billion (US$ 95 billion) bailout,[48] with conditions at least as harsh as those that Syriza had previously rejected. This political decision by the Syriza leadership was highly criticized by members of the party, including its Marxist former minister of finances Yanis Varoufakis, and led to a split and the creation of a new left party, Popular Unity.[49] Tsipras nonetheless led Syriza to victory in September after calling for new elections. Yet austerity was set to stay. Indeed, among the new government's priorities, BBC News noted, was a promise to "reinstate charges in state health service originally scrapped by Syriza."[50]

The direction of future events is difficult to discern, for the capitulations of 2015 may have only prolonged the day of reckoning. Though Greece eventually emerged from recession, its suffocating levels of unemployment, and resultant human misery, persisted.[51] The fate of its health care system, it is clear, is intertwined with the fate of its politics as a whole, and in particular with the ability of the Greek Left to counter the power of the international financial community.

SPAIN

Similar processes played out in Spain, another nation at the so-called periphery of the eurozone. Spain's economic position within the European Union laid the groundwork for austerity.[52] As in Greece, Spain's adoption of the euro led to a massive influx of capital from the wealthy EU nations, which in the case of Spain was mostly channeled into the housing sector. Low taxes on high incomes and wealth, in conjunction with tax evasion, left the nation's fiscal position vulnerable to economic disruption.[53] Spain suffered greatly after the bursting of its housing bubble, and the ensuing collapse of government revenues sent it into recession and austerity.[54]

Both the neoliberal Spanish Socialist Worker Party (Partido Socialista Obrero Español, PSOE)[55] and, to a greater extent, the Francoist right-wing People's Party (Partido Popular, PP)[56] adopted policies that moved the Spanish health system toward neoliberalism in multiple domains, as in Greece: health-system austerity, a retreat from universalism, cost sharing, and privatization.[57] During the summer of 2011, the PSOE agreed to modify the Spanish constitution to comply with the dictates of the EU,[58] a decision that set the stage for austerity following the 2011 elections that returned the conservative PP to power.[59]

PP prime minister Mariano Rajoy predictably justified austerity with the argument that the Spanish welfare state was not sustainable. Yet, in reality, Spain began the recession with a level of social spending well below the EU-15 average before the onset of the recession: 39 percent of its GDP compared to 46 percent for the fifteen core countries of the European Union.[60] With respect to health spending, in 2008 Spain was spending only 6.5 percent of its GDP on public health as compared with the 7.3 percent EU-15 average (conversely, Spanish private health expenditures were the highest in the EU-15).[61] Since 2009, austerity has been drastic in the health sector, with a €15 billion to €21 billion (US$21 billion to $29 billion) overall cut in health services funds.[62] Shortly after taking power, the PP government passed a law that significantly cut social spending, with reductions of 13.7 percent in 2012 and 16.2 percent in 2013.[63] Cuts affected all autonomous communities, though some were affected more than others, as in the case of Catalonia (now Republic of Catalonia).

Health care reforms and cuts included co-payments and a retreat from universal coverage through the denial of medical care to immigrants. Pensioners were the main target of co-payments, with non-poor retired people asked to pay 10 percent of the price of their drugs. Workers then had to pay a co-payment for drugs, and the system was extended to other benefits such as non-urgent ambulance services. Pensions already were insufficient to guarantee a modest living standard in Spain, with most pensioners receiving less than €650 (US$755) monthly in 2011. In fact, due to the staggering unemployment rate (more than 25 percent of the total adult workforce and

50 percent of the younger workforce at the height of the recession, and 17% and 38% respectively in 2017), many more families have had to rely on their pensions for their collective survival. This situation placed elderly pensioners in the unfortunate dilemma of choosing between drugs and other basic necessities.[64]

The effect of austerity on the Spanish health system has varied among Spain's seventeen autonomous communities (CCAA), each of which holds substantial control over its internal health administration, including spending decisions. Catalonia, the richest region of Spain, provides an important regional (now national) example of how the Great Recession translated into severe health care cuts, rising inequities, cost sharing, and privatization. Health-system austerity began early in Catalonia under the rule of a nationalist conservative coalition, Convergencia i Unio (CiU). Catalonia has a distinctive health care system with a substantial private presence.[65] Its regional government was one of the first to enact deep cuts in health spending.[66] The ruling CiU party used the recession to justify deep cuts but also to extend its privatization agenda. Although nominally state assets like hospitals cannot be directly transferred to private entities, changes to the mercantile law under which health care organizations operate have resulted in a degree of de facto privatization (that is, they can operate for profit and under private sector labor laws).[67] Former Harvard economics professor and Catalan minister of the economy Andreu Mas-Collel was candid when he told potential investors that the recession would bring opportunities for investment in the health sector.[68] Boi Ruiz, the CiU minister of health and former director of the association of private hospitals, encouraged citizens (on public TV) to join "mutuals," as Catalan private health care organizations are known. Under his watch the Catalan health care system suffered from severe cuts, 14 percent since 2010, or about €1.5 billion (US$1.7 billion).[69] Among the consequences of austerity, we find longer waiting lists for surgery, referrals to specialists, and primary care. In terms of overall performance, including finance, resources, pharmacy, and patient satisfaction, Catalonia ranked fifteenth out of the seventeen CCAAs in Spain.[70]

Of note, the government of Democratic Convergence of Catalonia (Convergencia Democrática de Cataluña, or CDC), a recent addition to the camp of pro-Catalan independence parties under the Democratic Party (PdCAT) name, has used the well-known observation that many aggregate health indicators tend to do well in recessions (for example, fewer occupational deaths and traffic deaths) to promote a positive spin on cuts and privatizations.[71] Many remained unconvinced, however, and, as in Greece, there have been major popular efforts to resist these changes. Local organizations such as Pasucat, La Marea Blanca, Dempeus per la Salut, media outlets such as Café amb Llet, and the Candidatures de Unio Popular (CUP)—the anti-capitalist, socialist, pro-independence, and feminist party in the Catalan Parliament—have challenged health care austerity in the streets, the media, the parliament, and the courts.[72]

In this struggle there have been some successes. Following a major corruption case involving the CDC that resulted in a conviction, the public became more aware of corruption, including in the health system.[73] Notorious CDC policies have included the channeling of public patients to private health providers;[74] the ceding of control of public assets to private providers;[75] a 25 percent cut in wages for workers in the public sector;[76] and the sale of medical records to private companies.[77] This state of affairs contributed to the successful toppling of the CDC president (Artur Mas) by the anti-capitalist and pro-Catalan independence CUP party.

Still, health care budget cuts totaling €1.5 billion (US$1.7 billion) between the years 2010 and 2014 translated into downsizing, closure of wards, reduced hours of operation, and increased waiting times, with resultant suffering and perhaps even preventable deaths. Staff reductions and wage cuts also have adversely affected the health care workforce. The privatization of the public health system has been pursued via the backdoor of consortia—entities with a majority of public ownership that can be privately managed to give control of public assets to for-profit businesses. Commodification occurs within poorly regulated public hospitals, where private, for-profit, after-hours business is encouraged using public assets as well as through double billing (by restricting access to covered services, the government effectually encourages enrollment in private health insurance). According to Marea Blanca (White Tide), an organization of left-wing health care workers, the transfer of public funds to private entities from 2011 to 2013 reached nearly €250 million (US$290 million).[78]

The Catalan government denied the charges of privatization, since assets were still nominally public, and further argued that the cuts were 1) the consequence of IMF, European Community, and ECB austerity policies toward the Spanish state; and 2) the Spanish state's long-standing imbalanced tax levy on Catalonia, which is often claimed to be around 9 percent of Catalan GDP, or €16 billion (US$18.8 billion). Such grievances including the turning down of anti-austerity policies passed by the Catalan parliament (against poverty and for gender equity in pay) have contributed to the chain of events resulting in the Catalan referendum of independence and the declaration of the Catalan Republic in October 2017.[79]

Turning from southern to northern Europe, we will see that though the economic situation in England is somewhat different, the neoliberal health policy agenda of the Conservative-led government is surprisingly similar to those of Greece and Spain.

ENGLAND

"You do not need to be a conspiracy theorist," wrote health policy scholar David Hunter in the *British Medical Journal* in 2013, "to conclude that from 1 April the NHS in England will never be the same again."[80] Hunter was referencing the date when the Health and Social Care Act, passed by the Conservative-led government in 2012, went into effect. The legislation sent the English NHS down a path of commercialization, privatization, and fragmentation, away from the universalist vision of its founder, Aneurin Bevan. Policy changes in the English NHS, coupled with ongoing austerity measures, are another instance of a neoliberal health policy "success" in Europe.

These developments have occurred in the context of neoliberal so-called reforms that stretch back to the government of Margaret Thatcher. For instance, Allyson Pollock and colleagues have critically examined commercialization within the English NHS that began with Thatcher and extended throughout the years of the New Labour government that came to power in 1997. Neoliberal reforms of the early Thatcher years extended along all four axes:[81]

- Health system austerity: a general squeeze on NHS spending, at least until later in the 1980s when funding was increased in conjunction with the implementation of the "internal market";
- Retreat from universalism: reduction in NHS services, specifically in dental care, eye care, and long-term care;
- Cost-sharing: increased user fees for drugs, eye care, and dental care;
- Privatization: top-down injection of a managerial culture drawn from the private sector, outsourcing of various hospital services to private corporations, and privatization of long-term care.

The most transformative policy shift, the so-called internal market, was conceived in Thatcher's later years but carried out under the administration of John Major. This reorganization of NHS funding and administration was partially inspired by the U.S. economist Alain Enthoven (whose influence in the United States, Europe, and Latin America is discussed in chapter 7). The impact of the internal market was twofold. First, by dividing the NHS into "buyers" of health services, consisting of select primary care practices together with local health authorities, and "sellers," comprising hospitals and secondary care providers, the internal market engineered an enormous rise in administrative and managerial expenses, funds that otherwise might have been spent on clinical care. Second, the establishment of the internal market, which Pollock and colleagues call a "seminal moment for the global health care industry," helped lay the groundwork for the later entry of commercial firms into the publicly funded health care business.[82]

Although the Labour Party ran successfully against Conservative health reforms in the 1997 elections, its victory brought no respite from privatization, but instead its acceleration, as historian Charles Webster notes. Blair's New Labour Party adopted Tory health care policy on three key levels: an acceptance of NHS austerity, an embrace of privatization, and a "policy of continuity" for the internal market.[83]

Other initiatives, for instance the "foundation trusts" that allowed public hospitals to function increasingly like private corporations, carried these initiatives forward.[84]

After the economic crisis of 2008, elections brought a coalition government to power that was led by David Cameron's Conservative Party. Cameron's government brought about change in health care in the United Kingdom, particularly England, along all four axes. First, and most visibly, was health-system austerity. Unlike Greece and Spain, which were subjected to the transnational economic and political might of the Troika, austerity was not forced upon the United Kingdom: the Conservative-led government elected to self-inflict it. As compared to the United States, where a degree of fiscal and monetary Keynesianism attenuated the impact of the recession through a huge, taxpayer-supported bailout of the largest private banks and industries, the United Kingdom embraced austerity with gusto.[85]

Compared to other areas of public spending, the NHS remained relatively protected. Still, a 2012 analysis described what the NHS potentially faced in the coming years if spending were merely maintained: "A decade of flat spending on health in real terms would be unprecedented in England, or indeed in other advanced Western economies."[86] The reality is that "flat" spending, or even the 0.9 percent annual increase that the NHS has received since 2010,[87] in a growing and aging society with rising demand for health services, is tantamount to financial strangulation. As the chief economist of the King's Fund, John Appleby, described, the NHS experienced the most meager growth in spending since its inception. Indeed, as a percent of GDP, he noted, NHS spending will fall in the coming decade.[88] This prediction is noteworthy because the NHS already has very low health spending. According to numbers from the Organisation for Economic Cooperation and Development (OECD), the United Kingdom spent 8.5 percent of GDP on health care in 2013, as compared to 16.4 percent in the United States (many Western European nations fall in between). The effects of this spending pattern included cuts in services, shutdowns, and a salary squeeze for the NHS workforce. In January 2015, for example, nearly twenty hospitals were forced to temporarily stop all elective surgeries.[89] "Junior doctors" went on strike in the face of a new adverse contract. Headlines continued to invoke NHS "overspending," but as many emphasized, the reality was that funds were insufficient in relation to the system's needs.[90] Moreover, a November 2015 spending review revealed that even though some areas of NHS spending will increase by 2020, others, in particular various public health programs, would see real cuts in coming years.[91]

Austerity policies also exerted their effects in the context of the 2012 Health and Social Care Act. The timely book, *NHS SOS*, provided a critical assessment of this law, as well as its context and impact.[92] The law advanced the neoliberal health agenda along all four axes, albeit in a relatively obscure manner. An analysis of the bill by lawyer Peter Roderick together with Pollock, David Price, and other colleagues contended that the bill would accomplish a more radical change than many realized, indeed essentially ending universal health care in England. As they argued, a fundamental legal foundation of the NHS since its inception in 1946 was the government's explicit responsibility to provide comprehensive health care throughout the country. A critical provision of the 2012 law terminated this legal responsibility. The duty of the NHS previously was carried out through administrative units accountable to the government and responsible for the care of everyone within their geographical "catchment areas." These long-standing units, which went by different names over the years, were replaced by the law with "Clinical Commissioning Groups" (CCGs) that were no longer responsible for all the residents in a defined area and which therefore had a much diluted accountability for the provision of comprehensive care for a set group of patients. These CCGs, like U.S. managed care organizations, were only responsible for their members.[93]

The authors of *NHS SOS* pointed out that as a result of these changes, the 2012 law endangered the very provision of free care in England, a hallmark of the NHS since its founding. The CCGs can determine which health care services the NHS will cover free of charge at the point of service, and which would be excluded. Those services that the CCGs elect not to cover would become prime pickings for the for-profit health service providers, sold to patients at a price in a medical marketplace. A provision that permitted NHS foundation trusts to receive nearly half their revenue from non-NHS care further fostered this move toward privatization, while at the same time another section of the law encouraged the "tendering" of health services to the private sector.[94] As a result, the law will "transform the NHS from a nationally mandated public service . . . into a service based on commercial contracting."[95] At the same time, expected reductions in services from cash-starved trusts may ultimately "reduce NHS-funded care to a basic package of services."[96]

To summarize, the trajectory has been one of ongoing austerity, falling quality, workforce strain, a reduced package of NHS services, and a growing for-profit health care sector. Such developments favor the emergence of a multi-tiered health care system. Even if the resulting system continues to provide universal coverage, it nonetheless represents a retreat from the model of a universal system that provided a unified, single tier of high quality care to all.

Again, as elsewhere, the ultimate outcome of these developments is far from certain. For instance, in 2016 "junior doctors," akin to interns and residents in the U.S. system, began launching strikes in response to a new contract that the Conservative government stated it would impose.[97] In 2015, a remarkable Labour primary election brought to the leadership of the party the leftist Jeremy Corbyn, who denounced NHS privatization in no uncertain terms. "The Tory Health and Social Care Act is designed to destroy the NHS and make it a service of last resort, instead of providing a universal service," Corbyn wrote.[98] He also argued in favor of adequately financing the NHS and terminating the private finance initiative (PFI) approach to hospital financing, with "an end to privatization in health," as his campaign website put it.[99] The commitment of the broader Labour Party leadership to a radical rejection of privatization and restoration of funding, however, remained less clear.[100] Moreover, in the wake of the historic "Brexit" referendum in June 2016, elites in the Labour Party launched an attempted coup to displace Corbyn from leadership of the party. It failed, however, and instead succeeded only in precipitating a huge influx of new members to Labour while strengthening the left-wing composition of Corbyn's shadow government.[101]

Subsequently, in 2017, Prime Minister Theresa May called a snap election, assuming Conservatives would coast to victory, congealing her government's mandate. But the results were humiliating for the Conservatives, who ceded seats to Labour, lost their majority, and hung on to power only by forming a coalition government with the reactionary Democratic Unionist Party of Northern Ireland. As this book goes to press, it is feasible that Corbyn could head the next government of the United Kingdom.

The fate of the NHS will depend on the outcome of these political contests. The continued squeeze on the NHS may result in its further disintegration or dismantling in the short-term. However, the resistance that austerity provokes, whether from health care workers, the populace at large, or more likely both, may open a window of opportunity for resistance and counterattack.

Conclusions

As we have seen, an offensive on public health systems in three European nations, propelled by conservative political parties working hand-in-hand with international financial institutions, accompanied the Great Recession and the austerity regime it produced. In each nation, the offensive unfolded along four axes of health care neoliberalism: austerity health spending, a rollback of universalism, a rise in payments required at time of use, and privatization of the delivery system itself. We can view these axes from the "reverse" perspective as well: the extent to which a health system receives adequate public funding (axis 1), is universal with respect to population coverage, provider access, and benefits offered (axis 2), lacks financial barriers to care at time of use (axis 3), and is removed from the command and control of profit-seeking capital (axis 4) is a measure of a social right to health care in a nation. Rather than placing health systems in one of two binary bins, those that deliver health care as a public good on the one hand and those that sell it as a commodity on the other, it may be more useful to construe systems along these multi-dimensional lines. Creating a social right to health care necessitates a universal public health system that delivers care as a social good, which in turn requires "de-commodification" in each of these four dimensions.

Unfortunately, the exact opposite has been occurring in the euro-zone. This is not surprising. Even when a strong system of public health care has been created, class interests and affiliated parties and policy actors will often seek its dismantling. There is, after all, a great deal of money to be made. The fate of "universal health care" is not predetermined, but depends on the outcome of ongoing political struggles, both at the grassroots and electoral levels.

From the U.S. perspective, a few lessons become apparent. First, even if and when a single-payer national health program is achieved, the possibility of reversal or at least a rollback will remain. Similarly, currently existing public health care programs such as Medicare and Medicaid remain threatened by these very same political dynamics. Indeed, Republican "Trumpcare" bills in 2017 aimed to decimate Medicaid. Second, in seeking to create a better health care system that draws on health care systems abroad, we must remain vigilant about the limitations and vulnerabilities of those models, so as not to replicate their weaknesses.

Finally, these transnational dynamics underscore the importance of movements of international solidarity in the protection and advancement of health care systems. Though divided by political borders, throughout the globe we are facing similar, albeit not identical, challenges from the neoliberal health care agenda. There is no doubt much to be gained in working collaboratively as internationalists, as we struggle toward health care systems based on solidarity rather than profitability.

PART FOUR

The Trajectory of Imperialism's Health Component

9—Imperialism's Health Component

Howard Waitzkin and Rebeca Jasso-Aguilar

Medicine and public health have played important roles in imperialism. With the emergence of the United States as an imperial power during the early twentieth century, linkages among imperialism, public health, and health institutions were forged through several key mediating institutions. Philanthropic organizations sought to use public health initiatives to address several challenges faced by expanding capitalist enterprises: labor productivity, safety for investors and managers, and the costs of care. From modest origins, international financial institutions and trade agreements eventually morphed into a massive structure of trade rules that have exerted profound effects on public health and health services worldwide. International health organizations have collaborated with corporate interests to protect commerce and trade. In this chapter, we clarify the connections among these mediating institutions and imperialism.

IMPERIALISM AND HEALTH

Although it is a complex, multifaceted phenomenon, imperialism in simple terms refers to an expansion of economic activities beyond national boundaries—especially investment, sales, extraction of raw materials, and labor to produce commodities and services—and to the social, political, and economic effects of this expansion. Empire yields many advantages for economically dominant nations. Ventures to build and to maintain empire have involved both capitalist and socialist countries (including the so-called social imperialism of the former Soviet Union). For centuries, imperialism included military conquest and the maintenance of colonies under direct political control. The decline of colonialism in the twentieth century, however, led to the emergence of political and economic "neocolonialism," by which poor countries provided similar advantages to richer countries as they had provided under the earlier, more formal versions of colonialism.

A fundamental characteristic of capitalist imperialism involves the extraction of raw materials and human capital, which move from the Global South to the economically dominant countries in the North. In the Global South, "underdevelopment of health" follows inevitably from this depletion of natural and human resources.[1] Under imperialist relationships, such extraction of wealth limits poorer countries' ability to construct effective health systems. These countries also face a net loss of health workers, who migrate to economically dominant nations after expensive training at home.

A cheap labor force also becomes an advantage for multinational corporations. The efficiency of labor became an important goal of public health programs sponsored abroad by philanthropies closely tied to expanding industries in the United States. The Rockefeller Foundation's activities in public health, for instance, sought improved health conditions, especially control of infectious diseases, as a way to enhance the productivity of labor.[2] Population-control programs initiated by the United States and other dominant countries also fostered a more reliable participation by women in the labor force. Through public health initiatives, a healthier, more predictable, and more productive labor force could enhance the fortunes of corporations seeking to expand in the Global South.

Another thrust of imperialism has involved the creation of new markets for products, including medical products, manufactured in dominant nations and sold throughout the rest of the world. This process, enhancing the accumulation of capital by multinational corporations, has appeared nowhere more clearly than in pharmaceutical and medical equipment industries.[3] The monopolistic character of these industries, as well as the stultifying impact that imported technology has exerted on local research and development, has led to advocacy for nationalized drug and equipment formularies in the Global South, with varying success. Such advocacy also has provided a framework for resistance to trade rules that protect patents and therefore enhance the financial interests of pharmaceutical and equipment corporations that operate in such countries.

Imperialism has reinforced international class relations, and medicine has contributed to this phenomenon. As in the United States, medical professionals in the Global South most often come from higher-income families; even when they do not, they frequently view medicine as a route of upward mobility. As a result, medical professionals tend to ally themselves with the capitalist class, the "national bourgeoisie," within these countries. They also frequently support cooperative links between the local capitalist class and business interests in economically dominant countries.[4] The class position of health professionals has led them to resist social change that would threaten current class structure, either nationally or internationally.[5]

Even after the decline of formal colonialism, imperialism frequently has involved military conquest, in addition to economic domination. Despite its benign profile, medicine has contributed to the military efforts of European countries and the United States. For instance, health workers have assumed armed or paramilitary roles in Indochina, North Africa, Iraq, and Afghanistan. Health institutions also have taken part as bases for counterinsurgency and intelligence operations in Latin America and Asia.[6]

The connections among imperialism, public health, and health services have operated particularly through several institutions that have mediated these connections: philanthropic foundations, international financial institutions, organizations that enforce trade agreements, and international health organizations.

Philanthropic Foundations

Notions about charitable contributions by wealthy people to the needy date back at least to the Greek practice of "philanthropy," but modern practices involving donations by foundations began in the early twentieth century. Andrew Carnegie, who accumulated his fortune mainly through the steel industry, took a leadership role in the creation of philanthropic foundations. His philanthropic ventures began with the establishment of Carnegie libraries in small U.S. towns and cities. In writings such as *The Gospel of Wealth*, published in 1901, Carnegie presented his opinions about the social responsibilities of wealth.[7]

Through his book, his speeches, and other efforts to influence his fellow barons of capitalism, Carnegie argued that contributing to the needs of society was consistent with good business practices. According to Carnegie, philanthropy provided several advantages for capitalists, including the achievement of favorable popular opinion about capitalist enterprises and individual entrepreneurs. More important, in Carnegie's view, the businessperson, by contributing intelligently to address social needs rather than squandering personal wealth, could assure entry into the heavenly realm. Thus the "gospel" of wealth. Among the book's many notable features, Carnegie distinguished between "imperialism" and the more virtuous "Americanism": "Imperialism implies naval and military force behind [*sic*]. Moral force, education, civilization are not the backbone of Imperialism. These are the moral forces which make for the higher civilization, for Americanism."[8] Through the Carnegie Endowment for International Peace and other interconnected foundations, Carnegie acted to achieve the fruits he preferred in the disposal of his earthly wealth and in his own heavenly future.

An important early extension of philanthropic foundations to health involved John D. Rockefeller and the Rockefeller Foundation. With a fortune based in oil, Rockefeller emulated Carnegie's philanthropic activities, despite their conflicts in the realm of monopolistic business practices. Rockefeller and associates moved to support public health activities and health services that would benefit the economic interests of Rockefeller-controlled corporations throughout the world.

To foster this goal, the Rockefeller Foundation initiated international campaigns against infectious diseases such as hookworm, malaria, and yellow fever. Between 1913, the year of its founding, and

1920, the Foundation supported the development of research institutes and disease eradication programs on every continent except
Antarctica. For capitalist enterprises expanding internationally,
infectious diseases proved troublesome for several reasons, which
became clear from the writings of Rockefeller and the managers of
the Rockefeller Foundation.[9] First, these infections reduced workers'
energy and therefore their productivity; from this perspective, hookworm became known as the "lazy man's disease." Secondly, endemic
infections in areas of the world designated for such efforts as mining,
oil extraction, agriculture, and the opening of new markets for the
sale of commodities made those areas unattractive for investors
and for managerial personnel. Third, when corporations assumed
responsibility for the care of workers, the costs of care escalated when
infectious diseases could not be prevented or easily treated.

Addressing these three problems, the Rockefeller Foundation's massive campaigns took on certain characteristics that persist to this day,
not only for Rockefeller but also for other foundations, international
public health organizations, and non-governmental organizations.
The Rockefeller Foundation emphasized "vertical" programs, initiated by the donor and focusing on specific diseases such as hookworm
or malaria. An alternative approach could encourage "horizontal"
programs, providing a broader spectrum of preventive and curative
services through a well-organized public health infrastructure of
clinics and hospitals. Rather than such broad public health initiatives
targeting disadvantaged populations, the Rockefeller Foundation's
vertical orientation favored a "magic bullet" approach, targeting new
vaccines and medications that could prevent and treat infectious
diseases.

A vertical orientation has continued in recent, large-scale efforts
by the Rockefeller Foundation, Gates Foundation, and other philanthropies to address public health problems like AIDS, tuberculosis,
malaria, and most recently the Ebola virus. The foundations often
frame their participation as attempts to improve economic development by "investing in health," a term first promoted by the World
Bank.[10] These initiatives usually encourage the participation of multinational pharmaceutical companies, which hold the patents for key

medications and vaccines used in infectious disease campaigns, and private insurance companies or managed care organizations, which assume responsibility and receive payment for delivering services in "public-private partnerships."

Currently, the Gates Foundation has emerged as the largest philanthropy worldwide focusing on public health. Its efforts continue to target specific infectious diseases, especially AIDS in Africa. Together with the World Health Organization, whose limited budget the Gates Foundation helps fund, and various non-governmental organizations also supported by Gates and Rockefeller, philanthropies have invested heavily in the control of infectious diseases through vaccines and other pharmaceutical products. In general, these strategies have left the insufficient public health infrastructures in many countries of the Global South relatively untouched, while lavish spending has occurred to support programs on AIDS, malaria, and tuberculosis.

As a result, access to medical and public health facilities remains inadequate for people who often face desperate circumstances. The contradictions of vertical programs, which persist as the legacy of the Rockefeller orientation in philanthropic support, lead to bizarre and tragic situations that have become well known to public health workers in the Global South. In countries devastated by AIDS, for instance, patients sick with other serious disorders, like cancer, feign or even intentionally get infected by HIV so they can receive medical care in well-funded AIDS programs. And when severe epidemics like Ebola strike, the vertically oriented investment policies of foundations leave countries in Africa without an urgently needed infrastructure of primary-care clinics and hospitals to care for critically ill patients.

INTERNATIONAL FINANCIAL INSTITUTIONS AND TRADE AGREEMENTS

The framework for modern international financial institutions and trade agreements began after the Second World War with the Bretton Woods agreements. These accords grew from meetings in Bretton Woods, New Hampshire, involving representatives of countries victorious in the war. The agreements initially focused on the economic reconstruction of Europe. Between 1944 and 1947, the Bretton Woods negotiations led to the creation of the International Monetary Fund (IMF) and the World Bank, as well as the establishment of the General Agreement on Tariffs and Trade (GATT).[11]

After Europe's recovery, these institutions and agreements gradually expanded their focus to the rest of the world. For instance, the World Bank adopted as its vision statement: "Our dream—a world without poverty."[12] However, because the IMF and World Bank provided most of their assistance through loans rather than grants, the debt burden of the poorer countries increased rapidly. By 1980, many countries in the Global South, including the poorest in the world, were spending on average about half their economic productivity, as measured by gross domestic product, on payment of their debts to international financial institutions, even though these institutions' goals usually emphasized the reduction of poverty. During the early 1980s, the international financial institutions embraced a set of economic policies known as "the Washington consensus." These policies, mainly advocated by the United States and the United Kingdom, involved deregulation and privatization of public services, which added to the debt crisis by reducing even further the public health efforts and health services that poorer countries could afford.

Initially, GATT aimed to reduce trade barriers among its twenty-three member countries by eliminating or cutting taxes and other fees on exports and imports. The fairly simple principles of GATT included "most favored nation treatment," according to which the same trade rules applied to all participating nations, and "national treatment," which required no discrimination in taxes and regulations between domestic and foreign goods.[13] GATT also established ongoing rounds of negotiations concerning trade agreements.

From their modest origins in GATT, international trade agreements eventually changed into a massive structure of rules that would exert profound effects on public health and health services worldwide. As the pace of international economic transactions intensified, facilitated by technological advances in communications and transportation, the World Trade Organization (WTO) in 1994 replaced the loose collection of agreements subsumed under

GATT. The burgeoning array of international trade agreements encompassed under WTO—seen also in recent negotiations concerning regional agreements such as the Trans-Pacific Partnership (on hold as of the early Trump presidency in the United States while still actively pursued by other participating countries) and the Trans-Atlantic Free Trade Agreement—expanded the purview of trade rules far beyond tariff barriers. Instead, the new trade agreements interpreted a variety of public health measures such as environmental protection, occupational safety and health regulations, quality assurance for foods and drugs, intellectual property restrictions pertaining to patented medications and equipment, and even public-sector health services themselves as potential barriers to trade. This perspective in trade agreements transformed the sovereignty of governments to regulate public health and to provide health services. Together with regional trade agreements initiated by the United States, WTO has sought to remove both tariff and "non-tariff" barriers to trade. The removal of non-tariff barriers to trade has affected the ability of national, state, and local governments to protect public health and medical services.

While tariff barriers to trade involve financial methods of protecting national industries from competition by foreign corporations, including import taxes, non-tariff barriers refer to non-financial laws and regulations affecting trade, particularly those that governments use to assure accountability and quality. In over 900 pages of rules, the WTO set criteria for permissible or impermissible non-tariff barriers, such as domestic policies governing environmental protection, food safety, and health services. Though aiming to achieve "free trade" across borders, the rules in trade agreements limit governments' regulatory authority over trade while enhancing the authority of international financial institutions and trade organizations.[14]

WTO rules (under general exceptions of GATT, Article 20) permit national and subnational "measures necessary to protect human, animal or plant life or health," but other provisions make this exception difficult to sustain in practice.[15] For example, a country could be required to prove that its laws and regulations constitute the alternatives least restrictive to trade, and that they are not in fact disguised barriers to trade.[16] These rules also restrict public subsidies, particularly those designated for domestic health programs and institutions, as potentially "trade distortive." Requiring that such subsidies apply equally to domestic or foreign companies that provide services under public contracts preempts public policies that direct subsidies to domestic companies and to public programs.

With relevance to public health, a key WTO provision requires "harmonization," which seeks to reduce variation in nations' regulatory standards for goods and services.[17] Proponents argue that harmonization can motivate some countries in the Global South to initiate labor and environmental standards where none previously existed.[18] But harmonization can also lead to erosion of existing standards, since it requires uniform global standards at the level least restrictive to trade.[19] The WTO encourages national governments to harmonize standards on issues as diverse as truck safety, pesticides, worker safety, community right-to-know laws about toxic hazards, consumer rights regarding essential services, banking and accounting standards, informational labeling of products, and pharmaceutical testing standards.

WTO and regional agreements such as the North American Free Trade Agreement (NAFTA) supersede member countries' internal laws and regulations, including those governing health. Under these agreements, governments at all levels faced a loss of sovereignty in policymaking pertinent to public health and health services. Traditionally, government agencies at the federal, state, county, and municipal levels maintain responsibility for protecting public health by assuring safe water supplies, controlling environmental threats, and monitoring industries for occupational health conditions. Trade agreements can reduce or eliminate such governmental activities, because the agreements treat these activities as potential barriers to trade.

For disputes, an appointed tribunal, rather than a local or national government, determines whether a challenged policy conforms to the rules of WTO or a regional trade agreement. The tribunal includes experts in trade but not necessarily in the subject matter of the cases, such as health or safety, or in the laws of the contesting countries.[20]

Documents and hearings remain closed to the public, press, and state and local elected officials. Because trade agreements treat federal governments as the only pertinent level of participation, only representatives of contesting countries can participate in the hearings, in addition to "experts" whose participation the tribunal requests.

When a tribunal finds that a domestic law or regulation does not conform to the rules of the WTO or a regional trade agreement, the tribunal orders that the disputed transaction proceed despite the wishes of government officials or public health experts. If a country fails to comply, the WTO or the commission with authority over a regional agreement like NAFTA can impose financial penalties and can authorize the "winning" country to apply trade sanctions against the "losing" country in whatever sector the winner chooses until the other country complies. In challenges decided by WTO or NAFTA tribunals, for instance, corporations and even individual investors have caused governments to suffer financial consequences and trade sanctions because of their efforts to pursue traditional public health functions. As they grapple with imposed sanctions, losing countries usually succumb to pressures for eliminating or changing the laws or regulations in question and not enacting similar laws in the future.

Chart 9.1 lists examples of decisions under trade agreements that have affected public health and health services. These show the immense scope of trade agreements' health-related impacts. Proposed trade agreements like the Trans-Pacific Partnership and the Trans-Atlantic Free Trade Agreement contain provisions that similarly remove or constrain governments' ability to protect public health.[21]

INTERNATIONAL HEALTH ORGANIZATIONS

The first approach to international public health organization arose in Europe during the Middle Ages. To block people from leaving or entering geographical areas affected by epidemics of infectious diseases, some governments established local, national, and international *cordons sanitaires*—guarded boundaries. Governments also imposed maritime quarantines that prevented ships from entering ports after

---

CHART 9.1: Examples of Actions under International Trade Agreements that Affect Public Health

---

- Occupational and environmental health:

  § Under Chapter 11 of the North American Free Trade Agreement (NAFTA), the Metalclad Corporation of the United States successfully sued the government of Mexico for damages after the state of San Luis Potosí prohibited Metalclad from reopening a toxic waste dump.

  § The Methanex Corporation of Canada sued the government of the United States in a challenge of environmental protections against a carcinogenic gasoline additive, methyl tertiary butyl ether (MTBE), banned by the state of California.

- Access to medications:

  § Acting on behalf of pharmaceutical corporations, the U.S. government invoked the Agreement on Trade-Related Aspects of Intellectual Property Rights (TRIPS) of the World Trade Organization (WTO) in working against attempts by South Africa, Thailand, Brazil, and India to produce low-cost anti-retroviral medications effective against AIDS.

- Safety and quality of products:

  § Canada challenged France's ban on asbestos imports under the WTO's Agreement on Technical Barriers to Trade (TBT). Although a WTO tribunal initially approved Canada's challenge, an appeal tribunal reversed the decision after international pressure.

- Safety and quality of food:

  § On behalf of the beef and biotechnology industries, the United States and Canada successfully challenged the European Union's ban of beef treated with artificial hormones under the WTO Agreement on the Application of Sanitary and Phyto-Sanitary Standards (SPS). The European Union still pays the United States and Canada more than $120 million annually in extra tariffs imposed due to the EU's decision to limit importation of hormone-treated beef.

- Medical and public health services:

  § The WTO General Agreement on Trade in Services (GATS) removes restrictions on corporate involvement in public hospitals, water, and sanitation systems. GATS affects state and national licensing requirements for professionals and can facilitate challenges to national health programs that limit participation by for-profit corporations.

visiting regions where epidemics were occurring. "Sanitary" authorities were appointed mostly on an ad hoc basis and remained active mainly when epidemics were present or anticipated.[22]

With the rise of export economies and the expansion of international trade during the late nineteenth and early twentieth centuries, conventional maritime public health went into decline. Instead, concerns about infectious diseases as detrimental to trade in the expanding reach of capitalist enterprise became a motivation for international cooperation in public health. An incentive for redesigning international public health emerged from a need to protect ports, investments, and land holdings such as plantations from infectious diseases.

The first formal international health organization appeared in the Americas. Founded in Washington, DC, during 1902, explicitly as a mechanism to protect trade and investments from the burden of disease, the International Sanitary Bureau focused on the prevention and control of epidemics.[23] Mosquito eradication campaigns and the implementation of a vaccine against yellow fever occupied public health professionals in this organization throughout the early twentieth century. During that period, plans proceeded for the construction of the Panama Canal, the development of agricultural enterprises in the "banana republics" of Central and northern South America, and the extraction of mineral resources as raw materials for industrial production from southern Mexico, Venezuela, Colombia, and Brazil. Work in the tropics demanded public health initiatives against mosquito-borne diseases like yellow fever and malaria, parasitic illnesses like hookworm, and the more common viral and bacterial illnesses like endemic diarrhea.

As the first modern international health organization, the International Sanitary Bureau devoted much of its early activities to infectious disease surveillance, prevention, and treatment, largely to protect trade and economic activities throughout the Americas. Later, during the 1950s, the International Sanitary Bureau became the Regional Office for the Americas within the World Health Organization (WHO) and in 1958 changed its name to the Pan American Health Organization (PAHO). Subsequently, PAHO's public health mission broadened.[24] PAHO has retained a focus on the protection of trade until the present day, and in general it supports the provisions of international trade agreements.

WHO emerged in 1948, as one of the component sub-organizations of the United Nations. Prevention and control of infectious disease epidemics remained a key objective throughout its history, but WHO did not frame its purpose in controlling infectious diseases as a way to protect trade and international economic transactions, as PAHO had done during its early history. Instead, during the 1970s, WHO prioritized the improved distribution of health services, especially primary health care. This orientation culminated in the famous WHO declaration on primary health care, issued at an international conference at Alma-Ata, USSR, in 1978.[25] As the principle of universal entitlement to primary care services became one of WHO's priorities, the organization advocated programs for improving access to care, especially in the poorest countries. This "horizontal" vision of public health policy gained substantial support worldwide, at least for a brief time.

However, during the 1980s WHO entered a chronic financial crisis produced largely because of the fragile financing provided for its parent organization, the United Nations. Because of ideological opposition to several programs operated by sub-organizations of the United Nations, especially those of the United Nations Educational, Scientific, and Cultural Organization (UNESCO), the Reagan administration withheld large portions of the United States' annual dues to the United Nations. As a result, the United Nations began to experience increasing budgetary shortfalls, which it needed to pass on to its component organizations, including WHO.

Into this financial vacuum entered the World Bank, which began to contribute a large part of WHO's budget. (Because WHO does not release its budget publicly, the precise degree of its dependency on the World Bank remains difficult to determine.) As WHO's financial base shifted more toward the World Bank and away from the United Nations, its policies also transformed to an orientation that more closely resembled those of international financial institutions and trade agreements. The financial crisis that originated in the non-payment of dues by the United States eventually led within WHO to a policy perspective regarding international trade that proved similar to PAHO's earlier orientation.

During the 1990s, the WHO pendulum swung back from a horizontal orientation toward the preference for vertical interventions. This renewed stance emphasized macroeconomic policies that involve national and international economic relationships, rather than the microeconomic policies pertinent to markets for specific goods and services, as well as the roles of public health and health services in these broad economic relationships. The orientation emerged largely from the efforts of the World Bank and affiliated international financial institutions, as well as key private foundations. Again attention turned to vaccines and medications as technological solutions to the health problems of the Global South. This orientation further facilitated the financial operations of multinational corporations in less developed countries.

The *Report of the Commission on Macroeconomics and Health: Investing in Health for Economic Development* (hereafter, *Report*), published by WHO in 2001, defined the relationships between health and the economy in the context of imperialism.[26] The *Report* led to a series of WHO projects on economic issues in health policy, health services, and public health. Many of the *Report*'s conceptual and methodological approaches mirrored the World Bank's orientation to health and economic development. Partly for that reason, the *Report* gave a revealing picture of the dominant ideology that shaped imperial health policies.

Most of the commissioners responsible for the *Report* had extensive experience with the World Bank, International Monetary Fund (IMF), or other international financial institutions. The commissioners had little background in collaborating with other types of social organizations. Notably absent among the commissioners were representatives of political parties, unions, professional organizations in medicine and public health, organizations of indigenous or ethnic/racial minorities, activists in occupational and environmental health, or members of the worldwide movement targeting economic globalization.

At the beginning the *Report* emphasized its central theme: "Improving the health and longevity of the poor is, in one sense, an end in itself, a fundamental goal of economic development. But it is also a means to achieving the other development goals relating to poverty reduction."[27] Therefore the goal of improving health conditions of the poor became a key element of economic development strategies. From this viewpoint, reducing the burden of the endemic infections that plagued the poorest countries—AIDS, tuberculosis, and malaria—would increase workforce productivity and facilitate investment.

A policy emphasis on "investing in health" (also in the *Report's* title) echoed the influential and controversial *World Development Report, Investing in Health*, published in 1993 by the World Bank.[28] The terminology of the title conveyed a double meaning: investing in health to improve health and productivity and investing capital as a route to private profit in the health sector. These two meanings of investment, complementary but distinct, pervaded the macroeconomic *Report*. As the Commission's chair Jeffrey Sachs (an economist previously known for "shock therapy" in the implementation of neoliberal policies of public sector cutbacks in Bolivia, Poland, and the former Soviet Union) stated in an address about the *Report's* public health implications at the American Public Health Association's annual meeting in 2001, "What investor would invest his capital in a malarial country?"[29]

In asserting that disease was a major determinant of poverty, the *Report* argued that investments to improve health composed a key strategy toward economic development, distancing itself from prior interpretations of poverty as a cause of disease. Instead, the *Report* emphasized various data on the "channels of influence from disease to economic development."[30] The *Report* deemphasized social determinants of disease, such as class hierarchies, inequalities of income and wealth, and racial discrimination. Although the *Report* referred to health as "an end in itself," the focus on economic productivity diminished the importance of health itself as a fundamental human right.

More recently, WHO has vacillated between two markedly different visions of global health. On the one hand, it has continued to pursue the vertically oriented emphasis on vaccines and medications rather than the horizontally oriented advocacy of comprehensive public health systems and access to services. With this orientation, WHO has collaborated with the WTO (with headquarters close to WHO's in Geneva) in trade agreements that limit governments' ability to protect public health and medical services.[31] On the other hand, WHO has responded intermittently to a worldwide constituency calling for greater attention to the social determinants of health. The latter orientation led to an influential report on social determinants and some suggestions about policy changes that would improve social conditions leading to ill health and early death.[32] In research and policy analysis, economic inequality consistently has emerged as the most important social determinant crying out for dramatic changes in policy. Meanwhile, existing policies continue to worsen inequality in the United States and most other countries.

The Ebola epidemic epitomizes the failures of WHO's leadership and the vertically oriented policies of the past. From its underfunded circumstances and dependency on the World Bank and the Gates Foundation, WHO mounted a delayed and hopelessly inadequate response to this epidemic. As usual, a race for the magic bullet emerged, with predictable financial bonanzas for the pharmaceutical industry. But because no effective vaccine or treatment of Ebola yet exists, an infrastructure of clinics and hospitals must provide supportive services like hydration and blood products, as well as educational efforts and simple supplies like adequate gloves and materials to block transmission of the virus. Such an infrastructure, nonexistent in West Africa largely due to the failure of past public health policies, would prove feasible if the powers that be would recognize the practical benefits of a horizontal approach to the development of public health infrastructure. But that approach contradicts a long tradition of top-down vertical policies that have nurtured the political and economic foundations of empire.

Recycling Public Health Interventions at the End of Empire

Throughout most of the twentieth century, the Rockefeller Foundation sponsored "vertical" campaigns against endemic infections: hookworm, yellow fever, tuberculosis, and malaria, among others. Rockefeller campaigns interpreted these infections as impediments to labor productivity, investment, and economic development. Rockefeller-funded programs also recognized that endemic infections blocked efforts to extract raw materials and to transport products and workers throughout the world. Such campaigns did not foster a broader, "horizontal" infrastructure that could provide integrated public health and primary care services. Instead, these interventions aimed to improve the economic circumstances of enterprises in the imperial countries by improving the health of the imperialized.

WHO's *Report on Macroeconomics and Health* updated this earlier Rockefellerism. Like the Rockefeller Foundation, its unacknowledged predecessor in macroeconomic thought, WHO through the *Report* called for investment to reduce poverty in poor countries while enhancing the economic prospects of the rich in both rich and poor countries alike. This approach also revived a vertical attack on specific diseases, rather than encouraging the development of integrated health care systems. Health as a fundamental human value, worthy of investment for its own sake, slipped from consciousness, as did the vision of redistributing wealth as a worthy goal in macroeconomic policy.

More recent efforts by WHO, the Gates Foundation, the International Fund for AIDS, the World Bank, and other agencies focusing on global health have replicated the failed policies of earlier eras.[33] Such influential programs that link public health, health services, and economic development generally emphasize vertical interventions based on technological fixes for specific diseases, rather than the horizontal enhancement of public health infrastructure. This old ideological wine continues to produce a familiar euphoria as it appears in new bottles.

But that age is ending. Conditions during the twenty-first century have changed to such an extent that a vision of a world without empire has become part of an imaginable future. In struggles throughout the world but especially in Latin America, a new consciousness rejects the inevitability of empire, even as the latter resurfaces where it apparently had been defeated.[34] This new consciousness also fosters a vision of medicine and public health constructed around principles of justice, not capital accumulation. Such scenarios convey a picture very different from that of the historical relation between imperialism and health, with less tolerance among the world's peoples for the public health policies of imperialism and a growing demand for public health systems grounded in solidarity rather than profitability and commodification.[35]

10—U.S. Philanthrocapitalism and the Global Health Agenda: The Rockefeller and Gates Foundations, Past and Present

Anne-Emanuelle Birn and Judith Richter

Afiercely competitive and enormously successful U.S. businessman turns his attention mid-career to worldwide public health. Historic curiosity? Or the most powerful contemporary actor in this field? As it turns out, both. At the beginning of the twentieth century, John D. Rockefeller used his colossal oil profits to create the Rockefeller Foundation (RF), staking a preeminent role in international health (as well as in medicine, education, social sciences, agriculture, and natural sciences). About a century later, the Bill and Melinda Gates Foundation (BMGF), endowed by the software magnate and his wife, had become the most influential agenda-setter in the global health and nutrition arena (and in agriculture, development, and education).

Each of these powerhouse foundations emerged at a decisive juncture in the history of international health. Each foundation was started by the richest, most driven capitalist of his day. Each businessman faced public condemnation for his unscrupulous, monopolistic business practices.[1] Both have been subject to adulation and skepticism regarding their philanthropic motives.[2] Sharing narrow, medicalized understandings of disease and its control, the RF sought to establish health cooperation as a legitimate sphere for intergovernmental action and shaped the principles, practices, and key institutions of the international health field,[3] while the BMGF appeared as global health governance was facing a crisis.

Both foundations and their founders were/are deeply political beings, recognizing the importance of public health to capitalism and of philanthropy to their reputations, while claiming the purportedly neutral technical and scientific basis of their efforts. However, there is one critical difference between them: the RF supported public health as a public responsibility, while BMGF actions have challenged the leadership and purview of public, intergovernmental agencies, fragmenting health coordination and allotting a massive global role for corporate and philanthropic "partners."[4]

Given the confluence of largesse and agenda setting at distinct historical moments, several questions emerge: How and why have U.S. mega-philanthropies played such an important role in producing and shaping knowledge, organizations, and strategies to address health issues worldwide? What are the implications for global health and its governance?

Such questions are particularly salient given that philanthrocapitalism is hailed as the means to "save the world" even as it depends on profits amassed from financial speculation, tax shelters, monopolistic pricing, exploitation of workers and subsistence agriculturalists, and destruction of natural resources—profits that are channeled, albeit indirectly, into yet more profiteering. The term philanthrocapitalism, coined by *The Economist*'s U.S. business editor, refers both to infusing philanthropy with the principles and practices of for-profit enterprise and as a way of demonstrating capitalism's benevolent potential through innovations that allegedly "benefit everyone, sooner or later, through new products, higher quality and lower prices."[5]

Most government entities are subject to public scrutiny, but private philanthropies are accountable only to their own self-selected boards. Just a few executives make major decisions that affect millions of people. In North America and various other jurisdictions, corporate and individual contributions to nonprofit entities are tax deductible, removing, for example, an estimated $40 billion from U.S. public coffers each year.[6] At least one-third (depending on the tax rate) of private philanthropies' endowments is thereby subsidized by the tax-paying public, which has no say in how such organizations' priorities are set or monies spent.

This chapter compares and contrasts the goals, modus operandi, and agenda-setting roles of the RF and BMGF. We propose that both the early twentieth-century RF and the contemporary BMGF have significantly shaped the institutions, ideologies, and practices of the international/global health field, sharing a belief in narrow, technology-centered, disease-control approaches. The RF, however, favored creation of a singular, public, coordinating agency for global health (eventually the World Health Organization/WHO), whereas the BMGF's privatizing approaches undermine WHO's constitutional mandate to promote health as a fundamental human right. Indeed, the BMGF's venture-philanthropy approach, applying methods from the venture capital field to charitable giving,[7] is emblematic of the business models that now penetrate the global public health field. These conditions have resulted in extensive private, for-profit influence over global health activities and have blurred boundaries between public and private spheres, representing a grave threat to democratic global health governance and scientific independence.[8]

ROCKEFELLER INTERNATIONAL HEALTH IN AN AGE OF IMPERIALISM

In 1913, as tropical health problems plagued imperial interests, oil mogul-cum-philanthropist John D. Rockefeller established the RF with the professed goal of "promot[ing] the well-being of mankind throughout the world." His efforts were part of a new American movement: scientific philanthropy. In his 1889 manifesto, *The Gospel of Wealth*, Scottish-born, rags-to-riches steel magnate Andrew Carnegie had called on the wealthy to channel their fortunes to the societal good by supporting organized social investments rather than haphazard forms of charity.[9]

Rockefeller followed this gospel by donating to the nascent field of public health, burnishing his social benefactor image in the process. His advisors advocated starting by tackling anemia-provoking hookworm disease, which was easily diagnosed and treated with medication and was viewed as central to the economic "backwardness" of the U.S. South, impeding industrialization and economic growth. That hookworm was not a leading cause of death, or that treatment occasionally provoked fatalities, seemed immaterial.

The handsomely funded Rockefeller Sanitary Commission for the Eradication of Hookworm Disease (1910–1914) showered eleven southern states with teams of physicians, sanitary inspectors, and laboratory technicians who administered deworming medication; promoted shoe wearing and latrine use; and disseminated public health materials, working through churches and agricultural clubs. (These activities brought favorable attention to the Foundation until a [false] rumor spread that the campaign aimed to sell shoes, prompting the Rockefeller name to fade into the background.)[10] Even if it did not "eradicate" the disease, the hookworm campaign ignited popular interest in public health, and the RF swiftly created an International Health Board to expand the work.

The RF's public health activities also served to counter negative publicity about the Rockefeller oil monopoly. Bad press mounted in 1914 when some two-dozen striking miners and their families were killed at the Ludlow, Colorado, mine, owned by a Rockefeller-controlled coal producer. Workers, investigative journalists, and the general public readily linked Rockefeller business and philanthropic interests, regarding the donations of "robber barons" as attempts to counter working-class unrest, political radicalism, and other threats to big business.[11]

The Rockefeller family was thus advised to engage in philanthropic spheres such as health, medicine, and education, perceived as neutral and unobjectionable. Over the next four decades, the RF dominated international health. Its staff, steered by active trustees and managers, initially overlapping with Rockefeller business advisors, oversaw a global enterprise of health cooperation through regional offices in Paris, New Delhi, Cali, and Mexico City. Hundreds of RF officers led its country-based public health work in scores of countries around the world.[12] By the time the International Health Division, as the International Health Board was renamed in 1927, was disbanded in

1951, it had spent the equivalent of billions of dollars on major tropical disease campaigns against hookworm, yellow fever, and malaria, plus smaller programs combatting yaws, rabies, influenza, schistosomiasis, and malnutrition, in almost a hundred countries and colonies. The Division also marshaled national commitment to its campaigns by obliging government co-financing, typically starting at 20 percent of costs and rising to the full amount within a few years. It also founded twenty-five schools of public health across the world and provided fellowships to 2,500 public health professionals to pursue graduate study, mostly in the United States.[13]

But the RF rarely addressed the most important causes of death, notably infantile diarrhea and tuberculosis, for which technical fixes were not then available and which demanded long-term, socially oriented investments, such as improved housing, clean water, and sanitation systems. The RF avoided disease campaigns that might be costly, complex, or time-consuming— other than yellow fever, which imperiled commerce. Most campaigns were narrowly construed so that quantifiable targets (insecticide spraying or medication distribution, for example) could be set, met, and counted as successes, then presented in business-style quarterly reports. In the process, RF public health efforts stimulated economic productivity, expanded consumer markets, and prepared vast regions for foreign investment and incorporation into the expanding system of global capitalism.

Alongside its disease campaigns, the RF sustained the international health field's evolving institutional framework. The League of Nations Health Organisation (LNHO), founded after the First World War, was modeled partially on the RF's International Health Board and shared many of its values, experts, and know-how in disease control, institution building, education, and research, even though the LNHO strove to challenge narrow, medicalized understandings of health. Instead of being supplanted by the LNHO, the RF became its major patron and lifeline.[14] Addressing the sociopolitical conditions underlying ill health was an important political rationale for public health in the 1930s climate of anti-fascist-, labor-, and socialist activism. The RF drew on, listened to, and even bankrolled certain progressive political perspectives, including those of avowed left-wing scientific researchers and public health experts,[15] although such support was always subordinate to its technical model and to bolstering U.S. capitalist power.

Yet the RF identified its most significant international contribution as "aid to official public health organizations in the development of administrative measures suited to local customs, needs, traditions, and conditions."[16] Thus its self-defined, broader gauge of success was its role in generating political and popular support for public health, creating national public health departments, and furthering the institutionalization of international health.

Philanthropic status conferred independence from public oversight; the RF was accountable only to its board. Its influence over agenda setting and institution building was enabled by its presence at the international level, bolstered by behind-the-scenes involvement in virtually every kind of public health activity and by missionary zeal in setting priorities. Yet, responding dynamically to shifting political, scientific, economic, cultural, and professional terrains, the RF's activities also involved extensive give and take, marked by moments of negotiation, co-optation, imposition, rejection, and productive cooperation. Uniquely for the era, the RF operated not only as a funding agency but simultaneously as a national, bilateral, multilateral, international, and transnational agency.[17]

The Cold War Interlude and the Rise of Neoliberalism

After WHO was established in 1948, the RF drew back from its leading role in international health, leaving a powerful but problematic legacy: it had generated political and popular support worldwide for public health and championed the institutionalization of international health, but it also entrenched outside agenda setting and a techno-biological approach. WHO inherited the RF's personnel, fellows, ideologies, practices, activities, and equipment, pursuing high-profile, vertical eradication campaigns against malaria, smallpox, and other diseases.[18]

During the Cold War, WHO was joined on the international health stage by bilateral agencies, international financial institutions, and other United Nations (UN) agencies, plus a dizzying array of humanitarian and non-governmental organizations (NGOs). Both the U.S. and Soviet blocs employed health infrastructure in their political and ideological rivalry, building hospitals, clinics, and pharmaceutical plants, sponsoring thousands of fellowships, and participating in RF-style disease campaigns.

In the 1970s, WHO's vertical approach began to be challenged. Its member states, especially newly decolonized countries not aligned with the Soviet Union or the United States, sought to address health sociopolitically. Halfdan Mahler, WHO Director-General from 1973 until 1988, provided the visionary leadership in this reorientation. The primary health care movement, enshrined in the seminal 1978 WHO-UNICEF Conference and Declaration of Alma-Ata and WHO's accompanying "Health for All" policy, called for health to be addressed as a fundamental human right through integrated social and public health measures that recognized the economic, political, social, and cultural contexts of health and focused on prevention rather than cure.[19] Health for All was also part of a larger UN effort, the New International Economic Order (NIEO), which also called on UN agencies to help regulate transnational corporations via binding international codes.

Just as WHO was trying to escape the RF's legacy of narrow health interventions, it became mired in political and financial crises. The economic situation in the late 1970s and early 1980s prevented many member countries from paying WHO dues. Meanwhile, U.S. resistance to what it portrayed as illegitimate "supra-national regulation," amid the overall rise of neoliberal political ideology, dampened support for publicly funded international health institutions. These conditions also contributed to a budget freeze in terms of dues paid by member states, which still remains in place. Moreover, U.S. president Ronald Reagan's administration unilaterally cut its assessed contributions to the UN by 80 percent in 1985 and then withheld its WHO member dues in 1986 to protest WHO's regulation of health-related commercial goods and practices,[20] particularly pharmaceuticals and infant foods.[21] By the early 1990s, less than half of WHO's budget came from member country dues, while many donors, now including a variety of private entities, stipulated the programs and specific activities to which they assigned funds. Today almost 80 percent of WHO's budget comes from donors who determine how their contributions are spent.

After the Cold War, international health efforts were justified on the grounds of promoting trade, disease surveillance, and health security.[22] By this time, WHO was being sidelined by the World Bank, armed with a far larger health budget and a drive to privatize health systems as well as water and other essential public services, and by an emerging paradigm forging UN "partnerships" with corporate actors. Many bilateral agencies, plus certain UN agencies such as UNICEF, bypassed WHO altogether.[23] With reduced intergovernmental spending, what was now dubbed "global health" philanthropy returned, its reemergence coinciding and intertwined with the rise of neoliberalism.

ENTER THE GATES FOUNDATION

By 2000, overall global health spending had become stagnant. Negative views of overseas development assistance were encouraged by political and economic elites and corporatized mass media. Many low- and middle-income countries (LMICs) were floundering under the multiple burdens of HIV/AIDS, reemerging infectious diseases, and burgeoning chronic diseases, all compounded by decades of World Bank and IMF-imposed cuts in social expenditures and the negative effects of trade and investment liberalization. Into this void a self-proclaimed savior for global health appeared, quickly molding its agenda within just a few years.

The BMGF was established in 2000 by Microsoft founder and long-serving CEO Bill Gates, the world's wealthiest person,[24] and his wife, Melinda, formerly a product development manager at Microsoft. As with Rockefeller, Gates's philanthropic entry coincided with bad press. He launched the Children's Vaccine Program, a BMGF precursor, in 1998,[25] when Microsoft was attracting negative publicity for lobbying to cut the U.S. Justice Department's budget at the same time that the company was mired in a federal antitrust suit.[26] In 1999,

Gates gave a $750,000 founding donation to the Global Alliance for Vaccines and Immunization (now GAVI, the Vaccine Alliance), an initiative announced at the World Economic Forum in Davos. Later that year Microsoft faced a class-action lawsuit for abusing its software monopoly on the part of millions of California consumers. BMGF-funded initiatives rapidly proliferated, even as Microsoft was facing further anti-competitive charges in the European Union. In 2002 the BMGF co-founded the Global Alliance for Improved Nutrition (GAIN) and became a major funder of the Global Fund to Fight AIDS, Tuberculosis, and Malaria (now called the Global Fund).

Today the BMGF, co-chaired by the couple together with Bill Gates, Senior, is by far the largest philanthropic organization involved in global health and the largest charitable foundation in the world. The BMGF spends more money on global health than any government except the United States.[27] Its 2016 endowment was $40.3 billion, including almost $20 billion donated thus far by U.S. mega-investor Warren Buffett, the BMGF's sole trustee other than Bill and Melinda Gates themselves.[28]

Through 2016, the BMGF had granted $41.3 billion in total; recent annual spending is around $6 billion. Approximately $1.2 billion goes into its "global health" program (covering HIV, malaria, and tuberculosis-control related activities) and $2.1 billion into its "global development" program (covering polio eradication, vaccine delivery, maternal and child health, family planning, and agricultural development), which, confusingly, involves considerable global health-related work. The BMGF's budget for global health-related activities has surpassed that of WHO in some recent years. Since 2008, the BMGF has been the largest private donor to WHO, with funding particularly earmarked for polio eradication.

The BMGF's stated global health aim is "harnessing advances in science and technology to reduce health inequities,"[29] encompassing both treatment, via diagnostic tools and drug development, and preventive technologies, such as vaccines and microbicides. Initially, the Seattle-based Gates Foundation focused on a few disease-control programs, mostly as a grant-making agency. Now its efforts reach over a hundred countries. It also maintains offices in several African countries, China, India, and the United Kingdom and has more than 1,400 staff members worldwide.

Echoing RF practices, the BMGF requires co-financing from its governmental "partners," designs technologically oriented programs to achieve positive results from narrowly defined goals, and emphasizes short-term achievements. The BMGF has developed an extraordinary capacity to marshal other donors to its efforts, including bilateral agencies, which collectively contribute ten times more resources to global health than the BMGF but with considerably less recognition.[30] The BMGF has been widely lauded for infusing cash and life into the global health field and encouraging other participants.[31] But even some of its supporters decry its lack of accountability and transparency (over what are, after all, taxpayer-subsidized dollars) and its undue power in setting the global health agenda.[32]

The BMGF Approach and Its Dangers

As a key funder of global health initiatives, the BMGF collaborates with a range of public, private, and intergovernmental agencies, as well as universities, corporations, advocacy groups, and NGOs. Like the RF, the BMGF sends the vast majority of its monies for global health to or through entities in high-income countries. Through 2016, three quarters of the total funds granted by its Global Health Program went to sixty organizations, 90 percent of which are located in the United States, United Kingdom, or Switzerland.[33]

A major focus of BMGF global health funding is vaccine distribution and development. In 2010 it committed $10 billion over ten years to vaccine research, development, and delivery. Vaccines are important and effective public health tools, especially when integrated into overall social improvements. Indeed, historical evidence demonstrates that even before most childhood vaccines were developed, significant mortality declines were achieved thanks to improved living and working conditions (including access to clean water, sanitation, occupational health and safety, fair wages, education, social protections, and primary health care) in the context of broad social and political struggles.[34]

The BMGF's reductionist approach emerged clearly in Bill Gates's keynote address in May 2005 to the fifty-eighth World Health Assembly, the annual gathering at which WHO member states set policy and decide on key matters. Gates invoked smallpox eradication through vaccination, the cost of which is low due to its non-patented status, in charting global health priorities: "Some . . . say that we can only improve health when we eliminate poverty. And eliminating poverty is an important goal. But the world didn't have to eliminate poverty in order to eliminate smallpox—and we don't have to eliminate poverty before we reduce malaria. We do need to produce and deliver a vaccine."[35] Gates's deceptively simple technological solution to the complex problem of malaria implies that approaches based on social justice can simply be ignored. Similarly, the BMGF's Grand Challenges in Global Health initiative funds scientists in nearly forty countries to carry out "bold," "unorthodox" research projects, which largely disregard the underlying social, political, and economic causes of ill health, including unprecedented accumulation and concentration of wealth among elites.[36]

To be sure, the BMGF has also supported other kinds of initiatives, albeit at a smaller scale. In 2006, for example, it gave a $20 million startup grant to the International Association of National Public Health Institutes and a $5 million grant to the WHO-based Global Health Workforce Alliance, which sought to address the shortage of health personnel in LMICs. BMGF funding has often had a privatizing impetus. More recently, the BMGF has begun funding "universal health coverage" (not the same as access to publicly funded universal health care, as discussed in chapter 7),[37] via a $2.2 million grant to the Results for Development Institute, which works to "remov[e] barriers impeding efficiency in global markets (for instance in health)."[38]

Despite the shortcomings of a technology-focused, disease-by-disease approach to public health problems, this model now prevails, shepherded by the BMGF's role in formal global health decision-making bodies. Its role grew in 2007 with the formation of the so-called H8: WHO, UNICEF, the UN Population Fund (UNFPA), UNAIDS, the World Bank, the BMGF, GAVI, and the Global Fund. Most are involved with and/or heavily influenced by the BMGF. The H8, akin to the former G8 (composed of eight powerful nations collaborating on economic policies and "security" issues: the United States, Japan, Germany, France, United Kingdom, Canada, Italy, and Russia; now the G7 without Russia) holds meetings behind closed doors to shape the global health agenda.[39]

Like the RF at its height, the BMGF's sway over the global health agenda stems from the magnitude of its donations, its ability to mobilize resources quickly and allocate substantial sums to large initiatives, the high profile of its patron, and the leverage it garners from the extraordinary range of organizations with which it partners. Yet Bill Gates's response to the 2014–15 Ebola outbreak in West Africa raises yet more questions about his vision. He called for a supranational, militarized global health authority, modeled on the North Atlantic Treaty Organization, to be mobilized in the event of future epidemics, usurping WHO's coordinating mandate while undercutting national sovereignty and democratic rule.[40]

The BMGF and Conflicts of Interest

Conflicts of interest in financing and staffing pervade the BMGF. In recent years it has been criticized for investing its endowment in polluting and unhealthy food and beverage industries and in private corporations that benefit from its support for particular global health and agriculture initiatives.[41] Although the BMGF sold many of its pharmaceutical holdings in 2009,[42] its financial interests in Big Pharma remain through Warren Buffett's Berkshire Hathaway holdings (almost half of the BMGF's endowment investments).

Overly close relationships between the BMGF and Big Pharma call into question the Foundation's stated aim of reducing health inequities, given that profiteering by these corporations impedes access to affordable medicines.[43] In addition, various senior BMGF executives once worked at pharmaceutical companies.[44] For instance, Dr. Trevor Mundel, president of the BMGF Global Health Program, was previously a senior executive at Novartis. His predecessor, Dr. Tachi Yamada, was an executive and board member of GlaxoSmithKline. Yet such "revolving-door" problems are rarely discussed publicly.[45]

Advocates for affordable life-saving medicines have also raised questions about the BMGF stance on intellectual property (IP). Gates admits that his Foundation "derives revenues from patenting of pharmaceuticals."[46] Microsoft has long been an ardent supporter of IP rights, which facilitate its worldwide capture of markets,[47] and has taken a leading role in assuring passage of the World Trade Organization's Agreement on Trade-Related Aspects of Intellectual Property Rights (TRIPS).[48] The BMGF and Microsoft are legally separate entities (as the RF and Rockefeller companies were), but linkages, such as BMGF's hiring of a Microsoft patent attorney in 2011 for its Global Health Program, are troubling.[49] The government of India became so concerned about the BMGF's pharmaceutical ties and related conflicts of interest that, in early 2017, it cut off all financial ties between the national advisory body on immunization and the BMGF.[50]

Such conflicts of interest also manifest at WHO, due to the increasing role of the BMGF as the main financier for WHO's budget. The problem of WHO's dependence on "voluntary" funding, its most fundamental institutional conflict of interest, remains unaddressed despite concerted efforts by civil society organizations.[51] It would take just $2.2 billion, which is only half that of New York-Presbyterian Hospital's budget,[52] to fully fund WHO through member state dues. Instead of lifting the freeze on WHO member dues, WHO's most recent reform produced the 2016 Framework of Engagement with Non-State Actors,[53] which further legitimized BMGF and corporate influence on WHO by specifically allowing philanthropic and corporate actors to apply for the "Official Relations" status that was originally meant for NGOs that shared the specific goals articulated in WHO's constitution.

THE BMGF, PUBLIC-PRIVATE PARTNERSHIPS, AND MULTI-STAKEHOLDER INITIATIVES

Among the levers through which the BMGF has garnered influence over agenda setting and decision making are "public-private partnerships" (PPPs). The generic term PPP covers a multitude of arrangements, activities, and relationships. In the early 1990s, PPPs were promoted as a way of funding and implementing global health initiatives in accordance with neoliberal prescriptions for privatizing public goods and services. By the late 1990s, UN agencies had classified a wide range of public-private interactions as "partnerships" or "multi-stakeholder initiatives" (MSIs). Both concepts lump all participants together, erasing key differences in the roles and objectives of those striving for human rights to health and nutrition, and those ultimately pursuing their bottom line.[54] Many of the major global health PPPs now in existence, with budgets ranging from a few million to billions of dollars—such as GAVI, Stop TB, Roll Back Malaria, and GAIN—were launched by the BMGF or have received funding from it.

These public-private hybrids encourage a close relationship between a public institution and business rather than an arm's-length one and promote a shared process of decision making among supposedly equal partners, or "stakeholders." Such arrangements have enabled business interests to obtain an unprecedented role in global health policymaking with inadequate public scrutiny or accountability[55] and are markedly different from the RF's past advocacy of public health as the responsibility of the public sector.

The BMGF's prominent role in the two most powerful PPPs—GAVI and the Global Fund, both H8 members—and its founding of GAIN underscore the primacy of the Foundation in shaping and enhancing the clout and business venture orientation of PPPs. GAVI has been the model for almost all global health PPPs. When Bill Gates first funded it, he was following the venture philanthropy model created in the mid-1990s by dot-com billionaires who advocated bringing business thinking and jargon into the public arena. The arrangements are characterized by the active involvement of donor entrepreneurs and Foundation staff in the recipient organizations and by board representation from the for-profit sector,[56] with some government representatives reporting that corporate presence creates an intimidating environment for public interest actors involved in these new arrangements.[57]

GAVI has been criticized for emphasizing new vaccines instead of ensuring that existing effective vaccination against childhood diseases is universally practiced. It has been characterized as a top-down arrangement emphasizing technical solutions that pay scant attention to local needs and conditions,[58] and underwriting already hugely profitable pharmaceutical corporations in the name of "saving children's lives."[59] Indeed, GAVI has subsidized companies such as Merck for already profitable products such as pneumococcal vaccine, while countries eligible for GAVI support are expected to take on an increasing proportion of costs, eventually losing both direct subsidies and access to lower-negotiated vaccine prices.[60]

Similar issues surround the Global Fund, the largest global health PPP in dollar terms. It received a $100 million startup grant from the BMGF, which has since given it almost $1.6 billion. Sidelining UN agencies, the Global Fund had disbursed $33 billion to fund programs in 140 countries as of early 2017, in the process further debilitating WHO and any semblance of democratic global health governance. WHO and UNAIDS have no voting rights on the board, but the private sector, currently represented by Merck and the BMGF, does. The Global Fund, like many PPPs, is known to offer "business opportunities," lucrative contracts and influence over decision making, as a prime feature of its work.

Similarly, since the BMGF and UNICEF founded GAIN, this PPP has popularized the term "micronutrient malnutrition" to justify its prime focus on food fortification and supplementation. GAIN argues that "in an ideal world we would all have access to a wide variety of nutrient-rich foods which provide all the vitamins and minerals we need. Unfortunately, for many people, especially in poorer countries, this is often not feasible or affordable."[61] This reasoning ignores food supply and distribution problems. Severe malnutrition prevails in regions with extremely fertile soil and advantageous growing conditions, producing some of the world's most nutritious crops, but these are largely for export markets, leaving local people on low incomes priced out of access to nutritious food.[62]

Overall, the PPP- and MSI-peppered global health architecture fragments and destabilizes the global health landscape, weakening WHO's authority and capacity to function and coordinate.[63] These arrangements allow private interests to frame the public health agenda, provide legitimacy to corporate and venture philanthropic involvement in the public domain, conflate corporate and public objectives, and raise multiple conflicts of interest, with most PPPs channeling public money into the private sector, not the other way around.[64] Most recently, a new global health campus built to house the headquarters of major PPPs, just a stone's throw from WHO, will further shift the node of global health governance physically and metaphorically away from UN agencies.[65]

OTHER AVENUES OF INFLUENCE

Little examined is the $3.5 billion in grants from the BMGF in recent years for "policy and advocacy" work. These grants fund extensive health and development media coverage, including BMGF-supported programs in outlets spanning the U.S. Public Broadcasting System to the United Kingdom's *Guardian* newspaper.[66] This coverage adds to the considerable self-publicity generated by Bill and Melinda Gates themselves, who have been featured in countless profiles over the years. Their 2017 annual letter, for instance, used cherry-picked evidence to promote an overly positive and misleading spin on the BMGF's achievements.[67] By contrast, the RF historically underplayed its public profile, largely because it was faced with a more vigilant media and a public skeptical about the intermixing of business and philanthropic interests and about the exertion of philanthropic influence at the highest political levels, behind closed doors.

Venture philanthropy funding from the BMGF increasingly influences civil society movements,[68] universities and researchers,[69] and government programs. This influence leads to modification of mandates, scientific research foci, and methodological approaches and also squeezes out more critical analyses. Indeed, the BMGF, via the Seattle-based Institute for Health Metrics and Evaluation, which it bankrolls, claims for itself a core WHO role: "diagnosing the world's health problems and identifying the solutions."[70] Meanwhile, critics within UN agencies, civil society organizations, and academia are silenced or excluded, depicted as holding outdated views. A 2015 Gates-funded evaluation report of the Scaling Up Nutrition multi-stakeholder initiative portrayed those who raised conflict-of-interest concerns as harboring "phobias" and "hostile feelings" toward industry, which could "potentially sabotage the prospects of multi-stakeholder efforts to scale up nutrition."[71]

Another telling illustration is a 2017 high-level Memorandum of Understanding (MOU) between the BMGF and the German development agency BMZ. This MOU commits BMGF and the BMZ to join forces in advancing the UN's 2030 Sustainable Development Goals (SDGs) through "revitalization" of global "partnership" approaches. Among other effects, this MOU opens BMZ's large network of contacts to the BMGF and invites staff exchanges between the organizations.[72] If this MOU becomes a model for future government-foundation relations, it will further undermine democratic and accountable decision making in the global health and development sphere.

PHILANTHROCAPITALISM REDUX: COMPARING THE RF AND THE BMGF

Philanthropic largesse and the social-entrepreneurial mission of twenty-first-century billionaires are today touted as unparalleled, as though capable of saving the world.[73] This is underscored by the ever more welcoming and enabling environments for corporate investment and "charitable" sponsorship of the UN's flagship SDGs, adopted in 2015 with the stated aim of ending poverty, reducing inequality, and advancing health, social well-being, and environmental sustainability.[74] The claims for selfless philanthropic generosity merit critical consideration,[75] for which comparisons with the past are illuminating.

Philanthropy circa 1900 derived from the profits and exploitative practices of oil, steel, railroad, and manufacturing interests. Similarly, the colossal profits earned during the 1990s and 2000s by investors in the information-technology, insurance, real estate, and financial sectors, as well as industries linked to mining, oil, and the military, were built on the rising inequality to which they contributed, abetted by massive, if often lawful, tax evasion.[76] In both eras, profits were amassed thanks to depressed wages and worsening labor conditions; trade and foreign investment practices obstructing and diluting protective regulations; illicit financial outflows; externalizing and transferring the social and environmental costs of doing business onto the public and future generations; and tacit support for military regimes to guarantee access to valuable raw materials and commodities.[77]

On the eve of launching his foundation, Bill Gates's net worth exceeded that of the total net worth of the bottom 40 percent of the U.S. population.[78] The company he created, and in which he and the BMGF still hold shares, was recently accused of heavily lobbying against reforms that would curtail corporate tax evasion.[79] Gates remains the wealthiest of eight mega-billionaires who are as rich as the poorest half of humanity.[80] Yet these men are celebrated for their philanthropy rather than scrutinized for their business practices.

The tenet that business models can resolve social problems, and are superior to redistributive, collectively deliberated policies and actions developed by elected governments, rests on the belief that the market is best suited to these tasks, despite ample evidence to the contrary. Still, the BMGF's support of such models and incentives diverges from that of the RF. Although following a business model and undergirding an expanding capitalist system, the RF explicitly called for public health to be just that—in the public sphere.

Tax-deductibility of philanthropic donations is an affront to democracy. The belief that charitable giving can change the world is just another variant of the decidedly undemocratic doctrine that the rich know best. Whereas "governments used to collect billions from tycoons and then decide democratically what to do with it,"[81] today they cede agenda setting for social priorities to the class that already wields undue economic and political power.

Applauding and encouraging the munificence of elites will not create equitable, sustainable societies. Ironically, people living on modest incomes are proportionately far more generous than the rich, often donating money and time at considerable personal sacrifice, without receiving comparable recognition or tax breaks for their contributions.[82] A century ago, the millions of people involved in social and political struggles for decent, fair societies were far more skeptical than many are today about big philanthropy and its effect on public policy making, including policies about public health.

In short, a plutocratic health governance system with authoritarian features is becoming entrenched. Fading independent critical media have facilitated the philanthrocapitalist onslaught, with the emergence of an engineered "consensus" claiming that the world's problems can only be solved through "partnerships" of all "stakeholders."

By contrast, through the 1940s, the RF supported a small number of left-wing advocates of social medicine even as it privileged a medicalized, reductionist approach; the BMGF, however, remains largely impervious to opposing viewpoints. As the premier international health organization of its day, the RF had an overarching purview and was instrumental in establishing the centrality of the field of public health to the realms of economic development, nation-building, diplomacy, scientific diffusion, and capitalism writ large, while institutionalizing lasting, if problematic, patterns of health cooperation. The BMGF, for its part, while reliant on the public sector to deliver many of its technology-focused programs,[83] appears largely indifferent to the survival of the "public" in public health.

A Rich Man's World: Must it Be?

These many examples demonstrate that capitalism trumps philanthropy—or "love of humankind," from the word's ancient Greek roots—making philanthrocapitalism an oxymoronic enterprise indeed. The pivotal, even nefarious, role it has played in global health depends on gargantuan resources enabled by profiteering of titanic proportions amid relentless ideological assaults on redistributive approaches, within a pro-corporate geopolitical climate of dominant, if currently cracking, global capitalism.

In the twenty-first century, it may still be a rich man's world, but we need not settle for a rich man's agenda. Collective activism to overturn philanthrocapitalism's hold on global health is an urgent necessity. This effort should draw from, and build upon, the resistance to the UN's promotion of "multi-stakeholder partnerships" and neoliberal global restructuring since the 1990s.[84] Those actors who have contributed either unwittingly, or through silent assent, or even with active collaboration to the global health plutocracy also share responsibility in re-democratizing it. Governments and UN agencies need to take their public mandates seriously. Scientists, scholars, activists, civil servants, international organizations' staff, parliamentarians, journalists, trade unionists, and ethical thinkers of all stripes have a duty to question and counter philanthrocapitalists' unjustified influence, work together for accountability and democratic decision making, and reclaim a global health agenda based on social justice rather than capital accumulation.

PART FIVE

The Road Ahead

11—Resisting the Imperial Order and Building an Alternative Future in Medicine and Public Health

Rebeca Jasso-Aguilar and Howard Waitzkin

Although medicine and public health have played important roles in the growth and maintenance of the capitalist system, conditions during the twenty-first century have changed to such an extent that a vision of a world without an imperial order has become part of an imaginable future.[1] Throughout the world, diverse struggles against the logic of capital and privatization illustrate the challenges of popular mobilization. In addition to these struggles, groups in several countries have moved to create alternative models of public health and health services. These efforts, especially in Latin America, have moved beyond the historical patterns fostered by capitalism and imperialism. (We have chosen not to address the Cuban case here, which is in many ways exceptional, and on which a great deal of previous work exists.[2]) All the struggles that we describe remain in a process of dialectic change and have continued to transform toward more favorable or less favorable conditions. However, the accounts show a common resistance to the logic of capital and a common goal of public health systems based in solidarity, not profitability.

Protagonists of struggles in Latin America have experienced the direct impacts of political and economic imperialism imposed by the

United States over the course of nearly two centuries. Policies that fortified U.S. dominance throughout the Americas originated formally with the Monroe Doctrine in 1823. Subsequently, U.S. economic and political elites succeeded in imposing a neocolonial environment, in which multinational corporations based in the United States could extract raw materials and open up new markets for the entire Western Hemisphere. The military forces of the United States protected the expanding U.S. empire through a series of invasions and other interventions throughout the nineteenth and twentieth centuries.

Latin American countries achieved political independence at various points in the past two hundred years, but economic independence has proven more elusive. Between the 1940s and 1970s Latin American countries attempted to establish their own economic thought and to follow their own economic paths. During this period, the region experimented with policies that favored state intervention to promote industrialization. Among other things, these policies allowed for the development and expansion of public services such as education and health care. While they did little to reduce poverty or inequality, they underscored the role of the state in national economic policy and its responsibility to provide a social safety net.

An ideological shift occurred in the 1980s, and Latin America became a laboratory for experimenting with the stringent economic programs that would become known as neoliberalism. Neoliberalism seeks to assert the superiority of the market over the state; it aims to reduce drastically the role of the state in the economy and to favor austerity, fiscal discipline, deregulation, privatization, and the dismantling of public social welfare initiatives.[3] Neoliberal policies were first imposed under military rule in Chile and later were introduced by elected governments in other Latin American countries, beginning with Bolivia in 1985. These "principles" were packaged as the "Washington Consensus" and were implemented under the watchful eyes of the International Monetary Fund and the World Bank. Between 1980 and 2010, privatization, deregulation, and liberalization led to a massive transfer of resources from the public to the private sector, the systematic elimination of the safety net, and the worsening of existing social and economic inequalities.

Due to a long history of confronting imperialism, Latin America became an especially fertile ground for resistance against neoliberalism. As a result, Latin American countries that were left in economic ruin because of neoliberal policies have led the struggle in the past fifteen years. Social movements in the region have unseated governments, appropriated factories, expelled corporations, sought autonomy and self-determination, engaged in electoral struggles, and shared broad demands of social justice.[4]

In this chapter, we analyze a series of popular struggles in which we have participated during the past decade as researchers and activists. These struggles include resistance against the privatization of health services in El Salvador and the privatization of water in Bolivia. We also analyze efforts to expand public sector health services in Mexico. Such scenarios convey resistance to the public health policies of imperialism and a growing demand for public health systems rooted in solidarity. These examples also reflect a larger phenomenon: the success of popular struggles to facilitate the participation of common citizens in social issues that are usually discussed and decided by political and economic elites. In practice this change has translated into demands to have a say in policies related to natural resources such as water and gas, as well as health services and medications. As one Bolivian participant put it, people have seized the right to decide on matters of the public sector: "el derecho de decidir sobre lo público."[5]

THE STRUGGLE AGAINST PRIVATIZATION OF HEALTH SERVICES IN EL SALVADOR

One of the first outbreaks of sustained resistance to imperial policies in public health and medicine took place during the late 1990s in El Salvador. This struggle focused on privatization policies initiated by the World Bank, in collaboration with the right-wing political party that then ruled El Salvador. Efforts to resist privatization of health services and the public health system there emerged as a model for analogous social movements elsewhere in Latin America. The Salvadoran example also illustrated similar processes that were to occur in many other countries throughout the world during the early twenty-first century, as imperial policies met with sustained resistance.

From 1998 to 1999, the health care sector in El Salvador fell into political turmoil, when conflict broke out over various issues. First, unionized workers from the Salvadoran Institute of Social Security (Instituto Salvadoreño del Seguro Social, ISSS) mobilized for a salary increase, after an agreement was reached but not honored by ISSS authorities. Second, an unfavorable revision of the collective bargaining contract further strained the relationship between workers and the ISSS administration. And third, the administration began to contract private entities for delivery of services—food, laundry, cleaning, and so on—to the ISSS hospitals. This outsourcing was the first signal of privatization within the ISSS. In line with this trend, two major public hospitals under renovation remained closed for several months, waiting to outsource their services to private entities instead of being returned to the management of the ISSS.[6]

Such actions were part of a strategy, favored by the World Bank, to privatize public hospitals and clinics. Simultaneously, the government tried to gather public sympathy for the privatization of health care on the basis of alleged corruption and inefficiency in the ISSS, all the while avoiding the term "privatization." But several conditions called into question the credibility of such allegations. For instance, during the previous thirteen years, those directly responsible for the functioning of the ISSS had been appointed by the party in power, the Republican Nationalist Alliance (Alianza Republicana Nacionalista, ARENA). These appointments included hospital directors and ISSS officials. Many ARENA politicians who supported privatization held a financial stake in this effort. In addition, the health budget was underspent, creating an artificial shortage of medications and delays in services, elements that proponents of privatization used to build the case for "modernization" and "democratization" of the health care system.[7]

These issues led to partial and temporary strikes in San Salvador. Workers mobilized in the vicinity of public hospitals. Those belonging to the Union of Workers of the Salvadoran Institute of Social Security

(Sindicato de Trabajadores del ISSS, STISSS) began a national strike, an indefinite, escalating strike. Negotiations between the ISSS administrative authorities and STISSS workers collapsed. This, combined with a growing concern among doctors about the privatization of health care, provided the ground for an alliance between the STISSS workers and the doctors of the recently created Medical Union of Workers of the Salvadoran Institute of Social Security (Sindicato Médico de Trabajadores del ISSS, SIMETRISSS). The medical profession, with little or no history of unionization, joined the national strike. The alliance of STISSS and SIMETRISSS produced a document titled "Historical Agreement for the Betterment of the National Health System" ("Acuerdo Histórico por el Mejoramiento del Sistema Nacional de Salud"). This document contained several points, including a demand for ending privatization in the national health system.[8]

A government commitment not to privatize health services ended the conflict temporarily. But instead of honoring the commitment, the Ministry of Health and the ISSS authorities continued to outsource hospital services, leading to ongoing conflict. For three years, workers from STISSS and doctors from SIMETRISSS organized strikes and rallies that gradually drew support from the larger civil society. Supporting organizations included teachers and blue-collar unions, students, feminist and environmentalist groups, bus drivers, market vendors, peasants, and coffee growers, the majority of them affiliated with the umbrella coalition Citizens Alliance Against Health Care Privatization.[9]

Strikes varied in length, and participants walked a fine line not to alienate the population at large. During strikes, doctors tended to acutely ill patients on the sidewalks, a strategic as much as a humanitarian action to gain the support of the general population. Another calculated action involved "handing the hospitals to the administrators" and walking out, a symbolic gesture to demonstrate that the hospitals could not run without doctors. The government responded with repression, using tear gas, rubber bullets, and water cannons against strikers. Doctors were fired and replaced with new personnel.[10]

Unparalleled solidarity and organization led to congressional approval of Decree 1024, in which the state guaranteed public health and social security. Decree 1024 stipulated that health care would remain public, prevented any future outsourcing of health care services, and effectively voided any prior outsourcing that the government had authorized since the beginning of the conflict. President Francisco Flores threatened to veto the decree, but coordinated pressure from sympathetic legislators in Congress and from civil society through mass collective action on the streets forced him to comply with it.[11]

This victory, however, was short-lived. Flores's party, ARENA, formed a congressional alliance that produced enough votes to repeal Decree 1024. The conflict continued for six more months, with several more marches and demonstrations taking place in San Salvador. These were massive rallies where demonstrators dressed in white as a symbol of peace and as a sign of solidarity with doctors and nurses wearing white coats. The demonstrations drew from 25,000 to 200,000 participants in a city of about 800,000 people. Many doctors sold their homes, cars, and home appliances to obtain the financial means to continue the struggle.[12]

The conflict ended when the World Bank reversed a privatization clause in a loan earmarked for modernizing the public health system. Union leaders and government representatives reached an agreement to stop the privatization of the public health system. Members of STISSS and SIMETRISSS were reinstated with their previous salaries and seniority, although some doctors who were replaced during the strike had to relocate. The agreement also established a follow-up commission on health reform, which included medical professionals, government officials, and representatives of unions and civil society.[13]

Efforts to maintain and to expand public-sector health care continued, especially after the election in 2009 of leftist Mauricio Funes as president, representing the political wing of the Farabundo Martí National Liberation Front (FMLN, the military wing of which had fought with ARENA during the long civil war in El Salvador during the 1980s and 1990s). Dr. María Isabel Rodríguez, a well-known leader of Latin American social medicine who lived in exile during much of the civil war, returned to direct public health and medical services as national minister of health. Funes markedly increased the government's consultation with civil society in economic and social policies. In health care, this orientation translated into a five-year strategic plan, for which the Citizens' Alliance Against Health Care Privatization was the main source. In this way, the Citizens' Alliance provided expertise for an independent movement engaged in pro-active, long-term actions. An independent National Health Forum also emerged, as members of civil society were invited to design and implement health care policies, and to hold the government account-able for its commitments. The Funes administration also incorporated voices that previously were marginalized, such as nurses, who have taken part with other groups in a new National Labor Roundtable. In addition, Funes brought more women into his cabinet, and these women used their positions to emphasize reproductive health.

Salvador Sánchez Cerén, a former guerrilla leader with the FMLN who won the election for president in 2014, pledged to consolidate the advances in health accomplished during the Funes presidency, and the Ministry of Health embarked on additional initiatives to strengthen the public sector in health services. Among other goals, these initia-tives have emphasized the continuing problems of violence that have plagued the country since the civil war and U.S. military intervention there. Supporting these efforts from a constructively critical posi-tion, a coalition of health professionals became active, inspired by the contributions to social medicine by Salvador Allende in Chile. The coalition honored Allende through its name, Dr. Salvador Allende Movement of Health Professionals (Movimiento de Profesionales de la Salud "Dr. Salvador Allende"). Although the coalition grew from the earlier struggles against neoliberal policies in El Salvador, younger health workers took leadership in the organization. They spearheaded the selection of San Salvador as the site of the November 2014 con-gress of the Latin American Social Medicine Association, which drew thousands of progressive health workers to advance the strug-gle against neoliberal policies and on behalf of alternative models to strengthen public services. Subsequently, the Allende Movement has continued to resist pressures for privatization in El Salvador and has acted in international solidarity with anti-privatization struggles in other countries.[14]

Resistance to Privatization of Water in Bolivia

Although clean water remains a fundamental goal of public health, the world's declining supplies of fresh water have emerged as a new frontier for corporate profit. Major corporations trying to sell water as a commodity have sought to privatize public water sources. In this context, the long-term resistance against privatization of water in Bolivia shows how a previously marginalized population can organize to win a struggle against powerful corporate forces that seek to commodify a critical public health resource.

Water availability in the province of Cochabamba, Bolivia, historically has posed serious problems. Climate and environmental conditions made this province a prime agricultural area. Agricultural workers (*regantes*, or those in charge of irrigation) managed dwindling water resources through irrigation practices rooted in cultural traditions known as *usos y costumbres* (uses and customs). Accelerated urbanization increased the demand for drinking water and water for domestic uses. Newer policies depleted underground water resources and favored urban development at the expense of the rural population.[15]

In 1997, the World Bank promoted privatization of Cochabamba's public water utility based on a rationale of eliminating public subsidies, securing capital for water development, and attracting skilled management. In its characteristic fashion, the Bank pressured the Bolivian government by making international debt relief in the amount of $600 million contingent on the privatization of water.[16] New legislation, Ley 2029, allowed a private corporation, Aguas del Tunari, to lease Cochabamba's public water and sewer company (Servicio Municipal de Agua Potable y Alcantarillado, SEMAPA). The contract effectively awarded Aguas del Tunari monopoly control over water services for forty years. The terms of the contract also prevented the *regantes* from using water in their traditional ways and allowed the company to appropriate any and all water sources, including neighborhood wells and rainwater. A few weeks after the contract was signed, water bills increased by an average of 200 percent, a change known as the *tarifazo*.

The Water War, a series of collective actions that took place during 2000, quickly ensued. The Coalition for the Defense of Water and Life (Coordinadora por la Defensa del Agua y la Vida) emerged to coordinate the mobilization of farmers, factory workers, professional people, neighborhood associations, teachers, retirees, the unemployed, and university students. These efforts included roadblocks, strikes, mass demonstrations and public assemblies, and a referendum. An intensive parallel investigation discovered among other things that Aguas del Tunari was a "ghost consortium" of enterprises grouped together under the control of Bechtel, a large U.S.-based corporation, in which prominent Bolivian politicians maintained economic interests. Making this information public allowed the Coordinadora to gather support.

During these contentious months, several developments strengthened the popular mobilization to block the privatization of water. The citizens of Cochabamba refused to pay their water bills, which they burned in highly symbolic public acts. On various occasions, the city was paralyzed by demonstrations, barricades, and strikes; economic activity was largely disrupted. The government responded with police and military actions, which led protestors to escalate their demands. A referendum organized in March showed an overwhelming rejection of the contract with Aguas del Tunari, revealing a deep concern over the privatization of water services and supplies. The government's response dismissed this democratic exercise. As protestors' demands escalated and mass mobilization intensified, the government took further repressive actions. It initiated a disinformation campaign, established martial law, and allowed the use of live ammunition in clashes with demonstrators. Protestors intensified mobilizations and citywide blockades, bringing the city to a halt. At the height of the conflict, a seventeen-year-old youth died and other protestors suffered injuries from gunfire. The youth's funeral drew tens of thousands of angry protestors. Later that day Aguas del Tunari announced that it was rescinding the contract and leaving Cochabamba.

SEMAPA remained a public company, and several policy changes occurred as a result of the struggle. The board of directors implemented community engagement and direct participation through the election of community representatives, who became accountable to social organizations and the population at large. These changes revealed a reappropriation of SEMAPA, a transformation into a public company under *control social*, meaning control exercised by the community. This effort by civil society to exercise control over public resources produced mixed results after the water struggle.[17] Nevertheless, it was a step that weakened the hegemony of neoliberal ideology, challenged the common sense of privatization policies, and opened the door to new forms of citizens' participation in political life.

The struggle to defeat privatization and to strengthen public water supplies constituted the first of a wave of mobilizations and uprisings that broke the trajectory of neoliberalism in Bolivia. Opposition to the commodification of water and the social reappropriation of SEMAPA signaled the people's commitment to new ways of doing politics. This new form of political participation characterized the social upheaval that swept Bolivia. During this period, citizens defeated a tax hike, challenged water policies in El Alto (a large suburb of Bolivia's capital, La Paz), unseated neoliberal president Gonzalo Sánchez de Lozada, and, in what came to be known as the Gas War, demanded participation in the decision-making process regarding the nation's gas resources. This chain of events made the defeat of neoliberalism seem possible. The Water War contributed substantially to this possibility, as it did to the election in 2005 and reelections in 2009 and 2014 of Evo Morales, Bolivia's first indigenous president.

Novel processes of democracy and participation have taken place during the Morales administration. At the request of the Coordinadora and activists representing various social movements, Morales committed to creating a new cabinet position: minister of water. This cabinet post dealt with pressing problems that remained after the recent water struggles and also aimed to encourage popular participation in government. The Ministry of Water included a social-technical commission formed by social movements, social organizations, and academics with expertise in water issues. The commission's charge was to discuss, reach consensus, and approve any projects, plans, and programs of the ministry. Again the commission was to exercise *control social.* The type of community control shown in the social reappropiation of SEMAPA evolved into a form of co-management between government and civil society. The commission originally held rights of discussion and voting on any project, plan, or program proposed by the Ministry. However, this role was limited from the beginning, and it became gradually more constrained under the argument that decisions made by others could not take precedence over the decisions of the Ministry. Although the commission eventually disappeared, it represented one of several exercises in community participation to exert control and demand accountability from the Bolivian government.

SOCIAL MEDICINE COMES TO POWER IN MEXICO CITY

Bold new health policies, linked to the election of a progressive government in Mexico City, illustrate what an alternative vision can accomplish under conditions of broad sociopolitical change. In the 2000 election, the left-oriented Party of the Democratic Revolution (Partido de la Revolución Democrática, PRD) gained control of the government in the Federal District of Mexico City, while the conservative Party of National Action (Partido de Acción Nacional, PAN) won the presidential election. Thus political life in Mexico during the first decade of the twenty-first century saw the strengthening of two distinct political and economic projects: an anti-neoliberal position in Mexico City, represented by Andrés Manuel López Obrador (known popularly as AMLO), and a neoliberal one at the federal level, embodied by President Vicente Fox. The two projects led to very different results.

As governor, AMLO initiated wide-ranging reforms of health and human services. To the post of secretary of health, López Obrador appointed Asa Cristina Laurell, a widely respected leader of Latin American social medicine.[18] Laurell and colleagues began a series of ambitious health programs, modeled according to social medicine principles. They first focused on senior citizens and the uninsured population, with a goal of guaranteeing the constitutional right to health protection.

The fourth article of the Political Constitution of Mexico and the thirty-fifth article of the federal health legislation granted this right, as well as universal coverage and free care through public institutions. However, because these documents did not clarify which entity had the obligation to provide health services, this right in practice often came to be seen as merely "good intentions." In contrast, an assumption underlying these documents was that public institutions should provide health protection. This assumption offered a legal justification to make the state, presumably the guardian of the public interest, the provider of this right.[19] The Mexico City Government (MCG) made use of this legal justification to design and implement health and human services policies that targeted vulnerable groups, thus making "the right to health protection a reality." Broad goals that guided the MCG's approach to health policy were:

> to democratize health care, reducing inequality in disease and death and removing economic, social, and cultural obstacles to access; to strengthen public institutions as the only socially just and economically sustainable option granting equal and universal access to health protection; to attain universal coverage; to broaden services for the uninsured population; to achieve equality in access to existing services; and to create solidarity through fiscal funding and the distribution of the costs of disease among the sick and the healthy.[20]

Health policies of the MCG derived from a concept of social rights. Leaders of the MCG saw the creation of social rights, those that the state is required to guarantee, as one of the most important gains achieved by the Mexican Revolution of 1910–1920.[21]

Two major programs initiated by the MCG aimed to improve public health and medical services. First, the Program of Food Support and Free Drugs for Senior Citizens created a social institution that granted all seniors a new social right. This program started in February 2001, and by October 2002 it had become virtually universal, covering 98 percent of Mexico City residents aged seventy years or more. Citizens received a monthly stipend amounting to the cost of food for one person (the equivalent of US$70) and free health care at the city government health facilities.[22]

A second initiative, the Program of Free Health Care and Drugs, focused on uninsured residents of Mexico City. By December 2002, about 350,000 among the 875,000 eligible families had enrolled. Later, by the end of 2005, 854,000 family units had registered in the program, which effectively amounted to universal coverage of the target population. The program provided all personal and public health services; MCG health facilities offered primary and hospital care for individuals and families.[23]

Financing these programs proved possible due to the MCG's commitment to curb administrative waste and corruption. An austerity program beginning in 2000 implemented a 15 percent pay cut for top government officials and eliminated superfluous expenses. The austerity measures yielded savings of $200 million in 2001 and $300 million in 2002. Simultaneously, the government undertook crackdowns against tax evasion and financial corruption. These savings allowed the government to increase the health budget by 67 percent, meaning that 12.5 percent of the Mexico City budget went for public health and health services.[24]

Such community-oriented initiatives won wide admiration and contributed to the PRD's electoral successes. Whereas in 2000 the PRD victory in Mexico City had been tight, by April 2003 the approval rate for AMLO reached an unprecedented 80 to 85 percent. The PRD swept the 2003 midterm election and took control of the Mexico City legislature. AMLO's austere and efficient administration, with zero tolerance for corruption and emphasis on social programs for the most vulnerable populations, earned him the support of Mexico's City's population in his 2006 national presidential bid. It also earned him the wrath of forces that supported the neoliberal status quo, including Mexico's political and financial elites who controlled the country's major media. Weeks after the election, the national electoral commission awarded the presidency to the PAN candidate, Felipe Calderón, even after widespread social mobilization to challenge the election due to extensive evidence of fraud.[25]

The movement that emerged to challenge the election (the *lopezobradorista* movement from here on) continued despite its failure to reverse the results. This movement led to the formation of the "Legitimate Government of Mexico." In this parallel, unofficial government, AMLO served as president and appointed a cabinet of intellectuals, social scientists, and politicians of leftist and anti-neoliberal ideology. Asa Cristina Laurell once again became the minister of health. The parallel government kept the social medicine vision alive as a viable policy alternative. According to Laurell, the Legitimate Government was "not a shadow government understood as a reaction to official actions of the other government . . . [it was] much more proactive, [with the capacity] to elaborate and discuss original proposals using as a starting point another idea of what we want our nation to be."[26]

In contrast, Popular Insurance (Seguro Popular), a federal health coverage program proposed and partly implemented by Vicente Fox's administration between 2003 and 2006, expanded during the Calderón administration between 2006 and 2012. This insurance program comprised a service package with limited coverage, cost-sharing by families, and gradual enrollment of the uninsured population. Limited coverage disrupted the provision of comprehensive care. Cost-sharing amounted to 6 percent of family income, a financial burden for poor families. Services not included had to be purchased through private insurance. The latter signaled a further push toward the privatization of health care, which was in line with Fox's and Calderón's neoliberal agendas.

The different ways in which Fox and Calderón on the one hand and AMLO on the other treated public health and health services policies illustrated two discordant visions of development. In 2006 the Mexican presidential election became so contested because it was a referendum on these different projects with the potential to create very different countries. As Laurell notes:

> In 2006 what was at play was not just the election of a candidate, the future of the country was at stake. . . . We lost the opportunity to rebuild our country and to make it less unequal, of building a

nation for everyone, in which social rights are guaranteed and built, that is what we lost with this electoral fraud.... What we are trying to do with the Legitimate Government and with the mobilization of citizens is to keep the hope alive.[27]

The *lopezobradorista* movement transformed itself into a social movement against neoliberalism and was for the social, political, and economic transformation of the country. This movement deterred Calderón's efforts to privatize energy during 2008 and during 2009 gained several seats in Congress, where they represented the only opposition to the neoliberal project. They questioned budgets and reforms, defended the movement's positions, and presented counterproposals.

As the movement continued to organize and promote an alternative national project, AMLO ran for president again in 2012. The 2012 presidential election was a replay of the 2006 struggle between two very different projects. One project attempted to maintain neoliberal hegemony; it was embodied in the candidate of the Revolutionary Institutional Party (Partido Revolucionario Institucional, PRI), Enrique Peña Nieto, and supported by the PAN, the corporate and business class, and the Church hierarchy. The other project represented a counter-hegemonic effort supported by the *lopezobradorista* movement, the PRD, and smaller progressive parties, and it posed a substantial challenge to the status quo. Corruption and fraud plagued this election also, through practices such as the use of cash and gift cards in exchange for people's votes in favor of the PRI candidate.

Neoliberal reforms and repression of social movements have become trademarks of Peña Nieto's government. His administration began with a labor reform that further eroded workers' rights and security, and throughout 2013 he pursued regressive reforms in education, energy, and fiscal policy. Yet the counter-hegemonic movement in Mexico has persisted, as the leadership (including AMLO, Laurell, and many others) and their constituencies continued the struggle in health and other arenas. Dissident teachers, for instance, have fought the imposition of neoliberal educational reform, with months of intense struggle that extended to several states in the country and gathered the support of large sectors of civil society. Chastised and dismissed by political and business elites, the teachers' struggle has been openly supported by just one political party, the leftist National Regeneration Movement (MORENA).

Emerging from the *lopezobradorista* movement, MORENA has been the most successful effort in the formal political arena during recent years. Officially formed in 2014, it participated in mid-term elections in 2015, winning a majority of seats in the congress of Mexico City and becoming the major political force in the city; it also won 8 percent of the national vote. These results overall are impressive for any party's first-time performance in electoral politics.

The party's platform is strongly oriented toward social justice rights, with education and health among its top priorities. MORENA's political gains translated, among other things, into the establishment of five public colleges and professional schools. One of them was a school of medicine located in the same geographical area in Mexico City where the mayor planned to develop "Ciudad Salud," an enclave of private hospitals, medical facilities, hotels, and restaurants that would cater to patients of economic means. A public school of medicine was an alternative to this neoliberal project, which ironically was promoted by a mayor belonging to the PRD, the party that was born as the leftist alternative to the neoliberal project imposed in Mexico by the PRI in 1988. Disappointment with the PRD's move to the center-right has led some critics and citizens to dismiss MORENA as a party that eventually will be co-opted and will abandon its leftist ideology. This is a dialectical process that will continue to play itself out in Mexico during coming years.[28]

Sociomedical Activism Against the Imperial Order

The struggles considered here confirm certain core principles of public health: the right to health care, the right to water and other components of a safe environment, and the reduction of illness-generating conditions such as inequality and related social determinants of poor health and early death. Affordable access to health care and clean water supplies provided by the state, for instance, have become the focus of activism throughout the world (including the United States, as described in chapters 14 and 15). Such struggles reinforce the principle of the right to organize at the grass roots and to have community voices heard and counted in policy decisions. Activism that seeks alternatives to neoliberalism and privatization encourages participation by diverse populations, an emphasis on solidarity, and a rejection of traditional political forms.

The challenge is to develop strategies for activism that can extend these "counter-hegemonic" spaces to broader social change. A goal of the social movements that we have described is not simply to win but to encourage public debate and raise the level of political consciousness. This new consciousness rejects the logic of capital and fosters a vision of medicine and public health constructed around principles of justice rather than commodification and profitability. No other path will resolve our most fundamental aspirations for healing.

12—The Failure of Obamacare and a Revision of the Single-Payer Proposal after a Quarter-Century of Struggle

Adam Gaffney, David Himmelstein, and Steffie Woolhandler

Since the mid-twentieth century, the U.S. health sector has undergone a steady transformation from small-scale enterprises controlled by doctors toward a corporatized industry controlled by giant firms. This dynamic retraces the path of other industries and fits Marx's description of movement from a so-called petit bourgeois organization to a fully capitalist mode. This transformation, however, has been neither simple nor complete. Indeed, it is riven with contradictions.

In this chapter, we explore the forces behind this shift, and their implications for the popular movement for a health care system focused on human needs rather than on profits. More than a quarter-century ago, two of us co-authored with other colleagues a "Physician's Proposal" for such a system, widely known as "single payer," that remains the central platform of the organization Physicians for a National Health Program (PNHP).[1] The profound changes in the intervening period, both the consolidation of corporate control of health care and the passage of President Barack Obama's Affordable Care Act (ACA), led to the recent drafting of a follow-up proposal, which was endorsed by more than 2,200 physicians and medical students.[2] Here, we seek to weave together an evaluation of how the trajectory of the health care sector intersects with this renewed vision for a single-payer system.

We trace how the encroachment of the interests of capital have shaped three key features of the U.S. health care system: (1) the rise of the for-profit managed care organization (MCO), (2) the emergence of high-deductible, "consumer-directed" health insurance, and (3) the consolidation of corporate ownership in much of the health care industry. It is worth noting that though for-profit entities must, by definition, have owners to whom profits can accrue, not-for-profit organizations can achieve surpluses of revenue over costs that may, somewhat similarly, be used for lucrative executive compensation. Although we focus on for-profit entities here, not-for-profit organizations can sometimes seek "profits" as aggressively as for-profit companies even though they lack shareholders. (See chapter 5 for more detail.)

Additionally, we will observe that popular pressure for "universal health care" helped lead to the passage of the first major health care reform legislation in a generation, the ACA. Yet while the ACA was a partial accommodation to pressure from "below" (that is, working- and middle-class support for health care reform), it was also, and to an even greater extent, an accommodation with power from "above" (that is, health care capital). The balance of power between these conflicting pressures culminated in a law that expanded health coverage to some of the poorest Americans, even while it solidified the role of corporate power in health care and perpetuated fundamental injustices within the U.S. health care system, including uninsurance, underinsurance, and the unfair and irrational distribution of health care facilities.

Much changed in 2016. The presidential election, which brought the billionaire Donald Trump to the presidency and gave Republicans continued control of Congress, opened the door for the reversal of even these relatively modest coverage gains. As we describe in the final part of this chapter, it may very well be that Republican health care meddling paradoxically wound up opening the door, in the intermediate term, to more progressive health care reform. We conclude with a description of the most prominent and promising progressive reform proposal, a single-payer national health program (NHP), and describe how it could address the deficiencies of the status quo, blocking the advance of capital in the realm of health care and facilitating the emergence of a humane and health-maximizing system.[3]

To understand the impediments to that vision, we will start by examining three pivotal turning points of health care capital that occurred in the late twentieth and early twenty-first centuries.

PIVOT I: THE MANAGED CARE STRATEGY AND THE RETREAT FROM NATIONAL HEALTH INSURANCE IN THE 1970s

Over the first three-quarters of the twentieth century, the health care landscape in the United States, initially dominated by independent practitioners and "charitable" hospitals, transformed into an organized, consolidated enterprise with great economic and political power. The medical profession, for instance, rose from a relatively modest institution in terms of earnings and influence to a position of "singular . . . economic power and cultural authority."[4] At the same time, charity hospitals—which, in truth, had relied on a more complex mix of funding than the "charity" label implied—increased their reliance on fees from paying customers and more generally adopted a profit-maximizing approach to medical care.[5] A burst of investment and construction in the early twentieth century turned hospitals into "one of the largest enterprises in the United States, outstripped only by the iron and steel industry, the textile industry, the chemical industry, and the food industry."[6]

Meanwhile, Blue Cross was founded by hospitals in Texas during the Great Depression and was explicitly designed to assure that the hospitals would be paid. During the Second World War, wage increases were banned, but unions and workers were allowed to bargain for expanded health benefits, encouraging the spread of employer-paid coverage, which was further stimulated by an Internal Revenue Service ruling that health benefits were not taxable.[7] In the post–Second World War period, the defeat of the national health insurance movement facilitated the rise of a powerful private health insurance industry. Though the non-profit "Blues" initially expanded to dominate the sector, in later years commercial insurers began to cherry-pick good-risk (healthier) workers, in the process becoming a formidable industry.[8] Finally, over the course of the century, the pharmaceutical industry slowly developed into one of the most profitable and powerful sectors in the world economy.

Together, the ascendency of the hospital, insurance, and drug industries—which together we and others call the "medical-industrial complex," with its growth as a major focus of capital accumulation within U.S. capitalism (discussed in chapter 5)—helps to explain why the United States entered the 1970s with no national health insurance plan. Medicaid and Medicare, passed in 1965, secured access to health care only for the elderly and some of the poor, groups unable to afford private insurance, and hence of little interest to insurers, despite their great medical needs. Still, many hoped that Medicare might become an initial step toward a universal program. And by the early 1970s, universal health care returned to the national political agenda, led in part by politicians such as Edward (Ted) Kennedy.

During the 1970s, a decade that saw the emergence of a neoliberal agenda in many fields, the U.S. health care sector underwent two crucial developments: first, the elaboration and championing of the "managed care strategy," and second, a declining vision of national health insurance or a national health service.[9] These developments were interconnected. Though MCOs are widely perceived as embodiments of pernicious corporate greed, what is less frequently understood is that the managed care strategy was explicitly formulated as a counter to national health insurance. It was also, as we shall see, conceptualized as a catalyst for the larger market-based transformation of U.S. health care.[10]

The early practice of "managed care," that is, physician groups that provided care to patients on a prepaid basis, stretches back to the early twentieth century.[11] However, a central feature of the modern MCO is a financial arrangement in which providers assume insurance risk, thereby giving them an incentive to reduce the overall health expenditures of their patients. The modern formulation of managed care can be traced to the physician and managed care theoretician Paul Ellwood.[12] In February 1970, Ellwood presented his plan for a national policy favoring managed care to representatives from President Nixon's Department of Health, Education and Welfare.[13] The administration was seeking solutions to a pair of pressing political issues: escalating government health care expenditures and burgeoning support in Congress for national health insurance.[14] Indeed, that same year, Senator Ted Kennedy and Representative Martha W. Griffiths introduced their "Health Security Bill," which would have established a single-payer national health insurance system that, like the British National Health Service and programs being enacted in Canadian provinces, would have been free at the time of use.[15] The managed care strategy was designed to counter this potent progressive threat.

Ellwood and colleagues said as much in a seminal article, published in 1971, which began by laying out the political predicament faced by the Nixon administration. The administration, they argued, had to pick one of two choices: submit to the opposition and "rely on continued or increased Federal intervention through regulation, investment, and planning," or embrace a managed care industry that would be "self-regulatory" and make "its own investment decisions."[16] The latter strategy, they argued, would necessitate larger delivery organizations, "risk sharing" among insurer, provider, and "consumer," and quality monitoring. This larger vision became clear in a critical sentence close to the end of the paper, in which they conceptualized MCOs as the gateway to a larger marketization within health care:

> The emergence of a free-market economy could stimulate a course of change in the health industry that would have some of the classical aspects of the industrial revolution—conversion to larger units of production, technological innovation, division of labor, substitution of capital for labor, vigorous competition, and profitability as the mandatory condition of survival.[17]

In other words, corporate MCOs, nurtured into existence by the government but subsequently "self-regulating," would compete in a burgeoning health care marketplace and thereby drive down health costs, while maintaining quality through the reporting of performance statistics to vigilant consumers. MCOs would thereby keep the partisans of national health insurance at bay while ushering in a revolutionary marketization on behalf of the medical-industrial complex. (For more on the role of Ellwood and colleagues in the development of neoliberal health policies, see chapter 7.)

Though this vision faltered in the short term, it would triumph in the long run, especially in the realm of ideology. Despite Nixon's endorsement, for instance, MCOs evolved sluggishly during the 1970s. National legislation in 1973 set a fairly high regulatory bar for MCO plans to qualify for federal aid, and few did.[18] Though amendments to the 1973 act later in the decade loosened these regulations and made it easier to qualify,[19] it was not until the 1980s that large corporate MCOs rose to prominence. Additionally, a combination of political factors, rather than the logic of the managed care strategy, led to the failure in the 1970s of both Kennedy's health care plans and Nixon's counterproposals for expanded coverage (although the structure of Ellwood's and Nixon's approach formed the model for later health care reforms, including the ACA; for details, see chapter 7). Ultimately, it was the election of President Ronald Reagan that unleashed the corporate MCO. Like the election of Margaret Thatcher across the Atlantic, that event opened a political window of opportunity for the well-prepared advocates of a neoliberal health care agenda.

PIVOT I COMPLETED: THE CORPORATE MCO COMES AND GOES, 1980s–1990s

Many have described the harmful impacts of the Reagan administration on public health, through cuts in social spending, weakening support for occupational and environmental health protection, reduced funding for public hospitals and community health centers, and other regressive policies.[20] The administration's role as midwife for the corporate MCO is less appreciated, however. Early in his first term, Reagan's team succeeded in passing an important new law that aimed for active promotion of MCOs as "an opportunity for investors."[21] MCOs grew in number, size, and market share over the course of the next decade, and although most were initially nonprofit, by 1986 they were predominantly run by for-profit corporations.[22] By the middle of the 1990s, MCOs covered about a third of workers.[23]

Yet the growth of the managed care model catalyzed resistance to it. In order to increase profitability and contain costs, MCOs corrupted the process of medical decision making, using financial carrots and sticks to discourage physicians from prescribing needed but expensive health services for their patients.[24] Patients and physicians came to see MCOs as financially extractive and predatory. In 1997, two popular films, *As Good As It Gets* and *The Rainmaker*, portrayed denials of care by insurers.[25] Superimposed on these developments, however, was the reemergence of the health care reform debate. The unanticipated victory of Harris Wofford, who favored single-payer reform, to the U.S. Senate from Pennsylvania showed the depth of support for reform. Polling demonstrated that his position on national health reform was an important factor in his victory, and his election put reform back on the national political agenda.[26]

Democratic candidate Bill Clinton soon embraced the cause, though after he became president the protracted and secretive deliberations of the task force led by Hillary Clinton produced a complex plan that retreated from earlier, more universal proposals. The Clintons' "Health Security Plan" would have preserved the "disintegrating private financing system," while at the same time bolstering "the movement toward managed care."[27] It incorporated a vision of "managed competition" inspired by business professor Alain Enthoven, who had participated in conferences with policy analysts and industry insiders at Paul Ellwood's retreat home in Jackson Hole, Wyoming, during the early 1990s (for more on Enthoven, see chapter 7).[28] But for reasons others have explored in detail,[29] the campaign imploded, seriously harming the political standing of Bill Clinton and the Democratic Party in the process.

Though the growth of MCOs continued for several years following Clinton's health care reform fiasco,[30] widespread popular anger at corporations' restrictions on care continued to heat up, culminating in a flood of bills designed to protect patients.[31] Even as public anger contributed to the dropping of unpopular tools like utilization controls, this period cemented the consolidation of the insurance and hospital industries,[32] in line with Ellwood's vision of the "conversion to larger units of production." In some senses, the death of the MCO was, to use the phrase often attributed to Mark Twain, "greatly exaggerated."

Later the managed care ethos spread into other private health insurance products and government programs. For instance, the populations covered by Medicaid and Medicare—poor and older individuals—had been unprofitable for private insurers. But federal and state initiatives during the 1980s and 1990s, including a loosening of restrictions by Congress during the Reagan administration, led to a major rise in Medicaid MCOs.[33] Privatized Medicare plans, now called Medicare Advantage, likewise grew in the 1990s and 2000s. In other words, private insurers were increasingly drawing on public funds to provide managed care coverage under both Medicaid and Medicare. And from a broader perspective, the dynamic of consolidation and integration of health care delivery catalyzed by the managed care revolution became even more entrenched.

Thus this first pivot of health care capital left behind a larger, more consolidated health insurance industry. It also paved the way for the next important pivot: the move toward high-deductible health insurance, or what some would cheerily call "consumer-directed health care."

Pivot II: Enter Consumer-Directed Health Care, 1990s–2000s

The fluctuations and disturbances in the health insurance marketplace in the late 1990s necessitated a dynamic response from corporations in the early twenty-first century. The story of Aetna helps elucidate some of the larger trends during this transitional period. Aetna entered the 1990s as a conventional commercial insurer, focused on traditional health insurance, even while the corporate managed care model seemed ascendant. The company's leaders then dove into acquisitions and mergers, in the process becoming a dominant managed care model insurer.[34]

Just as managed care was dominating the insurance marketplace, however, anger at MCOs was reaching a boiling point. Physicians, for instance, were suing insurers for payments and sometimes leaving MCOs altogether. (Disclosure: two of us, DH and SW, led a movement against an infamous physician-gag clause imposed by U.S. Healthcare, now Aetna U.S. Healthcare.) Aetna's revenues declined, its stock price sank, and its big investors were soon calling for blood on the boardroom floor. Aetna's response was multifold. First, it moved away from attempting to control costs by constraining payments to doctors (the previous approach to gaining market share), and instead accepted that it would simply pass on rising costs to employers in the form of rising premiums. It also sought to pass along rising costs to "consumers," by increasing patients' out-of-pocket exposure through co-payments, deductibles, and coinsurance.[35]

The push for greater cost sharing went quickly beyond Aetna. Around this time, patients' out-of-pocket exposure costs began to rise throughout the industry. A new insurance product, the "consumer-directed health plan" (CDHP), emerged in the marketplace. CDHPs were defined as high-deductible plans that were combined with an option for some sort of tax-advantaged savings account. In practice, individuals in higher tax brackets generally opened these accounts. Additionally, high-deductible plans proved particularly unattractive for the sick, who experienced greater medical needs and faced greater out-of-pocket expenses.[36] Thus, CDHPs became part of another long-standing insurer strategy of recruiting healthier patients and avoiding sicker ones, so-called cherry picking.

The history of "cost sharing" and "consumer-directed health care" is far less linear and straightforward than the rise of corporate MCOs. In the era before health insurance, for instance, essentially all private health care spending was out-of-pocket.[37] Consumer-driven health care enthusiasts, however, saw the imposition of higher cost-sharing as little less than a revolution.[38] The ideological and academic foundation of consumer-driven healthcare had been laid with decades of research and commentary, going back to the famous RAND health insurance experiment in the 1970s, which was initially conceived as a study to guide the design of a national health insurance program.[39] Though the results of this huge policy experiment were mixed and in many respects ambiguous, many concluded from it that out-of-pocket exposure to health care costs would reduce health utilization, lower spending, and yet not harm health. So an argument became prevalent that people actually had too much health insurance, which caused them to use health care they did not need.

The idea that overinsurance is the fundamental flaw in American health care gained currency through the work of prominent economists and health policy experts.[40] The term "moral hazard," previously used to describe fraudulent practices such as buying fire insurance before burning down your barn, was increasingly applied to patients' use of medical services paid for by their insurance. Conservative economist Milton Friedman, for instance, argued in a 2001 article, "How to Cure Health Care," in favor of high-deductible insurance plans attached to health savings accounts. After all, he noted, "nobody spends somebody else's money as wisely or as frugally as he spends his own."[41] Notably, the "Cadillac Tax" of the ACA, which penalizes expensive (generally more comprehensive) health care plans, is based on this "moral hazard" ideology.

Like the MCO, however, the "victory" of cost sharing was incomplete. On the one hand, these sorts of plans covered more and more workers over the past decade, rising from 4 percent of workers with employer-provided health insurance in 2006 to 24 percent in 2015.[42] Yet although CHDPs covered only a fraction of workers, the impact of this approach became much larger, with growing cost sharing for workers, whether or not they were in a plan explicitly labeled as a CDHP.[43] Moreover, employers shifted the costs of premiums to workers. Between 2005 and 2015, premiums for employer-sponsored health plans for families rose 61 percent, with a disproportionate 83 percent rise in workers' contribution.[44]

Critically, the ACA did not aim to slow this trend toward rising out-of-pocket costs. On the contrary, the law accommodated high cost sharing. In the marketplaces (exchanges), it created a system of four metallic-tiers of coverage, which ranged in actuarial value from 60 percent (bronze) to 90 percent (platinum), meaning that insurance would, on average, pay between 60 percent and 90 percent (respectively) of medical bills, with households paying the remaining 40 percent to 10 percent in co-payments, deductibles, and coinsurance.[45]

But it is important to place this development in a larger context. For progressive health activists, the elimination of financial barriers to care has long been a critical element of "true" universal health care. For instance, in the 1940s, the creation of universally "free" health care was the largely uncontested core of health care reform in Great Britain.[46] And, as we saw earlier, Kennedy's earliest health care proposal, the Health Security Bill of 1970, proposed first-dollar universal coverage.[47] Removing health care entirely from the cash nexus, to a large extent, is tantamount to its de-commodification.[48] In contrast, health care in the United States remains a commodity, purchased for a price, albeit often with substantial public subsidies. This brings us to the third pivot of the health care sector: the consolidation of the health care industry itself.

PIVOT III: THE MULTI-DIMENSIONAL CONSOLIDATION OF HEALTH CARE CAPITAL

In the 1970s, progressives, including scholars such as Vicente Navarro and activists in Health-PAC and the Health Marxist Organization, drew attention to the emerging corporatization and consolidation of the American medical-industrial complex (discussed in chapter 5). Later, in his 1982 book *The Social Transformation of American Medicine*, Paul Starr described five "dimensions" along which such health corporatization was unfolding: (1) a transition in ownership status from nonprofit (and public) to for-profit; (2) horizontal integration (for example, the integration of multiple hospitals into a single health care system); (3) the rise of large enterprises consisting of both profit and nonprofit arms; (4) vertical integration (for example, the integration of health care providers with insurance companies); and (5) the development of regionally or nationally concentrated health care markets.[49] And in 1980, Arnold Relman, editor of the *New England Journal of Medicine*, issued a warning against the "medical industrial complex."[50]

More recently, these processes accelerated. For instance, for-profit conversions became commonplace in the health insurance industry, with most transitioning to for-profit status since for-profit conversions of Blue Cross plans began in 1994.[51] Two large for-profit chains came to own the vast majority of kidney dialysis facilities, and an increasing number of hospitals changed to for-profit ownership.[52] Moreover, most nonprofit hospitals were integrated into larger health systems, which in turn increasingly acquired physician groups, home health services, and other health care providers. The wave of hospital mergers and acquisitions—or horizontal integration—resulted in about half of hospital markets meeting criteria for being "highly concentrated," with many markets having a single dominant hospital system and a few smaller ones.[53] A drive for greater revenue and new investments motivated these developments. A system that failed to expand risked losing market share to competitors in a health services marketplace characterized by aggressive advertising for insured patients. Horizontal consolidation, moreover, gives regionally dominant hospital systems the leverage to command higher prices from insurers. The bigger the system, the higher the price.[54] The acquisition by health care systems of physician practices is a similar strategy to diminish competition and increase leverage, but the impact of this trend on prices is less clear.[55]

Consolidation also has been underway in the health insurance industry. In the summer of 2015, two massive health insurer acquisitions were announced: Anthem's plan to buy Cigna (for $54.2 billion) and Aetna's to acquire Humana (for $37 billion).[56] Had they gone through, only three major nationwide insurers would have remained. However, in 2017, federal judges blocked both mergers. Nonetheless, the possibility for insurance industry consolidation in the future remains. Though the insurers correctly contended that these acquisitions would allow them to "negotiate lower prices with doctors and hospitals,"[57] there is little reason to believe that consumers will benefit from these reductions through lower premiums.[58] Indeed, premiums may even rise. In essence, this wave of insurance mergers amounts to an "arms race"[59] between two competing sectors of the medical industrial-complex: insurance corporations and large provider organizations.

What is the next stage of this arms race? Probably even greater consolidation, specifically the fusion of health care systems with insurance corporations. To some extent, this is nothing new. Kaiser Permanente, for instance, has long served as both insurer and provider to large numbers of Californians. Yet that system is a regionally delimited, not-for-profit organization. But will the new giant health care systems, often with an aggressive business approach regardless of their for-profit or not-for-profit status, also become insurance corporations?

In a few geographical areas, health care systems morphed in this way. Colorado-based Catholic-Health Initiatives, Long Island–based North Shore-LIJ Health System (recently renamed Northwell), and the large Missouri-headquartered Ascension system spun off corporate subsidiaries or subdivisions that have sold health insurance policies, though some systems have retreated from their insurance operations.[60] According to a September 2015 report from Moody's Investors Service, "In the next several years an increasing number of not-for-profit hospitals will enter the commercial health insurance business, looking to improve care management and gain market share."[61] Meanwhile, from the opposite direction, insurance companies have made moves to acquire health care providers and facilities in the United States and internationally.[62] In 2012, for instance, the mega-insurer UnitedHealth Group purchased most of Amil, the largest integrated insurer/hospital system company in Brazil, for $4.3 billion.[63] Its CEO subsequently said that he "could see" buying hospital systems in the United States as well.[64]

Meanwhile, a wave of mergers and acquisitions has led to consolidation in the pharmaceutical industry, As a result, the number of member firms in Big Pharma's lobbying group (Pharmaceutical Research and Manufacturers of America, or PhRMA) fell from 42 in 1988 to 11 in 2014.[65] Simultaneously, four big firms have come to dominate the generic drug industry. And 2017 saw the announcement of a potential merger of a new type: retail pharmacy giant CVS—which also serves as a "pharmacy benefit manager," an intermediary between drug companies and insurers, and runs a chain of walk-in clinics—announced plans to acquire Aetna, one of the largest health insurers, in a $60 billion deal that would be "one of the largest in the history of the health industry."[66]

The Affordable Care Act and the Advance of Health Care Capital

The ACA incorporated huge concessions to corporate health interests, including the pharmaceutical and insurance industries.[67] Coverage did improve for some people with low incomes. The expansion of Medicaid in some states and sliding-scale subsidies for the purchase of private health insurance through state exchanges resulted in a reduction in the number of uninsured.[68] Yet the ACA did not deliver "universal health care." Twenty-eight million remained uninsured in 2016,[69] and a similar number are expected to remain uninsured indefinitely,[70] even if the Republican goal to repeal the ACA never comes to fruition. Thus, though the ACA was a partial accommodation to long-standing popular demands for universal health care, it was to no small degree an accommodation with health care capital. Beyond these concessions to health care industries, the ACA also enshrined into law some of the least favorable characteristics that occurred previously during the three critical pivots of the health care sector.

First, the law promoted Accountable Care Organizations (ACOs), which are essentially modified versions of the corporate MCOs that, as we have traced, rose in the 1970s and crashed in the 1990s. The term ACO first appeared in the medical literature in a 2007 paper[71] arguing that an integrated health system, centered around a hospital, would permit accurate measurement of quality and could "improve the overall experience of care."[72] The ACA subsequently encouraged the formation of ACOs. It created a new program, the Medicare Shared Savings Program, that, along with the Medicare Pioneer ACO program, paid health systems using a formula that offered rewards to those that spent less on their patients and penalized those that spent more.[73] This risk sharing, of course, creates perverse financial incentives that encourage denial of care to patients who need services.

The movement toward ACOs, which started with Medicare, has

been joined en masse by private insurers. In various configurations, ACOs are even emerging worldwide.[74] Moreover, the ACO payment strategy is fueling the consolidation and integration of health care providers. Several factors have contributed to this. First, to be classified as an ACO under Medicare, systems must care for a certain minimum number of beneficiaries. Second, as we have discussed, size matters: larger systems may allow ACOs to negotiate higher payments from private insurers. As a result, health care in most U.S. regions and cities seems likely to be dominated by a few "mega-ACOs" in the years to come.[75] (On consolidation, see chapter 5.)

In addition, the ACA codified the move to increased patient cost sharing—the second pivot toward health care commodification— through high co-payments, deductibles, and co-insurance. For instance, deductibles averaged $5,731 for individual Bronze plans purchased through the ACA's insurance exchanges in 2016.[76] Thus, in addition to the 27 million people expected to remain uninsured over the next decade, an estimated 31 million are already considered underinsured.[77] In sum, the ACA's concessions to corporations have strengthened their hold on the health care system, even while reducing the number of the uninsured. Reversing this dynamic will require more fundamental change.

A New Vision for a Single-Payer National Health Program in the Age of Trump

The ACA's shortcomings and the increasing corporate dominance of health care motivated PNHP's most recent revised proposal for a single-payer reform.[78] All of the PNHP proposals, however, reject the pivots of health care neoliberalism as described in this chapter. They each outline the structure of a comprehensive national health program based on the principles of equity and universalism, in which health care is made available on the basis of health needs, not financial means.

First, the proposals call for comprehensive, first-dollar coverage for everyone in the country. The publicly funded and administered national health program (NHP) would cover all health services—physician care, pharmaceuticals, supplies, nursing care, hospital care, dental care, mental health care, and long-term care—thereby replacing the fragmented public and private patchwork of coverage. Currently, even the insured often lack access to many of these services, in particular long-term care.

The NHP additionally would delink access to health care from individual or household finances through the elimination of cost sharing, that is, co-payments, deductibles, and co-insurance paid at time of health care use. Though cost sharing is the norm in the United States, it is known from the experiences of other nations that such user fees can be eliminated even as costs are controlled. The elimination of these payments would end underinsurance and its ugly manifestations, like medical bankruptcies. At the same time, by covering all, including undocumented immigrants, the NHP would bring an end to uninsurance in the United States. Finally, the NHP would effectively provide "one big network" of doctors and hospitals, putting an end to the insurance networks that separate patients from the providers of their choice and foster the segregation of care. The aim thus would be both universality and equality of access.

The envisioned NHP would also reverse the ascendency of corporate control in the health care system. As in Canada, insurance plans that duplicated the NHP coverage would be prohibited, leaving little residual role for private insurers. For-profit health facilities that participated in the NHP would be required to convert to not-for-profit governance. And when a single integrated health care system achieved regional dominance constituting an effective monopoly, it would be placed under public control, a new element in the latest proposal designed to deal with the problem of increasingly large and dominating health systems.

The proposals also lay out an explicit plan for the construction of new health care facilities and other capital investments. Currently, budgets for operating expenditures and capital expenditures come from a single revenue stream. As a result, new facilities and equipment are built where profits are high, not necessarily where they are needed. In contrast, the NHP would separate operating and capital payments: new capital expenditures would be regionally planned and publicly funded, allowing a planned distribution of new facilities and equipment based on medical needs, not profitability. Such explicit health care planning would help reduce regional inequalities in access to health care facilities and technology, bringing us toward the goal of health care equity.

From the perspective of cost control, the unified and greatly simplified payment system would facilitate the elimination of the enormous administrative waste intrinsic to a privatized, fragmented system.[79] In particular, the global budgeting of hospitals would permit the essential elimination of hospital billing activities, which currently consume 25 percent of hospital expenditures, almost double that of single-payer nations.[80] Additionally, hospitals would be precluded from using these funds for advertising or on exorbitant executive salaries. As mentioned, for-profit hospitals would be excluded from the NHP altogether. Finally, as in other nations, the NHP would use its purchasing clout to bring down drug costs, generating substantial savings. Together, the vast savings that such reforms would generate would easily meet the additional costs of the expanded coverage. In particular, the elimination of administrative waste could free up an approximate $500 billion a year, funds that could then be spent on covering those who lack insurance and broadening and improving coverage for the remainder.[81]

Public funds would, however, still need to be raised to replace the money currently spent on private health insurance premiums and cost sharing. While a mix of payroll taxes and general progressive taxes might accomplish this aim during a transitional period, as with previous proposals, the latest proposal notes that progressive taxation would be a more equitable approach to health system funding. In fact, such a funding system could help to reduce economic inequality itself, which is an increasingly important determinant of poor health.

By happenstance, the publication of the revised PNHP proposal in May 2016 coincided with the Democratic presidential primary campaign. Health care was a major issue dividing the candidates. In contrast to Hillary Clinton, who favored maintaining and perhaps building upon the ACA, Senator Bernie Sanders endorsed single-payer reform along the general lines envisioned in PNHP's proposal.

For a moment, single-payer became a central issue in the political discourse, and the prospects for its achievement seemed to be rising. Sanders's defeat in the primary was thus a major disappointment for many single-payer supporters. The largely unpredicted victory in the general election of Trump, a reactionary billionaire who promised the repeal of the ACA, rattled many health care justice advocates to the core.

The Republican government's assault on health has quickly unfolded in numerous domains. Environmental protections have been rolled back and reproductive health care access has been threatened, while Trump's xenophobic agenda has endangered the health of immigrants. And the government's economic agenda, if achieved, would no doubt greatly exacerbate economic inequality, itself a cause of health inequality.

In the realm of medical care, in 2017 Trump and the Republican Congress tried—and failed—to repeal the ACA, and replace it with something meaner and more regressive. The "American Health Care Act" (AHCA) and its Senate companions would have preserved the basic infrastructure of the ACA, though they would have drastically reduced federal funding of state Medicaid programs, made the ACA's subsidies less generous and more regressive, defunded Planned Parenthood, and inflicted other harms. The resultant savings would have been routed to the wealthy and to health care corporations in the form of tax cuts adding up to more than $800 billion over a decade.[82] Although passed narrowly by the House, and actively supported by Trump, the Republican effort died in the Senate (as of this writing), due in no small part to the efforts of progressive activists who hammered Trumpcare as an assault on health and dignity.

It is unclear whether Republicans will make another go at a full health care bill. But whether or not they do, it seems clear that efforts to defend the status quo will serve as a poor shield against right-wing assault, and will do nothing to advance the larger goal of health care justice. In light of the glaring injustice of the health care status quo, it is understandable that many Americans want something new. That sentiment has crystallized in a growing consensus that the next step for progressives should be a push for single-payer.

During 2017, the fortunes of single-payer rose rapidly. The single payer bill in the House of Representatives gained 120 co-sponsors, the most ever in the bill's history, and more than half of all House Democrats. Senator Sanders made headlines with the release of a new single-payer bill, which was cosponsored by 16 other senators (including leading contenders for the Democratic presidential nomination in 2020), an increase from zero cosponsors for Sanders's previous single-payer bill. Thus, as dark as these times may seem, there is hope on the horizon, especially if political movements in support of single-payer continue to flourish and grow. Now may be an optimal time to coalesce around a more egalitarian alternative.

Political progress necessitates that we look both backwards and forwards. Capitalist health care in the twenty-first century, as we have aimed to show in this chapter, is the product of a decades-long process of corporatization and consolidation. These developments were built first on the failure of universal health care reform and second on the hegemony of the neoliberal health care agenda. The NHP that PNHP proposes, in contrast, seeks both the universalization and the de-commodification of health care in the United States. Understanding and confronting the ascendency of health care capital is a first and necessary step toward this vision. Laying out an explicit vision for a more egalitarian health system is another important step. But actually creating such a program is the final—and by far most difficult—undertaking ahead of us.

13—Overcoming Pathological Normalcy: Mental Health Challenges in the Coming Transformation

Carl Ratner

The troubling condition that has become our "new normal" needs to be rendered intelligible. It is evident that the normal is shot through with pathologies in numerous domains and forms. These pathologies call for an explanation of them as a totality. Normal, or normative, is pathological in certain ways. Pathological normalcy is akin to Marx's construct of the "mode of production." These constructs capture the underlying essence of a social structure that generates the features of individual elements within that structure.

Of course, different normal conditions are pathological in different ways and generate different individual pathologies. Pathological normalcy under capitalism differs from that under fascism, or under slavery, or under autocratic "socialism." The pathological normalcy of a society provides a common target and suggests a common struggle to eradicate the totality of individual pathologies.

This chapter presents a cultural-medical model of contemporary pathology. I explain the nature of that pathology, the kinds of treatment necessary to bring about health, and what health consists of, given that the new normal is pathological. The cultural-medical model contrasts with the conventional, individualized, biomedical model of disease, treatment, and health. I argue that the cultural-medical model reflects the actual causes of pathology better than the conventional model. This model also offers more effective treatments, which will bring about more fulfilling societal, psychological, and physical health. The model goes beyond criticizing the biomedical model; it replaces it with a more valid model that is urgently needed.

The prior, traditional model appears in Figure 13.1. This model associates normality with health and fulfillment. The association encompasses psychology, biology, ecology, and society. This pattern characterizes the vast bulk of the population. Alongside this happy, healthy normality are a few outliers that happen to have suffered debilitating idiosyncratic biopsychological problems, or debilitating idiosyncratic personal experiences, such as having parents killed in a car accident. These random, unusual, idiosyncratic events occur outside normal, healthy social institutions, psychology, and biology. Treatment for these idiosyncratic outliers involves bringing them into the fold of normal society, which will remedy their deficient biology and debilitating personal experiences.

FIGURE 13.1: The Traditional Biomedical Model

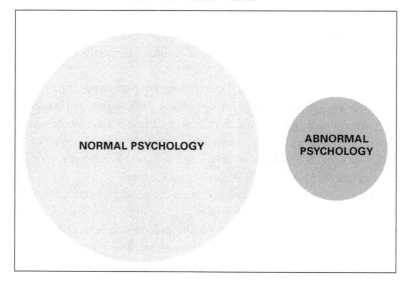

The cultural-medical model portrays pathology and health in a different configuration. It shows that what is commonly viewed as normal is actually pathological in many ways (not entirely, of course). Erich Fromm articulated this construct in his 1964 book, *The Pathology of Normalcy*.[1] Pathological normalcy is a compound term that refers to psychological phenomena and social-cultural phenomena simultaneously. It assumes that social conditions are basic to psychological and biological pathology, health, and treatment, just as the biomedical model implicitly does. The difference in the models is the assumption about the actual nature of social conditions—pathological versus beneficent. This difference generates contradictory notions about health, pathology, and treatment. Figure 13.2 depicts the cultural-medical model.

This cultural-medical model greatly reduces the number of genuinely healthy people. The malevolent pressures of pathologically normal society and psychology generate more intense, extreme forms of abnormal psychology. Abnormal psychology is now drawn into normal society while healthy psychology is forced out, into other protective social domains.

FIGURE 13.2: The Cultural-Medical Model

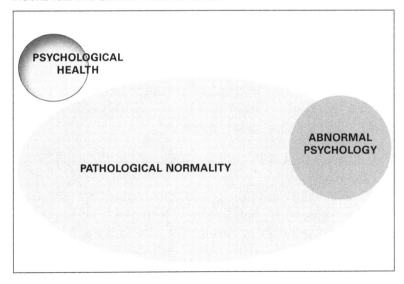

Fromm's model applies to pathologies in general. Consider respiratory disorders. If the normal environment is polluted, then minor respiratory diseases will be prevalent: the normal will be pathological, and pathology will be normal. In addition, normal pollution will aggravate abnormal respiratory diseases and intensify their prevalence. Normal air pollution is killing 3.3 million people a year worldwide.[2] In China alone, a 2015 study estimated that air pollution contributed to approximately 1.6 million deaths a year, or about 4,400 people a day.[3]

This calculation makes normal pollution deadlier than war. Wars do not kill 3.3 million every single year. Pollution also reduces the prevalence of respiratory health. Health will be confined to people who live in protected microclimates where pollution is low, or who have strong biological resistance to respiratory disease.

Pathological normalcy is a critical construct that calls for improving normal society. It is appealing to social activists, though it is rejected by those who favor the status quo. Howard Waitzkin reports that Chilean president Salvador Allende was a medical pathologist who applied pathological normalcy to explaining medical disease.[4] Revolutionary psychologists such as Ignacio Martín-Baró and Frantz Fanon espoused this perspective in understanding the psychological suffering of peasants in Central America and colonized Africans.[5]

NORMAL SOCIETY AND NORMAL PSYCHOLOGY

Pathological normalcy denotes the conditions under which healthy, fulfilling experiences change to pathological, debilitating experiences.[6] I will list only a few examples.

- We have seen that our natural environment is polluted to the point of pathology.
- The political system in the United States and many other countries is pathological, dominated as it is by corporate corruption, campaign financing that distorts elections, lobbying that shapes legislative decisions, dysfunctional political parties, and many other conditions that make democracy unworkable.

- The U.S. economy is pathological in terms of rapidly increasing inequality and the reduction in the standard of living of the masses. "Half of New York City residents say they are struggling economically, making ends meet just barely, if at all."[7] The three wealthiest people in the United States own more wealth than the bottom half of the U.S. population combined, a total of 160 million people.[8] In 2014, the median income of middle class households was 4 percent less than in 2000. Moreover, because of the Great Recession of 2007–2009, median wealth (minus debts) fell by 28 percent from 2001 to 2013. In 2015, 20 percent of U.S. adults were in the lowest income tier, up from 16 percent in 1971.[9]
- Chapters in this book document the crisis of the health care system that is increasingly commodified and individualized.
- The criminal justice system is pathological, fraught with injustice, brutality, and oppressive mass incarceration.
- Education is increasingly class stratified and privatized to exclude marginalized people from educational opportunities. Punishment and control increasingly supplant genuine education in schools: New York City has more than five thousand police officers patrolling the city's schools, which is more than the combined number of school guidance counselors and social workers. Nationwide, more than 17,000 police work in schools. California spends more money on prisons than it does on education.
- Work is pathological in being autocratic and dangerous; work-related illnesses kill 50,000 workers annually in the United States.

If pathology is normal, it is not anomalous or accidental, which is how the medical model portrays it. Pathology must be profitable and useful for the social system, that is, for the dominant class that is enriched and empowered by the system, not for the populace.

The Relative Destructiveness of Pathological Normalcy and Abnormal Behavior

Pathological normalcy explains abnormal psychology in new terms. What we call mental illness is largely rooted in the pathological normality of society and psychology.[10] Oftentimes, the stressors of normalcy become very intense and directly generate abnormal psychology. Unemployment, dangerous work, and low wages often cause abnormal psychology. Research over many decades demonstrates that abnormal psychology (mental illness) is proportional to such social stressors. The intensity of disturbance is highly correlated with the number of social stressors. Stressors, in turn, are a function of social-class position, which itself is correlated with mental illness.[11]

In addition to normal pathology directly causing abnormal psychology and behavior, normal stress aggravates vulnerabilities that may be innate in certain individuals. These two processes are ways that normal pathology exacerbates abnormal psychology. Normal forms of pathology always surround and underlie abnormal, extreme forms. Abnormal behavior is neither discontinuous with, nor anomalous to, normal behavior.

Extreme, abnormal violence is an outgrowth of normal violence. Neoliberal, market-driven public institutions promote antisocial thinking or behavior and inure individuals to inequity and cruelty. Violence is ubiquitous in modern society, from the marketing of the military to imposing financial austerity to the economic decimating of communities, to the exploitation of employees and devaluing human worth at work.[12] Since the United States was founded in 1776, it has been at war during 218 out of its 240 years of existence.

Normal violence stems from the frustrations that irritate people, the lack of social solutions, and individual destructiveness to cope with these conditions. For instance, mass shootings are abnormal-pathological acts. They appear to be the workings of irrational, non-social individuals. However, historical evidence reveals that mass killings in the United States are rooted in changing normal social conditions. In addition, most perpetrators of gun violence are pathologically normal, not psychologically abnormal or mentally ill. "Fewer than 6 percent of the 120,000 gun-related killings in the United States between 2001 and 2010 were perpetrated by people diagnosed with mental illness. Our research finds that across the board, the mentally ill are 60 to 120 percent more likely than the average person to be the victims of violent crime rather than the perpetrators."[13] Most perpetrators of mass killings are alienated angry young men, but these risk factors also describe thousands of people who never commit a mass killing.[14]

Cancer is an abnormality in human biology. Normal environmental contaminants are often the cause. Variations in the toxicity of the environment lead to cultural and geographical differences in cancer prevalence. For instance, exposure to normal indoor residential insecticides is associated with a 47 percent increased risk for childhood leukemia and a 43 percent increased risk for childhood lymphomas. Outdoor pesticides and herbicides are associated with a 26 percent increased risk for brain tumors.[15] Children are not becoming increasingly susceptible to these serious diseases because of increased individual, innate vulnerability in genes.

Abnormal economic crises are similarly the direct and logical outcome of pathological-normal economic and financial practices. The Great Recession exemplifies this point. Most factors that precipitated it were legal, normal acts. Politicians such as Ronald Reagan and Bill Clinton approved laws that made it legal for banks to mix risky, high-profit loans with stable, secure "working capital." Easy credit led people to increase their personal borrowing. Speculative building and buying led to risky loans. New financial instruments such as credit default swaps allowed the commodifying of financial risk to facilitate easier disposing and disguising of it.

In certain cases, extreme events are precipitated or prolonged by a natural basis that is worsened by pathologically normal activities. This tendency is manifested in a variety of phenomena. Global warming is a natural cyclical phenomenon, but natural cyclical warming trends are exacerbated to dangerous levels by pathologically normal ecological conditions, which produce their own social and health problems. For instance, they intensified the recent California drought by 25 percent, according to research from Columbia University, and contributed to the devastating fires that in 2017 destroyed homes and habitat in California and the Pacific Northwest.[16] The Fukushima nuclear catastrophe in March 2011 was precipitated by a natural earthquake and tsunami. However, it was greatly worsened by the normal, profit-driven, financial decisions that minimized safety concerns in the construction and maintenance of the nuclear reactors. Those are what transformed the tsunami from a misfortune to a catastrophe.

We usually think that extreme, abnormal behavior is more destructive than normal problems because this is what the medical model presents. However, pathological normality reverses this relationship. The social effect of pathologically normal violence is far greater than the effects of abnormal violence. Pathologically normal violence includes war. Presidents and secretaries of defense who authorize and plan wars are not mentally ill. Nor are the soldiers who fight in wars and kill opponents. Yet the damage they cause far exceeds the damage from abnormal violence by "berserk" gunmen. Pathologically normal economic practices, the daily manipulation, cheating, speculation, de-skilling, outsourcing, tax code revisions, and exploitation, are all more destructive than the criminal thief.

Extreme unusual events receive the most attention. People believe that extreme, abnormal behavior is the most fearful threat to normal social life and psychology. It is supposed to make normal life pathological by overrunning it with abnormal elements from outside. This is how the Islamic State in Iraq and Syria (ISIS) is portrayed. The truth is the opposite: rising normal pathology is more destructive, and it produces increasingly abnormal behavior. Normal U.S. foreign policy generated ISIS. And normal policies that govern unemployment, working conditions, and pollution generate more deaths in the United States than extreme terrorists do. Contrary to popular opinion, extreme events are highlighted in news media because they are minor problems that are not the basis of social ills and demand no changes in pathological normalcy. Leaders highlight them to appear concerned with social health, while they allow real problems of pathological normalcy to persist, thereby enriching and empowering themselves and other elites.

PSYCHOLOGICAL TREATMENT AND INTERVENTION

In oppressive, pathologically normal social conditions, pathology cannot be treated according to the biomedical model. Pathology in the biomedical model is readily treated by individual interventions to eradicate individual pathogens. The normal environment in which people live is healthy and fulfilling, and it reinforces the individual treatment of pathogens. It protects the recovering patient from relapse.

Pathological normality falsifies this scenario because the lived environment is toxic. Individual treatment of abnormal disorders remains contradicted by toxic normality, which continually pushes the patient back into pathology.[17] Such treatment deforms the patient to adjust to toxic normalcy. For instance, psychotropic medication desensitizes or tranquilizes the individual to social stressors and makes them less perceptible. Medication does not eliminate the stressors, the pollution, the junk food, or other pathogens so that the patient will attain a healthy and fulfilled state.[18]

The more that normal society is pathological, the less effective "normal" treatments become. Such treatments strive to adjust the individual patient to mainstream society, or to make minor policy adjustments to enhance individual success. More fundamental solutions require transforming the broader social conditions that constitute pathological normalcy.[19]

DENYING PATHOLOGICAL NORMALCY AND LEGITIMATING THE STATUS QUO

Preserving the status quo and its leadership requires that the social system appears healthy and that pathology is defined as deviating from normality.[20] There are two strategies for constructing this misleading picture.

First, the biomedical model interprets pathology as an isolated, separate realm of abnormality, unrelated to normal society or psychology. One strategy for cleansing normalcy from pathology is to misdiagnose it as abnormal psychology. For instance, the Diagnostic and Statistical Manual used for psychiatric diagnosis describes using marijuana as an abnormal disorder ("cannabis use disorder"). A long list of behavioral criteria includes use in larger amounts or over a longer period than was originally intended. Such mundane behaviors become defined as abnormal psychology. Similarly, more than ten thousand U.S. children younger than two years old are prescribed the psychotropic drugs risperidone (Risperdal) and fluoxetine (Prozac). Health care providers have given a diagnosis of attention deficit hyperactivity disorder to at least 10,000 children age two or three and then have prescribed medications such as amphetamine-dextroamphetamne (Adderall).[21] The "disorders" that inspire this prescribing are generally normal temper tantrums or other socially generated acts. Under conditions of pathological normality, such mundane behaviors become classified as abnormal psychology.

In addition to conceptually classifying pathological normalcy as abnormal psychology, psychiatry distances disturbed individuals from normal society by social and physical means. Psychiatry treats such people in special institutions such as prisons and long-term and short-term recovery facilities. Psychotropic medication for serious disturbances renders many of those patients unfit for full social participation. This social and medical segregation of patients from normal society creates a social and physical "Other" in which pathology is diagnosed and separated from non-pathology. Such segregation then uses the socially created Other to justify the notion that psychopathy is something naturally apart from normal society and must be given special treatment. Medication and psychotherapy bolster this notion by treating psychopathy as an individual disease that is individually treated. High recidivism seems to confirm this assumption of individual abnormality, because even after professional treatment, the disturbed still cannot function normally.

Denying and obscuring pathological normalcy is common in how extreme events are reported. News reports of extreme behavior isolate the perpetrator from normal society. They typically state that the perpetrator was mentally ill. This approach is designed to end discussion of social causes because mental illness is portrayed as accidental, random, or rooted in esoteric, biochemical dysfunction or traumatic individual experience. The news then searches the personal life and motives of the perpetrator. Societal conditions usually are not mentioned as a cause. Instead, society is portrayed as the victim, and greater security is imposed to protect it. This portrayal only protects the pathological normalcy that caused the extreme behavior in the first place.

Gun violence is portrayed as a product of individual disturbance or terrorism. This distracts from the fact that 13,000 gun homicides are committed annually in the United States. Construing gun violence as abnormal limits solutions to prohibiting disturbed, risky individuals from buying guns. This construction allows the vast violence of normal society and normal people to continue unabated.

A second strategy for de-pathologizing the normal is to redefine pathology as healthy or fulfilling. For example, concern about obesity is condemned as prejudice against overweight people.[22] Obesity is construed as a lifestyle choice, as valuable as any other, and deserving of respect and tolerance. De-pathologization ignores the causes of obesity under current social conditions, especially the role of food producers aiming to increase consumption and profit. Food manufacturers add salt and sugar to stimulate food consumption, knowing that these ingredients are unhealthy.[23] This problem is disregarded by accepting food consumption as personal choice, ideologically shifting social structural issues to individual issues.

Pathological normalcy is the cause of most abnormal pathology. The cultural-medical model critiques pathological normalcy as our existential condition. This model leads to transformative politics because its critique of purportedly normal society leads inexorably to calling for societal transformation. We must not shy away from criticizing pathologically normal behavior as pathological. We are not criticizing the individuals themselves; we are utilizing their pathologies as indictments of "normal" society. Individuals are victims of "normality."

This approach leads to a critique of pathologically normal society and testifies to a need for revolutionary change. Social critique is also behavioral-psychological critique because it recognizes that systemic problems are manifested in individual behavior and psychology. Conversely, behavioral problems of individuals are grist for the revolutionary mill, if they are recognized as calling for social transformation that moves beyond the pathological normalcy of twenty-first century capitalism.

POLITICAL ACTION FOR SOCIAL IMPROVEMENT

It is commonly believed that improving society depends upon mitigating abnormal, antisocial acts that disturb healthy normality. However, because pathological normalcy is more destructive than abnormal behavior, social improvement depends upon changing the structure of normal society and psychology.

A healthy normal social system will generate fulfilling, beneficent behaviors throughout social domains. This radically different situation will supplant the need for individual strategizing about how to overcome pathologically normal influences. For example, when food is wholesome, with junk food minimized, eating what is available becomes much healthier. The individual does not have to navigate, negotiate, resist, and strategize how to eat well.

Individual treatment, like all individualistic strategies for improvement, is inefficient and expensive because each individual must be sought out and treated, one by one. Or each individual must treat himself or herself, through personal resources and efforts. And each person must waste time sifting through multiple private insurance plans, instead of having one simple national plan that covers everyone. Additionally, individual efforts will be counteracted by pathological social conditions. Such conditions, for instance, account for most dieters' failure to lose weight over the long run, because junk food remains widely available.

Rather than trying to circumvent pathological conditions of society through individual counteractions, the more effective solution is to transform pathological normalcy so that social conditions support psychological, physical, and ecological health. It is impossible to solve specific pathologies in education, health care, government, news, entertainment, policing, incarceration, international relations, ecology, and the like because pathological normalcy reinforces a given social system and the dominant social class that runs and profits by it. Reforms that are acceptable to the status quo are inadequate for solving problems, and reforms that truly solve problems are unacceptable to the status quo. Adequacy and acceptability are antithetical in pathological normality. Indeed, acceptability is a sign of inadequacy.

Instead of proposing new policies within the status quo to improve it, a different social system must be built that eradicates pathological normalcy by transforming it. All solutions to individual pathologies must fall within this broad objective. The criterion for addressing a social problem is whether the alternative will inspire an alternative normality, not whether it is feasible within the existing normality. We must acknowledge that problems of pathological normalcy cannot be solved within its own parameters. Minor technical improvements within the status quo are possible and helpful, but they do not solve larger problems. Cancer screening and radiation treatments may prolong life, but they do not solve those problems of cancer that could be solved by de-polluting the environment. Raising the minimum wage does not eradicate class hierarchy.

Although proposals can be offered to the pathological status quo as improvements for social problems, they generally will be rejected or co-opted to the extent that pathological normalcy is functional for a dominant social class, which resists change. This perspective means that the construct of pathological normalcy calls for a revolutionary praxis aiming to eradicate it. The path beyond capitalism, as suggested in the last chapter of this book, involves a conscious struggle to replace pathological normalcy with a post-capitalist normalcy where social conditions foster mental health rather than undermine it.

14—Confronting the Social and Environmental Determinants of Health

Carles Muntaner and Rob Wallace

As critics of Obamacare and global "universal health coverage" efforts have noted, not even universal access and the elimination of for-profit corporations from health care would guarantee health equity in the United States, or anywhere else for that matter.[1] Social relations, encompassing economic, political, and cultural interrelationships, are the most important determinants of population health.[2] The forty-year difference in life expectancy between Chad (around fifty years) and Monaco (around ninety) cannot be explained by access to health care alone.

Indeed, social determinants encapsulate even health care systems themselves. Although access to care contributes to longevity and quality of life, access does not in itself achieve those ends.[3] Social and environmental determinants of health are embedded in humanity's social structures and exert an overwhelming impact on health, routinely explaining the greatest part of the variation in health outcomes.[4]

From our species' origins onward, infectious diseases, historically the greatest source of human mortality, have repeatedly emerged with major shifts in economic, political, and cultural practices.[5] Domesticated animals served as sources for human diphtheria, influenza, measles, mumps, plague, pertussis, rotavirus A, tuberculosis, sleeping sickness, and visceral leishmaniasis.[6] Ecological changes brought upon landscapes by human modification have caused spillovers of cholera from algae, malaria from birds, and HIV/AIDS, dengue fever, malaria, and yellow fever from wild primates such as monkeys.

Each round of new infections stimulated innovations in medicine and public health, including individual treatment and prevention, as well as population level interventions, including land and marine quarantines, compulsory burial, isolation wards, water treatment, and subsidies for the sick and unemployed.[7] Indeed, as classic work by John McKinlay, Sonja McKinlay, and Thomas McKeown showed, the declines in infectious diseases that eventually marked the first half of the twentieth century in industrial countries resulted primarily from public health interventions and less so from medical advances.[8] Each series of agricultural and industrial inventions through history, including those focusing specifically on health, accelerated demographic shifts and new settlement, placing susceptible host populations close to novel sources of infection and environmental exposure.[9]

In this chapter, we consider contemporary examples in which social and environmental determinants, often lost in the debates around health care, have affected population health. Without a broader revolution in how communities live, work, and relate, even a single-payer plan would fail to stem poor health outcomes. Let us emphasize that health services and broader public health interventions are not mutually exclusive but rather need to be addressed together in the struggles ahead.[10]

SOCIAL DETERMINANTS OF HEALTH

Despite their contribution to longevity and quality of life, health services nowadays are considered only one social determinant of health.[11] The social environment shapes health and disease through pregnancy, child development, education, work, housing, and community, among other impacts.[12] Yet much research on social determinants analyzes them in isolation from one another, as if they were independent risk factors.[13]

Without a more systemic approach, the way society shapes health and disease remains elusive. Strong and reliable associations between racial categories and mortality, for instance, might suggest underlying causes yet speak little about how racism imposes itself on health. Generalized gradients of occupational rank and health might suggest social mechanisms but by themselves omit the exploitation, domination, discrimination, and other relevant social processes that explain health inequalities. This is where the Marxian tradition, starting with Engels's *The Condition of the Working Class in England*, can provide greater insights by uncovering the illness-generating social conditions that do not fit the pragmatic framework built largely around descriptions, gradients, and associations.[14]

There are examples where public health policies that explicitly address social determinants have achieved marked successes. For instance, some countries require the participation of other government sectors, such as transportation, in addition to health departments.[15] Such health policy strategies, known as intersectoral action (ISA) or Health in All Policies (HiAP), have achieved a variety of population health improvements over several decades.[16] The recent example of the Canadian "Housing First" ISA intervention among homeless persons with severe mental disorders eliminated preconditions for housing.[17] HiAP meanwhile reduced cardiovascular mortality in North Karelia, Finland, an effort that combined the education sector, the media, and producers of dairy goods.[18]

ISA has been implemented in a variety of countries, with leadership on the approach from low- and middle-income countries such as India, Jamaica, Sri Lanka, and Thailand.[19] With HiAP added, the list now includes Cuba, Brazil, Malaysia, Iran, Colombia, Ecuador, Morocco, Uganda, Venezuela, and Chile, in addition to some high-income countries such as Finland, Australia, Canada, Belgium, the United Kingdom, New Zealand, Sweden, and Norway.[20]

Countering the Effects of Capitalist Production: Traffic Mortality

Interventions in road and traffic mortality offer another example. The impact of transportation on mortality, injuries, and mental health is a growing area of research in the field of social determinants.[21] Global road and traffic fatalities number 1.2 million a year, a number increasing over time, with most concentrated in the Global South.[22] Motor vehicle mortality has been rising with globalization.[23] Economic growth entails greater labor exploitation, putting more workers on the road and leading to more injuries and fatalities.[24] Several interventions have been proposed.[25] But while officials and policymakers increasingly acknowledge the impact of transport on population health, their approaches have often favored capital accumulation and private modes of transportation over public health goals that specifically focus on eliminating injuries and fatalities.

In contrast, "Vision Zero," an ISA in traffic safety, has been implemented across multiple countries, including in Sweden where road traffic deaths are dropping as a result.[26] Vision Zero applies the egalitarian principles of public health, namely that the preservation of life takes precedence over other objectives of the traffic system, any road traffic fatality is unacceptable, and the government must assume responsibility for road traffic deaths. The Swedish case provides evidence that social determinants of health can be tackled with policies that both improve population health and reduce inequities in health, since the working and middle classes tend to suffer disproportionately from road traffic injuries.[27]

In addition to transportation, ISA or HiAP initiatives have addressed nutrition, education, urban planning, employment, and housing programs in mostly high- and middle-income countries.[28] While such programs are implemented in cities, provinces, and other subnational units, other macroeconomic, political, and cultural policies tackle the determinants of health at the national, regional, or global levels.[29] As we will touch on next, such macro-level policies address the most fundamental social determinants of health, or what are known as "the causes of the causes."[30]

Policies to Improve Population Health

At the national level, good-faith approaches aimed at addressing the social determinants of health historically have achieved successes for social democratic and socialist governments.[31] Countries in the Global South have taken the lead in the field of health equity. Kerala

State in India, Sri Lanka before the civil war, and more recently, the Bolivarian Misiones (Missions) in Venezuela, the Plan Nacional del Buenvivir (National Plan of Good Living) in Ecuador, and the Bolsa Família (Family Allowance) in Brazil have offered advances in ISA and HiAP.[32]

Several northern European countries meanwhile have used their wealth, science, technology, and social democratic governance to implement policies that have targeted social determinants.[33] These policies entail relatively high levels of social spending, public sector services (under the rubric of de-commodification), prevention, policy integration, decentralization, consensus building, and evaluation. The social determinants acted upon include child development, education, housing, neighborhood environments, traffic, nutrition, employment and working conditions, family policy, social exclusion, aging, and gender.[34] The policies have led to poverty reduction, income inequality reduction, and improvements in some health outcomes.[35] Threats to these achievements include austerity policies of the European Union and new free trade agreements (for details, see chapter 8).

ENVIRONMENTAL DETERMINANTS OF HEALTH

In contrast to social determinants of health, environmental determinants usually refer to "abiotic," or non-living, chemical or physical components of the environment that impact health. Such determinants include air pollution, water quality, climate and climate change, flooding, altitude, geomagnetic activity, heavy metals, agricultural chemicals, and other largely geophysical impacts.[36] The term "environmental determinants" embodies something of a false dichotomy, as environmental inputs, whatever their geneses before human society, are at this point in history often socially determined.[37] In this context, we next explore three examples: the effects of privatization on water quality; the epidemiological damage that deforestation causes; and the emergence of virulent infectious diseases from industrialized livestock. (We do not include the enormous problem of climate change in this analysis because its impact as an environmental determinant of health receives the wide attention it deserves elsewhere.)[38]

Potable Water without Protection

The lead crisis in Flint, Michigan, offers a quintessential example clarifying the social origins of our abiotic environments. Following up residents' complaints about discoloration, taste, and smell, Virginia Tech researchers tested 271 Flint homes for lead levels in their tap water.[39] Investigators found levels from 27 parts per billion (ppb), five times greater than concentrations considered safe—an exposure leading to cardiovascular problems, kidney damage, and neurological morbidity—to levels as high as over 5,000 ppb, a level the Environmental Protection Agency defines as "toxic waste."[40] The state reported additional increases in levels of carcinogenic "total trihalomethanes"—disinfectants chloroform, bromoform, bromodichloromethane, and dibromochloromethane—above EPA standards.[41]

Pediatrician Mona Hanna-Attisha and colleagues determined that the proportion of Flint infants and children with above-average levels of lead doubled since 2014 and in some areas even tripled, with likely lifelong impact on cognition and motor skills.[42] The state also announced a spike in Legionella bacterium in the water, with eighty-seven reported infections, ten of them fatal.[43]

How did such a public health crisis come about in a modern industrial city? In 2011, citing Flint's $15 million deficit, Michigan governor Rick Snyder placed the city under emergency management.[44] Unelected appointees took over responsibilities that democratically elected officials previously exercised over the city's budget, local law, and public sector union contracts.[45] In one of the nation's poorest cities, historically victimized by environmental injustice associated with the auto industry, one appointee, Darnell Earley, doubled residential water rates to twice the state average—twice that of New York City, seven times that of Miami, and ten times that of Phoenix, a city built in the middle of a desert.[46]

Michigan decided to save another $20 million over eight years by switching Flint off Detroit water.[47] Instead of keeping Flint connected for the two years a new pipeline to Lake Huron was to be built, Earley, with approval from the Michigan Department of Environmental

Quality (DEQ), turned about-face on the state's previous position and decided to source the heavily polluted Flint River.[48] The DEQ advised the city to follow a protocol for treating water from the Flint River that was intended for new water systems, leaving out a crucial corrosion-control chemical, standard in cities across the country, that prevents lead from leaching out of older pipes at a total cost of $140 a day.[49]

As environmental engineer Terese Olson explained, an environmental health disaster quickly followed from this quest to save money:

> The Flint River is naturally high in corrosive chloride. Therefore, iron pipes in the water distribution system began corroding immediately after the initial switch from Detroit water. The iron that was released from the corroding pipes reacted with residual chlorine that is added to kill microorganisms, making it unavailable to function as a disinfectant.
>
> Because chlorine, which reacted with the iron pipes, could not act as a disinfectant, bacteria levels spiked. When coliform bacteria were detected in distribution system water samples, water utility managers were obliged by law to increase the levels of chlorine. The higher levels of chlorine, while reducing coliform counts, led to the formation of more trihalomethanes.[50]

Michigan learned of the damage early. Upon noticing its engine parts were rusting under the new water regime in 2014, the General Motors plant in Flint, which helped pollute the river in the first place, obtained a variance to switch back to Detroit water, costing the state of Michigan $440,000 in operational costs to do so.[51] In the face of its assurances to Flint residents throughout 2015 that their water was safe to drink, emails as early as January showed the state so concerned about its own employees' safety that it had purified water delivered to the city's state office building.[52] DEQ officials meanwhile gamed residents' complaints about the water by refusing to retest homes that scored high for lead and demanding owners of test homes flush their lines before water sampling, diluting readings.[53] The stonewalling led residents to contact the Virginia Tech team that discovered and, unlike the state government, shared the extent of the crisis. Much of the blood testing since has been financed by lawyers preparing to sue the state.[54]

The notion that mass poisoning could be tagged as accident, negligence, or even cover-up fails to square with a larger context. A broader program of neoliberal expropriation frames the crisis. Preceding Flint's water switch, the Detroit Water and Sewer Department (DWSD) offered Flint a deal that would have saved the emergency-managed city millions of dollars.[55] Flint could have continued on the Detroit pipeline it had used for over fifty years. The state rejected the offer because, insiders reported, Governor Snyder was intent on breaking up DWSD and privatizing its operations.[56] Whatever Snyder's plans, the state, in a water war of its own making, intended to break Flint away from the DWSD, a safer source of water based in the public sector.[57] (Chapter 11 analyzes the water war in Bolivia as an example of struggles to come.)

The pallets of bottled water that celebrities and others eventually donated with good intentions—water Flint residents drank and bathed in amid continued reports of rashes, itchiness, and hair loss—represented another manifestation of the economic mechanics that poisoned the water supply in the first place.[58] Daniel Jaffee and Soren Newman analyze the shift in bottled water from niche product to ubiquitous staple as emblematic of what John Bellamy Foster and colleagues have presented as Lauderdale's Paradox, in which the loss or enclosure of a freely available resource adds to its exchange value.[59] "Municipal tap water networks," write Jaffee and Newman,

> pose substantial barriers to capital accumulation, leading one influential scholar to frame water as an "uncooperative commodity." However, bottled water's characteristics enable it to evade many of these constraints, rendering it a "more perfect commodity" for accumulation. Second, expansion of the market good of bottled water alters the prospects for the largely publicly provided good of tap water. We conclude that the growth of this relatively new commodity represents a more serious threat to the project of universal public drinking water provision than that posed by tap water privatization.[60]

The poisoning of Flint's children for the sake of bondholders and other investors covering the costs of the new pipeline shows that the two threats of privatization and commodification of water are not mutually exclusive. Jaffee and Newman's point illuminates the extent to which capital aims at fencing off the commons to include even the water we drink.

Forests without Disease Resilience

A Flint bereft of political power during a fight over the commodification of water loses the protection of the most basic of shared resources. West Africa or Bahia, Brazil, stripped of its forest by export-led mining, logging, and monoculture agriculture, loses the ecosystemic relationships that routinely control its deadliest pathogens.

In late 2013 an Ebola outbreak emerged from the agroforest of southern Guinea.[61] The molecular characteristics of the virus proved little different from previous variants. Yet the outbreak strain would propagate across the region, infecting 28,000 people and killing 11,000, leaving bodies in the streets of capital cities Monrovia, Liberia, and Conakry, Guinea.[62] How to explain this apparent phase shift from intermittent forest killer, taking out a village here and there, to an infection that threatened to turn into a pandemic?

Some commentators have noted the structural adjustment to which West Africa has been subjected, a divestiture of public health infrastructure that would permit even a deadly infection to go ill-treated or even unnoticed once it spilled over from its animal reservoir.[63] However, as Rob Wallace and colleagues describe, the source of the outbreak appears to extend back into the forest itself.[64] Shifts of land use in forested Guinea during the past decade depended in large part on neoliberal efforts at opening the region to global circuits of capital. Continental Africa represents about 60 percent of the world's last farmland frontier. The World Bank characterizes the Guinea Savannah Zone, stretching across West Africa, as "one of the largest underused agricultural land reserves in the world."[65] The Bank views the Savannah as best developed on the industrial model, mainly by multinational agribusiness corporations.

From the new agricultural regime, an archipelago of hybrid oil palm plots has emerged in and around the Guéckédou area, the Ebola outbreak's apparent ground zero.[66] The characteristic landscape is a mosaic of villages surrounded by dense vegetation and interspersed by crop fields of oil palm and patches of open forest and regenerated young forest. The general pattern can be discerned at a finer scale as well west of the town of Meliandou, where the index cases of the new Ebola were identified. The landscape may embody a growing interface between humans and fruit-eating bats, a key reservoir for Ebola, including hammer-headed bats, little collared fruit bats, and Franquet's epauletted fruit bats.[67] Nur Shafie and colleagues document a variety of disturbance-associated fruit bats attracted to oil palm plantations.[68] Bats migrate to oil palm for food and shelter from the heat, while the plantations' wide trails permit easy movement between roosting and foraging sites. As the forest disappears, multiple species of bat shift their foraging behavior to the food and shelter that are left.

Almudena Marí Saéz and others have since proposed that the initial Ebola spillover in Guinea occurred outside Meliandou when children, including the putative index case, caught and played with Angolan free-tailed bats in a local tree.[69] The bats are an insectivore species also previously documented as an Ebola virus carrier. As Rodrick Wallace and colleagues describe, whatever the specific reservoir source, shifts in agroeconomic context still appear a primary cause.[70] Previous studies show the free-tailed bats also attracted to expanding cash crop production in West Africa, including sugarcane, cotton, and macadamia.[71]

Indeed, nearly every Ebola outbreak to date appears connected to capital-driven shifts in land use, including logging, mining, and agriculture, back to the first outbreak in Nzara, Sudan, in 1976, where a British-financed factory spun and wove local cotton.[72] When Sudan's civil war ended in 1972, the area rapidly repopulated and much of Nzara's local rain forests and bat ecology was reclaimed for subsistence farming, with cotton returning as the area's dominant cash crop.[73] Hundreds of bats were roosting in the factory itself and several workers became infected.

The ostensible "background" of the forest from which Ebola and other pathogens emerge, the sum of chance interactions across agroecological actors, may be a key explanation for the outbreak.[74] Neotropical forests are complicated environments marked by complex ecological webs of pathogens and hosts, prey and predators, competitors and mutualists, among other functional relationships. Most pathogens rarely get the chance to line up enough susceptible hosts into the chain of transmission that the disease agent needs to make it out of the forest. There appears an inbuilt environmental inertia that cushions outbreaks. For Ebola, a gorilla troop or a human village or two every couple of years suffers a spillover event, a terrible thing, but the outbreak spreads no farther. When forests are stripped out by logging and monoculture crops, most pathogens die out along with their hosts. But other strains hit the veritable jackpot. These disease agents, Ebola now among them, are no longer constrained by the forest ecosystem and their hosts adjust to the new opportunity, helping produce much wider outbreaks.

A similar dynamic appears to help account for the emergence of Zika in urban Brazil.[75] Zika is a mosquito-borne RNA virus of the Flavivirus group that has caused a broad outbreak of infant microcephaly and adult Guillain-Barré syndrome, among other neuropathies. At one point, the World Health Organization projected Zika to infect four million Latin Americans.[76]

Although an urban disease, Zika's success appears in part connected to capital-led changes in the periurban landscape as far away as the edge of the neotropical forest. Geographer Christian Brannstrom reported that two million square kilometers of the grassland-woodland Cerrado savannah of western Bahia in Brazil has been converted to a "neoliberal frontier" of ranch and farmland, often properties in excess of 5,000 hectares.[77] Farmers raise soy, cotton, coffee, and fruit crops for the export market, with the Bahia government subsidizing infrastructure cost-sharing, value-added tax discounts, and rebates on finance charges for the largest projects.

Cleide de Albuquerque and colleagues recorded a coincidental shift in mosquito community ecology on the heavily populated coast, with the arrival of Aedes albopictus in the native forests of Recife, which became the urban epicenter for Zika-associated microcephaly in the state of Pernambuco.[78] Albopictus joined the already established Aedes aegypti and Culex quinquefasciatus, and what were for researchers a surprising variety of other novel vector species, reported carriers of filariasis, dengue, Rocio virus, Mayaro virus, and yellow fever.[79] In short, much as with the bats in West Africa, the mosquitoes of Brazil may have shifted their geographic range in response to development driven by global circuits of capital, with profound impacts on novel or reemergent pathogens.

Megafarms without Natural Selection

Whereas many pathogens are emerging out of forests where multinational corporations are mining, logging, and raising export crops and livestock, the kinds of megafarms with which forests are replaced are also sources of new infections. Among such emergent pathogens are industrial Campylobacter, Nipah virus, Q fever, hepatitis E, Salmonella enteritidis, foot-and-mouth disease, and a variety of novel influenza variants, including H1N1 (2009), H1N2v, H3N2v, H5N1, H5N2, H6N1, H7N1, H7N3, H7N7, H7N9, and H9N2.[80] Global consumption of largely cosmetic antimicrobials in industrial cattle, chickens, and pigs is projected to increase 67 percent from approximately 63,000 to 106,000 tons each year until 2030, selecting for the kind of total antibiotic resistance already emerging in human patients.[81]

By its business model and logistics, industrial livestock production offers a powerful mechanism of selecting for greater deadliness in circulating strains of viruses and bacteria.[82] Research that models the evolution of virulence shows that increases in livestock and poultry populations, increases in the rate of harvest, increases in the geographic extent of commodity production, and decreases in variation of genetic immunity, all central to industrial production, select for increases in pathogen deadliness.[83]

The diversity of influenza has long played an important role in the way the virus is able to evolve new characteristics in nature.[84] The same can now be said for industrial poultry and livestock. In 1982 virologist Kennedy Shortridge recorded 46 among what were then 108 possible combinations of influenza virus strains at a single poultry factory in Hong Kong.[85] More recently, a consortium tracked the various H1 and H3 subtypes moving through Hong Kong swine, including classical swine influenza, European or Eurasian swine flu, the triple-reassortant swine flu (H1N1, 2009), and seasonal H1N1 and H3N2 influenza.[86] Guan Yi's group showed that influenza A (H5N1) underwent a population increase and spike in diversity only when the virus entered populations of domestic poultry in China.[87]

The influenzas of increasing evolutionary diversity transitioning into and supported by poultry are also spilling over into humans.[88] For decades human populations supported influenza serotypes of only the H1, H2, and H3 classes, which are commonly known as seasonal influenzas. Now a broad variety of H5, H6, H7, and H9 serotypes, for which human populations express little individual or herd immunity, are appearing rapidly.

An increasing diversity of pathogens is driven in part by the changing economics of the livestock sector. Three of swine flu H1N1's genomic segments originated in the classical swine influenza (HA, NP, NS), three segments from a North American H3N2-avian-swine recombinant (PB2, PB1, PA), and two from a Eurasian swine recombinant (NA, M).[89] In short, every one of H1N1's genetic segments proved most closely related to those of influenzas circulating among swine, together originating on wholly different continents. That is a geographic range that no small farming operation can explain. Only multinational corporations can facilitate such profound biological changes over very long distances. And unlike avian influenza, for which industrial apologists blame wild waterfowl, there are no wild pigs to blame.

Consolidation in industrial agriculture meanwhile affects the evolution and spread of influenza viruses in other ways. Nearly three-quarters of the world's poultry breeding is in the hands of a few multinational corporations.[90] The primary breeders, who engineer the first three generations of poultry for cooking ("broiler lines") that commercial firms ("multiplier companies") subsequently market, declined from eleven companies in 1989 to four in 2006. The ten companies producing chickens that lay eggs ("layer lines") in 1989 were consolidated to two by 2006: the Erich Wesjohann Group and Hendrix Genetics. The value of the products that these primary breeders provide is biologically "locked" by offering multiplier companies only the males of the male lines and females of the female line.[91] As a result, batches of hybrid chickens, whose genetic makeup is a trade secret, must be purchased continuously from the primary breeder. By this industrial cascade, from producer to many multiplier companies, a single-source chicken can serve as the progenitor for millions of broiler progeny, largely bred for their sellable characteristics alone: fast-growing, large breasts, etc.

This practice in effect removes natural selection as a self-correcting (and free) ecological service.[92] When farmers or public health officials kill off those poultry that avoided being struck dead by the virus as a safety precaution, the culling has no bearing on the development of immune resistance to the pathogens identified, as these birds, broilers and layers alike, do not breed on site and are unable to evolve in response. In other words, the failure to accumulate natural resistance to circulating pathogens is built into the industrial model before a single outbreak occurs. Such circumstances, putting profit before epidemiology, are likely to cultivate devastating epidemics across animal and human populations alike in the decades to come.

OUR HEALTH IS A SHARED COMMONS

The condition of our health care system is an important input for population health. In organizing medical care around extracting profit, neoliberal policies trade broad health coverage across populations for just-in-time expediency, benefiting mainly patients who can afford it. Inequities in access become another of the social determinants that, along with the determinants we have discussed here, drive population health.

But even a socialized health care system that fills those gaps would represent an insufficient service. As global road and traffic mortalities, collapses of municipal water quality, and epidemics produced by multinational agribusiness show, social and environmental determinants impact health outcomes for billions of people, which even the very best health care systems can treat only on the back end. A truly socialized medicine would integrate public health as a shared commons across populations.

Presently, ecologies that connect neighborhoods, water, land, and disease have been so alienated from their locales as to turn many a landscape into economic ideology incarnated. Geographer Jason Moore goes so far as to propose that capitalist production does not have an ecology so much as it is an ecology, one divorced from the most basic of organismal needs.[93] As if humans, and the animal populations on which we depend, can eat stock options and drink investment. As if housing, food, and water, in some natural order of capitalism, must be made available only to those who can pay for what previously constituted our open commons. The damage extends beyond expropriation. The sociopathologies at the heart of what James O'Connor analyzed as the second contradiction of capitalism, gutting the very environmental inputs upon which capitalism depends, are ramifying through multiple ecosystems, with profound impacts on human health.[94]

There are alternatives. Another world is emerging around or from underneath the wreckage, including community-led water protection and flood control (using bunds, leaky dams, and culverts), conservation agriculture, and landscape disease ecologies organized around mitigating pathogen evolution and spread.[95] Each effort, affecting millions of people, embodies reintegrating the commons, as both moral ideal and economic reality, back into the landscape.

15—Conclusion: Moving beyond Capitalism for Our Health

Adam Gaffney and Howard Waitzkin

The contradictory politico-medical landscape gives cause for both anguish and hope. People in nations around the world continue to rely on inequitable and inadequate health systems. An increasingly transnational corporate health care industry, meanwhile, aggressively aims to exploit the gaps left open by underfunded or nonexistent public provision, furthering commercialization and fragmentation. In the United States, the first major health reform in decades, the Affordable Care Act (ACA), has expanded health insurance coverage to a substantial degree even while it preserves many of the most pernicious injustices of the system. And the 2016 presidential election brought to power billionaire Donald Trump at the head of a right-wing government that is aggressively seeking to slash the health care safety net, eliminating many of the law's beneficial provisions while funneling enormous wealth to the very rich.

Yet there is also evidence that the United States and some other nations are undergoing a historic political realignment, which may create an opportunity for more fundamental transformation in coming years. A more egalitarian health care alternative, a single-payer national health program, returned to the political discussion in the context of the U.S. presidential primary campaign of 2015–2016, and again after the Republicans' effort at repealing and replacing the ACA crumbled. More broadly, awareness of and anger at the deleterious impact of the neoliberal agenda has become widespread, along with a growing willingness to take bold steps to confront it. From the perspective of health care, the ACA's failure to achieve the goal of universal health care is obvious to many. Families still go bankrupt from medical bills, inequalities in access persevere, costs continue to squeeze the stagnant incomes of the working class, and many millions remain uninsured. Yet rising discontent alone will not change the status quo. In this concluding chapter, we examine some of the ways forward.

Here is our approach. First, we outline, in broad strokes, some political dynamics shaping health care reform in the United States. Second, we consider how one part of the health care workforce—doctors—can play a key role in advancing the progressive health agenda. Third, we address "democratization" and emphasize new communal structures that focus on health care as part of a broader transformational struggle in our societies. Fourth, we consider how health care fits into activism that moves beyond the current realities and restrictions of the U.S. two-party system.

As the failure of the ACA to create a system of universal health care becomes more obvious and as Republican efforts to repeal the law either flounder or make things far worse, achieving clarity about such political dynamics could contribute to the goal of a more democratized and egalitarian health care system, and through it, to our larger ambition of a more equitable and healthier society.

Some Political Realities

To expand on reasons for anguish and hope: In the United States, as in some other countries, the politics and policies of the right have become increasingly reactionary, as evidenced by Trump's successful misogynistic, xenophobic, and racist campaign. Moreover, a consensus within the mainstream Republican Party aims to dismantle much of the existing welfare state devoted to health care. This consensus seeks, for instance, further commodification of the already highly corporatized U.S. health care system, through the voucherization of Medicare, the privatization or rollback of Medicaid, additional financialization of health care through the promotion of "health savings accounts," and similar approaches. Along these lines, the House and Senate ACA repeal bills would have sharply reduced federal Medicaid funding, reduced the generosity of premium subsidies, and funded tax breaks for the rich, sending the number of the uninsured soaring while exacerbating economic inequality.[1] Over the course of 2017, these bills failed, though they could be resurrected in the future.

Democrats, on the other hand, have been more divided on health care. The 2016 Democratic presidential primary, for instance, saw the embrace of two distinct health care visions by the two candidates, Hillary Clinton and Bernie Sanders. Clinton basically defended the status quo, that is, the ACA, an approach that amounts to the acceptance of the many injustices in the U.S. health care system. For without further change, about 10 percent of the U.S. population will remain perpetually uncovered,[2] "underinsurance" will become the norm among health insurance plans, and corporate consolidation will deepen.

Self-described democratic socialist Bernie Sanders, in contrast, wholeheartedly embraced a far different vision, namely a fundamental transformation of the U.S. health care system through the creation of a universal, single-payer national program. As in the legislation he previously introduced in the U.S. Senate, his proposal echoed other single-payer proposals, including that of Physicians for a National Health Program,[3] in calling for a universal right to comprehensive medical services for all without cost-sharing—no co-payments, deductibles, or co-insurance. The surprising historic success of his campaign helped thrust health reform back into the national discussion, which in turn prompted many commentators in the Clinton camp into a vigorous defense of the ACA and vociferous, frequently inaccurate attacks on single-payer reform.[4]

Sanders's relative success—as well as the rising prominence of single-payer over the course of 2017—reflects a sea change in U.S. politics. Many, especially younger Americans,[5] increasingly reject neoliberal centrism within the Democratic Party in exchange for more progressive alternatives. Regarding health care, polls continue to demonstrate wide public support of single-payer reform.[6] Despite this growing belief in the need for major societal change, however, major obstacles remain, especially the lobbying might of corporate capital and health care capital in particular. Majorities supporting change, including single-payer reform, cannot in themselves overcome the power and financial resources of the opposition. For fundamental change to happen, organization will be necessary around several poles of popular power. One critical pole involves the huge health care workforce. In the following section, we focus on a single group of health workers, doctors. Other groups of health workers are, needless to say, no less important, but we highlight doctors here due to the profession's historically conservative influence and the potential for this to change in the new political economy of health care.

HEALTH WORKERS, INCLUDING DOCTORS, IN SOCIAL MOVEMENTS

The unique class position of their profession structures the political role of doctors. However, this position is neither static nor uniform, as the location of physicians within the class hierarchy has varied significantly across time and space. In the United States during the twentieth century, doctors saw an enormous increase in their influence and income, and as a result could exert a formidable influence on the U.S. health system.[7] In light of this sharp social and economic ascendency, the profession, or at least its establishment organizations, long had a conservative impact on national policies. The American Medical Association (AMA) worked against national health reform, most famously in its successful opposition to the post–Second World War campaign for national health insurance.[8] Due to its previous capitulation to racial discrimination in medicine, together with its continued opposition to a national health program, many have viewed the AMA as a reactionary organization.

Yet the profession is no monolithic bloc, and throughout history and in different places, physicians have joined a wide variety of progressive causes, often explicitly articulating a link between their political and medical work. The famous German pathologist Rudolf

Virchow is one of the earliest examples of the progressive political tradition in medicine. Virchow was a scientist and a physician, but also a revolutionary and a political thinker. His report on the Silesian typhus epidemic is a foundational work in social medicine thought, though he also wrote in favor of universal health care during the revolutionary year of 1848, when he joined the barricades.[9]

We cannot do justice to the multitude of progressive health care movements over the last century and a half since Virchow, but a few warrant special mention. For instance, even as the AMA smeared national health insurance from coast to coast, the New York City–based "Physicians Forum" remained steadfast in support of it, with many of its members ultimately falling victim to McCarthyite repression in the 1950s as a result.[10] The civil rights era saw the development of a potent medical activist movement, with one group, the Medical Committee of Human Rights, functioning as a medical support group for the civil rights movement, and later becoming what has been called the "medical arm of the new left."[11] U.S. health care workers have also served as internationalists during revolutionary moments, in nations ranging from Spain during its civil war to Mozambique during its struggle for national liberation.[12] In so doing, they sometimes risked their lives. Such varied instances of medico-political activism, whether domestic or international, to some extent flowed from common intellectual and political traditions.[13]

In more recent years, health care workers, including doctors, continue to take part in key health-related political campaigns, sometimes in alliance with grassroots and labor organizations, in countries throughout the globe. In El Salvador during the late 1990s, for instance, the right-wing ARENA (Republican Nationalist Alliance) government tried to push through the privatization of public hospitals with support from the World Bank. This action precipitated a strike among health workers organized within the social security union. Physicians, also concerned about the privatization agenda, formed a coalition with these workers and joined the strike. In 2002, huge demonstrations took place. The campaign ended in victory: the World Bank withdrew the requirement for health care privatization, and public-sector hospitals and clinics grew stronger as a result.[14] (For more on struggles against neoliberal health policies in El Salvador and other countries, see chapter 11.)

Activism by health care workers also has figured prominently in recent organizing that focuses on austerity policies (as described in chapter 8). During the Great Recession, several nations in Europe, including Spain, Greece, and the United Kingdom, experienced sharp reductions in government spending, straining their public health systems. In addition to reduced health spending, these countries saw a retreat from the universal reach of their health care systems, the imposition of new user fees, and attempts at health sector privatization. Social movements served as key sites of resistance to these attacks, and health workers played important roles in such struggles. In Spain, for instance, after passage of a law in 2012 that would have restricted the ability of undocumented immigrants to use the health system, some 1,300 physicians and nurses pledged to defy the law and to continue to provide care to these individuals.[15] Additionally, the financial crisis and austerity policies sparked a large grassroots political movement, the 15-M movement, or *Indignados*.[16] The *Indignados* rejected the establishment parties and called for more fundamental democratic change, but also for protection against health care austerity and privatization. The movement "mounted demonstrations to defend the public health care system (the so called Marea Blanca, or White Tide), and occupied health facilities."[17] It included health care workers, among them physicians, who protested and implemented a strike in Madrid to protest the privatization of hospitals and primary care centers,[18] forcing the municipal government to withdraw its plans.[19]

In the United Kingdom, the National Health Service (NHS), particularly the English NHS, has faced similar challenges. Following the economic crisis, the NHS was grossly underfunded by the Conservative government of David Cameron. This austerity funding coincided with passage of a new law that facilitated the further privatization and fragmentation of the NHS.[20] In late 2015 and early 2016, the government provoked a conflict with the country's "junior doctors" (equivalent to residents in the U.S. system) in seeking to impose a new adverse contract.[21] Though to some extent the anger of the junior doctors related to a decrease in pay and an increase in "antisocial hours" (that is, required work on weekends and nights) under the new contract, the junior doctors' strikes also figured as part of a broader mobilization against the attack on the NHS.[22]

In the United States, doctors' changing social-class position affects their willingness to support and to participate in progressive movements for change. As mentioned above, the U.S. medical profession underwent an enormous change from the nineteenth century to the mid-twentieth century, and the profession gained in prestige, wealth, and power.[23] Yet more recent decades have seen the rise of powerful corporate interests, which have challenged the sovereignty of the profession.[24] For decades, some have described this corporate transformation as leading to the "proletarianization" of physicians.

In 1985, for instance, sociologists John B. McKinlay and Joan Arches argued that a process of physician proletarianization was already underway, albeit in its early stages.[25] They cited ongoing bureaucratization, de-skilling, unionization efforts, and the rising role of computer technology. The authors argued that high salaries alone did not mean that proletarianization was not happening; what mattered more, they contended, was the value of physicians' labor taken as surplus value by the employer. For example, physicians making $100,000 a year could be producing $1 million a year in revenues for the health system for which they work.[26] Others remained skeptical about proletarianization. Though work within a corporate medical system "will necessarily entail a profound loss of autonomy," and though "there will be more regulation of the pace and routines of work," sociologist Paul Starr contended in 1982 that the need for the "active cooperation of physicians" will limit the extent to which proletarianization might unfold.[27]

More than three decades later, the situation remains unstable. On the one hand, physicians continue to occupy highly privileged economic ground, earning substantially more than their peers in other high-income nations. Indeed, by one calculation, more than a fifth of physicians live in the top 1 percent of households by income.[28] At the same time (as documented in chapter 12), recent decades have seen the further evolution of health system consolidation and corporatization. One aspect of this change has been so-called vertical integration, the purchasing or incorporation of physicians' practices into large health systems. As a result, physicians increasingly work as the salaried employees of both for-profit and not-for-profit systems. At the same time they face heavy administrative burdens, coupled with what they perceive as burdensome demands for electronic documentation. Such changes have led to a marked decline in autonomy and in control over working conditions, a process of workplace proletarianization, albeit at a high pay rate. This transformation has given rise to dissatisfaction and resentment among "doctor workers," which has increased resistance, union organizing, and activism. (Part One of this volume analyzes proletarianization in depth.)

The goal here is not to turn back the clock. Picturing the age of the black bag–toting solo practitioner who would visit patients in their homes and provide treatment free from the constraints of managed care organizations or hospital administrators as a golden era for medicine is inaccurate. Every era of U.S. medicine has contained dark features, and progress occurred on several fronts during the twentieth century, such as the passage of Medicaid and Medicare, and the decline of de jure racial segregation in medicine. Moreover, larger health organizations are not inherently problematic, nor is a turn to salaried from fee-for-practice practice. Indeed, salaries have many advantages as a form of payment.[29] More important than the particular size of the health care organization or the specific method of physician payment is the political economy of the health system itself.

Reconfigurations should take place on both macro and micro levels. By the macro level, we mean national level health system changes. Specifically, a single-payer national health program that provides equal access to comprehensive care for everybody in the country remains a crucially needed reform. At the same time, fundamental changes must happen at the level of the health care organization. Specifically, we have in mind changes that will result in participatory decision making and communal ownership of health care organizations in which social solidarity replaces capital accumulation as the guiding motivation.

COMMUNAL HEALTH CARE ORGANIZATIONS

Political power, it has been argued, emanates from two poles: "constituted" power (the established power of the state) and "constituent" power (popular power from below). Though constituent power plays a critical role in the making of political change, including revolutions, historically it has become subsequently marginalized by victorious, newly constituted power. However, in both theory and practice, some have then sought to shift power back from the constituted to the constituent. The "communal state" envisioned by the late Venezuelan President Hugo Chávez, in which bottom-up "communes" played a key role in the political transition of the nation, serves as an example where "constituent" power is embraced instead of sidelined.[30]

At this point in history, the notion of the communal, a concept influenced by the work of the political theorist István Mészáros, who served as one of Hugo Chávez's most trusted advisers,[31] can help guide strategies in health care. What practical lessons emerge from this concept? What is the meaning of "constituent" power in health care? Might we further democratize health care by working to shift power downward, to the communities and individuals who work in and who use a particular health care organization?

In truth, a bottom-up orientation in health care is not at all a novel concept. In 1978, most famously, the Declaration of Alma Ata called for ground-up, community-oriented, primary care–centered health systems. "The people have the right and duty to participate individually and collectively," the Declaration asserted, "in the planning and implementation of their health care."[32] During subsequent years, a variety of participatory, communal projects have embraced the spirit of Alma Ata. In the United States, the Lincoln Collective, in which over one hundred health care workers struggled to remake one South Bronx hospital into a more community-accountable institution, is a prominent example.[33] Multiple efforts to build communal health care organizations have also taken place in Latin America. In revolutionary Nicaragua, for instance, large-scale participation in health projects on the community level, including volunteer efforts by people organized into brigades (*brigadistas*), led to accomplishments combining health care with community empowerment.[34]

Communal organization also figured as a guiding principle in Venezuela's innovative experiments that restructured health services at the community level. Under Chávez's presidency, Venezuela enacted pathbreaking innovations based on social medicine principles. Influenced partly by leaders in Latin American social medicine, the country embarked on a far-reaching series of organizational changes.[35] Although Chávez and his government advocated accessible, public-sector health services as part of its program after winning the national election in 1999, several barriers stood in the way of achieving that vision. First, the ministry of health in the Chávez government continued to operate in a top-down, bureaucratic manner that impeded outreach to underserved urban and rural communities. Secondly, the Venezuelan medical profession opposed proposals to expand public sector services.

In the impasse, the Libertador Municipality within the boundaries of Caracas initiated a grassroots effort to improve services for the poor. The municipality issued a call for physicians to live and work in the community. When few Venezuela doctors responded, the municipality's mayor, Freddy Bernal, approached the Cuban Embassy, and within several months a contingent of Cuban doctors arrived.[36]

This approach spread throughout Venezuela. The name of the initiative, Misión Barrio Adentro (Mission of the Community Within), refers to the grassroots, bottom-up emergence of a parallel public-sector health system. Low-income communities throughout the country organized to provide health services on the local level, with the assistance of more than 20,000 primary care physicians from Cuba. Communities constructed their own health facilities and designed services that addressed the perceived needs of specific neighborhoods. A new innovative system of Barrio Adentro–based community medical education—Medicina Integral Comunitaria—aimed to produce a socially conscious Venezuelan primary care workforce. These changes occurred with some support but for the most part independently from the national ministry of health.[37] Misión Barrio Adentro later attracted attention as a model for change in many other Latin American countries, particularly in Bolivia under the presidency of Evo Morales. The late health economist Gavin Mooney, meanwhile, contextualized Misión Barrio Adentro as a "very real shift in power to the people in the Venezuelan health-care system."[38]

At the time of this writing, however, Venezuela has faced a crisis that extends to its health system. A deterioration in economic conditions has resulted from a variety of internal and external factors that are beyond the scope of this chapter.[39] Among the latter factors are ongoing destabilization efforts ranging from disinformation campaigns to the activities of U.S.-supported opposition groups. This multifaceted economic crisis has been accompanied by reports of severe health system strain, shortages, and worsening health conditions following the gains of the Chávez era.[40] A historic malaria epidemic in the country also pointed to a deteriorating public health landscape.[41] Additionally, the lack of integration of Barrio Adentro into the overall public health care system, together with competition from a large private health care system with which it vied for resources and personnel, could be seen as weaknesses.[42] Still, despite these developments and the uncertainty of the future, the Barrio Adentro system has functioned as a critical network of free, community-based care for a population that previous governments had entirely shunned, as well as a unique demonstration of communal health care in practice.[43]

Lessons can be drawn from this and other similar experiences. From a broader perspective, for instance, Gavin Mooney called for a new "communitarian" approach to health care:

> The key considerations here involve a shift in power to citizens; genuine participation of citizens in health and health-care planning; an emphasis on the community and in turn on communitarianism; and communitarian claims. The power shift is what really holds the key. Most fundamentally this involves the recognition that there are issues where it is critically informed people, citizens, who must be

allowed to have their voice heard in what is their health-care system and their society.[44]

He described how different forms of "deliberative democracy" allow community members to take part directly in health care policy and planning issues.[45] Mooney favored one such method, citizens' juries, in which randomly selected community members participate in a process of informed, deliberative decision making on community health issues, including those pertaining to issues of equity.[46]

Further democratization of health care should become an important component of the progressive political agenda. A hospital, community health center, or other organization responsible for the care of a group of people in a particular area should respond to the wishes of patients as well as members of the community more broadly. A reorganization of "constituted" health care, along the lines of a national health program, is of course necessary. At the same time, a shift toward "constituent" power, embracing the organized political agency of community members, needs greater emphasis. For instance, when a health system becomes a private monopoly, community accountability usually gets trumped by the profit motive. For this reason, another element of "constituent" power in health care involves placing health systems with regional dominance under public control.[47] Similar approaches to constituent power in health care have taken place in Nicaragua and Venezuela, which we consider here, but also in other revolutionary contexts such as Cuba and Chile, which have been described elsewhere.[48] Reinvigorating constituent power in health care through communal organizations should be an important goal in the road ahead.

POLITICAL CHANGE, THE TWO-PARTY SYSTEM, AND THE AGE OF THE TWIN INEQUALITIES

We must talk honestly about the current reality of political power in the United States, including two distinct obstacles to progressive change in health care: the unique structure of the U.S. two-party system, and the right-wing government that took power in 2017.

First, regarding the former issue, it is important to acknowledge that powerful working-class parties, which the United States has long lacked, have played critical roles in advancing the cause of universal health care in other nations.[49] In the United Kingdom, for instance, it was the Labour Party that ultimately pushed through that nation's unique system of universal health care, the NHS. Though some argue that an overall consensus on health care reform had already formed over the course of the Second World War, there can be little doubt that the precise form it took, including complete universalism, free care at time of use, and the nationalization of hospitals, reflected to no small extent the party that formulated the law.[50] Similarly, in the Canadian province of Saskatchewan, it was the left-wing Cooperative Commonwealth Federation (later, the New Democratic Party) that undertook the first crucial movement toward a provincial single-payer system.[51]

The United States, in contrast, lacks a potent labor or left-wing party. Moreover, during the neoliberal era, the Democratic Party shifted rightward (as did Labour in the United Kingdom), embracing a pro-corporate line exemplified by the rise of the Democratic Leadership Council and the presidency of Bill Clinton. And as the Democratic Party shifted rightward, so too did its health care policy. For instance, many prominent Democrats were supportive of a national health insurance plan in the post–Second World War decades, from Harry S. Truman to Ted Kennedy. During subsequent decades, however, Democrats increasingly embraced a more neoliberal approach to health policy. Instead of advocating for national health insurance, Democrats from Bill Clinton to Barack Obama proposed hybrid-type plans that incorporated elements of the "managed competition" ideas of Alain Enthoven as well as initially conservative ideas like the employer mandate and the individual mandate (for details, see chapter 7).[52] Yet, as noted earlier, the Sanders campaign in the 2015–2016 Democratic presidential primary took things in a different direction. While other Democratic presidential primary candidates embraced single-payer in the past, Sanders put this proposal back into the limelight, even while Hillary Clinton described it as an idea "that will never, ever come to pass."[53] Even in defeat,

Sanders's success may prove to be a harbinger of growing popular struggle in the United States.

This brings us to the second development that proponents of progressive change in health care must confront: the right has taken control of the political stage. Trump, who came to power in part by deviating from Republican orthodoxy and embracing the discourse of economic populism, and in part by appealing to deeply rooted racist and xenophobic sentiment, delivered the executive branch to Republicans. Combined with Republican control of both Senate and House, this development has shut the door to progressive health care change in the near term. Yet Republicans' attempt to remake the American health care system through various ACA-repeal bills faced embarrassing defeats. Sanders launched a new single-payer bill, earning an impressive number of co-sponsors, in a moment widely seen as a watershed, even if the political circumstances necessary for its achievement lay in the future.

Still, those trying to advance a progressive health care agenda, including a national health program, cannot idly wait for some future, undefined electoral turn to push ahead. The urgent work is to construct a powerful, multicentric coalition—including unions and labor campaigns, organizations centered around the health professions, racial justice groups, and other grassroots activist organizations—that can offer a vision of change, while at the same time shaping, prodding, and supporting progressive political actors and parties. Moving a bold progressive health reform agenda forward, including instituting a national health program, may additionally require creating a new working-class party (or parties), a process that imposes unique challenges.[54] This process will require a broad, potent, multi-focal popular movement pushing for change from below. If this development sounds unlikely, we would counter that another dynamic will make it both possible and necessary in coming years: the continued rise of the twin inequalities, the first economic and the second, related one of health.

Rising economic inequality has spurred political movements and change for years, an early and important manifestation of which was the global Occupy movement. Increasingly, however, there is a growing awareness of rising health inequality. Racial health inequalities remain entrenched and insidious.[55] In addition, a variety of studies have demonstrated a widening of health inequalities along the divide of social class, beginning around the onset of the neoliberal era.[56] Differentials in life expectancy by income are continuing to widen even in the twenty-first century.[57] Indeed, in recent years we have witnessed an increase in mortality in one subgroup, middle-aged whites,[58] even while whites still enjoy significantly better health than blacks. Rising health inequality, like rising economic inequality, should be seen as a product of the neoliberal era, with each inequality likely contributing to the other.

And though health care is only one contributor to health, the struggle for a non-exploitative, accessible health care system can address both these inequalities. Organizing to make equitable health care available to all, free at the point of use, targets inequalities in health, while organizing to achieve this goal through a progressively funded, single-payer system targets the more fundamental economic inequalities of our society.

As Obamacare is increasingly recognized as insufficient and inadequate, the demand for such fundamental change in capitalist health care, as well as the economic system that shapes both health care and health itself, will continue to grow. We have highlighted several facets of the struggles ahead: organizing among health workers including physicians; building communal, democratic structures and processes within health care organizations; and transforming political parties and social movements so they become forces that can achieve fundamental change in health care and in capitalist society. Such struggles also must target the social and environmental pathologies that capitalist society constructs as normal and that impact health in ways even more important than health care.

The forces that resist these changes command wealth and power that emanate from a tiny part of the U.S. population (less than the 1 percent made famous by the Occupy movement) and an even tinier part of the world's population. Those in this minority will no doubt continue to fight ferociously to preserve the profound advantages they gain from the status quo, of which capitalist health care figures as only one part. Though the power of this small number should not be underestimated, neither should ours. The road ahead is a steep one, but given the fragility of our harsh capitalist system together with the discontent and suffering it breeds, it is one that we can and must surmount.

We are in the midst of a struggle to create a fundamentally more just and equal society, "a world to build"[59] that is both healthier and happier. To build that world, we must move beyond capitalism for our health. If we fail and the tiny group that benefits from current arrangements prevails, it will be because we have allowed that to happen, so let us choose to win.

Contributors

MATTHEW ANDERSON is a family physician working in the Bronx, New York, and on the faculty of the Montefiore Residency Program in Social Medicine. He is co-editor of the bilingual journal *Social Medicine/ Medicina Social*.

ANNE-EMANUELLE BIRN is Professor of Critical Development Studies at the University of Toronto. She is lead author of the *Textbook of Global Health*, fourth edition (Oxford University Press, 2016) and co-editor of *Comrades in Health: US Health Internationalists, Abroad and at Home* (Rutgers University Press, 2013). In 2014 she was recognized as one of the top one hundred Women Leaders in Global Health.

ROBB BURLAGE is the founder of the Health Policy Advisory Center and the *Health/PAC Bulletin*. He also founded the Joint Graduate Degree Program in Public Health and Urban Planning at Columbia University. With Students for a Democratic Society, he was active in the civil rights movement in the South and in advocacy for occupational and environmental health among mineworkers. He is Senior Management Consultant to the New York City Department of Health and Hospitals.

ADAM GAFFNEY is a writer, physician, single-payer activist, and researcher. He is a pulmonary and critical care physician at the Cambridge Health Alliance in Massachusetts and is a board member of Physicians for a National Health Program. He writes widely on issues of health policy, politics, and history.

IDA HELLANDER has served as Executive Director and then Director of Health Policy and Programs at Physicians for a National Health Program (http://www.pnhp.org) and is a long-term activist for a single-payer system in the United States.

DAVID HIMMELSTEIN and STEFFIE WOOLHANDLER are professors of Public Health at City University of New York at Hunter College, and primary care physicians in the South Bronx. Among their best known research is work on the high administrative costs in the U.S. health care system, medical bankruptcy, and access to medical care for the oppressed. They co-founded Physicians for a National Health Program, an organization that advocates single-payer national health insurance for the United States.

REBECA JASSO-AGUILAR holds a PhD in Sociology and is affiliated with the University of New Mexico as a Visiting Scholar. She has co-authored several articles with Howard Waitzkin on the subject of neoliberalism and health care. Currently she is engaged in ongoing research on social movements against neoliberalism in Latin America, with a focus on Mexico and Bolivia, and is an active participant in the National Regeneration Movement (MORENA) in Mexico.

JOEL LEXCHIN teaches health policy at York University in Toronto and is an emergency physician at the University Health Network, also in Toronto.

CARLES MUNTANER, originally from Catalonia, is a professor of Nursing, Public Health and Psychiatry at the University of Toronto. He has worked on social inequalities in health and health equity in Europe, North America, the Middle East, East Asia, and West Africa. His research centers around Marxian class analysis and class politics to understand and eliminate global health inequalities. He has collaborated with ministries of health around the world including those of the Bolivarian Republic of Venezuela and the Republic of Chile.

CARL RATNER specializes in cultural psychology, or the manner in which macro cultural factors organize human psychology. He has written on the psychology of oppression. Among his books and papers is *Macro Cultural Psychology: A Political Philosophy of Mind* (Oxford University Press, 2012). He has worked and lived in China, where he was a visiting professor at Peking University.

JUDITH RICHTER is an independent scholar working for democratic health governance. She has served as a consultant for civil society organizations and networks, United Nations agencies, and research institutes.

Her publications include *Holding Corporations Accountable: Corporate Conduct, International Codes, and Citizen Action* (Zed Books).

GORDON SCHIFF is general internist and Associate Director of the Brigham and Women's Hospital Center for Patient Safety Research and Practice. He is an Associate Professor of Medicine at Harvard Medical School.

HOWARD WAITZKIN is Distinguished Professor Emeritus of Sociology at the University of New Mexico and Adjunct Professor of Internal Medicine at the University of Illinois. For many years he has been active in the struggles for national health programs in the United States and Latin America. He is the author of *Medicine and Public Health at the End of Empire* (Paradigm, 2011) and other books.

ROB WALLACE is an evolutionary biologist presently visiting the University of Minnesota's Institute for Global Studies. His research has addressed the evolution and spread of influenza, the agroeconomics of Ebola, the social geography of HIV/AIDS in New York City, and the evolution of infection life history in response to antiviral medications. Wallace is co-author of *Farming Human Pathogens* and *Neoliberal Ebola: Modeling Disease Emergence from Finance to Forest and Farm* (both with Springer), and author of *Big Farms Make Big Flu* (Monthly Review Press).

SARAH WINCH is a health ethicist. She is Head of the Discipline of Medical Ethics, Law and Professionalism at the University of Queensland Medical School in Australia.

Notes

Introduction

1. "Dr. Martin Luther King on Health Care Injustice," http://www.pnhp.org/news/2014/october/dr-martin-luther-king-on-health-care-injustice.

2. Howard Waitzkin and Ida Hellander, "The Neoliberal Model Comes Home to Roost in the United States—If We Let It," *Monthly Review* 68/1 (May 2016): 1–18.

3. Samir Amin, *The Implosion of Contemporary Capitalism* (New York: Monthly Review Press, 2013).

4. John Bellamy Foster, Brett Clark, and Richard York, *The Ecological Rift: Capitalism's War on the Earth* (New York: Monthly Review Press, 2011); Naomi Klein, *This Changes Everything: Capitalism vs. the Climate* (New York: Simon & Schuster, 2014).

5. Harry Braverman, *Labor and Monopoly Capital* (New York: Monthly Review Press, 1998).

6. For the distinction between Global South and Global North, we are indebted to the work of Samir Amin, who has illuminated the historical and contemporary importance of the exploited peripheries in the South and exploiting centers in the North; for instance: Samir Amin, "Revolution from North to South," *Monthly Review* 69/3 (July-August 2017): 113-27.

7. István Mészáros, *Beyond Capital* (New York: Monthly Review Press, 1995).

8. Howard Waitzkin and Barbara Waterman, *The Exploitation of Illness in Capitalist Society* (Indianapolis: Bobbs-Merrill, 1974).

1. Disobedience: Doctor Workers, Unite!

1. Epigraph: Erich Fromm, *On Disobedience* (New York: Harper, 2010). A briefer version of this chapter originally appeared in *Medscape*, May 20, 2016, http://www.medscape.com/viewarticle/863297. To protect confidentiality, I have deleted all personal names and have fictionalized the names of all organizations; "eDocuments of Disobedience," available on request, include memoranda intended as illustrations for doctor

workers to use in contemplating or executing acts of disobedience.

2. Further details and analyses of proletarianization in medicine appear in chapters 2, 3, 4, and 7.

3. John D. Stoeckle, "Working on the Factory Floor," *Annals of Internal Medicine* 107/2 (1987): 250–51.

4. Carol Peckham, "Medscape Physician Compensation Report 2016," *Medscape*, April 1, 2016.

5. Carol Peckham, "Medscape Lifestyle Report 2016: Bias and Burnout," *Medscape*, January 13, 2016, http://www.medscape.com/features/slideshow/lifestyle/2016/public/overview#page=1.

6. "Physician Burnout Is a Public Health Crisis, Ethicist Says," *Medscape,* March 4, 2016,http://www.medscape.com/viewarticle/859300.

7. Hannah Arendt, *Eichmann in Jerusalem: A Report on the Banality of Evil* (New York: Viking, 1968).

8. Pamela Hartzband and Jerome Groopman, "Medical Taylorism," *New England Journal of Medicine* 374/2 (2016):106–8.

9. American Medical Association, *Code of Medical Ethics,* 2016, http://www.ama-assn.org/ama/pub/physician-resources/medical-ethics/code-medical-ethics/opinion8115.

10. Noam Scheiber, "Doctors Unionize to Resist the Medical Machine," *New York Times,* January 9, 2016, http://www.nytimes.com/2016/01/10/business/doctors-unionize-to-resist-the-medical-machine.html.

11. I am deeply indebted to my friend Mark Teismann, who provided inspiration, encouragement, and critical feedback for me as I wrote this article while he was dying; and to my partner and co-conspirator, Mira Lee, who offered constructive suggestions and reminders that disobedience can transform the world.

2. Becoming Employees: The Deprofessionalization and Emerging Social-Class Position of Health Professionals

1. Epigraph: Franz Kafka, *The Trial* (Harmondsworth and London: Penguin, 1953), p. 243.

2. Karl Marx, "Estranged Labor," in *Economic and Philosophical Manuscripts of 1844,* https://www.marxists.org.

3. Barbara Starfield et al., "Contribution of Primary Care to Health Systems and Health," *Milbank Quarterly* 83/3 (2005): 457–502; James Macinko et al., "Quantifying the Health Benefits of Primary Care Physician Supply in the United States," *International Journal of Health Services* 37/1 (2007): 111–26.

4. Barbara Starfield et al., "The Effects of Specialist Supply on Populations' Health: Assessing the Evidence," *Health Affairs* 24, Web Exclusive (2005): W5-97-WE-107.

5. "OECD Health Statistics 2016: Country Statistical Profiles," Organization for Economic Cooperation and Development, http://www.oecd.org.

6. John D. Goodson, "Unintended Consequences of Resource-Based Relative Value Scale Reimbursement," *JAMA* 298/19 (2007): 2308–10.

7. Calvin Sia et al., "History of the Medical Home Concept," *Pediatrics* 113, Supp. 4 (2004): 1473–78.

8. See also: Kurt C. Stange et al., "Defining and Measuring the Patient-Centered Medical Home," *Journal of General Internal Medicine* 25/6 (2010): 601–12.

9. H. Jack Geiger, "Community-Oriented Primary Care: A Path to Community Development," *American Journal of Public Health* 92/11 (2002): 1713–16.

10. Pieter Van Herck et al., "Systematic Review: Effects, Design Choices, and Context of Pay-for-Performance in Healthcare," *BMC Health Services Research* 10 (2010): 247.

11. Catherine M. DesRoches et al., "Electronic Health Records' Limited Successes Suggest More Targeted Uses," *Health Affairs* 29/4 (2010): 639–46.

12. Pamela Hartzband and Jerome Groopman, "Off the Record: Avoiding the Pitfalls of Going Electronic," *New England Journal of Medicine* 358/16 (2008): 1656–58.

13. Press Ganey Associates, Inc., "Patient Voice: Every Patient Matters, Every Voice Counts," https://helpandtraining.pressganey.com.

14. Donald T. Campbell, "Assessing the Impact of Planned Social Change," Public Affairs Center, Dartmouth College, Occasional Paper Series, December 1976, https://www.globalhivmeinfo.org.

15. American Academy of Family Physicians, "Sugar Substitutes: What You Need to Know," http://familydoctor.org.

16. American Academy of Pediatrics, "Corporate Friends of Children Fund Members," http://www.aap.org.

17. National Heart, Lung, and Blood Institute, "Corporate Partners," http://www.nhlbi.nih.gov.

18. Eric G. Campbell et al., "Institutional Academic–Industry Relationships," *JAMA* 298/15 (2007): 1779–86.

19. Mary Carmichael, "Bitter Pills: Harvard Medical School and Big Pharma," *Boston Magazine*, November 2009.

20. American Medical Student Association, "AMSA Scorecard 2014," http://amsascorecard.org/.

21. Matthew Stewart, *The Management Myth: Why the Experts Keep Getting It Wrong.* (New York: W. W. Norton, 2009).

3. The Degradation of Medical Labor and the Meaning of Quality in Health Care

1. Joseph Rabatin, Eric Williams, Linda Baier-Manwell, Mark Schwartz, Roger Brown, and Mark Linzer, "Predictors and Outcomes of Burnout in Primary Care Physicians," *Journal of Primary Care and Community Health* 7/1 (2016): 41–43; Stewart Babbott, Linda Manwell, Roger Brown et al., "Electronic Medical Records and Physician Stress In Primary Care: Results From the MEMO Study," *Journal of the American Medical Informatics Association* 21/e1, (2014): e100–06; Perry An, Joseph Rabatin, Linda Manwell et al., "Burden of Difficult Encounters in Primary Care: Data From the Minimizing Error, Maximizing Outcomes Study," *Archives of Internal Medicine* 169/4 (2009): 410–14; Doris Vahey, Linda Aitken, Douglas Sloane et al., "Nurse Burnout and Patient Satisfaction," *Medical Care* 42/2 Suppl. (2004): 1157–66.

2. Karl Marx, *The Marx-Engels Reader,* vol. 4 (New York: W. W. Norton, 1972).

3. Harry Braverman, *Labor and Monopoly Capital: The Degradation of Work in the Twentieth Century* (New York: Monthly Review Press, 1998); R. Jamil Jonna and John Bellamy Foster, "Beyond the Degradation of Labor: Braverman and the Structure of the US Working Class," *Monthly Review* 66/5 (2014): 1–24.

4. Gordon Schiff and Norbert Goldfield, "Deming Meets Braverman: Toward a Progressive Analysis of the Continuous Quality Improvement Paradigm," *International Journal of Health Services* 24/4 (1994): 655–73.

5. Gordon Schiff, "Crossing Boundaries: Violation or Obligation?" *Journal of the American Medical Association,* 310/12 (2013): 1233–34.

6. Bernie Monegain, "Burnout Rampant in Healthcare: Survey Reveals 60% of Healthcare Workers Experience Burnout," *HealthcareIT News,* April 30, 2013, http://healthcareitnews.com/news/burnout-rampant-healthcare.

7. Bonnie Jennings, Margarete Sandelowski, and Melinda Higgins, "Turning Over Patient Turnover: An Ethnographic Study of Admissions, Discharges, and Transfers," *Research in Nursing and Health* 36/6 (2013): 554–66.

8. Thomas Bodenheimer and Christine Sinsky, "From Triple to Quadruple Aim: Care of the Patient Requires Care of the Provider," *Annals of Family Medicine* 12/6 (2013): 573–76.

9. Thomas Bodenheimer, "Primary Care: Will I Survive?" *New England Journal of Medicine* 355/9 (2009): 861–64. On the prior pattern of professional dominance, see Eliot Freidson, *Professional Dominance* (New York: Taylor & Francis, 1970) and *Profession of Medicine* (Chicago: University of Chicago Press, 1988).

10. Charles Kenney, *Transforming Health Care: Virginia Mason Medical Center's Pursuit of the Perfect Patient Experience* (New York: CRC Press, 2011); Craig C. Blackmore and Gary S. Kaplan, "Lean and the Perfect Patient Experience," *BMJ Quality & Safety* (2016), doi: 10.1136/bmjqs-2016-005273.

11. Sarah Winch and Amanda Henderson, "Making Cars and Making Healthcare: A Critical Review," *Medical Journal of Australia* 191/1 (2009): 28–29.

12. Bozena Poksinska, Malgorzata Fialkowska–Filipek, and Jon Engström, "Does Lean Healthcare Improve Patient Satisfaction? A Mixed-Method Investigation into Primary Care," *BMJ Quality and Safety* (February 10, 2016), doi: 10.1136/bmjqs-2015-004290.; Chris Huxley, "Three Decades of Lean Production: Practice, Ideology, and Resistance," *International Journal of Sociology* 45/2 (2015): 133–51; Mike Parker and Jane Slaughter, "Management by Stress," *Technology Review* 91/7 (1998): 37–44.

13. Cedric Lomba, "Beyond the Debate Over "Post" vs "Neo" Taylorism: The Contrasting Evolution of Industrial Work Practices," *International Journal of Sociology* 20/1 (2005): 71–91.

14. Leo Panitch and Colin Leys, *Morbid Symptoms: Health Under Capitalism, Socialist Register* (London: Merlin Press, 2009); David Coburn, "Neoliberalism and Health," *The Wiley Blackwell Encyclopedia of Health, Illness, Behavior, and Society* (2014): 1678–83, doi: 10.1002/9781118410868.wbehibs149.

15. Mary Walton, *The Deming Management Method* (New York: Penguin, 1988).

16. Antonio D'Andreamatteo, Luca Ianni, Federico Lega, and Massimo Sargiacomo, "Lean in Healthcare: A Comprehensive Review," *Health Policy* 119/9 (2015): 1197–209.

17. Terry Tudor, Steven Bannister, Sharon Butler et al., "Can Corporate Social Responsibility and Environmental Citizenship Be Employed in the Effective Management of Waste?: Case Studies From the National Health Service (NHS) in England and Wales," *Resources, Conservation and Recycling* 52/5 (2008): 764–74; Naomi Klein, *This Changes Everything: Capitalism vs. the Climate* (New York: Simon and Schuster, 2015).

18. Julian Tudor Hart, "The Inverse Care Law," *The Lancet* 297/7696 (1971): 405–12.

19. Lawrence Casalino, Arthur Elster, Andy Eisenberg, Evelyn Lewis, John Montgomery, and Diana Ramos, "Will Pay-For-Performance and Quality Reporting Affect Health Care Disparities?" *Health Affairs* 26/3 (2007): 405–14.

20. Joshua Vest, Jangho Yoon, and Brian Bossak. "Changes to the Electronic Health Records Market in Light of Health Information Technology Certification and Meaningful Use," *Journal of the American Medical Informatics Association* 20/2 (2013): 227–32.

21. Sherry Turkle, "The Flight from Conversation," *New York Times*, April 21, 2012; Sherry Turkle, *Alone Together: Why We Expect More from Technology and Less from Each Other* (New York: Basic Books, 2012); Nancy Brown, "Driving EMR Adoption: Making EMRs a Sustainable, Profitable Investment," *Health Management Technology* 25/5 (2005): 47–48.

22. Michel Foucault, *Discipline and Punish: The Birth of the Prison* (New York: Vintage, 1977); Foucault, "Governmentaility," in *The Foucault Effect: Studies in Governmentality,* ed. Graham Burchell, Colin Gordon, and Peter Miller (Chicago: University of Chicago Press, 1991); Alan McKinlay and Ken Starkey, "Managing Foucault," in *Foucault, Management and Organization Theory: From Panopticon to Technologies of Self,* ed. Alan McKinlay and Ken Starkey (London: Sage Publications, 1998).

23. Fitzhugh Mullan, "A Founder of Quality Assessment Encounters a Troubled System Firsthand: Interview with Dr. Avedis Donabedian," *Health Affairs* 20, no. 1 (2001): 137–41.

24. Robert Wachter, "How Measurement Fails Doctors and Teachers," *New York Times,* January 16, 2016.

25. James Reason. *Managing the Risks of Organizational Accidents,* vol. 6 (Burlington, VT: Ashgate Publishing, 1997).

26. Antonio Gramsci, *Prison Notebooks,* vol. 2 (New York: Columbia University Press, 1992).

27. Donald Berwick, "The Stories Beneath," *Medical Care* 45/12 (2007): 1123–25; Asaf Bitton, Gregory Schwartz, Elizabeth Stewart et al., "Off the Hamster Wheel? Qualitative Evaluation of a Payment-Linked Patient-Centered Medical Home (PCMH) Pilot," *Milbank Quarterly* 90/3 (2012): 484–515; Benjamin Crabtree, Sabrina Chase, Christopher Wise et al., "Evaluation of Patient-Centered Medical Home Practice Transformation Initiatives," *Medical Care* 49/1 (2011): 10–16, doi: 10.1097/MLR.0b013e3181f80766.

28. Lawrence Casalino, David Gans, Rachel Weber et al., "US Physician Practices Spend More than $15.4 Billion Annually To Report Quality Measures," *Health Affairs (Millwood)* 35/3 (2016): 401–6.

29. Donald Berwick, "Health Services Research, Medicare, and Medicaid: A Deep Bow and a Rechartered Agenda," *Milbank Quarterly* 93/4 (2015): 659–62.

30. David Himmelstein and Steffie Woolhandler, "Quality Improvement:

'Become Good at Cheating and You Never Need To Become Good at Anything Else,'" *Health Affairs Blog,* August 27, 2015, http://healthaffairs. org/blog/2015/08/27/quality-improvement-become-good-at-cheat-ing-and-you-never-need-to-become-good-at-anything-else/.

31. Wachter, "How Measurement Fails Doctors and Teachers."

32. Gordon D. Schiff, Andrew B. Bindman, and Troyen A. Brennan, "A Better-Quality Alternative: Single-Payer National Health System Reform," *Journal of the American Medical Association* 272/10 (1994): 803–8; Adam Gaffney, Steffie Woolhandler, Marcia Angell, and David Himmelstein, "Moving Forward from the Affordable Care Act to a Single-Payer System," *American Journal of Public Health* 106/6 (2016): 987–88.

33. Julian Tudor Hart, "Two Paths for Medical Practice," *Lancet* 340 (1992): 772-75.

5. The Transformation of the Medical-Industrial Complex: Financialization, the Corporate Sector, and Monopoly Capital

This chapter is based on a panel that was held at the 2015 Left Forum on the medical-industrial complex. Panelists discussed health care in the United States and suggested fault lines: contradictions that could become opportunities for organizing toward a system of Health for All—a publicly funded health care system built on protecting the health of all citizens and residents, while also addressing the social determinants of health. Our thanks to John Ehrenreich, Robert Padgog, Oli Fein, and Carmelita Blake.

1. Robert Burlage, *New York City's Municipal Hospitals: A Policy Review* (Washington, DC: Institute for Policy Studies, 1967).

2. The complete Health/PAC archives are available at the Health/PAC Digital Archive, http://www.healthpacbulletin.org.

3. Merlin Chowkwanyun, "The New Left and Public Health: The Health Policy Advisory Center, Community Organizing, and the Big Business of Health, 1967–1975," *American Journal of Public Health* 101/2 (2011): 238–49.

4. Barbara Ehrenreich and John Ehrenreich, *The American Health Empire: Power, Profits, and Politics* (New York: Vintage Books,1970).

5. "Editorial: The Medical Industrial Complex," *Health/PAC Bulletin* (November 1969): 1–2.

6. President Dwight D. Eisenhower, "Eisenhower's Farewell Address to the Nation," January 17, 1961, http://www.americanrhetoric.com/speeches/dwightdeisenhowerfarewell.html.

7. Ehrenreich and Ehrenreich, *The American Health Empire*, p. 252.

8. Ibid., vi.

9. Margaret Davis and Sally T. Burner. "Three Decades of Medicare: What the Numbers Tell Us," *Health Affairs* 14 (1995): 231–43.

10. Peggy Gallagher, "Back to the Drawing Boards: Redefining Some Grand Designs," *Health/PAC Bulletin* 16/5 (Fall 1985): 7–8.

11. Nate Leskovic, "Saving Family Medicine at Columbia," *Primary Care Progress*, October 20, 2015, http://www.primarycareprogress.org/blogs/16/559.

12. Anoop Raman et al., "Guest Editorial: Trial by Firings—Lessons in Organizing at New York–Presbyterian," *American Academy of Family Physicians*, October 19, 2015, http://www.aafp.org/news/opinion/20151019guested-nypfmresidency.html.

13. Arnold S. Relman, "The New Medical-Industrial Complex," *New England Journal of Medicine* 303/17 (1980): 963–70. Most sources cite Relman as the source of the term medical-industrial complex, although this is incorrect. Relman did not cite Health/PAC.

14. Arnold S. Relman, "The Health Care Industry: Where Is It Taking Us?" *New England Journal of Medicine* 325/12 (1991): 854–59.

15. Charles Ornstein, Lena Groeger, Mike Tigas, and Ryann Grochowski Jones, "Dollars for Docs: How Industry Dollars Reach Your Doctors," *ProPublica*, May 1, 2016, https://projects.propublica.org/docdollars/.

16. Larry Husten, "Newly Elected President of Institute of Medicine Is on the Pepsico Board of Directors," Forbes.com, February 19, 2014, http://www.forbes.com/sites/larryhusten/2014/02/19/newly-elected-president-of-institute-of-medicine-is-on-the-pepsico-board-of-directors/#15c5c406d97d.

17. "Weill Cornell Dean Remains on Corporate Payrolls, Sparking Debate about Industry's Role in Academia," *Cornell Daily Sun*, November 30, 2012, https://www.utmb.edu/newsroom/article8099.aspx.

18. "Petition to Relocate Dana Farber Cancer Institute fundraiser from Mar-a–Lago Club," February 2017, https://medium.com/@hmsadvocacy/petition-to-relocate-dana-farber-cancer-institute-fundraiser-from-mar-a-lago-club-5d01dc36ded0.

19. Timothy Anderson, Chester B. Good, and Walid F. Gellad, "Prevalence and Compensation of Academic Leaders, Professors, and Trustees on Publicly Traded US Healthcare Company Boards of Directors: Cross Sectional Study," *BMJ* 351 (2015): h4826, doi: 10.1136/bmj.h4826.

20. John Ehrenreich, *Third Wave Capitalism: How Money, Power, and the Pursuit of Self-Interest Have Imperiled the American Dream* (Ithaca, NY: Cornell University Press, 2016).

21. Judith E. Bell, "Saving Their Assets: How to Stop Plunder at Blue Cross and Other Nonprofits," *American Prospect* online, May–June, 1996, http://prospect.org/article/saving-their-assets-how-stop-plunder-blue-cross -and-other-nonprofits.

22. James Peltz, "Health Net Wins For-Profit Status: The State Lets the Woodland Hills–Based HMO Convert from a Nonprofit Organization After It Agrees to Cede Majority Ownership to a Foundation," *Los Angeles Times*, February 8, 1992, http://articles.latimes.com/1992-02-08/business/fi-1192_1_health-net.

23. Michael Hiltzik and David Olmos, "Are Executives at HMOs Paid Too Much Money?" *Los Angeles Times*, August 30, 1995, http://articles.latimes.com/1995-08-30/news/mn-40469_1_hmo-executive.

24. Mark A. Hall, and Christopher J. Conover, "The Impact of Blue Cross Conversions on Accessibility, Affordability, and the Public Interest," *Milbank Quarterly* 81/4 (2003): 509–42.

25. Thomas Farragher and Liz Kowalczyk, "Fueled by Profits, a Healthcare Giant Takes Aim at Suburbs," *Boston Globe,* December 12, 2008, http://www.bostonglobe.com/specials/2008/12/21/fueled-profits-healthcare-giant-takes-aim-suburbs/hVExi2njp1hUFhQIyRUmuO/story.html.

26. Editorial, "The Risks of Hospital Mergers," *New York Times*, July 7, 2014, http://www.nytimes.com/2014/07/07/opinion/the-risks-of-hospital-mergers.html.

27. Scott Allen and Marcella Bombardieri, "A Handshake That Made Healthcare History," *Boston Globe*, December 28, 2008, http://archive.boston.com/news/local/massachusetts/articles/2008/12/28/a_handshake_that_made_healthcare_history/.

28. Scott Allen and Thomas Farragher, "Partners, Insurer Under Scrutiny," *Boston Globe,* January 23, 2009, http://archive.boston.com/news/local/massachusetts/articles/2009/01/23/partners_insurer_under_scrutiny/.

29. "Attorney General Martha Coakley's Office Releases Report on Health Care Cost Drivers," Website of the Attorney General of Massachusetts, January 2010, http://www.mass.gov/ago/news-and-updates/press-releases/2010/ago-releases-report-on-health-care-cost-drivers.html.

30. Molly Gamble, "15 Things to Know about the Deal between Partners HealthCare, Massachusetts AG Martha Coakley," *Becker's Hospital Review,* July 14, 2014, http://www.beckershospitalreview.com/hospital-transactions-and-valuation/15-things-to-know-about-massachusetts-settlement-with-partners-healthcare.html.

31. The Trustees of Columbia University, Website of Columbia University, April 10, 2016, http://secretary.columbia.edu/trustees-columbia-university.

32. Aaron Fisher, Sasha Zients, and Garrett Donnelly,"Ties that Bind: Checking on the Manhattanville Benefits Agreement, Six Years Later," *Columbia Spectator,* March 25, 2015, http://features.columbiaspectator.com/eye/2015/03/25/ties-that-bind/.

33. Caroline Humer,"Exclusive: Makers Took Big Price Increases on Widely Used U.S. Drugs," Reuters Online, April 5, 2016, http://www.reuters.

com/article/us-usa-healthcare-drugpricing-idUSKCN0X10TH.

34. Steven Witt, "Valeant Pharmaceuticals' Novel Business Approach Made It a Wall Street Darling—Then a Pariah," *New York Magazine,* January 11, 2016, http://nymag.com/daily/intelligencer/2016/01/valeant-wall-st-darling-to-pariah.html.

35. Andrew Pollack and Sabrina Tavernise,"Valeant's Drug Price Strategy Enriches It, but Infuriates Patients and Lawmakers," *New York Times,* October 5, 2010, http://www.nytimes.com/2015/10/05/business/valeants-drug-price-strategy-enriches-it-but-infuriates-patients-and-lawmakers.html.

36. Dan McCrum, "Valeant and the IRS," *Financial Times Online,* August 15, 2014, http://ftalphaville.ft.com/2014/08/15/1903532/valeant-and-the-irs/.

37. James Surowiecki, "The Roll-Up Jacket," *The New Yorker,* April 4, 2016, http://www.newyorker.com/magazine/2016/04/04/inside-the-valeant-scandal.

38. John Bellamy Foster, "The Financialization of Capital and the Crisis," *Monthly Review* 59/11 (April 2008): 1–19.

39. Paul M. Sweezy, "More (or Less) on Globalization," *Monthly Review* 49/4 (September 1997): 1–5.

40. Alan Walks, "Bailing Out the Wealthy: Responses to the Financial Crisis, Ponzi Neoliberalism and the City," *Human Geography* 3/3 (2010): 54–84.

6. The Pharmaceutical Industry in the Context of Contemporary Capitalism

1. Harriet Washington, *Deadly Monopolies* (New York: Anchor Books, 2011); Richard Anderson, "Pharmaceutical Industry Gets High on Fat Profits," November 6, 2014, http://www.bbc.com/news/business-28212223.

2. Donald W. Light and Joel Lexchin, "Foreign Free Riders and the High Price of US Medicines," *BMJ* 331 (2005): 958–60.

3. Prescrire Editorial Staff, "New Drugs and Indications in 2014," *Prescrire International* 24 (2015): 107–10.

4. Joseph A. DiMasi, Henry G. Grabowski, and Ronald W. Hansen, "Innovation in the Pharmaceutical Industry: New Estimates of R&D Costs," *Journal of Health Economics* 47 (2016): 20–33.

5. Donald W. Light and Rebecca N. Warburton, "Extraordinary Claims Require Extraordinary Evidence," *Journal of Health Economics* 24 (2005): 1030–33.

6. Stanley Finkelstein and Peter Temin, *Reasonable Rx: Solving the Drug Price Crisis* (Upper Saddle River, NJ: FT Press, 2008).

7. Greg Miller, "Is Pharma Running Out of Brainy Ideas?," *Science* 329

(2010): 502–4; David Holmes, "Skies Darken Over Drug Companies," *Lancet* 379 (2012): 1863–64.

8. Pedro Cuatrecasas, "Drug Discovery in Jeopardy," *Journal of Clinical Investigation* 116 (2006): 2837–42.

9. Belen Pedrique, Nathalie Strub-Wourgaft, Claudette Some, Piero Olliaro, Patrice Trouiller, Nathan Ford, Bernard Pécoul, and Jean-Hervé Bradol, "The Drug and Vaccine Landscape for Neglected Diseases (2000–11): A Systematic Assessment," *Lancet Global Health* 1 (2013): e371–79.

10. Daniel M. Hartung, Dennis N. Bourdette, Sharia M. Ahmed, and Ruth H. Whitham, "The Cost of Multiple Sclerosis Drugs in the US and the Pharmaceutical Industry," *Neurology* 84 (2015): 2815–22.

11. Andrew Pollack, "Doctors Denounce Cancer Drug Prices of $100,000 a Year," *New York Times,* April 25, 2013.

12. Hank McKinnell, *A Call to Action: Taking Back Healthcare for Future Generations* (New York: McGraw Hill, 2005).

13. World Health Organization, *The World Medicines Situation* (Geneva: WHO, 2004).

14. Patricia McGettigan, Peter Roderick, Rushikesh Mahajan, Abhay Kadam, and Allyson M. Pollock, "Use of Fixed Dose Combination (FDC) Drugs in India: Central Regulatory Approval and Sales of FDCs Containing Non-Steroidal Anti-Inflammatory Drugs (NSAIDs), Metformin, or Psychotropic Drugs," *PLoS Medicine* 12 (2015): e1001826.

15. Courtney Davis and John Abraham, *Unhealthy Pharmaceutical Regulation: Innovation, Politics and Promissory Science* (Hampshire, UK, and New York: Palgrave Macmillan, 2013).

16. John Abraham, "Sociology of Pharmaceuticals Development and Regulation: A Realist Empirical Research Programme," *Sociology of Health & Illness* 30 (2008): 869–85.

17. Davis and Abraham, *Unhealthy Pharmaceutical Regulation.*

18. James L. Zelenay, Jr. "The Prescription Drug User Fee Act: Is a Faster Food and Drug Administration Always a Better Food and Drug Administration?," *Food and Drug Law Journal* 60 (2005): 261–338.

19. John Abraham, *Science, Politics and the Pharmaceutical Industry: Controversy and Bias in Drug Regulation* (London: UCL Press, 1995).

20. Daniel Carpenter, Evan James Zucker, and Jerry Avorn, "Drug-Review Deadlines and Safety Problems," *New England Journal of Medicine* 358 (2008):1354–61.

21. John Abraham and Graham Lewis, "Europeanization of Medicines Regulation," in *Regulation of the Pharmaceutical Industry*, ed. John Abraham and Helen Lawton Smith (Hampshire, UK: Palgrave Macmillan, 2003), 42–81.

22. Ibid.

23. House of Commons, Health Committee, *The Influence of the Pharmaceutical Industry: Fourth Report of Session 2004-05,* vol. 1 (London: Stationery Office Limited, April 5, 2005).

24. Joel Lexchin, "Pharmaceuticals, Patents and Politics: Canada and Bill C-22," *International Journal of Health Services* 23 (1993): 147–60.

25. Ameet Sarpatwari, Jerry Avorn, and Aaron S Kesselheim, "Progress and Hurdles for Follow-On Biologics," *New England Journal of Medicine* 372 (2015): 2380–82.

26. James Love, "TPP, Designed to Make Medicine More Expensive, Reforms More Difficult," 2015, https://medium.com/@jamie_love/tpp-designed-to-make-medicine-more-expensive-reforms-more-difficult-e6a94a5d4a18.

27. Kazi Stastna, "Eli Lilly Files $500M NAFTA Suit against Canada Over Drug Patents," September 13, 2013, http://www.cbc.ca/news/business/eli-lilly-files-500m-nafta-suit-against-canada-over-drug-patents-1.1829854.

28. Hazel Moir, Deborah H. Gleeson, Brigitte Tenni, and Ruth Lopert, *Assessing the Impact of Alternative Patent Systems on the Cost of Health Care: The TPP and HIV Treatment in Vietnam* (Sydney, Australia: Asia-Pacific Innovation Conference, 2014).

29. Peter Drahos, "Expanding Intellectual Property's Empire: The Role of FTAs," November 2003, http://www.ictsd.org/downloads/2008/08/drahos-fta-2003-en.pdf.

30. Jean O. Lanjouw and William Jack, "Trading Up: How Much Should Poor Countries Pay to Support Pharmaceutical Innovation?," *CGD Brief* 4 (2004): 1–7.

31. Campaign for Access to Essential Medicines, *Untangling the Web of Antiretroviral Price Reductions* (Geneva: Médecins Sans Frontières, 2010).

32. Ellen F 't Hoen, "TRIPS, Pharmaceutical Patents, and Access to Essential Medicines: A Long Way From Seattle to Doha," *Chicago Journal of International Law* 3 (2002): 27–48.

33. Stephanie Rosenberg, *Comparative Chart of Pharmaceutical Patent and Data Provisions in the TRIPS Agreement, Free Trade Agreements Between Trans-Pacific FTA Negotiating Countries and the U.S., and the U.S. Proposal to the Trans-Pacific FTA* (Washington, DC: Public Citizen, 2011).

34. Youn Jung and Soonman Kwon, "The Effects of Intellectual Property Rights on Access to Medicines and Catastrophic Expenditure," *International Journal of Health Services* 45 (2015): 507–29.

35. Ellen F 't Hoen, *The Global Politics of Pharmaceutical Monopoly Power:*

Drug Patents, Access, Innovation and the Application of the WTO Doha Declaration on TRIPS and Public Health (Diemen, NL: AMB, 2009).

36. *Daily Mail*, "'We Didn't Make This Medicine for Indians . . . ,'" January 24, 2014, http://www.dailymail.co.uk/news/article-2545360/Pharmaceutical-chief-tries-stop-India-replicating-cancer-treatment.html.

37. Writing Group for the Women's Health Initiative Investigators, "Risks and Benefits of Estrogen Plus Progestin in Healthy Postmenopausal Women: Principal Results from the Women's Health Initiative Randomized Controlled Trial," *JAMA* 288 (2002): 321–33.

38. Adam L Hersh, Marcia L. Stefanick, and Randall S. Stafford, "National Use of Postmenopausal Hormone Therapy: Annual Trends and Response to Recent Evidence," *JAMA* 291 (2004): 47–53.

39. Marc-André Gagnon, *The Nature of Capital in the Knowledge-Based Economy: The Case of the Global Pharmaceutical Industry* (Toronto: Political Science, York University, 2009).

40. Antonio Nieto, Angel Mazon, Rafael Pamies, Juan J. Linana, Amparo Lanuza, Fernando Oliver Jiménez, Alejandra Medina-Hernandez, and Javier Nieto, "Adverse Effects of Inhaled Corticosteroids in Funded and Nonfunded Studies," *Archives of Internal Medicine* 167 (2007): 2047–53.

41. Joseph A DiMasi, "Success Rates for New Drugs Entering Clinical Testing in the United States," *Clinical Pharmacology & Therapeutics* 58 (1995): 1–14; Bruce M. Psaty and Drummond Rennie, "Stopping Medical Research to Save Money: A Broken Pact with Researchers and Patients," *JAMA* 289 (2003): 2128–31.

42. "WMA Declaration of Helsinki: Ethical Principles For Medical Research Involving Human Subjects," 2008, http://www.wma.net/en/30publications/10policies/b3/.

43. Ibid.

44. Bruce M. Psaty and Richard A. Kronmal, "Reporting Mortality Findings in Trials of Rofecoxib for Alzheimer Disease or Cognitive Impairment: A Case Study Based on Documents from Rofecoxib Litigation," *JAMA* 299 (2008): 1813–17.

45. Peter Lurie and Sidney M Wofle, "Misleading Data Analyses in Salmeterol (SMART) Study," *The Lancet* 366 (2005): 1261–62.

46. James M. Wright, Thomas L. Perry, Kenneth L. Bassett, and G. Keith Chambers, "Reporting of 6-Month vs 12-Month Data in a Clinical Trial of Celecoxib," *JAMA* 286 (2001): 2398–99.

47. Natasha Singer, "Medical Papers by Ghostwriters Pushed Therapy," *New York Times*, August 5, 2009.

48. Eric H. Turner, Annette M. Matthews, Efthia Linardatos, Robert A. Tell, and Robert Rosenthal, "Selective Publication of Antidepressant

Trials and Its Influence on Apparent Efficacy," *New England Journal of Medicine* 358 (2008): 252–60.

49. Dirk Eyding, Monika Lelgemann, Ulrich Grouven, Martin Härter, Mandy Kromp, Thomas Kaiser, Michaela F. Kerekes, Martin Gerken, and Beate Wiseeler, "Reboxetine for Acute Treatment of Major Depression: Systematic Review and Meta-Analysis of Published and Unpublished Placebo and Selective Serotonin Reuptake Inhibitor Controlled Trials," *BMJ* 341 (2010): e4737.

50. Jon Jureidini, Leeman B McHenry, and Peter R Mansfield, "Clinical Trials and Drug Promotion: Selective Reporting of Study 329," *International Journal of Risk & Safety in Medicine* 20 (2008): 73–81.

51. Martin B. Keller, Neal D. Ryan, Michael Strober et al., "Efficacy of Paroxetine in the Treatment of Adolescent Major Depression: A Randomized, Controlled Trial," *Journal of the American Academy of Child and Adolescent Psychiatry* 40 (2001): 762–72.

52. S. Swaroop Vedula, Lisa Bero, Roberta W Scherer, and Kay Dickersin, "Outcome Reporting in Industry-Sponsored Trials of Gabapentin for Off-Label Use," *New England Journal of Medicine* 361 (2009): 1963–71.

53. Sergio Sismondo, "'You're Not Just a Paid Monkey Reading Slides': How Key Opinion Leaders Explain and Justify Their Work," Edmund J Safra Working Papers, Harvard University, No. 26 (2013).

54. John W. Norton, "Is Academic Medicine for Sale?" *New England Journal of Medicine* 343 (2000): 508.

55. Alan Maynard, personal communication, 2001.

56. Donald W. Light and Antonio F. Maturo, *Good Pharma: The Public-Health Model of the Mario Negri Institute* (New York: Palgrave Macmillan, 2015).

57. James Love, *What's Wrong with Current System of Funding R&D, and What Are Ideas for Reforms?* (Washington, DC: Knowledge Ecology International, 2015).

58. Arthur Schafer, "Biomedical Conflicts of Interest: A Defence of the Sequestration Thesis—Learning from the Cases of Nancy Olivieri and David Healy," *Journal of Medical Ethics* 30 (2004): 8–24.

59. Tracy R Lewis, Jerome H. Reichman, and Anthony Deh-Chuen So, "The Case For Public Funding and Public Oversight of Clinical Trials," *Economists' Voice* 4 (2007): 1–4; Marcia Angell, *The Truth About the Drug Companies: How They Deceive Us and What to Do About It* (New York: Random House, 2004).

60. Lewis, Reichman, and So, "The Case For Public Funding and Public Oversight of Clinical Trials."

61. Dean Baker, "The Benefits and Savings from Publicly Funded Clinical

Trials of Prescription Drugs," *International Journal of Health Services* 38 (2008): 731–50.

62. Patented Medicine Prices Review Board, *Regulating Prices* (Ottawa: PMRPB, 2014), http://www.pmprb-cepmb.gc.ca/english/View.asp?x= 1440.

63. Patented Medicine Prices Review Board, *Annual Report 2012* (Ottawa: PMPRB, 2013).

64. OECD, *Health at a Glance 2015: OECD Indicators* (Paris: OECD Publishing, 2015).

65. Productivity Commission, 2003, *Evaluation of the Pharmaceutical Industry Investment Program, Research Report* (Canberra, Australia: AusInfo, 2003).

66. Pharmaceutical Management Agency, *Annual Review 2012* (Wellington, NZ: PHARMAC, 2013).

67. As this book went to press, two physician organizations, one in the United States (Physicians for a National Health Program) and one in Canada (Canadian Doctors for Medicare), have developed a comprehensive strategy to restrict the power of the pharmaceutical industry and to improve access to medications (proposals submitted for publication, November 2017).

7. Obamacare: The Neoliberal Model Comes Home to Roost

An earlier version of this chapter appeared in *Monthly Review* 68/1 (May 2016): 1–18.

1. Congressional Budget Office, "Insurance Coverage Provisions of the Affordable Care Act," March 2015, https://www.cbo.gov/sites/default/ files/cbofiles/attachments/43900-2015-03-ACAtables.pdf; Rachel Nardin, Leah Zallman, Danny McCormick, Steffie Woolhandler, and David Himmelstein, "The Uninsured after Implementation of the Affordable Care Act: A Demographic and Geographic Analysis," *Health Affairs Blog*, June 6, 2013, http://healthaffairs.org/blog/2013/06/06/ the-uninsured-after-implementation-of-the-affordable-care-act-a- demographic-and-geographic-analysis/.

2. Robert Pear, "Many Say High Deductibles Make Their Health Law Insurance All but Useless ," *New York Times*, November 14, 2015, http:// www.nytimes.com/2015/11/15/us/politics/many-say-high-deductibles -make-their-health-law-insurance-all-but-useless.html.

3. David Himmelstein and Steffie Woolhandler, "The Post-Launch Problem: The Affordable Care Act's Persistently High Administrative Costs," *Health Affairs Blog*, May 27, 2015, http://healthaffairs.org/ blog/2015/05/27/the-post-launch-problem-the-affordable-care-acts- persistently-high-administrative-costs/; David U. Himmelstein et al.,

"A Comparison of Hospital Administrative Costs in Eight Nations: US Costs Exceed All Others By Far," *Health Affairs* 33/9 (2014): 1586–94; Steffie Woolhandler, Terry Campbell, and David U. Himmelstein, "Costs of Health Care Administration in the United States and Canada," *New England Journal of Medicine* 349/8 (2003): 768–75.

4. "Health Insurance CEO Pay Skyrockets in 2013," Health Care NOW!, May 5, 2014, http://www.pnhp.org/news/2014/may/health-insurance-ceo-pay-skyrockets-in-2013.

5. Centers for Medicare and Medicaid Services, "National Health Expenditure Projections 2012–2022," https://www.cms.gov/Research-Statistics-Data-and-Systems/Statistics-Trends-and-Reports/NationalHealthExpendData/Downloads/Proj2012.pdf.

6. Richard A. Young and Jennifer E. DeVoe, "Who Will Have Health Insurance in the Future? An Updated Projection," *Annals of Family Medicine* 10/2 (2012): 156–62.

7. Howard Waitzkin, *Medicine and Public Health at the End of Empire* (Boulder, CO: Paradigm Publishers, 2011), chap. 8.

8. Howard Waitzkin and Celia Iriart, "How the United States Exports Managed Care to Third World Countries," *Monthly Review* 52/1 (May 2000): 21–35; Karen Stocker, Howard Waitzkin, and Celia Iriart, "The Exportation of Managed Care to Latin America," *New England Journal of Medicine* 340/14 (1999): 1131–36.

9. Waitzkin and Iriart, "How the United States Exports Managed Care to Third World Countries."

10. Alain C. Enthoven and K. Wayne Smith, *How Much Is Enough? Shaping the Defense Program, 1961–1969* (New York: Harper & Row, 1971).

11. For more on the sources of neoliberal health reform in the military, see Howard Waitzkin, "The Strange Career of Managed Competition: Military Failure to Medical Success?" *American Journal of Public Health* 84/3 (1994): 482–89; Alain C. Enthoven, "Commentary: Setting the Record Straight—A Reply to Howard Waitzkin," *American Journal of Public Health* 84/3 (1994): 490–93; Howard Waitzkin, "A Rejoinder [to commentary by Alain Enthoven]," *American Journal of Public Health* 84/3 (1994): 493–94. For a more recent packaging of the same perspective, see Alain C. Enthoven, "Market Forces and Efficient Health Care Systems," *Health Affairs (Millwood)* 23/2 (March–April 2004): 25–27; Alain C. Enthoven and Wynand P.M.M. van de Ven, "Going Dutch: Managed-Competition Health Insurance in the Netherlands," *New England Journal of Medicine* 357/24 (2007): 2421–23.

12. Waitzkin, "The Strange Career of Managed Competition."

13. Alain C. Enthoven, "Consumer-Choice Health Plan," *New England Journal of Medicine* 298/12–13 (1978): 650–58, 709–20; Enthoven,

Health Plan: The Only Practical Solution to the Soaring Cost of Medical Care (Reading, MA: Addison-Wesley, 1980).

14. Alain C. Enthoven, *Theory and Practice of Managed Competition in Health Care Finance* (Amsterdam: North-Holland, 1988); Alain C. Enthoven and Richard Kronick, "A Consumer Choice Health Plan for the 1990s," *New England Journal of Medicine* 320/1–2 (1989): 29–37, 94–101; Paul Ellwood, Alain Enthoven, and Lynn Etheredge, "The Jackson Hole Initiatives for a Twenty-First-Century American Health Care System," *Health Economics* 1/3 (1992): 149–68.

15. For information about Obama's switch from single-payer to market-oriented principles and the campaign contributions that supported this conversion, see "Barack Obama on Single Payer in 2003," http://www.pnhp.org/news/2008/june/barack_obama_on_sing.php; Brad Jacobson, "Obama Received $20 Million from Healthcare Industry in 2008 Campaign," *The Raw Story*, http://rawstory.com/2010/01/obama-received-20-million-healthcare-industry-money-2008/. Obama's support from the insurance industry deteriorated slightly in 2012. See Center for Responsive Politics, "2012 Presidential Race," https://www.opensecrets.org/pres12/.

16. Deborah Levine and Jessica Mulligan, "Overutilization, Overutilized," *Journal of Health Politics, Policy and Law* 40/2 (2015): 421–37.

17. "Health Policy Brief: The CO-OP Health Insurance Program (updated)," *Health Affairs*, updated January 23, 2014, http://www.healthaffairs.org/healthpolicybriefs/brief.php.

18. Entidad Promotora de Salud Organismo Cooperativo SALUDCOOP, Directorio de Empresas, Colombia, http://www.informacion-empresas.co/empresa_entidad-promotora-salud-organismo-cooperativo-salu-dcoop.html.

19. Kip Sullivan, "How to Think Clearly about Medicare Administrative Costs: Data Sources and Measurement," *Journal of Health Politics, Policy and Law* 38/3 (2013): 479–504.

20. Sharita R. Thomas, Brystana G. Kaufman, Randy K. Randolph, Kristie Thompson, Julie R. Perry, and George H. Pink, "A Comparison of Closed Rural Hospitals and Perceived Impact," North Carolina Rural Health Research Program, University of North Carolina, April 2015, http://www.shepscenter.unc.edu/wp-content/uploads/2015/04/AfterClosureApril2015.pdf; Chad Terhune, "Closure of Three Southland Hospitals May Be Part of a Trend," *Los Angeles Times*, April 3, 2013, http://articles.latimes.com/2013/apr/03/business/la-fi-pacific-hospitals-closing-20130404.

21. Waitzkin, *Medicine and Public Health at the End of Empire*, chaps. 9 and 10.

22. Himmelstein and Woolhandler, "The Post-Launch Problem."

23. "Are Health Insurers Making Huge Profits?" *The Economist*, May 5, 2010. http://www.economist.com/blogs/democracyinamerica/2010/03/insurance_costs_and_health-care_reform.

24. Nicole Lurie, Nancy B. Ward, Martin F. Shapiro et al., "Termination of Medi-Cal Benefits," *New England Journal of Medicine* 314/19 (1986): 1266–68.

25. Ursula Giedion and Manuela Villar Uribe, "Colombia's Universal Health Insurance System," *Health Affairs (Millwood)* 28/3 (May–June 2009): 853–63.

26. *World Health Report 2000. Health Systems: Improving Performance* (Geneva: World Health Organization, 2000), http://www.who.int/whr/2000/en/whr00_en.pdf. For critiques, see Celia Almeida, Paula Braveman, Marthe Gold et al., "Methodological Concerns and Recommendations on Policy Consequences of the World Health Report 2000," *The Lancet* 357/9269 (2001): 1692–97; Vicente Navarro, "Assessment of the World Health Report 2000," *The Lancet* 356/9241 (2000): 1598–601.

27. Felicia M. Knaul, Eduardo González-Pier E, Octavio Gómez-Dantés et al., "The Quest for Universal Health Coverage: Achieving Social Protection for All in Mexico," *The Lancet* 380/9849 (2012): 1259–79; Waitzkin, *Medicine and Public Health at the End of Empire*, chap. 9; Asa Cristina Laurell, "Three Decades of Neoliberalism in Mexico: The Destruction of Society," *International Journal of Health Services* 45/2 (2015): 246–64.

28. Julio Frenk, "Leading the Way toward Universal Health Coverage: A Call to Action," *The Lancet* 385/9975 (2015): 1352–58.

29. Howard Waitzkin, "Universal Health Coverage: The Strange Romance of *The Lancet*, MEDICC, and Cuba," *Social Medicine/ Medicina Social* 9/2 (2015): 93–97.

30. Nila Heredia, Asa Cristina Laurell, Oscar Feo et al, "The Right to Health: What Model for Latin America?," *The Lancet* 385/9975 (2015): e34-7. doi: 10.1016/S0140-6736(14)61493-8.

31. Waitzkin, *Medicine and Public Health at the End of Empire*, chap. 9; Laurell, "Three Decades of Neoliberalism in Mexico"; Amit Sengupta. "Universal Health Coverage: Beyond Rhetoric," Ottawa, Ont.: International Development Research Centre. Occasional Paper No. 20, November 2013, http://www.municipalservicesproject.org/sites/municipalservicesproject.org/files/publications/OccasionalPaper20_Sengupta_Universal_Health_Coverage_Beyond_Rhetoric_Nov2013_0.pdf; David Stuckler, Andrea B. Feigl, Sanjay Basu, and Martin McKee, "The Political Economy of Universal Health Coverage," background paper for the Global Symposium on Health

Systems Research. November 16–19, 2010, Montreux, World Health Organization. http://www.pacifichealthsummit.org/downloads/UHC/the%20political%20economy%20of%20uhc.PDF.

32. Giedion and Villar Uribe, "Colombia's Universal Health Insurance System."

33. Amanda L. Glassman, María-Luisa Escobar, Antonio Giuffrida, and Ursula Gliedion, *From Few to Many: Ten Years of Health Insurance Expansion in Colombia* (Washington, DC: Inter-American Development Bank, 2009).

34. Thomas C. Tsai, "Second Chance for Health Reform in Colombia," *The Lancet* 375/9709 (2010): 109–10.

35. Ingrid Vargas, María Luisa Vázquez, Amparo Susana Mogollón-Pérez, and Jean-Pierre Unger, "Barriers of Access to Care in a Managed Competition Model: Lessons from Colombia," *BMC Health Services Research* 10/297 (2010): 1–12.

36. César E. Abadía-Barrero, "Neoliberal Justice and the Transformation of the Moral: The Privatization of the Right to Health Care in Colombia," *Medical Anthropology Quarterly* (October 21, 2014), doi: 10.1111/maq.12161.

37. Senator Jorge Robledo, "SALUDCOOP: The Greatest Robbery of Public Assets," speech in a plenary session of the Colombian Senate, September 9, 2014, http://colombiasupport.net/2014/10/saludcoop-the-greatest-robbery-of-public-assets/.

38. Himmelstein and Woolhandler, "The Post-Launch Problem."

39. Adam Gaffney, Steffie Woolhandler, Marcia Angell and David U. Himmelstein, "Moving Forward From the Affordable Care Act to a Single-Payer System," *American Journal of Public Health* 106/6 (2016): 987–88; David U. Himmelstein, Steffie Woolhandler et al., "A National Health Program for the United States: A Physicians' Proposal," *New England Journal of Medicine* 320/ 2 (1989): 102–8; Kevin Grumbach, Thomas Bodenheimer, David U. Himmelstein, and Steffie Woolhandler, "Liberal Benefits, Conservative Spending: The Physicians for a National Health Program Proposal," *JAMA* 265/19 (1991): 2549–54; Charlene Harrington, Christine Cassel, Carroll L. Estes et al., "A National Long-Term Care Program for the United States: A Caring Vision," *JAMA* 266/21 (1991): 3023–29.

40. Gerald Friedman, "Funding HR 676: The Expanded and Improved Medicare for All Act: How We Can Afford a National Single-Payer Health Plan," http://www.pnhp.org/sites/default/files/Friedman%20Executive%20Summary.pdf.

41. "New Poll on Single Payer and a Medicare Buy-In," *Progressive Change Institute, Conducted by GBA Strategies, January 9-15, 2015,*

http://www.pnhp.org/news/2015/january/new-poll-on-single-payer-and-a-medicare-buy-in.

42. Physicians for a National Health Program, "The Expanded & Improved Medicare For All Act (H.R. 676)," http://www.pnhp.org/publications/united-states-national-health-care-act-hr-676.

43. Barbara Ehrenreich and John Ehrenreich, "The Real Story Behind the Crash and Burn of America's Managerial Class," *Alternet*, February 13, 2013, http://www.alternet.org/economy/barbara-and-john-ehrenreich-real-story-behind-crash-and-burn-americas-managerial-class; Barbara and John Ehrenreich, "The Professional-Managerial Class," *Radical America* 11/2 (March–April 1977): 7–31.

44. Carol Peckham, "Medscape Physician Compensation Report 2015," http://www.medscape.com/features/slideshow/compensation/2015/public/overview#page=9; Elisabeth Rosenthal, "Apprehensive, Many Doctors Shift to Jobs with Salaries," *New York Times*, February 13, 2014, ,http://www.nytimes.com/2014/02/14/us/salaried-doctors-may-not-lead-to-cheaper-health-care.html.

45. Dante Morra, Sean Nicholson, Wendy Levinson, David N. Gans, Terry Hammons and Lawrence P. Casalino, "US Physician Practices versus Canadians: Spending Nearly Four Times as Much Money Interacting with Payers," *Health Affairs*, August 2011, http://content.healthaffairs.org/content/early/2011/08/03/hlthaff.2010.0893.

46. John B. McKinlay and Joan Arches, "Toward the Proletarianization of Physicians," *International Journal of Health Services* 15/2 (1985): 161–95; Adam Reich, "Disciplined Doctors: The Electronic Medical Record and Physicians' Changing Relationship to Medical Knowledge," *Social Science & Medicine* 74/7 (2012): 1021–28.

47. Eric Hobsbawm, "Lenin and the 'Aristocracy of Labor,'" *Monthly Review* 64/7 (December 2012): 26–34.

48. Samir Amin, "Contra Hardt and Negri: Multitude or Generalized Proletarianization?," *Monthly Review* 66/6 (November 2014): 25–36.

49. In this sense, the financial flows of health insurance cohere with John Bellamy Foster's comment: "At the more stratospheric level represented by contemporary finance, the general formula for capital, or M-C-M', is being increasingly supplanted by the circuit of speculative capital, M-M', in which the production of use values disappears altogether and money simply begets more money." John Bellamy Foster, "The Epochal Crisis," *Monthly Review* 65/6 (October 2013): 1–12.

8. Austerity and Health Care

1. Consider, for instance, the faltering steps toward health care universalism taken by Ireland in recent years, as described by Sara Ann Burke

et al., "From Universal Health Insurance to Universal Healthcare? The Shifting Health Policy Landscape in Ireland since the Economic Crisis," *Health Policy* 120/3 (2016): 235–40. For a brief perspective on the assault on universal health care in Europe, see Aaron Reeves, Martin McKee, and David Stuckler, "The Attack on Universal Health Coverage in Europe: Recession, Austerity and Unmet Needs," *European Journal of Public Health* 25/3 (2015): 364–65.

2.   Joseph E. Stiglitz, *Freefall: America, Free Markets, and the Sinking of the World Economy* (New York: W. W. Norton, 2010); Richard D. Wolff, *Capitalism Hits the Fan: The Global Economic Meltdown and What to Do About It* (Northampton, MA: Olive Branch Press, 2010).

3.   Vicente Navarro and Carles Muntaner, eds., *The Financial and Economic Crises and Their Impact on Health and Social Well-Being*, Policy, Politics, Health and Medicine Series (Amityville, NY: Baywood Publishing, 2014); Anna Maresso, et al., eds., *Economic Crisis, Health Systems and Health in Europe: Country Experience* (Brussels: WHO Regional Office for Europe/European Observatory on Health Systems and Policies, 2015).

4.   However, even the salutary effects of recession on mortality (as with the reduction in workplace fatalities) may depend on changes in technology, such as a move to service industries. This is suggested by recent analyses, which have found more muted effects on macroeconomic change and mortality. Christopher J. Ruhm, "Recessions, Healthy No More?," *Journal of Health Economics* 42 (2015): 17–28.

5.   David Stuckler and Sanjay Basu, *The Body Economic: Why Austerity Kills* (New York: Basic Books, 2013); Veronica Toffolutti and Marc Suhrcke, "Assessing the Short-Term Health Impact of the Great Recession in the European Union: A Cross-Country Panel Analysis," *Preventative Medicine* 64 (2014): 54–62; Mahiben Maruthappu et al., "Economic Downturns, Universal Health Coverage, and Cancer Mortality in High-Income and Middle-Income Countries, 1990–2010: A Longitudinal Analysis," *The Lancet* (2016), doi: http://dx.doi.org/10.1016/S0140-6736(16)00577-8.

6.   Together with Stucker and Basu's book (which focuses more broadly on the impact of austerity on health, and how a nation's response to economic crisis impacts health), a number of papers have examined this issue, which are cited in the relevant sections below. Two good references dealing with how austerity may impact universal health systems must be cited at the outset: Martin McKee et al., "Universal Health Coverage: A Quest for All Countries but Under Threat in Some," *Value Health* 16/1 (2013): S39–45; Martin McKee et al., "Austerity: A Failed Experiment on the People of Europe," *Clinical Medicine* 12/4 (2012):

346–50. In the first, the authors synthesize ideas about how universal health care came about politically, but also point to the looming threat to universal health care in Europe. In the second, they briefly describe health system changes in Greece, Spain, Portugal, and Italy.

7. Some material in this article was presented at a talk on "Global Neoliberal Attack on Public Health Systems" given by Adam Gaffney at the 2015 American Public Health Association annual meeting.

8. This definition is that of Vicente Navarro, in "Neoliberalism as a Class Ideology; Or, the Political Causes of the Growth of Inequalities," *International Journal of Health Services* 37/1 (2007): 47–62. For a revealing historical analysis of the ideological roots of neoliberalism, see Daniel Stedman Jones, *Masters of the Universe: Hayek, Friedman, and the Birth of Neoliberal Politics* (Princeton: Princeton University Press, 2012). For a discussion on neoliberalism in health care, see also Ronald Labonte and David Stuckler, "The Rise of Neoliberalism: How Bad Economics Imperils Health and What to Do about It," *Journal of Epidemiology and Community Health* 70/3 (2016): 312–18.

9. Others have described "neoliberal" changes in health systems proceeding generally along these lines. For instance, Holden described a process of progressive privatization of health services in developing, post-communist, and developed nations (axis 4). He also makes note of efforts to increase cost sharing in some nations (axis 3). Many have also described how decreasing public funding for the welfare state (axis 1) or its universality (axis 2) can undermine the welfare state politically. McKee and Stuckler, for instance, in "The Assault on Universalism," discuss how governments can undermine generally popular benefits—including public health care—by restricting universal benefits to the poor. Grouping these four "axes" together under the umbrella of neoliberalism seems to us conceptually valid. Movement along each axis takes a nation toward the marketization and commercialization of its health system. Additionally, they all work in tandem: austerity, for example, can reduce the quality of public services and thereby promote the private provision of these services. Along similar lines, John Lister's excellent book explores neoliberal attacks on health care systems throughout the globe, including in developing countries, with an emphasis on the role of international bodies like the World Bank. See Chris Holden, "Privatization and Trade in Health Services: A Review of the Evidence," *International Journal of Health Services* 35/4 (2005): 675–89; Martin McKee and David Stuckler, "The Assault on Universalism: How to Destroy the Welfare State," *British Medical Journal* 343/7837 (2011): d7973, doi: 10.1136/bmj.d7973; John Lister, *Health Policy Reform: Global Health versus Private Profit*

(Farringdon, UK: Libri Publishing, 2013); Labonte and Stuckler, "The Rise of Neoliberalism: How Bad Economics Imperils Health and What to Do about It."

10. This has been recognized by others outside the United States and Europe. For instance, Canadian Doctors for Medicare was formed in 2006 given concerns about "the increased privatization in Canadian health care and the development of a two-tier health care system." Canadian Doctors for Medicare, "Background of CDM," http://www.canadiandoctorsformedicare.ca/Who-We-Are.

11. Charalampos Economou et al., "The Impact of the Crisis on the Health System and Health in Greece," *Economic Crisis, Health Systems, and Health in Europe: Country Experience* (Brussels: European Observatory on Health Systems and Policies, World Health Organization, 2015); Alexander Kentikelenis et al., "Greece's Health Crisis: From Austerity to Denialism," *The Lancet* 383/9918 (2014): 748–53.

12. Vicente Navarro, "Report from Spain: The Political Contexts of the Dismantling of the Spanish Welfare State," *International Journal of Health Services* 45/3 (2015): 405–14; Vicente Navarro, "The Crisis and Fiscal Policies in the Peripheral Countries of the Eurozone," *International Journal of Health Services* 42/1 (2012): 1–7.

13. This paragraph's discussion of the history of Greece's health care system relies on Charalampos Economou, "Greece: Health System Review," *Health Systems in Transition* 12/7 (2010): 17–25.

14. Yanis Varoufakis, "From Contagion to Incoherence: Toward a Model of the Unfolding Eurozone Crisis," *Contributions to Political Economy* 32/1 (2013): 51–71.

15. Mark Blyth, *Austerity: The History of a Dangerous Idea* (Oxford: Oxford University Press, 2013), 5, 73; Louise Story, Landon Thomas, and Nelson D. Schwartz, "Wall St. Helped to Mask Debt Fueling Europe's Crisis," *New York Times*, February 13, 2010, http://www.nytimes.com/2010/02/14/business/global/14debt.html.

16. Blyth, *Austerity*, 60–64; Paul Krugman, "The Austerity Delusion," *The Guardian*, April 29, 2015, http://www.theguardian.com/business/ng-interactive/2015/apr/29/the-austerity-delusion.

17. Blyth, *Austerity*, 73.

18. Anna Maria Santiago, "Fifty Years Later: From a War on Poverty to a War on the Poor," *Social Problems* 62/1 (2015): 2–14; Jon Stone, "Austerity Is Being Used as a Cover-Story for Class War Against the Poor, Yanis Varoufakis Says," *The Independent*, September 25, 2015, http://www.independent.co.uk/news/uk/politics/austerity-is-being-used-as-a-cover-story-for-class-war-against-the-poor-yanis-varoufakis-says-10516247.html; Robe Urie, "Greece and Global Class War,"

Counterpunch, July 3 2015, http://www.counterpunch.org/2015/07/03/greece-and-global-class-war; Paul Krugman, "The Austerity Delusion," *The Guardian*, April 29 2015, http://www.theguardian.com/business/ng-interactive/2015/apr/29/the-austerity-delusion.

19. "Greece's Debt Crisis Explained," *New York Times*, October 17, 2015, http://www.nytimes.com/interactive/2016/business/international/greece-debt-crisis-euro.html; Ned Resnikoff, "Who Is Really Being Bailed Out in Greece?" *Al Jazeera America*, July 2, 2015, http://america.aljazeera.com/articles/2015/7/1/greek-bailout-money-went-to-banks-not-greece.html.

20. Stuckler and Basu, *The Body Economic*, 84.

21. Annika Breidthardt and Jan Strupczewski, "Europe Seals New Greek Bailout but Doubts Remain," Reuters, February 21, 2012, http://www.reuters.com/article/usgreece-idUSTRE8120HI20120221.

22. Economou et al., "The Impact of the Crisis on the Health System and Health in Greece," 110–11.

23. Suzanne Daley, "Fiscal Crisis Takes Toll on Health of Greeks," *New York Times*, December 26, 2011, http://www.nytimes.com/2011/12/27/world/europe/greeks-reeling-from-health-care-cutbacks.html.

24. Stuckler and Basu, *The Body Economic*, 86; Elias Kondilis et al., "Economic Crisis, Restrictive Policies, and the Population's Health and Health Care: The Greek Case," *American Journal of Public Health* 103/6 (2013): 973–79.

25. Dimitris Niakas, "Greek Economic Crisis and Health Care Reforms: Correcting the Wrong Prescription," *International Journal of Health Services* 43/4 (2013): 597–602; Economou et al., "The Impact of the Crisis on the Health System and Health in Greece," 116.

26. The schemes intended to shore up the uninsured fell short, according to Alexander Kentikelenis, in "Bailouts, Austerity and the Erosion of Health Coverage in Southern Europe and Ireland," *European Journal of Public Health* 25/3 (2015): 365–66.

27. Economou et al., "The Impact of the Crisis on the Health System and Health in Greece," 114.

28. Ibid., 114–15, 122.

29. Alexander Kentikelenis et al., "Health Effects of Financial Crisis: Omens of a Greek Tragedy," *The Lancet* 378/9801 (2011): 1457–58; Angelique Chrisafis, "Greek Debt Crisis: 'Of All the Damage, Healthcare Has Been Hit the Worst,'" *The Guardian*, July 9, 2015, https://www.theguardian.com/world/2015/jul/09/greek-debt-crisis-damage-healthcare-hospital-austerity; Effie Simou and Eleni Koutsogeorgou, "Effects of the Economic Crisis on Health and Healthcare in Greece in the Literature from 2009 to 2013: A Systematic Review," *Health Policy*

115/ 2 (2014): 111–19; Economou et al., "The Impact of the Crisis on the Health System and Health in Greece,"125.

30.   Stuckler and Basu, *The Body Economic*, 85.

31.   Alexander Kentikelenis et al., "Greece's Health Crisis: From Austerity to Denialism," *The Lancet* 383/9918 (2014): 748–53.

32.   In the face of public protest, however, the hospitalization co-payment of €25 (US$29) was reversed. John Zarocostas, "Rise in User Fees in Greece Could Reduce Access to Healthcare, Charity Warns," *British Medical Journal* 342 (2011): d200; Alexander Kentikelenis et al., "Greece's Health Crisis"; Economou et al., "The Impact of the Crisis on the Health System and Health in Greece," 115.

33.   Economou et al., "The Impact of the Crisis on the Health System and Health in Greece," 115.

34.   Note that implementation of these measures has been "limited" thus far. Economou et al., "The Impact of the Crisis on the Health System and Health in Greece," 117–18.

35.   Economou et al., "The Impact of the Crisis on the Health System and Health in Greece," 132.

36.   Kondilis et al., "Economic Crisis, Restrictive Policies, and the Population's Health and Health Care: The Greek Case."

37.   Marina Karanikolos and Alexander Kentikelenis, "Health Inequalities after Austerity in Greece," *International Journal for Equity in Health* 15 (2016): 83.

38.   Dimitris Zavras, Athanasios I. Zavras, Ilias-Ioannis Kyriopoulos, and John Kyriopoulos, "Economic Crisis, Austerity and Unmet Healthcare Needs: The Case of Greece," *BMC Health Services Research* 16 (2016): 309.

39.   Karanikolos and Kentikelenis, "Health Inequalities after Austerity in Greece."

40.   Economou et al., "The Impact of the Crisis on the Health System and Health in Greece," 124.

41.   Simou and Eleni Koutsogeorgou, "Effects of the Economic Crisis on Health and Healthcare in Greece in the Literature from 2009 to 2013: A Systematic Review."

42.   Charles C Branas, et al., "The Impact of Economic Austerity and Prosperity Events on Suicide in Greece: A 30-Year Interrupted Time-Series Analysis." *BMJ Open* 5, no. 1 (January 1, 2015).

43.   Kondilis et al., "Economic Crisis, Restrictive Policies, and the Population's Health and Health Care: The Greek Case."

44.   Dimitris Zavras, Vasiliki Tsiantou, Elpida Pavi, Katerina Mylona, and John Kyriopoulos, "Impact of Economic Crisis and Other Demographic and Socio-Economic Factors on Self-Rated Health in Greece," *European Journal of Public Health* 23, no. 2 (Apr 2013): 206–10.

45. Eva Karamanoli, "Greek Government Plans Health System Overhaul," *The Lancet* 385/9970 (2015): 761–62; Chrisafis, "Greek Debt Crisis"; Charalampos Economou, "Syriza's Ambitious Plan to Rescue the Greek Health System," *The Conversation*, January 26, 2015, http://the-conversation.com/syrizas-ambitious-plan-to-rescue-the-greek-health -system-36735.

46. Renee Maltezou, Deepa Babington, and Toby Chopra, "Greece Scraps Hospital Visit Fee, to Hire Health Workers," Reuters, April 2, 2015, http:// www.reuters.com/article/2015/04/02/eurozone-greece-health-idUSL6 N0WZ1P420150402#PVQJdIYuLV61MHme.97.

47. Yanis Varoufakis, *Adults in the Room: My Battle with Europe's Deep Establishment* (London: Bodley Head, 2017).

48. Karl Stagno Navarra, Ian Wishart, and Rebecca Christie, "Greece Capitulates to Creditors' Demands to Cling to Euro," *Bloomberg Business*, July 13, 2015, http://www.bloomberg.com/news/articles/2015-07-13/ eu-demands-tsipras-capitulation-as-bailout-costs-spiral-ic1mkgo3.

49. Stathis Kouvelakis, "Introducing Popular Unity," *Jacobin*, August 21, 2015, https://www.jacobinmag.com/2015/08/popular-unity-syriza-left-platform-lafazanis; phillip inman, "Yanis Varoufakis: Bailout Deal Allows Greek Oligarchs to Maintain Grip," *The Guardian*, August 17, 2015, http://www.theguardian.com/business/2015/aug/17/yanis-varo-ufakis-bailout-deal-greek-oligarchs-maintain-grip-eu-leaders-greece.

50. "Greece Election: Alexis Tsipras Hails 'Victory of the People'," BBC News, September 21, 2015, http://www.bbc.com/news/ world-europe-34307795.

51. Yanis Varoufakis, *And the Weak Suffer What They Must?: Europe, Austerity and the Threat to Global Stability* (New York: Nation Books, 2016).

52. Vicente Navarro, *Ataque a la Democracia y al Bienestar* (Barcelona: Anagrama, 2012).

53. Indeed, just a few years before the crisis, the leader of the then ruling socialist party (Partido Socialista Obrero Español, PSOE) had famously argued that paying less tax was "socialist."

54. Navarro, "The Social Crisis of the Eurozone"; Navarro, *Ataque a la democracia y al bienestar.*

55. The PSOE was already strong during the second Spanish republic before Franco's coup in 1936. When the dictatorship ended in 1977, with help from external supporters the PSOE became one of the two majoritarian parties to alternate power. The PSOE quickly moved toward the political center, embracing NATO and neoliberalism.

56. The PP is the major right-wing party in Spain, a large umbrella organization that includes neoliberals as well as neofascists. Its origins

are rooted in Franco's National Catholicism, with many of its leaders having personal ties to Franco's regime.

57. Maresso, et al., *Economic Crisis, Health Systems and Health in Europe: Country Experience.*

58. Violeta Ruiz Almendral, "The Spanish Legal Framework for Curbing the Public Debt and the Deficit," *European Constitutional Law Review* 9/2 (2013): 189–204.

59. Navarro, *Ataque a la Democracia y al Bienestar.*

60. Navarro, "The Social Crisis of the Eurozone: The Case of Spain"; Navarro, *Ataque a la democracia y al bienestar*, 125.

61. Vicente Navarro, "Los Recortes en la Sanidad Pública," *El Plural*, November 13, 2011, http://www.elplural.com/2011/11/13/los-recortes-en-la -sanidad-publica.

62. Federación de Asociaciones para la Defensa de la Sanidad Pública, "Los Servicios Sanitarios De Las CCAA. Informe 2015 (XII Informe)," http://www.fadsp.org/index.php/sample-sites/manifiestos/1111-los-servicios-sanitarios-de-las-ccaa-informe-2015-xii-informe.

63. Helena Legido–Quigley et al., "Erosion of Universal Health Coverage in Spain," *The Lancet* 382/9909 (2013): 1977.

64. This paragraph relies on Gonzalo Casino, "Spanish Health Cuts Could Create 'Humanitarian Problem,'" *The Lancet* 379/9828 (2012): 1777.

65. Catalonia has its own political institutions and a majoritarian sovereign movement. Regional elections in 2015, which were interpreted in terms of referendum, gave a majority of seats to independent parties, which won 48 percent of the popular vote. The proportion supporting sovereignty is actually greater than 80 percent. The different stance toward health care cuts and privatizations has been a major source of conflict between the anti-capitalist left and Convergencia, thwarting an independentist alliance to break away from Spain.

66. Fourteen percent or €1.5 million (US$1.76 million) since 2010. Catalana Taraffa, Davide Malmusi, Josep Martí Valls, "Mai Mes pot Passar el que ha Passat Amb la Sanitat Catalane," *Catalunya Plural*, January 15, 2016, http://www.eldiario.es/catalunyaplural/opinions/Mai-passar-passat-sanitat-catalana_6_473562657.html.

67. Marine Caralp, "Puerta Abierta a la Actividad Privada con la Autorización de la Generalitat al Consorcio del Clínic," *Catalunya Plural*, July 15, 2015, http://www.eldiario.es/catalunya/diarisanitat/Puerta-autorizacion-Govierno-Consorcio-Clinic_6_409169103.html.

68. "CiU Stepped up the Privatization of Public Health Care," *Café amb Llet*, February 8, 2015.

69. Taraffa, Malmusi, and Valls, "Mai Mes pot Passar el que ha Passat Amb la Sanitat Catalane."

70. Federación de Asociaciones para la Defensa de la Sanidad Pública, "Los Servicios Sanitarios De Las CCAA. Informe 2015 (XII Informe)."

71. Observatori del Sistema de Salut de Catalunya, *Determinants Social I Economics de la Salut Efectes de la Crisi Econòmica Sobre la Salut de la Població De Catalunya Generalitat de Catalunya* (2014), http://observatorisalut.gencat.cat/web/.content/minisite/observatorisalut/contingutsadministratius/observatori_efectes_crisi_salut_document.pdf.

72. Julia de Jodar and David Fernandez, *Cop de Cup* (Barcelona: Edicions S.A., 2012).

73. Jesús García, "Condenado el Exalcalde de Lloret por Aceptar Sobornos de un Empresario," *El Pais*, November 6, 2015, http://ccaa.elpais.com/ccaa/2015/11/06/catalunya/1446805995_762086.html.

74. Jordi Mumbrú, "La CUP Denuncia la Privatización Oculta del Hospital Clínic desde 2009," *Catalunya Plural*, January 10, 2013, http://www.eldiario.es/catalunya/CUP-privatizacion-Hospital-Clinic-beneficiada_0_181282095.html.

75. "Isabel Vallet (CUP): 'No Aguantem que Boi Ruiz Digui que no hi ha Evidències de Privatització de la Sanitat,'" *ARA Barcelona*, April 15, 2015, http://www.ara.cat/politica/Vallet-CUP-Boi_Ruiz-sanitat-privatitzacio_0_1339666135.html.

76. Taraffa, Malmusi, and Valls, "Mai Mes pot Passar el que ha Passat Amb la Sanitat Catalane."

77. "CUP Denuncia que Visc+ Sólo Busca el Lucro para Ciertos Agentes de la Salud," *El Periódico*, February 20, 2015, http://www.elperiodico.com/es/noticias/sanidad/cup-denuncia-visc-busca-lucro-ciertos-agentes-3955304.

78. This paragraph, including the €1.5 billion figure at the beginning, draws on Marea Blanca, *Balanç De Les Polítiques Sanitàries Del Govern Del Sr. Mas (CiU) Amb El Suport Del Sr. Jonqueres (Erc)* (Barcelona: Marea Blanca, 2015), http://www.mareablanca.cat/comunicat-durgencia-de-la-comissio-de-coordinacio-de-la-marea-blanca-de-catalunya/.

79. CUP Alternativa D'esquerres, *Un peu la parlament de Catalunya* (Paisos Catalans: Novoprint, 2015).

80. David J. Hunter, "Will 1 April Mark the Beginning of the End of England's NHS? Yes," *British Medical Journal* 346 (2013): f1951, doi: 10.1136/British Medical Journal.f1951.

81. The following four-point summary draws upon "Privatising the NHS: An Overview," a chapter in Allyson Pollock, *NHS Plc: The Privatisation of Our Health Care* (London; New York: Verso, 2004), 34–80. Also, Charles Webster, *The National Health Service: A Political History* (New York: Oxford University Press, 2002), 140–252.

82. This discussion of the internal market in this paragraph relies on

Pollock, *NHS Plc*, 17–22, 41–42, quote page 17; Webster, *The National Health Service*, 187–92.

83. Ibid., 209–18, 231, 240–41, quote on 210.

84. For critical descriptions of foundation trusts, see Pollock, *NHS Plc*, 71–72; Julian Tudor Hart, *The Political Economy of Health Care: Where the NHS Came From and Where It Could Lead*, 2nd ed. (Bristol, UK: Policy Press, 2010), 141.

85. Paul Krugman, "The Austerity Delusion," *The Guardian*, April 29, 2015, http://www.theguardian.com/business/ng-interactive/2015/apr/29/the-austerity-delusion.

86. Adam Roberts, Louise Marshall, and Anita Charlesworth, *A Decade of Austerity: The Funding Pressures Facing the NHS from 2010/11 to 2021* (London: Nuffield Trust, 2012), http://www.nuffieldtrust.org.uk/sites/files/nuffield/publication/121203_a_decade_of_austerity_summary_1.pdf.

87. John Appleby, "UK's Health and Social Care Spending Plans: More of the Same?," *British Medical Journal* 351 (2015), doi: http://dx.doi.org/10.1136/bmj.h6458.

88. John Appleby, "NHS Spending: Squeezed as Never Before," *The Kings Fund Blog*, October 20, 2015, http://www.kingsfund.org.uk/blog/2015/10/nhs-spending-squeezed-never.

89. Sarah Neville, "The NHS: On Life Support," *The Financial Times*, September 17, 2015, http://www.ft.com/cms/s/0/96838d4a-df8e-11e4-a6c4-00144feab7de.html#axzz4E21szZSf.

90. For instance, as NHS consultant physician David Oliver wrote in response to a report in the *British Medical Journal*, "One person's 'overspend' is another's 'underfunding with services not paid enough to cover their activity costs' depending on how you spin it." Response to Gareth Iacobucci, "NHS Hospitals Post Record Pound 1.6bn Overspend in First Six Months of Year," *British Medical Journal* 351 (2015), doi: http://dx.doi.org/10.1136/bmj.h6305.

91. Appleby, "UK's Health and Social Care Spending Plans: More of the Same?"

92. Raymond Tallis and Jacky Davis, eds., *NHS SOS: How the NHS Was Betrayed—And How We Can Save It* (London: Oneworld, 2013).

93. Both this and the next paragraph rely on the arguments of Allyson Pollack writing with colleagues Peter Roderick, David Price, and others in a number of publications: Allyson M Pollock et al., "A Flawed Bill with a Hidden Purpose," *The Lancet* 379/9820 (2012): 999; Allyson M. Pollock, David Price, and Peter Roderick, "Health and Social Care Bill 2011: A Legal Basis for Charging and Providing Fewer Health Services to People in England," *BMJ* 344 (2012) e1729; Allyson M. Pollock et al.,

"How the Health and Social Care Bill 2011 Would End Entitlement to Comprehensive Health Care in England," *The Lancet* 379/9814 (2012): 387–89; Allyson M. Pollock and David B. Price, "From Cradle to Grave," in *NHS SOS*, 174–203; Allyson. M. Pollock and Peter Roderick, "Why the Queen's Speech on 19 May Should Include a Bill to Reinstate the NHS in England," *British Medical Journal* 350 (2015) h2257; Peter Roderick and Allyson M. Pollock, "A Wolf in Sheep's Clothing: How Monitor Is Using Licensing Powers to Reduce Hospital and Community Services in England under the Guise of Continuity," *British Medical Journal* 349 (2014):g5603, doi: 10.1136/bmj.g5603.

94. This paragraph relies on the publications of Pollock and colleagues as cited in the previous note.

95. Allyson M. Pollock and David B. Price, "From Cradle to Grave," in *NHS SOS*, 188.

96. Peter Roderick and Allyson M. Pollock, "A Wolf in Sheep's Clothing."

97. Adam Gaffney, "Saving the NHS," *Jacobin*, April 26, 2016, https://www.jacobinmag.com/2016/04/nhs–junior–doctors–strike–health–privatization/.

98. Jeremy Corbyn, "Jeremy Corbyn: Thank You All for Making This Happen," *People's Daily Morning Star*, September 13, 2015, https://www.morningstaronline.co.uk/a-d997-Jeremy-Corbyn-Thank-you-all-for-making-this-happen#.VpE6D5MrIcg.

99. "Jeremy Corbyn Launches 'Standing to Deliver,'" http://www.jeremy-forlabour.com/jeremy_corbyn_launches_standing_to_deliver; Jeremy Corbyn, "Labour Must Clean Up the Mess It Made with PFI, and Save the Health Service," *The Guardian*, August 26, 2015, http://www.the-guardian.com/commentisfree/2015/aug/26/pfi-labour-nhs-health-service-private-finance-initiative.

100. As John Lister noted in an interview in *Jacobin*, the Labour Party even under Corbyn has not been as aggressive as it could have been in advancing the cause of the NHS. Gaffney, "Saving the NHS."

101. Richard Seymour, "Anatomy of a Failed Coup in the UK Labour Party," *Telesur*, July 7, 2016, http://www.telesurtv.net/english/opinion/Anatomy-of-a-Failed-Coup-in-the-UK-Labour-Party-20160707-0009.html.

9. Imperialism's Health Component

An earlier version of this chapter appeared in *Monthly Review* 67/3 (July–August 2015): 114–29.

1. Vicente Navarro argued this perspective in an important early work, "The Underdevelopment of Health or the Health of Underdevelopment: An Analysis of the Distribution of Human Health Resources in Latin America," *Politics & Society* 4 (1974): 267–93.

2.   E. Richard Brown, *Rockefeller Medicine Men: Medicine and Capitalism in the Progressive Era* (Berkeley: University of California Press, 1979).

3.   Howard Waitzkin, *The Second Sickness: Contradictions of Capitalist Health Care,* 2nd ed. (Lanham, MD: Rowman & LIttlefield, 2000), chap. 4; Milton Silverman, Mia Lydecker, Philip R. Lee, *Bad Medicine: The Prescription Drug Industry in the Third World* (Stanford, CA: Stanford University Press, 1992); Peter Davis, ed., *Contested Ground: Public Purpose and Private Interest in the Regulation of Prescription Drugs* (Oxford: Oxford University Press, 1996).

4.   William I. Robinson, *A Theory of Global Capitalism: Production, Class, and State in a Transnational World* (Baltimore: Johns Hopkins University Press, 2004); *Latin America and Global Capitalism: A Critical Globalization Perspective* (Baltimore: Johns Hopkins University Press, 2008).

5.   Waitzkin, *The Second Sickness*, chap. 2.

6.   See Barry S. Levy and Victor W. Sidel, eds., *War and Public Health* (New York: Oxford University Press, 2008).

7.   Andrew Carnegie, *The Gospel of Wealth & Other Timely Essays* (New York: The Century Company, 1901).

8.   Ibid., 176.

9.   Brown, *Rockefeller Medicine Men;* Anne-Emanuelle Birn, *Marriage of Convenience: Rockefeller International Health and Revolutionary Mexico* (Rochester, NY: Rochester University Press, 2006); Anne-Emanuelle Birn, Yogan Pillay, Timothy H. Holtz, eds., *Textbook of International Health: Global Health in a Dynamic World* (New York: Oxford University Press, 2009), chap. 2; Marcus Cueto, ed., *Missionaries of Science: The Rockefeller Foundation and Latin America* (Bloomington: Indiana University Press, 1994).

10. Howard Waitzkin, "Report of the World Health Organization's Commission on Macroeconomics and Health: A Summary and Critique," *The Lancet* 361 (2003): 523–26, and *Medicine and Public Health at the End of Empire* (Boulder, CO: Paradigm Publishers, 2011); Anne-Emanuelle Birn, "Gates's Grandest Challenge: Transcending Technology as Public Health Ideology," *The Lancet* 366 (2005): 514–19.

11. Ellen R. Shaffer, Howard Waitzkin, Rebeca Jasso-Aguilar, and Joseph Brenner, "Global Trade and Public Health," *American Journal of Public Health* 95 (2005): 23–34.

12. World Bank, "Poverty Overview," http://www.worldbank.org/en/topic/poverty/overview.

13. Shaffer et al., "Global Trade and Public Health."

14. Ilona Kickbusch, "The Development of International Health Policies—Accountability Intact?" *Social Science & Medicine* 51 (2000): 979–89.

15. "The General Agreement on Tariffs and Trade," GATT 1947, Articles 27–38, https://wto.org.

16. Lori Wallach and Patrick Woodall, *Whose Trade Organization?: A Comprehensive Guide to the WTO* (New York: New Press, 2004).

17. WTO, *World Trade Report 2012*, https://wto.org.

18. Nick Drager and Carlos Vieira, *Trade in Health Services: Global, Regional, and Country Perspectives* (Washington, DC: Pan American Health Organization, 2002).

19. Lori Wallach, "Accountable Governance in the Era of Globalization: The WTO, NAFTA, and International Harmonization of Standards," *University of Kansas Law Review* 50 (2002): 823–65.

20. Wallach and Woodall, *Whose Trade Organization?*

21. Ronald Labonté, Ashley Schram, and Arne Ruckert, "The Trans–Pacific Partnership Agreement and Health: Few Gains, Some Losses, Many Risks," *Globalization and Health* 12/25 (2016): 1–7, doi: 10.1186/s12992-016-0166-8.

22. Marcos Cueto, *The Value of Health: A History of the Pan American Health Organization* (Rochester, NY: Rochester University Press, 2007), chap. 1.

23. Ibid., chap. 2.

24. Ibid., chap. 5; Elizabeth Fee and Theodore M. Brown, "100 Years of the Pan American Health Organization," *American Journal of Public Health* 92 (2002): 12–13.

25. World Health Organization, "Declaration of Alma-Ata: International Conference on Primary Health Care," Alma-Ata, USSR, September 6–12, 1978, http://www.who.int/publications/almaata_declaration_en.pdf; Marcos Cueto, "The Origins of Primary Health Care and Selective Primary Health Care," *American Journal of Public Health* 94 (2004): 1884–93.

26. Commission on Macroeconomics and Health, *Macroeconomics and Health: Investing in Health for Economic Development* (Geneva: World Health Organization, 2001).

27. Ibid., 1.

28. World Bank, *World Development Report: Investing in Health* (New York: Oxford University Press, 1993).

29. Jeffrey Sachs, "The Report of the Commission on Macroeconomics and Health," paper presented at the annual meeting of the American Public Health Association, Atlanta, Georgia, 2001. See also Japhy Wilson, *Jeffrey Sachs: The Strange Case of Dr Shock and Mr Aid* (London and New York: Verso, 2014), chap. 6.

30. Commission on Macroeconomics and Health, *Macroeconomics and Health*, 30–40.

31. World Trade Organization Secretariat and World Health Organization, *WTO Agreements and Public Health: A Joint Study by the WHO and the WTO Secretariat* (Geneva: World Trade Organization, 2002).

32. World Health Organization, *Closing the Gap in a Generation. Commission on Social Determinants of Health* (Sterling, VA: Stylus Publishing, 2008); also available at http://www.who.int/social_determinants/final_report/en/.

33. Anne-Emanuelle Birn, "Gates's Grandest Challenge: Transcending Technology as Public Health Ideology," *The Lancet* 366 (2005): 514–19; Birn, Pillay, and Holtz, *Textbook of International Health*, chap. 2.

34. Countries where progressive governments consolidated and made important gains have always been under relentless attacks from powerful domestic and international neoliberal actors, but these have intensified in the past few years. As we write (fall 2017), countries like Venezuela, Brazil, and Argentina are in social, political, and economic turmoil. In Venezuela, the neoliberal opposition has sought to depose Hugo Chávez's successor, President Nicolás Maduro, with the complaisance of the Organization of American States (OAS) and the European Union. In Brazil, a political elite has impeached President Dilma Rouseff—President Lula Da Silva's successor—on unproved charges of corruption. In Argentina, a neoliberal president was elected after the progressive administrations of Nestor and Cristina Kirchner. The progressive governments of Ecuador and Bolivia remain under permanent threat. In all these countries progressive achievements are at risk, including important gains made in access to health care and public health.

35. Rebeca Jasso-Aguilar and Howard Waitzkin, "Resisting Empire and Building an Alternative Future in Medicine and Public Health," *Monthly Review* 67/3 (July–August 2015): 114–29. See update in chapter 11 of this volume.

10. U.S. Philanthrocapitalism and the Global Health Agenda: The Rockefeller and Gates Foundations, Past and Present

This piece was adapted and updated from Anne-Emanuelle Birn, "Philanthrocapitalism, Past and Present: The Rockefeller Foundation, the Gates Foundation, and the Setting(s) of the International/ Global Health Agenda," *Hypothesis* 12/1 (2014): e8.

We are grateful to Sarah Sexton, Alison Katz, Esperanza Krementsova, Mariajosé Aguilera, Jens Martens, and Lída Lhotská for their support and suggestions.

1. Ron Chernow, *Titan: The Life of John D. Rockefeller, Sr.* (New York: Random House, 1998); William H. Page and John E. Lopatka, *The*

Microsoft Case: Antitrust, High Technology, and Consumer Welfare (Chicago: University of Chicago Press, 2009).

2. William Wiist, *Philanthropic Foundations and the Public Health Agenda* (New York: Corporations and Health Watch, 2011), http://corporationsandhealth.org/2011/08/03/philanthropic-foundations-and-the-public-health-agenda/.

3. Josep Lluís Barona, *The Rockefeller Foundation, Public Health and International Diplomacy, 1920–1945* (New York: Routledge, 2015).

4. Judith Richter, *Public-Private Partnerships and International Health Policy Making: How Can Public Interests Be Safeguarded?* (Helsinki: Ministry for Foreign Affairs of Finland, Development Policy Information Unit, 2004); Jens Martens and Karolin Seitz, *Philanthropic Power and Development: Who Shapes the Agenda?* (Aachen/Berlin/Bonn/New York: Brot für die Welt/Global Policy Forum/MISEREOR, 2015). https://www.globalpolicy.org/images/pdfs/Newsletter/newsletter_15_09_25.pdf.

5. Matthew Bishop and Michael Green, *Philanthrocapitalism: How Giving Can Save the World* (New York: Bloomsbury Press, 2009). The original 2008 subtitle of this book, *How the Rich Can Save the World*, was changed in the wake of the 2008 global financial crisis when it became apparent that the rich were harming rather than saving the world. See website: http://philanthrocapitalism.net/about/faq/.

6. George Joseph, "Why Philanthropy Actually Hurts Rather than Helps Some of the World's Worst Problems," *In These Times*, December 28, 2015, http://inthesetimes.com/article/18691/Philanthropy_Gates-Foundation _Capitalism.

7. David Callahan, *The Givers: Money, Power, and Philanthropy in a New Gilded Age* (New York: Alfred A. Knopf, 2017).

8. This is magnified by other actors, in particular the World Economic Forum's Global Redesign Initiative (WEF GRI), a corporate-led campaign that set out in 2009 to restructure the architecture of global decision making so that UN agencies become just one of many stakeholders in "multi-stakeholder governance." See Judith Richter, "Time to Turn the Tide: WHO's Engagement with Non-State Actors and the Politics of Stakeholder-Governance and Conflicts of Interest," *BMJ* 348 (2014): g3351, http://www.bmj.com/content/348/bmj.g3351; Flavio Valente, "Nutrition and Food: How Government for and of the People Became Government for and by the TNCs," *Transnational Institute*, January 19, 2016, https://www.tni.org/en/article/nutrition-and-food-how-government-for-and-of-the-people-became-government-for-and-by-the.

9. Andrew Carnegie, "The Gospel of Wealth," *North American Review* 148 (1889): 653–54. Carnegie later expanded this presentation to a book, published in 1901; see discussion in chapter 9.

10. John Ettling, *The Germ of Laziness: Rockefeller Philanthropy and Public Health in the New South* (Cambridge, MA: Harvard University Press, 1981).

11. Philanthropy also played an ambiguous role in struggles over government-guaranteed social protections by promoting "voluntary," charity-based, efforts instead. To this day, both nonprofit and for-profit private sectors in the United States play a large part in providing social services, curbing the size and scope of the U.S. welfare state *and* giving private interests undemocratic purview over social welfare.

12. John Farley, *To Cast Out Disease: A History of the International Health Division of the Rockefeller Foundation, 1913–1951* (New York: Oxford University Press, 2004).

13. Marcos Cueto, ed., *Missionaries of Science: The Rockefeller Foundation and Latin America* (Bloomington: Indiana University Press, 1994).

14. Iris Borowy, *Coming to Terms with World Health: The League of Nations Health Organisation 1921–1946* (Frankfurt: Peter Lang, 2009).

15. Anne-Emanuelle Birn and Theodore M. Brown, eds., *Comrades in Health: U.S. Health Internationalists Abroad and at Home* (New Brunswick, NJ: Rutgers University Press, 2013).

16. League of Nations Health Organisation, "International Health Board of the Rockefeller Foundation," *International Health Yearbook* (Geneva: LNHO, 1927).

17. Anne-Emanuelle Birn, *Marriage of Convenience: Rockefeller International Health and Revolutionary Mexico* (Rochester, NY: University of Rochester Press, 2006).

18. Anne-Emanuelle Birn, "Backstage: The Relationship between the Rockefeller Foundation and the World Health Organization, Part I: 1940s–1960s," *Public Health* 128/2 (2014): 129–40.

19. The RF resurfaced at this time to play a small but instrumental role in promoting *selective* primary health care (SPHC), emphasizing scaled-down "cost-effective" approaches, such as immunization and oral rehydration; these became the main plank of UNICEF's child survival campaigns during the 1980s under director James Grant, the son of an eminent RF man, creating bitter and lingering divisions between WHO and UNICEF.

20. Nitsan Chorev, *The World Health Organization between North and South* (Ithaca, NY: Cornell University Press, 2012).

21. Judith Richter, *Holding Corporations Accountable* (London: Zed Books, 2001).

22. Eeva Ollila, "Global Health Priorities—Priorities of the Wealthy?" *Globalisation and Health* 1/6 (2005): 1–5.

23. Debabar Banerji, "A Fundamental Shift in the Approach to International

Health by WHO, UNICEF, and the World Bank: Instances of the Practice of 'Intellectual Fascism' and Totalitarianism in Some Asian Countries," *International Journal of Health Services* 29/2 (1999): 227–59.

24. Deborah Hardoon, "An Economy for the 99%," (Oxford: Oxfam International, 2017), https://www.oxfam.org/en/research/economy-99.
25. Martens and Seitz, *Philanthropic Power and Development*.
26. Page and Lopatka, *The Microsoft Case*.
27. Mark Curtis, "Gated Development—Is the Gates Foundation Always a Force for Good?," Global Justice Now, 2016, http://www.globaljustice. org.uk/sites/default/files/files/resources/gated-development-global-justice-now.pdf.
28. https://www.gatesfoundation.org/Who-We-Are/General-Information/ Foundation-Factsheet. In 2006, Buffett pledged 10 million shares of his Berkshire Hathaway stock to the BMGF, at the time worth US$31 billion. The shares are paid in annual installments. https://www.gates-foundation.org/Who-We-Are/General-Information/Leadership/ Executive-Leadership-Team/Warren-Buffett.
29. Bill and Melinda Gates Foundation, "Global Health Data Access Principles," April 2011, https://docs.gatesfoundation.org/Documents/ data-access-principles.pdf.
30. Anne-Emanuelle Birn, Yogan Pillay, and Timothy H. Holtz, *Textbook of Global Health*, 4th ed. (New York: Oxford University Press, 2017).
31. Bishop and Green, *Philanthrocapitalism*.
32. Linsey McGoey, *No Such Thing as a Free Gift: The Gates Foundation and the Price of Philanthropy* (New York: Verso Books, 2015).
33. David McCoy, Gayatri Kembhavi, Jinesh Patel, and Akish Luintel, "The Bill and Melinda Gates Foundation's Grant-Making Program for Global Health," *The Lancet* 373/9675 (2009): 1645–53; Birn, Pillay, and Holtz, *Textbook of Global Health*. Between 1998 and 2016, for example, Seattle-based PATH (Program for Appropriate Technology in Health), PATH Drug Solutions, and PATH Vaccine Solutions, together the BMGF's largest grantee, received over US$2.5 billion, about 12 percent of the global health and global development grants it disbursed.
34. Birn, Pillay, and Holtz, *Textbook of Global Health*.
35. Bill Gates, "Prepared Remarks, 2005 World Health Assembly," http:// www.gatesfoundation.org/speeches-commentary/Pages/bill-gates-2005-world-health-assembly.aspx.
36. Anne-Emanuelle Birn, "Gates's Grandest Challenge: Transcending Technology as Public Health Ideology," *The Lancet* 366/9484 (2005): 514.
37. Anne-Emanuelle Birn, Laura Nervi, and Eduardo Siqueira, "Neoliberalism Redux: The Global Health Policy Agenda and the Politics

of Co-optation in Latin America and Beyond," *Development and Change* 47/4 (2016): 734–59.

38. Results for Development, "Our Approach," http://www.r4d.org/ about-us/our-approach.

39. Martens and Seitz, *Philanthropic Power and Development*.

40. Jacob Levich, "The Gates Foundation, Ebola, and Global Health Imperialism," *American Journal of Economics and Sociology* 74/4 (2015): 704–42.

41. David Stuckler, Sanjay Basu, and Martin McKee, "Global Health Philanthropy and Institutional Relationships: How Should Conflicts of Interest Be Addressed?" *PLoS Medicine* 8/4 (2011): 1–10.

42. Jessica Hodgson, "Gates Foundation Sells Off Most Health-Care, Pharmaceutical Holdings," *Wall Street Journal*, August 14, 2009, http:// online.wsj.com/article/SB125029373754433433.html.

43. William Muraskin, "The Global Alliance for Vaccines and Immunization: Is It a New Model for Effective Public-Private Cooperation in International Public Health?" *American Journal of Public Health* 94/11 (2004): 1922–25.

44. Reuters, "Merck Exec to Be Gates Foundation CFO," March 31, 2010, http://www.reuters.com/article/idUSN3120 892820100331.

45. See McCoy et al., "The Bill and Melinda Gates Foundation's Grant-Making Program for Global Health." A few investigative journalists and online sites serve as courageous exceptions.

46. William New, "Pharma Executive to Head Gates' Global Health Program," *Intellectual Property Watch*, September 14, 2011, http:// www.ip-watch.org/2011/09/14/pharma-executive-to-head-gates-global -health-program/.

47. Page and Lopatka, *The Microsoft Case*.

48. Curtis, "Gated Development."

49. New, "Pharma Executive to Head Gates' Global Health Program."

50. Anubhuti Vishnoi, "Centre Shuts Health Mission Gate on Bill & Melinda Gates Foundation," *Economic Times*, February 9, 2017.

51. Arun Gupta and Lída Lhotska, "A Fox Building a Chicken Coop?— World Health Organization Reform: Health for All, or More Corporate Influence?" APPS (Asia & Pacific Policy Society) Policy Forum, December 5, 2015, http://www.policyforum.net/a-fox-building-a-chicken-coop/; Catherine Saez, "WHO Engagement with Outside Actors: Delegates Tight-Lipped, Civil Society Worried," *Intellectual Property Watch*, May 24, 2016, https://www.ip-watch.org/2016/05/24/who-engagement-with-outside-actors-delegates-tight-lipped-civil-society-worried/.

52. Donald G. McNeil Jr., "The Campaign to Lead the World Health Organization," *New York Times*, April 3, 2017, https://www.nytimes.

com/2017/04/03/health/the-campaign-to-lead-the-world-health-organization.html.

53. World Health Organization, "Framework of Engagement with Non-State Actors," WHO, 2016, Document WHA69.10, http://www.who.int/about/collaborations/non-state-actors/A69_R10-FENSA-en.pdf.

54. Ann Zammit, "Development at Risk: Rethinking UN-business Partnerships," Geneva, UN Research Institute for Social Development, 2003, http://www.unrisd.org/80256B3C005BCCF9/%28httpPublicat ions%29/43B9651A57149A14C1256E2400317557?OpenDocument; Richter, *Public-Private Partnerships.*

55. Marian L. Lawson, "Foreign Assistance: Public-Private-Partnerships (PPPs)," Congressional Research Service, 2013, http://www.fas.org/sgp/crs/misc/R41880.pdf.

56. Judith Richter, *"We the Peoples" or "We the Corporations"? Critical Reflections on UN-Business "Partnerships"* (Geneva: IBFAN/GIFA, 2003), http://www.ibfan.org/art/538-3.pdf; Eeva Ollila, *Global Health–Related Public-Private Partnerships and the United Nations,* Globalism and Social Policy Programme (GASPP), University of Sheffield, 2003, http://www.aaci-india.org/Resources/GH-Related-Public-Private-Partnerships-and-the-UN.pdf.

57. Katerini T. Storeng, "The GAVI Alliance and the 'Gates Approach' to Health System Strengthening," *Global Public Health* 9/8 (2014): 865–79.

58. William Muraskin, *Crusade to Immunize the World's Children: The Origins of the Bill and Melinda Gates Children's Vaccine Program and the Birth of the Global Alliance for Vaccines and Immunization* (Los Angeles: Global Bio Business Books, 2005).

59. Anne-Emanuelle Birn and Joel Lexchin, "Beyond Patents: the GAVI Alliance, AMCs, and Improving Immunization Coverage through Public Sector Vaccine Production in the Global South," *Human Vaccines* 7/3 (2011): 291–92.

60. Doctors Without Borders, *The Right Shot: Bringing Down Barriers to Affordable and Adapted Vaccines* (New York: MSF Access Campaign, 2015).

61. Global Alliance for Improved Nutrition (GAIN), "Large Scale Food Fortification," http://www.gainhealth.org/programs/initiatives/.

62. Lucy Jarosz, "Growing Inequality: Agricultural Revolutions and the Political Ecology of Rural Development," *International Journal of Agricultural Sustainability* 10/2 (2012): 192–99.

63. Germán Velásquez, "Public-Private Partnerships in Global Health: Putting Business before Health?," Genevan South Centre, 2014, http://www.southcentre.int/wp-content/uploads/2014/02/RP49_PPPs-and-PDPs-in-Health-rev_EN.pdf.

64. Eeva Ollila, "Restructuring Global Health Policy Making: The Role of Global Public-Private Partnerships," in *Commercialization of Health Care: Global and Local Dynamics and Policy Responses,* ed. Maureen Mackintosh and Meri Koivusalo (Basingstoke, UK: Palgrave Macmillan, 2005).

65. Catherine Saez, "Geneva Health Campus: New Home for Global Fund, GAVI, UNITAID by 2018," *Intellectual Property Watch,* February 14, 2017, https://www.ip-watch.org/2017/02/14/new-geneva-health-campus-new-homes-global-fund-gavi-unitaid-2018/.

66. Sandi Doughton and Kristi Helm, "Does Gates Funding of Media Taint Objectivity?," *Seattle Times,* February 19, 2011.

67. Martin Kirk and Jason Hickel, "Gates Foundation's Rose-Colored World View Not Supported by Evidence," *Humanosphere,* March 20, 2017, http://www.humanosphere.org/opinion/2017/03/gates-foundations-rose-colored-world-view-not-supported-by-evidence/.

68. Shack/Slum Dwellers International, "Partners," http://knowyourcity.info/partners/.

69. Callahan, *The Givers.*

70. McNeil, "The Campaign to Lead the World Health Organization."

71. Judith Richter, "Conflicts of Interest and Global Health and Nutrition Governance: The Illusion of Robust Principles," *BMJ* 349 (2014): g5457, http://www.bmj.com/content/349/bmj.g5457/rr.

72. BMZ and the Bill and Melinda Gates Foundation, "Memorandum of Understanding between the German Federal Ministry for Economic Cooperation and Development and the Bill & Melinda Gates Foundation," (Berlin: BMZ and Seattle: BMGF), http://www.bmz.de/de/zentrales_downloadarchiv/Presse/1702145_BMZ_Memorandum.pdf.

73. Bishop and Green, *Philanthrocapitalism.*

74. UN Division for Sustainable Development, "Sustainable Development Goals," 2016, https://sustainabledevelopment.un.org.

75. McGoey, *No Such Thing.*

76. Linda McQuaig and Neil Brooks, *The Trouble with Billionaires* (London: Oneworld Publications, 2013).

77. William I. Robinson, *Global Capitalism and the Crisis of Humanity* (New York: Cambridge University Press, 2014).

78. Russell Mokhiber and Robert Weissman, *Corporate Predators: The Hunt for Mega-Profits and the Attack on Democracy* (Monroe, ME: Common Courage Press, 1999).

79. Curtis, "Gated Development."

80. Hardoon, "An Economy for the 99%."

81. Robert Reich cited in Peter Wilby, "It's Better to Give than Receive," *New Statesman,* March 19, 2008, http://www.newstatesman.com/society/2008/03/philanthropists-money.

82. Alex Daniels and Anu Narayanswamy, "The Income-Inequality Divide Hits Generosity," *Chronicle of Philanthropy*, October 5, 2014, http://www.philanthropy. com/article/The-Income-Inequality-Divide/152551.

83. David McCoy and Linsey McGoey, "Global Health and the Gates Foundation—in Perspective," in *Health Partnerships and Private Foundations: New Frontiers in Health and Health Governance*, ed. Owain D. Williams and Simon Rushton (Basingstoke, UK: Palgrave, 2011).

84. Kenny Bruno and Joshua Karliner, "Tangled Up in Blue: Corporate Partnerships at the United Nations," San Francisco, Transnational Resource & Action Center, 2000, http://www.corpwatch.org/article.php?id=996;

11. Resisting the Imperial Order and Building an Alternative Future in Medicine and Public Health

An earlier version of this chapter appeared in *Monthly Review* 67/3 (July–August 2015): 129–42.

1. Howard Waitzkin and Rebeca Jasso-Aguilar, "Imperialism's Health Component," *Monthly Review* 67/3 (July–August 2015): 114–29.

2. Howard Waitzkin, *Medicine and Public Health at the End of Empire* (Boulder, CO: Paradigm Publishers, 2011), chap. 4.

3. Susanne Soederberg, "From Neoliberalism to Social Liberalism: Situating the National Solidarity Program within Mexico's Passive Revolution," *Latin American Perspectives* 28 (2001): 104–23; Héctor Guillén Romo, *La Contrarrevolución Neoliberal en México* (México City: Ediciones Era, 1997), 13.

4. The work of Samir Amin and Marta Harnecke has influenced our own, for instance, Samir Amin, "Popular Movements toward Socialism," *Monthly Review* 66/2 (June 2014): 1–32; Marta Harnecker, *A World to Build: New Paths Toward Twenty-First Century Socialism* (New York: Monthly Review Press, 2015).

5. Observations in the sections on El Salvador, Bolivia, and Mexico derive from the participatory fieldwork of Rebeca Jasso-Aguilar and the sources cited below.

6. STISS (Sindicato de Trabajadores del Instituto Salvadoreño del Seguro Social, the Union of Workers of the Salvadoran Institute of Social Security) internal document detailing the chronology of the movement (San Salvador: STISS, 2002), in author's possession; Leslie Schuld, "El Salvador: Who Will Have the Hospitals?" *NACLA Report on the Americas 36* (2003): 42–45.

7. Schuld, "El Salvador."

8. SIMETRISSS, "Historical Agreement for the Betterment of the National Health System," Working Paper, San Salvador: SIMETRISSS, 2002).

9.   Lisa Kowalchuck, "Mobilizing Resistance to Privatization: Commun-
     ication Strategies of Salvadoran Health-Care Activists," *Social
     Movement Studies* 10 (2011): 151–73.

10. STISS, internal document.

11. SIMETRISS, "Historical Agreement for the Betterment of the National
     Health System."

12. Ibid.

13. Leslie Schuld, "El Salvador: Anti-Privatization Victory," *NACLA Report
     on the Americas* 37 (2003): 1; Kowalchuck, "Mobilizing Resistance to
     Privatization."

14. Opinión Allendista, "ALAMES Se Suma a la Movilización Mundial
     Contra la Privatización de la Salud," April 10, 2017, http://mpsalvador-
     allendestana.blogspot.com.

15. Alberto García Orellana, Fernando García Yapur, and Luz Quiton
     Heras, *La Guerra del Agua, Abril de 2000: La Crisis de la Política en
     Bolivia* (La Paz: Fundación PIEB, 2003); William Assíes, "David versus
     Goliath en Cochabamba: Los Derechos del Agua, el Neoliberalismo,
     y la Renovación de la Protesta Social en Bolivia," *Tinkazos* 4 (2001):
     106–31.

16. Jim Shultz, "La Guerra del Agua y sus Secuelas," in *Desafiando la
     Globalización: Historias de la Experiencia Boliviana,* ed. Jim Shultz and
     Melissa Crane Draper (La Paz: Plural Editores, 2008), 17–51.

17. This process included the democratic election of a community member
     from each of the three zones in which the city of Cochabamba is
     divided. The Water War victory had energized the community and ini-
     tial participation was high, but enthusiasm and engagement declined
     after a couple of years. A few years later only the southern zone (Zona
     Sur) had sustained a high level of participation, and SEMAPA again
     was plagued by issues of corruption and mismanagement. Analyses
     and explanations of this disengagement and persistent corruption are
     beyond the scope of this chapter, but it is important to underscore one
     key issue: the difficulty of sustaining community engagement in the
     absence of vigorous organization and the construction of a counter-
     hegemonic alternative. The population in the Zona Sur has a history
     of organization and collective action around water issues. People in
     the other two zones do not share such history. Their involvement in
     the water struggle was the result of weariness from weeks of on-and-
     off disruptive protests and outrage at the death of the young protestor,
     and they did not necessarily have an ideological commitment to the
     struggle against privatization or to the transformation of SEMAPA.

18. Howard Waitzkin, Celia Iriart, Alfredo Estrada, and Silvia Lamadrid,
     "Social Medicine in Latin America: Productivity and Dangers Facing

the Major National Groups," *The Lancet* 358 (2001): 315–23; Howard Waitzkin, Celia Iriart, Alfredo Estrada, and Silvia Lamadrid, "Social Medicine Then and Now: Lessons from Latin America," *American Journal of Public Health* 91 (2001): 1592–601.

19. Asa Cristina Laurell, "Interview with Dr. Asa Cristina Laurell," *Social Medicine* 2 (2007): 46–55; Asa Cristina Laurell, "Health Reform in Mexico City, 2000–2006," *Social Medicine* 3 (2008): 145–57.

20. Asa Cristina Laurell, "What Does Latin American Social Medicine Do When It Governs? The Case of the Mexico City Government," *American Journal of Public Health* 93 (2003): 2028–31.

21. Ibid.

22. Ibid.

23. Laurell, "Health Reform in Mexico City, 2000–2006."

24. Ibid.

25. Héctor Díaz-Polanco, *La Cocina del Diablo: El Fraude de 2006 y los Intelectuales* (México City: Editorial Planeta Mexicana, 2012).

26. Laurell, "Interview with Dr. Asa Cristina Laurell."

27. Ibid.

28. For an in-depth analysis of such dialectical process see Rebeca Jasso-Aguilar, "Anti-Neoliberal Struggles in the 21st Century: Gramsci Revisited," *PArtecipazione e COnflitto* 7/3 (2014): 616–56, http://siba-ese.unisalento.it/index.php/paco/article/view/14349/12500; and Rebeca Jasso-Aguilar, "¿Revolución Pasiva, Transformismo, Cesarismo? Una Explicación Gramsciana Alternativa de los Gobiernos Progresistas de América Latina," in Boaventura de Sousa Santos y José Manuel Mendes (orgs.), *Demodiversidad: Imaginando Nuevas Posibilidades Democráticas* (Madrid, Spain: Akal, 2017).

12. The Failure of Obamacare and a Revision of the Single-Payer Proposal after a Quarter-Century of Struggle

1. David U. Himmelstein, Steffie Woolhandler, and the Writing Committee of the Working Group on Program Design, "A National Health Program for the United States: A Physicians' Proposal," *New England Journal of Medicine* 320/2 (1989): 102–8; Steffie Woolhandler, David U. Himmelstein, Marcia Angell, Quentin D. Young, and the Physicians' Working Group for Single-Payer National Health Insurance, "Proposal of the Physicians' Working Group for Single–Payer National Health Insurance," *Journal of the American Medical Association* 290/6 (2003): 798–805.

2. Adam Gaffney, Steffie Woolhandler, David U. Himmelstein, and Marcia Angell, "Moving Forward from the Affordable Care Act to a Single Payer System," *American Journal of Public Health* 106/6 (2016): 987–88.

3. The views expressed in this article are those of the authors, and do not necessarily reflect the views of Physicians for a National Health Program or its members. The exception is our discussion of a national health program, which draws on proposals that have been endorsed by the organization.

4. Paul Starr, *The Social Transformation of American Medicine* (New York: Basic Books, 1982), 3–29, at 29.

5. Indeed, much of this change had already occurred by the early twentieth century. Rosemary Stevens, *In Sickness and in Wealth: American Hospitals in the Twentieth Century* (New York: Basic Books, 1989), 17–51.

6. Ibid., 111.

7. Jill S. Quadagno, *One Nation, Uninsured: Why the U.S. Has No National Health Insurance* (New York: Oxford University Press, 2005), 50–52.

8. Paul Starr, *Remedy and Reaction: The Peculiar American Struggle over Health Care Reform*, revised edition (New Haven: Yale University Press, 2013), 43; Colin Gordon, *Dead on Arrival: The Politics of Health Care in Twentieth-Century America* (Princeton: Princeton University Press, 2005), 75.

9. On the latter development, see Adam Gaffney, "The Neoliberal Turn in American Health Care," *International Journal of Health Services* 45/1 (2015): 33–52.

10. These two points were made in Paul Ellwood's seminal managed care proposal; see Paul M. Ellwood Jr. et al., "Health Maintenance Strategy," *Medical Care* 9/3 (1971): 291–98.

11. Starr, *Remedy and Reaction*, 54.

12. Bradford H. Gray, "The Rise and Decline of the HMO: A Chapter in U.S. Health Policy History," in *History and Health Policy in the United States: Putting the Past Back In*, ed. Rosemary Stevens, Charles E. Rosenberg, and Lawton R. Burns (New Brunswick, NJ: Rutgers University Press, 2006), 318. For the history of the managed care organization (health maintenance organization, or HMO, was the term used earlier for MCO), we largely rely on Gray's work.

13. Philip J. Funigiello, *Chronic Politics: Health Care Security from FDR to George W. Bush* (Lawrence: University Press of Kansas, 2005), 174; Gray, "The Rise and Decline of the HMO," 318.

14. Gray, "The Rise and Decline of the HMO," 318.

15. Starr, *The Social Transformation of American Medicine*, 394.

16. Ellwood et al., "Health Maintenance Strategy," 291.

17. Ibid., 298.

18. Gray, "The Rise and Decline of the HMO," 320.

19. Ibid., 321.

20. Anthony Robbins, "Can Reagan Be Indicted for Betraying Public Health?," *American Journal of Public Health* 73/1 (1983): 12–13.

21. Gray, "The Rise and Decline of the HMO," 323.

22. Ibid., 315.

23. Henry J. Kaiser Family Foundation, *The 2016 Employer Health Benefits Survey*, http://kff.org/health-costs/report/2016-employer-health-benefits -survey/

24. Quadagno, *One Nation, Uninsured*, 161; David U. Himmelstein and Steffie Woolhandler, "Global Amnesia: Embracing Fee-for-Non-Service-Again," *Journal of General Internal Medicine* 29/5 (2014): 693–95. Regarding the problematic impact of for-profit care more generally, see Steffie Woolhandler and David U. Himmelstein, "When Money Is the Mission—the High Costs of Investor-Owned Care," *New England Journal of Medicine* 341/6 (1999): 444–46.

25. Responding to the paltry asthma treatment received by her son, Helen Hunt's character in *As Good As It Gets* exclaims, "Fucking HMO bastard pieces of shit," to which the non-HMO physician responds shortly thereafter, "It's okay. Actually, I think that's their technical name." See Diane Levick, "In Real Life, as in Film, HMO's Image Is Ailing," *Hartford Courant*, November 26, 1997, http://articles.courant.com/1997-11-26/news/9711260206_1_managed-kaiser-hmos-health.

26. Regarding Wofford, see Funigiello, *Chronic Politics*, 203.

27. Jacob S. Hacker, "The Historical Logic of National Health Insurance: Structure and Sequence in the Development of British, Canadian, and U.S. Medical Policy," *Studies in American Political Development* 12/1 (1998): 124.

28. This was the Jackson Hole Group, which produced the "Jackson Hole Plan" of managed competition, adopted but modified by Clinton. Funigiello, *Chronic Politics*, 206.

29. Among others, Vicente Navarro, *The Politics of Health Policy: The US Reforms, 1980–1994* (Cambridge, MA: Blackwell, 1994).

30. Joseph White, "Markets and Medical Care: The United States, 1993–2005," *Milbank Quarterly* 85/3 (2007): 395–448.

31. Samuel H. Zuvekas and Joel W. Cohen, "Paying Physicians by Capitation: Is the Past Now Prologue?," *Health Affairs* 29/9 (2010): 1666–61; Robert J. Blendon et al., "Understanding the Managed Care Backlash," *Health Affairs* 17/4 (1998): 80–94.

32. White, "Markets and Medical Care," 415.

33. Michael Sparer, "Medicaid Managed Care: Costs, Access, and Quality of Care," in *The Synthesis Project* (Princeton, NJ: Robert Wood Johnson Foundation, 2012), http://www.rwjf.org/content/dam/farm/reports/reports/2012/rwjf401106, 3–4.

34.   The discussion of Aetna in this and the following paragraph is based on a methodical 2004 case study of Aetna authored by health economist James Robinson, who undertook interviews with insiders as well as extensive financial analyses. James C. Robinson, "From Managed Care to Consumer Health Insurance: The Fall and Rise of Aetna," *Health Affairs* 23/2 (2004): 43–55.

35.   Robinson, "From Managed Care to Consumer Health Insurance."

36.   Steffie Woolhandler and David U. Himmelstein, "Consumer Directed Healthcare: Except for the Healthy and Wealthy It's Unwise," *Journal of General Internal Medicine* 22/6 (2007): 879–81.

37.   A point made by Timothy S. Jost, *Health Care at Risk: A Critique of the Consumer-Driven Movement* (Durham, NC: Duke University Press, 2007), 42.

38.   For instance, as discussed in various venues by Regina Herzlinger at the Harvard Business School.

39.   Robert H. Brook et al., "Does Free Care Improve Adults' Health? Results from a Randomized Controlled Trial," *New England Journal of Medicine* 309/23 (1983): 1426–34.

40.   For instance, see Martin S. Feldstein, "The Welfare Loss of Excess Health Insurance," *Journal of Political Economy* 81/2 (1973): 251–80.

41.   Milton Friedman, "How to Cure Health Care," *Public Interest*, no. 142 (2001), http://www.thepublicinterest.com/archives/2001winter/article1.html.

42.   Henry J. Kaiser Family Foundation, *The 2016 Employer Health Benefits Survey*.

43.   Ibid. For example, only 10 percent of workers faced general annual deductibles of $1,000 (for single coverage) in 2006; by 2015, nearly half did.

44.   Ibid.

45.   Actuarial value refers to the average percent cost of health care costs paid for by the insurer, with the remainder the responsibility of the insured individual or family in the form of cost sharing. Co-payments, deductibles, and co-insurance are three different types of cost sharing. Co-payments are a flat fee for a medical service or drug. Deductibles consist of a sum of money that the insured individual pays out of pocket over a time period (generally a year) before insurance "kicks in." Co-insurance is a percent of a medical service or drug paid by the insured individual, with the insurer paying the remainder.

46.   Rudolf Klein, *The New Politics of the NHS*, 7th ed. (London: Radcliffe, 2013), 19.

47.   Starr, *The Social Transformation of American Medicine*, 394.

48.   Esping-Andersen discusses de-commodified social rights within one of the three types of capitalist welfare states. In this book, however,

the implications of de–commodified *health care* receive little attention. Gøsta Esping–Andersen, *The Three Worlds of Welfare Capitalism* (Princeton, N.J.: Princeton University Press, 1990).

49. Starr, *The Social Transformation of American Medicine*, 429.

50. The groundwork for this viewpoint had been laid by Health/PAC. Arnold S. Relman, "The New Medical-Industrial Complex," *New England Journal of Medicine* 303/17 (1980): 963–70.

51. Milt Freudenheim, "Blue Cross Lets Plans Sell Stock," *New York Times*, June 30, 1994, http://www.nytimes.com/1994/06/30/business/blue-cross-lets-plans-sell-stock.html.

52. Ashok Selvam, "For-Profits Rising: Investor-Owned Hospitals Add Market Share, Along with Growing Numbers of Ventures with Not-for-Profit Counterparts," *Modern Healthcare*, March 3, 2012, http://www.modernhealthcare.com/article/20120303/MAGAZINE/303039958.

53. David M. Cutler and Fionna Scott Morton, "Hospitals, Market Share, and Consolidation," *JAMA* 310/18 (2013): 1964–70.

54. Martin Gaynor and Robert Town, "The Impact of Hospital Consolidation," *The Synthesis Project* (Princeton: Robert Wood Johnson Foundation, 2012), http://www.rwjf.org/en/library/research/2012/06/the-impact-of-hospital-consolidation.html; Zack Cooper et al., "The Price Ain't Right? Hospital Prices and Health Spending on the Privately Insured," *National Bureau of Economic Research Working Paper Series no. 21815* (2015): 1–37.

55. Gaynor and Town, "The Impact of Hospital Consolidation." However, a more recent study found that hospital ownership of physician practices allows these systems to command higher health care prices. See Laurence C. Baker, M. K. Bundorf, and Daniel P. Kessler, "Vertical Integration: Hospital Ownership of Physician Practices Is Associated with Higher Prices and Spending," *Health Affairs* 33/5 (2014): 756–63.

56. Ankur Banerjee and Ransdell Pierson, "Anthem to Buy Cigna, Creating Biggest U.S. Insurer," Reuters, July 24, 2015, http://www.reuters.com/article/2015/07/24/us-cigna-m-a-anthem-idUSKCN0PY12B20150724.

57. Ibid.

58. Leemore Dafny, "The Risks of Health Insurance Mergers," *Harvard Business Review,* September 24, 2015, https://hbr.org/2015/09/the-risks-of-health-insurance-company-mergers.

59. Herman quotes Erik Gordon, professor of business at the University of Michigan, who tells him: "It's a cyclical arms race, until antitrust steps in and says that's enough." Bob Herman, "Providers Fear Insurance Mergers Will Intensify Rate Pressures," *Modern Healthcare*, June 27, 2015, http://www.modernhealthcare.com/article/20150627/MAGAZINE/306279934.

60. Melanie Evans, "Expect More Health Systems to Get in the Insurance Game," *Modern Healthcare,* September 28, 2015, http://www.modern-healthcare.com/article/20150928/NEWS/150929889.

61. Quoted in ibid.

62. Melanie Evans, "Cutting out the Middleman: Systems Buying and Developing Insurance Plan," *Modern Healthcare,* March 23, 2013, http://www.modernhealthcare.com/article/20130323/MAGAZINE/303239976; Steven Brill, *America's Bitter Pill: Money, Politics, Backroom Deals, and the Fight to Fix Our Broken Healthcare System* (New York: Random House, 2015), 447.

63. Anna Wilde Mathews and Jon Kamp, "UnitedHealth to Buy 90% of Brazil's Amil for $4.3 Billion," *Wall Street Journal,* October 8, 2012, http://www.wsj.com/articles/SB10000872396390444897304578044390351511894.

64. According to Brill, based on his interview with the CEO, in *America's Bitter Pill,* 447.

65. "Consolidation Efforts Transform the Pharmaceutical Industry," *Blooomberg,* May 1, 2014, https://www.bloomberg.com/graphics/info-graphics/pharma-mergers.html.

66. Andrew Ross Sorkin, Michael de La Merced, and Katie Thomas, "CVS Is Said to Be in Talks to Buy Aetna in Landmark Acquisition," *New York Times,* October 26, 2017, https://www.nytimes.com/2017/10/26/business/dealbook/cvs-aetna.html?_r=0.

67. Brill, *America's Bitter Pill,* 101, 144, 127; Starr, *Remedy and Reaction,* 204–5.

68. Henry J. Aaron and Gary Burtless, *Potential Effects of the Affordable Care Act on Income Inequality* (Washington, DC: Brookings Institute, 2014), http://www.brookings.edu/research/papers/2014/01/potential-effects-affordable-care-act-income-inequality-aaron-burtless.

69. Robin A. Cohen, Emily Zammitti, and Michael E Martinez, *Health Insurance Coverage: Early Release of Estimates from the National Health Interview Survey, 2016.* Washington DC: National Center for Health Statistics, 2017. https://www.cdc.gov/nchs/data/nhis/earlyrelease/insur201705.pdf.

70. Congressional Budget Office, *Insurance Coverage Provisions of the Affordable Care Act—CBO's March 2015 Baseline,* https://www.cbo.gov/sites/default/files/recurringdata/51298-2015-03-aca.pdf.

71. "Health Policy Brief: Next Steps for ACOs," *Health Affairs,* January 31, 2012, http://www.healthaffairs.org/healthpolicybriefs/brief.php?brief_id=61.

72. Elliot S. Fisher et al., "Creating Accountable Care Organizations: The Extended Hospital Medical Staff," *Health Affairs* 26/1 (2007): w44-w57.

73. *Summary of Final Rule Provisions for Accountable Care Organizations Under the Medicare Shared Savings Program* (Washington DC: Department of Health and Human Services and Center for Medicare & Medicaid Services, 2014), https://www.cms.gov/medicare/medi-care-fee-for-service-payment/sharedsavingsprogram/downloads/aco_summary_factsheet_icn907404.pdf.

74. Richard M. Scheffler, "Accountable Care Organizations: Integrated Care Meets Market Power," *Journal of Health Politics, Policy and Law* 40/4 (2015): 633–38.

75. Himmelstein and Woolhandler, "Global Amnesia."

76. HealthPocket, "2016 Affordable Care Act Market Brings Higher Average Premiums for Unsubsidized," https://www.healthpocket.com/healthcare-research/infostat/2016-obamacare-premiums-deductibles - .Vlymi9-rQch.

77. Sara R. Collins et al., "The Problem of Underinsurance and How Rising Deductibles Will Make It Worse—Findings from the Commonwealth Fund Biennial Health Insurance Survey," Commonwealth Fund, May 2015, http://www.commonwealthfund.org/publications/issue-briefs/2015/may/problem-of-underinsurance.

78. The following discussion draws on this proposal as well as the organizations' previous two proposals. Himmelstein, Woolhandler et al., "A National Health Program for the United States: A Physicians' Proposal"; Woolhandler et al., "Proposal of the Physicians' Working Group for Single-Payer National Health Insurance"; Gaffney et al., "Moving Forward from the Affordable Care Act to a Single-Payer System."

79. Steffie Woolhandler, Terry Campbell, and David U. Himmelstein, "Costs of Health Care Administration in the United States and Canada," *New England Journal of Medicine* 349/8 (2003): 768–75; David U. Himmelstein et al., "A Comparison of Hospital Administrative Costs in Eight Nations: US Costs Exceed All Others by Far," *Health Affairs* 33/9 (2014): 1586–94; Aliya Jiwani et al., "Billing and Insurance-Related Administrative Costs in United States' Health Care: Synthesis of Micro-Costing Evidence," *BMC Health Services Research* 14 (2014): 556, doi: 10.1186/s12913-014-0556-7.

80. Himmelstein et al., "A Comparison of Hospital Administrative Costs in Eight Nations: US Costs Exceed All Others by Far."

81. Steffie Woolhandler and David Himmelstein. "Single-Payer Reform: The Only Way to Fulfill the President's Pledge of More Coverage, Better Benefits, and Lower Costs," *Annals of Internal Medicine* 166/8 (2017): 587–588.

82. *H.R. 1628, the American Health Care Act, Incorporating Manager's*

Amendments 4, 5, 24, and 25 (Washington DC: Congressional Budget Office, 2017), https://www.cbo.gov/publication/52516.

13. Overcoming Pathological Normalcy: Mental Health Challenges in the Coming Transformation

This chapter has been adapted from a longer article, Carl Ratner, "The Generalized Pathology of Our Era," in *International Critical Thought* 7/1 (2017), DOI: 10.1080/21598282.2017.1287586.

1. Erich Fromm, *The Pathology of Normalcy* (New York: American Mental Health Foundation Books, 2010).

2. Jos Lelieveld et al., "The Contribution of Outdoor Air Pollution Sources to Premature Mortality on a Global Scale," *Nature* 525 (Sept. 17, 2015): 367–71, doi:10.1038/nature15371.

3. Dan Levin, "Air Pollution in China Is Tied to 1.6 Million Deaths a Year," *New York Times*, August 14, 2015.

4. Howard Waitzkin, "The Commodification of Health Care and the Search for a Universal Health Program in the United States," October 12, 2012, http://www.pnhp.org/news/2012/october/howard-waitzkin-on-commodification-and-the-search-for-a-universal-health-program.

5. Carl Ratner, "Recovering and Advancing Martin-Baro's Ideas about Psychology, Culture, and Social Transformation," *Theory and Critique of Psychology,* 2015, http://www.teocripsi.com; available at www.sonic.net/~cr2.

6. See Jennifer M. Silva, *Coming Up Short: Working-Class Adulthood in an Age of Uncertainty* (New York: Oxford University Press, 2015), for an excellent ethnography of this condition.

7. Alexander Burns and Giovanni Russonello, "Half of New Yorkers Say They Are Barely or Not Getting By, Poll Shows," *New York Times,* November 19, 2015, http://www.nytimes.com/2015/11/19/nyregion/half-of-new-yorkers-say-they-are-barely-or-not-getting-by-poll-shows.html.

8. Chuck Collins and Josh Hoxie, "Billionaire Bonanza: The Forbes 400 and the Rest of US," Institute for Policy Studies, November 2017, https://inequality.org/wp-content/uploads/2017/11/BILLIONAIRE-BONANZA-2017-Embargoed.pdf; Noah Kirsch, "The 3 Richest Americans Hold More Wealth than Bottom 50% of the Country, Study Finds," *Forbes*, November 9, 2017, https://www.forbes.com/sites/noahkirsch/2017/11/09/the-3-richest-americans-hold-more-wealth-than-bottom-50-of-country-study-finds/#346860f33cf8;

9. "The American Middle Class Is Losing Ground," Pew Research Center, December 9, 2015, http://www.pewsocialtrends.org/2015/12/09/the-american-middle-class-is-losing-ground/.

10. Carl Ratner and El-Sayed El-Badwi, "A Cultural Psychological Theory of Mental Illness, Supported by Research in Saudi Arabia," *Journal of Social Distress and the Homeless* 20/3–4 (2011): 217–74, www.sonic. net/~cr2.

11. Carl Ratner, *Vygotsky's Cultural-Historical Psychology and Its Contemporary Applications* (New York: Plenum, 1991), chap. 6; Carl Ratner, *Macro Cultural Psychology: A Political Philosophy of Mind* (New York: Oxford University Press, 2012), 194–97.

12. Vicente Berdayes and John W. Murphy, *Neoliberalism, Economic Radicalism, and the Normalization of Violence* (New York: Springer, 2016).

13. Henry A. Giroux, "Murder, Incorporated: Guns and the Growing Culture of Violence in the US," *Truthout,* October 7, 2015, http://www.truth-out.org/news/item/33127-murder-incorporated-guns-and-the-growing-culture-of-violence-in-the-us. See also Sharon Lafraniere, Sarah Cohen, and Richard A. Oppel Jr., "How Often Do Mass Shootings Occur? On Average, Every Day, Records Show," *New York Times,* December 2, 2015, http://www.nytimes.com/2015/12/03/us/how-often-do-mass-shootings-occur-on-average-every-day-records-show.html.

14. N. R. Kleinfield, Russ Buettner, David W. Chen, and Nikita Stewart, "Killers Fit a Profile, but so Do Many Others," *New York Times*, October 2, 2014, http://www.nytimes.com/2015/10/04/us/mass-murderers-fit-profile-as-do-many-others-who-dont-kill.html.

15. Nicholas Bakalar, "Childhood: Pesticides Tied to Youth Cancer," *New York Times,* September 22, 2015, http://well.blogs.nytimes.com/2015/09/21/pesticides-tied-to-childhood-cancers/.

16. Darryl Fears, "Global Warming Worsened the California Drought, Scientists Say," *Washington Post*, August 20, 2015, https://www.washingtonpost.com/news/energy-environment/wp/2015/08/20/scientists-say-global-warming-has-made-californias-drought-25-percent-worse/?utm_term=.5fe197a4287a.

17. Ratner, *Vygotsky's Cultural-Historical Psychology and Its Contemporary Applications*, 281–82.

18. Drugs widely prescribed to treat severe post-traumatic stress symptoms for veterans are no more effective than placebos and come with serious side effects, including weight gain and fatigue: Benedict Carey, "Anti-Psychotic Use Is Questioned for Combat Stress," *New York Times,* August 3, 2011. Regarding the limited evidence of effectiveness for other psychotropic medications, see Marcia Angell, "The Epidemic of Mental Illness: Why?," *New York Review of Books* 58/11 (June 23, 2011): 20–22; Robert Whitaker, *Anatomy of an Epidemic: Magic Bullets,*

Psychiatric Drugs, and the Astonishing Rise of Mental Illness in America (New York: Crown, 2011).

19. Philip Cushman, "Confronting Sullivan's Spider: Hermeneutics and the Politics of Therapy," *Contemporary Psychoanalysis* 30 (1994): 801–44.

20. Joel Best, "Whatever Happened to Social Pathology? Conceptual Fashions and the Sociology of Deviance," *Sociological Spectrum* 26 (2006): 533–46.

21. Alan Schwarz, "Still in a Crib, Yet Being Given Antipsychotics," *New York Times*, December 11, 2015, http://www.nytimes.com/2015/12/11/us/psychiatric-drugs-are-being-prescribed-to-infants.html.

22. Jason Whitesel, *Fat Gay Men: Girth, Mirth, and the Politics of Stigma* (New York: New York University Press, 2014); May Friedman, "Mother Blame, Fat Shame, and Moral Panic: 'Obesity' and Child Welfare," *Fat Studies* 4 (2015): 14–27.

23. Michael Moss, *Salt, Sugar, Fat: How the Food Giants Hooked Us* (New York: Random House, 2013).

14. Confronting the Social and Environmental Determinants of Health

1. Mark Hall and Richard Lord, "Obamacare: What the Affordable Care Act Means for Patients and Physicians," *BMJ* 349/7 (2014): g5376, doi: 10.1136/bmj.g5376; Rifat Atun et al., "Health-System Reform and Universal Health Coverage in Latin America," *The Lancet* 385/9974 (2015): 1230–47; Howard Waitzkin and Ida Hellander, "Obamacare: The Neoliberal Model Comes Home to Roost in the United States—If We Let It," *Monthly Review* 68/1 (2016): 1–18. See also chapter 7 in this volume.

2. Commission on Social Determinants of Health, *Closing the Gap in a Generation: Health Equity through Action on the Social Determinants of Health: Final Report of the Commission on Social Determinants of Health* (Geneva: World Health Organization, 2008).

3. Stephen Frankel, "Commentary: Medical Care and the Wider Influences upon Population Health: A False Dichotomy," *International Journal of Epidemiology* 30/6 (2001): 1267–68.

4. Commission on Social Determinants of Health, *Closing the Gap in a Generation*.

5. William H. McNeill, *Plagues and Peoples* (New York: Anchor, 2010).

6. Jessica Pearce-Duvet, "The Origin of Human Pathogens: Evaluating the Role of Agriculture and Domestic Animals in the Evolution of Human Disease," *Biological Reviews* 81/3 (2006): 369–82; Nathan D. Wolfe, Claire P. Dunavan, and Jared Diamond, "Origins of Major Human Infectious Diseases," *Nature* 447/7142 (2007): 279–83.

7. Sheldon J. Watts, *Epidemics and History: Disease, Power, and Imperialism* (New Haven: Yale University Press, 1997); James Colgrove, "The McKeown Thesis: A Historical Controversy and Its Enduring Influence," *American Journal of Public Health* 92/5 (2002): 725–29.

8. John B. McKinlay and Sonja M. McKinlay, "The Questionable Contribution of Medical Measures to the Decline of Mortality in the United States in the Twentieth Century," *Milbank Memorial Fund Quarterly* 55/3 (1977): 405–28; Thomas McKeown, *The Role of Medicine: Dream, Mirage or Nemesis?* (Oxford: Basil Blackwell, 1979).

9. Richard Kock, Robyn Alders, and Robert G. Wallace. "Wildlife, Wild Food, Food Security and Human Society," in *Animal Health and Biodiversity—Preparing for the Future: Illustrating Contributions to Public Health,* Compendium of the OIE Global Conference on Wildlife, Paris, February 23–25, 2011, 71–79.

10. Patricia O'Campo and James R. Dunn, eds., *Rethinking Social Epidemiology: Towards a Science of Change* (New York: Springer, 2011).

11. Commission on Social Determinants of Health, *Closing the Gap in a Generation.*

12. Michael Marmot, *The Health Gap: The Challenge of an Unequal World* (London: Bloomsbury Publishing, 2015).

13. Richard G. Wilkinson and Michael Marmot, *Social Determinants of Health: The Solid Facts* (Geneva: World Health Organization, 2003).

14. Friedrich Engels, *The Condition of the Working Class in England* (London: Penguin, 1987); Carles Muntaner et al., "Two Decades of Neo-Marxist Class Analysis and Health Inequalities: A Critical Reconstruction," *Social Theory & Health* 13/3–4 (2015): 267–87; Carles Muntaner, "On the Future of Social Epidemiology—A Case for Scientific Realism," *American Journal of Epidemiology* 178/6 (2013): 852–57.

15. Don Nutbeam, "Inter-Sectoral Action for Health: Making It Work," *Health Promotion International* 9/3 (1994): 143–44.

16. Joy E. Lawn et al., "Alma-Ata 30 Years On: Revolutionary, Relevant, and Time to Revitalize," *The Lancet* 372/9642 (2008): 917–27; Ketan Shankardass et al., "A Scoping Review of Intersectoral Action for Health Equity Involving Governments," *International Journal of Public Health* 57/1 (2016): 25–33; Hege Hofstad, "The Ambition of Health in All Policies in Norway: The Role of Political Leadership and Bureaucratic Change," *Health Policy* 120/5 (2016): 567–75.

17. Stephen W. Hwang et al., "Ending Homelessness among People with Mental Illness: The At Home/Chez Soi Randomized Trial of a Housing First Intervention in Toronto," *BMC Public Health* 12/1 (2012): 787.

18. Timo Ståhl et al., *Health in All Policies. Prospects and Potentials* (Helsinki:

Finnish Ministry of Social Affairs and Health, 2006); Shankardass et al., "A Scoping Review of Intersectoral Action for Health Equity Involving Governments."

19. Halfdan Mahler, "Blueprint for Health for All," *WHO Chronicle* 31/12 (1977): 491–98; G. Gunatilleke et al., *Intersectoral Action for Health: Sri Lanka Study* (Sri Lanka: Marga Institute, 1984); Public Health Agency of Canada and World Health Organization, *Health Equity through Intersectoral Action: An Analysis of 18 Country Case Studies* (Ottawa, Ont.: PHAC & WHO, 2008).

20. PHAC and WHO, *Health Equity through Intersectoral Action*; Carles Muntaner and H. Chung, "Political Commitment for Intersectoral Action on Health Equity in Urban Settings," Proceedings of the Seventh Global Conference on Health Promotion. Promoting Health and Development: Closing the Implementation Gap, Nairobi, Kenya, 2009; Kimmo Leppo et al., *Health in All Policies: Seizing Opportunities, Implementing Policies* (Helsinki: Ministry of Social Affairs and Health, 2013); Shankardass et al., "A Scoping Review of Intersectoral Action for Health Equity Involving Governments."

21. Mark MacCarthy, "Transport and Health," in *Social Determinants of Health*, ed. Richard Wilkinson and Michael Marmot (Oxford: Oxford University Press, 2003).

22. World Health Organization, *Global Status Report on Road Safety 2015* (Geneva: WHO, 2015), http://apps.who.int/iris/bitstream/.10665/189242/1/9789241565066_eng.pdf; Sharon Chekijian et al., "The Global Burden of Road Injury: Its Relevance to the Emergency Physician," *Emergency Medicine International* (2014):139219, doi: 10.1155/2014/139219.

23. Rafael Lozano et al., "Global and Regional Mortality from 235 Causes of Death for 20 Age Groups in 1990 and 2010: A Systematic Analysis for the Global Burden of Disease Study 2010," *The Lancet* 380/9859 (2013): 2095–128.

24. José A. Tapia and Ana V. Diez Roux, "Life and Death during the Great Depression," *Proceedings of the National Academy of Sciences* 106/41 (2009): 17290–5.

25. MacCarthy, "Transport and Health."

26. Matts-Åke Belin, Per Tillgren, and Evert Vedung, "Vision Zero—A Road Safety Policy Innovation," *International Journal of Injury Control and Safety Promotion* 19/2 (2012): 171–79; Lars Hultkrantz, Gunnar Lindberg, and Camilla Andersson, "The Value of Improved Road Safety," *Journal of Risk and Uncertainty* 32/2 (2006): 151–70; World Health Organization, *Global Status Report on Road Safety 2013: Supporting a Decade of Action* (Geneva: World Health Organization, 2013).

27. Patrick Morency et al., "Neighborhood Social Inequalities in Road Traffic Injuries: The Influence of Traffic Volume and Road Design," *American Journal of Public Health* 102/6 (2012): 1112–19.
28. World Health Organization, *Health in All Policies: Helsinki Statement. Framework for Country Action* (Geneva: WHO, 2014).
29. Sandro Galea, ed., *Macrosocial Determinants of Population Health* (New York: Springer, 2007); Carles Muntaner and Vicente Navarro, "Conclusion: Political, Economic, and Cultural Determinants of Population Health—A Research Agenda," in *Political and Economic Determinants of Population Health and Well-Being: Controversies and Developments*, ed. Vicente Navarro and Carles Muntaner (Amityville, NY: Baywood Publishing, 2004); Howard Waitzkin, "Political Economic Systems and the Health of Populations: Historical Thought and Current Directions," in *Macrosocial Determinants of Population Health*, ed. Sandro Galea (New York: Springer, 2007).
30. Michael Marmot, "Social Determinants of Health Inequalities," *The Lancet* 365/9464 (2005): 1099–104.
31. Vicente Navarro et al., "Politics and Health Outcomes," *The Lancet* 368/9540 (2006): 1033–37; Marta Harnecker, *A World to Build: New Paths toward Twenty-First Century Socialism* (New York: Monthly Review Press, 2015).
32. G. Gunatilleke et al., *Intersectoral Action for Health: Sri Lanka Study* (Sri Lanka: Marga Institute, 1984); Carles Muntaner et al., "History Is Not Over: The Bolivarian Revolution, Barrio Adentro, and Health Care in Venezuela," in *The Revolution in Venezuela: Social and Political Change under Chávez*, ed. Thomas Ponniah and Jonathan Eastwood (Cambridge, MA: Harvard University Press, 2011); Daniel López-Cevallos, Chunhuei Chi, and Fernando Ortega, "Equity-Based Considerations for Transforming the Ecuadorian Health System," *Revista de Salud Pública* 16/3 (2014): 347–60; Davide Rasella et al., "Effect of a Conditional Cash Transfer Programme on Childhood Mortality: A Nationwide Analysis of Brazilian Municipalities," *The Lancet* 382/9886 (2013): 57–64.
33. Marie-France Raynault and Dominique Côté, *Scandinavian Common Sense: Policies to Tackle Social Inequalities in Health* (Montreal: Baraka Books, 2015).
34. Ibid.; Olle Lundberg et al., *The Nordic Experience: Welfare States and Public Health (NEWS)*, Health Equity Studies No. 12 (Stockholm: Centre for Health Equity Studies, 2008).
35. Lundberg et al., *The Nordic Experience*.
36. Andrea Gazzinelli et al., "A Research Agenda for Helminth Diseases of Humans: Social Ecology, Environmental Determinants, and

Health Systems," *PLoS Neglected Tropical Diseases* 6/4 (2012): e1603; Takashi Nakaoka et al., "Glocalization of Social and Environmental Determinants of Health," *Journal of Socialomics* 2/1 (2013), http://dx.doi.org/10.4172/2167-0358.1000101; Catherine Machalaba et al., "Climate Change and Health: Transcending Silos to Find Solutions," *Annals of Global Health* 81/3 (2015): 445–58.

37. Richard Levins and Cynthia Lopez, "Toward an Ecosocial View of Health," *International Journal of Health Services* 29/2 (1999): 261–93.

38. Among other sources on climate change and health, see those of the American Public Health Association and World Health Organization at https://www.apha.org/topics-and-issues/climate-change; http://www.who.int/mediacentre/factsheets/fs266/en/. The U.S. government previously provided key sources on this topic but websites have been modified or removed under the Trump administration.

39. Siddhartha Roy, "Lead Results from Tap Water Sampling in Flint, MI During the Flint Water Crisis," Flint Water Study Updates, December 1, 2015, http://flintwaterstudy.org/2015/12/complete-dataset-lead-results-in-tap-water-for-271-flint-samples/.

40. Christopher Ingraham, "This Is How Toxic Flint's Water Really Is," *Washington Post,* January 15, 2016, https://www.washingtonpost.com/news/wonk/wp/2016/01/15/this-is-how-toxic-flints-water-really-is/.

41. David C. Bellinger, "Lead Contamination in Flint—An Abject Failure to Protect Public Health," *New England Journal of Medicine* 374/12 (2016): 1101–3.

42. Mona Hanna-Attisha et al., "Elevated Blood Lead Levels in Children Associated with the Flint Drinking Water Crisis: A Spatial Analysis of Risk and Public Health Response," *American Journal of Public Health* 106/2 (2016): 283–90.

43. Roxanne Nelson, "Crisis in Flint: Lead and Legionnaires' Disease," *Lancet Infectious Diseases* 16/3 (2016): 298–99.

44. Spencer Kimball, "How Austerity Poisoned the People of Flint, Michigan," *DW,* January 22, 2016, http://www.dw.com/en/how-austerity-poisoned-the-people-of-flint-michigan/a-18997520.

45. Sean Crawford, "Viewpoint: The Flint Water Crisis from the Ground Up," *Labor Notes,* January 22, 2016, http://www.labornotes.org/blogs/2016/01/viewpoint-flint-water-crisis-ground.

46. David Rosner, "Flint, Michigan: A Century of Environmental Injustice," *American Journal of Public Health* 106/2 (2016): 200–1; Christopher Ingraham, "Flint's Poisoned Water Was Among the Most Expensive in the Country," *Washington Post,* February 16, 2016, https://www.washingtonpost.com/news/wonk/wp/2016/02/16/flints-poisoned-water-was-the-most-expensive-in-the-country/.

47. Crawford, "Viewpoint: The Flint Water Crisis from the Ground Up."
48. Curt Guyette, "Exclusive: Gov. Rick Snyder's Men Originally Rejected Using Flint's Toxic River," *Daily Beast,* January 24, 2016, http://www.thedailybeast.com/articles/2016/01/24/exclusive-gov-rick-snyder-s-men-originally-rejected-using-flint-s-toxic-river.html.
49. Terese Olson, "The Science Behind the Flint Water Crisis: Corrosion of Pipes, Erosion of Trust," *The Conversation,* January 28, 2016, http://theconversation.com/the-science-behind-the-flint-water-crisis-corrosion-of-pipes-erosion-of-trust-53776.
50. Ibid.
51. Brianna Owczarzak, "GM Says No to Flint Water," October 14, 2014, http://www.wnem.com/story/26785625/gm-says-no-to-flint-water; Michael Moore, "10 Things They Won't Tell You About the Flint Water Tragedy," n.d., http://michaelmoore.com/10FactsOnFlint/.
52. Liam Stack, "Michigan Gave State Employees Purified Water as It Denied Crisis, Emails Show," *New York Times,* January 29 2016, http://www.nytimes.com/2016/01/30/us/flint-michigan-purified-water.html.
53. John P. Leary, "Flint's Bottom Line," *Jacobin,* January 27, 2016, https://www.jacobinmag.com/2016/01/flint-lead-water-crisis-michigan-snyder -emergency-contamination/.
54. Ryan Garza, "These Photos of Flint Kids Will Break Your Heart," *Detroit Free News,* January 23, 2016, http://www.freep.com/story/news/local/michigan/flint-water-crisis/2016/01/23/flint-water-crisis-photos/79244792/.
55. Steve Neavling, "Gov. Snyder Lied: Flint Water Switch Was Not about Saving Money, Records Suggest," *Motor City Muckrake,* January 23, 2016, http://motorcitymuckraker.com/2016/01/23/gov-snyder-lied-flint-water-switch-was-not-about-money-records-show/.
56. Ibid.
57. Paul Eagan, "'Sweetheart' Bond Deal Aided Flint Water Split from Detroit," *Detroit Free Press.* May 12, 2016, http://www.freep.com/story/news/local/michigan/flint-water-crisis/2016/05/11/did-state-give-flint-break-its-water/84238120/.
58. Abby Goodnough, "In Flint, Fears of Showering Bring Desperate Measures," *New York Times,* April 13 2016, http://www.nytimes.com/2016/04/14/us/in-flint-rashes-stirfears-of-showering-as-scientists-hunt-forculprit.html.
59. Daniel Jaffee and Soren Newman, "A More Perfect Commodity: Bottled Water, Global Accumulation, and Local Contestation," *Rural Sociology* 78/1 (2013): 1–28. Jaffee and Newman also draw on Karl Polanyi's concept of fictitious commodities and David Harvey's vision of accumulation by dispossession. On Lauderdale's Paradox, see John

Bellamy Foster and Brett Clark, "The Paradox of Wealth: Capitalism and Ecological Destruction," *Monthly Review* 61/6 (2009), https://monthlyreview.org/2009/11/01/the-paradox-of-wealth-capitalism-and-ecological-destruction/, and John Bellamy Foster, Brett Clark, and Richard York, *The Ecological Rift: Capitalism's War on the Earth* (New York: Monthly Review Press, 2010). See also Robert G. Wallace and Richard A. Kock, "Whose Food Footprint? Capitalism, Agriculture and the Environment," *Human Geography* 5/1 (2012): 63–83.

60. Jaffee and Newman, "A More Perfect Commodity."

61. Sylvain Baize et al., "Emergence of Zaire Ebola Virus Disease in Guinea," *New England Journal of Medicine* 371 (15) (2014): 1418–25; Hiroshi Nishiura and Gerardo Chowell, "Early Transmission Dynamics of Ebola Virus Disease (EVD), West Africa, March to August 2014," *Eurosurveillance* 19/36 (2014): 1–6.

62. World Health Organization, "WHO Ebola Situation Report," August 12, 2015, http://apps.who.int/iris/bitstream/10665/182071/1/ebolasitrep_ 12Aug2015_eng.pdf.

63. Alexander Kentikelenis, Lawrence King, Martin McKee, and David Stuckler, "The International Monetary Fund and the Ebola Outbreak," *Lancet Global Health* 3/2 (2015): e69-e70; Mosoka Fallah et al., "Strategies to Prevent Future Ebola Epidemics," *The Lancet* 386/9989 (2015): 131.

64. Robert G. Wallace et al., "Did Ebola Emerge in West Africa by a Policy-Driven Phase Change in Agroecology?," *Environment and Planning* 46/11 (2014): 2533–42.

65. Michael Morris et al., *Awakening Africa's Sleeping Giant: Prospects for Commercial Agriculture in the Guinea Savannah Zone and Beyond* (Washington, DC: World Bank Publications, 2009).

66. Wallace et al., "Did Ebola Emerge in West Africa by a Policy-Driven Phase Change in Agroecology?"

67. Juliet R. Pulliam et al., "Agricultural Intensification, Priming for Persistence and the Emergence of Nipah Virus: A Lethal Bat-Borne Zoonosis," *Journal of the Royal Society, Interface/The Royal Society* 9/66 (2012): 89–101; Kevin J. Olival and David T. Hayman, "Filoviruses in Bats: Current Knowledge and Future Directions," *Viruses* 6/4 (2014): 1759–88; Raina K. Plowright et al., "Ecological Dynamics of Emerging Bat Virus Spillover," *Proceedings of the Royal Society* 282/1798 (2015): 2014–24.

68. Nur J. Shafie et al., "Diversity Pattern of Bats at Two Contrasting Habitat Types along Kerian River, Perak, Malaysia," *Tropical Life Sciences Research* 22/2 (2011): 13–22.

69. Almudena M. Saéz et al., "Investigating the Zoonotic Origin of the West African Ebola Epidemic," *EMBO Molecular Medicine* 7/1 (2015): 17–23.

70. Rodrick Wallace et al., "Ebola in the Hog Sector: Modeling Pandemic Emergence in Commodity Livestock," in *Neoliberal Ebola: Modeling Disease Emergence from Finance to Forest and Farm*, ed. Robert G. Wallace and Rodrick Wallace (Switzerland: Springer, 2016).

71. Christina L. Noer et al., "Molossid Bats in an African Agro-Ecosystem Select Sugarcane Fields as Foraging Habitat," *African Zoology* 47/1 (2012): 1–11; Peter J. Taylor, Ara Monadjem, and Jacobus N. Steyn, "Seasonal Patterns of Habitat Use by Insectivorous Bats in a Subtropical African Agro-Ecosystem Dominated by Macadamia Orchards," *African Journal of Ecology* 51/4 (2013): 552–61; Christin Stechert et al., "Insecticide Residues in Bats along a Land Use-Gradient Dominated by Cotton Cultivation in Northern Benin, West Africa," *Environmental Science and Pollution Research* 21/14 (2014): 8812–21.

72. Report of a WHO/International Study Team, "Ebola Haemorrhagic Fever in Sudan, 1976," *Bulletin of the World Health Organization* 56/2 (1978): 247; Eric Bertherat et al., "Leptospirosis and Ebola Virus Infection in Five Gold-Panning Villages in Northeastern Gabon," *American Journal of Tropical Medicine and Hygiene* 60/4 (1999): 610–65; J. M. Morvan et al., "Forest Ecosystems and Ebola Virus," *Bulletin de la Société de Pathologie Exotique* 93/3 (2000): 172–75; Allison Groseth, Heinz Feldmann, and James E. Strong, "The Ecology of Ebola Virus," *Trends in Microbiology* 15/9 (2007): 408–16.

73. David Roden, "Regional Inequality and Rebellion in the Sudan," *Geographical Review* 64/4 (1974): 498–516; D. H. Smith et al., "The Nzara Outbreak of Viral Haemorrhagic Fever," in *Ebola Virus Haemorrhagic Fever: Proceedings of an International Colloquium on Ebola Virus Infection and Other Haemorrhagic Fevers*, ed. S.R. Pattyn (Amsterdam: Elsevier, 1978).

74. Robert G. Wallace et al., "Did Neoliberalizing West African Forests Produce a New Niche for Ebola?," *International Journal of Health Services* 46/1 (2016): 149–65.

75. Robert G. Wallace, "Losing Zika for the Trees," *Farming Pathogens* blog, February 26, 2016, https://farmingpathogens.wordpress.com/2016/02/26/losing-zika-for-the-trees/; Rodrick Wallace, Luis Chaves, Luke Bergmann, Constância Ayres, Lenny Hogerwerf, Richard Kock, and Robert G. Wallace, *Clear-Cutting Disease Control: Capital-Led Deforestation, Public Health Austerity, and Vector-Borne Infection.* (Switzerland: Springer, 2018)

76. Greg Botelho, "Zika Virus 'Spreading Explosively,' WHO Leader Says," February 20, 2016, http://www.cnn.com/2016/01/28/health/zika-virus-global-response/.

77. Christian Brannstrom, "South America's Neoliberal Agricultural

Frontiers: Places of Environmental Sacrifice or Conservation Opportunity," *AMBIO: A Journal of the Human Environment* 38/3 (2009): 141–49.

78.   Cleide M. de Albuquerque et al., "Primeiro Registro de Aedes Albopictus em Área da Mata Atlântica, Recife, PE, Brasil," *Revista de Saúde Pública* 34/3 (2000): 314–15.

79.   Nádia C. Aragão et al., "A List of Mosquito Species of the Brazilian State of Pernambuco, including the First Report of Haemagogus Janthinomys (Diptera: Culicidae), Yellow Fever Vector and 14 Other Species (Diptera: Culicidae)," *Revista da Sociedade Brasileira de Medicina Tropical* 43/4 (2010): 458–59; Roberto G. Carvalho, Ricardo Lourenço de Oliveira, and Ima A. Braga, "Updating the Geographical Distribution and Frequency of Aedes Albopictus in Brazil with Remarks Regarding Its Range in the Americas," *Memórias do Instituto Oswaldo Cruz* 109/6 (2014): 787–96.

80.   Jonathan Epstein et al., "Nipah Virus: Impact, Origins, and Causes of Emergence," *Current Infectious Disease Reports* 8/1 (2006): 59–65; Kendall P. Myers et al., "Are Swine Workers in the United States at Increased Risk of Infection with Zoonotic Influenza Virus?" *Clinical Infection and Disease* 42/1 (2006): 14–20; Jay P. Graham et al., "The Animal-Human Interface and Infectious Disease in Industrial Food Animal Production: Rethinking Biosecurity and Biocontainment," *Public Health Reports* 123/3 (2008): 282–99; Jessica H. Leibler et al., "Industrial Food Animal Production and Global Health Risks: Exploring the Ecosystems and Economics of Avian Influenza," *EcoHealth* 6/1 (2009): 58–70; Bryony A. Jones et al., "Zoonosis Emergence Linked to Agricultural Intensification and Environmental Change," *Proceedings of the National Academy of Sciences* 110/21 (2013): 8399–404; Salah Uddin Khan et al., "Epidemiology, Geographical Distribution, and Economic Consequences of Swine Zoonoses: A Narrative Review," *Emerging Microbes and Infection* 2/12 (2013): e92.

81.   Thomas P. Van Boeckel et al., "Global Trends in Antimicrobial Use in Food Animals," *Proceedings of the National Academy of Sciences* 112/18 (2015): 5649–54; Yi-Yun Liu et al., "Emergence of Plasmid-Mediated Colistin Resistance Mechanism MCR-1 in Animals and Human Beings in China: A Microbiological and Molecular Biological Study," *Lancet Infectious Diseases* 16/2 (2016): 161–68; Patrick McGann et al., "*Escherichia coli* Harboring *mcr-1* and *bla*CTX-M on a Novel IncF Plasmid: First Report of *mcr-1* in the USA," *Antimicrobial Agents and Chemotherapy* 60/7 (2016): 4420–21.

82.   Katie Atkins et al., *Livestock Landscapes and the Evolution of Influenza Virulence*, Virulence Team Working Paper No. 1 (Rome: Food and

Agriculture Organization of the United Nations, 2010); Robert G. Wallace, "Breeding Influenza: The Political Virology of Offshore Farming," *Antipode* 41/5 (2009): 916–51; Rob Wallace, *Big Farms Make Big Flu: Dispatches on Infectious Disease, Agribusiness, and the Nature of Science* (New York: Monthly Review Press, 2016).

83. Clayton E. Cressler et al., "The Adaptive Evolution of Virulence: A Review of Theoretical Predictions and Empirical Tests," *Parasitology* 143/7 (2016): 915–30; Samuel Alizon et al., "Virulence Evolution and the Trade-Off Hypothesis: History, Current State of Affairs and the Future," *Journal of Evolutionary Biology* 22/2 (2009): 245–59; Erik E. Osnas, Paul J. Hurtado, and Andrew P. Dobson, "Evolution of Pathogen Virulence across Space during an Epidemic," *American Naturalist* 185/3 (2015): 332–42.

84. Neus Latorre-Margalef et al., "Long-Term Variation in Influenza A Virus Prevalence and Subtype Diversity in Migratory Mallards in Northern Europe," *Proceedings of the Royal Society B: Biological Sciences* 281/1781 (2014): 20140098, doi: 10.1098/rspb.2014.0098.

85. Kennedy F. Shortridge, "Avian Influenza A Viruses of Southern China and Hong Kong: Ecological Aspects and Implications for Man," *Bulletin of the World Health Organization* 60 /1 (1982): 129.

86. Dhanasekaran Vijaykrishna et al., "Long-Term Evolution and Transmission Dynamics of Swine Influenza A Virus," *Nature* 473/7348 (2011): 519–22.

87. Dhanasekaran Vijaykrishna et al., "Evolutionary Dynamics and Emergence of Panzootic H5N1 Influenza Viruses," *PLoS Pathogens* 4/9 (2008): e1000161.

88. Sarah H. Olson et al., "Sampling Strategies and Biodiversity of Influenza A Subtypes in Wild Birds," *PLoS One* 9/3 (2014): e90826; Centers for Disease Control, *Transmission of Influenza Viruses from Animals to People*, August 19, 2014, http://www.cdc.gov/flu/about/viruses/transmission.htm.

89. Rebecca J. Garten et al., "Antigenic and Genetic Characteristics of Swine-Origin 2009 A(H1N1) Influenza Viruses Circulating in Humans," *Science* 325/5937 (2009): 197–201.

90. Susanne Gura, *Livestock Genetics Companies: Concentration and Proprietary Strategies of an Emerging Power in the Global Food Economy* (Ober-Ramstadt, Ger.: League for Pastoral Peoples and Endogenous Livestock Development, 2007), http://www.pastoralpeoples.org/docs/livestock_genetics_en.pdf.

91. Glenn E. Bugos, "Intellectual Property Protection in the American Chicken-Breeding Industry," *Business History Review* 66/1 (1992): 127–68; Ilse Koehler-Rollefson, "Concentration in the Poultry Sector,"

presentation at "The Future of Animal Genetic Resources: Under Corporate Control or in the Hands of Farmers and Pastoralists?" International Workshop, Bonn, Germany, October 16, 2006, http://www.pastoralpeoples.org/docs/03Koehler-RollefsonLPP.pdf.

92. Wallace, *Big Farms Make Big Flu.*

93. Jason Moore, *Capitalism in the Web of Life: Ecology and the Accumulation of Capital* (New York: Verso, 2015).

94. James O'Connor, *Natural Causes* (New York: Guilford Press, 1998).

95. Geofrey Lean, "UK Flooding: How a Yorkshire Town Worked with Nature to Stay Dry," *The Independent,* January 2, 2016, http://www.independent.co.uk/news/uk/home-news/uk-flooding-how-a-yorkshire-flood-blackspot-worked-with-nature-to-stay-dry-a6794286.html.; Robert G. Wallace and Richard A. Kock, "Whose Food Footprint? Capitalism, Agriculture and the Environment," *Human Geography* 5/1 (2012): 63–83; Robert G. Wallace et al., "The Dawn of Structural One Health: A New Science Tracking Disease Emergence along Circuits of Capital," *Social Science & Medicine* 129, Special Issue (2015): 68–77, http://dx.doi.org/10.1016/j.socscimed.2014.09.047.

15. Conclusion: Moving beyond Capitalism for Our Health

1. Congressional Budget Office, *H.R. 1628, the American Health Care Act, Incorporating Manager's Amendments 4, 5, 24, and 25,* https://www.cbo.gov/publication/52516; Congressional Budget Office. "H.R. 1628: Better Care Reconciliation Act of 2017," https://www.cbo.gov/system/files/115th-congress-2017-2018/costestimate/52849-hr1628senate.pdf.

2. Congressional Budget Office, Federal Subsidies for Health Insurance Coverage for People under Age 65: 2016 to 2026, March 2016, https://www.cbo.gov/sites/default/files/114th-congress-2015-2016/reports/51385-HealthInsuranceBaseline.pdf, 17.

3. Steffie Woolhandler, David U. Himmelstein, Marcia Angell, Quentin D. Young, and the Physicians' Working Group for Single-Payer National Health Insurance, "Proposal of the Physicians' Working Group for Single-Payer National Health Insurance," *JAMA* 290//6 (2003): 788–805; Adam Gaffney, Steffie Woolhandler, David U. Himmelstein, and Marcia Angell, "Moving Forward from the Affordable Care Act to a Single-Payer System," *American Journal of Public Health* 106/6 (2016): 987–88.

4. Adam Gaffney, "How Liberals Tried to Kill the Dream of Single-Payer," *The New Republic,* March 8, 2016, https://newrepublic.com/article/131251/liberals-tried-kill-dream-single-payer.

5. Many commentators have made note of this change. For instance, Matthew Yglesias, "Bernie Sanders Is the Future of the Democratic

Party," *Vox*, February 9, 2016, http://www.vox.com/2016/2/9/10940718/bernie-sanders-future-demographics.

6. Frank Newport, "Majority in U.S. Support Idea of Fed-Funded Healthcare System," Gallup, May 16, 2016, http://www.gallup.com/poll/191504/majority-support-idea-fed-funded-healthcare-system.aspx?g_source=Politics&g_medium=newsfeed&g_campaign=tiles.

7. Paul Starr, *The Social Transformation of American Medicine* (New York: Basic Books, 1982), 8.

8. Monte M. Poen, *Harry S. Truman versus the Medical Lobby: The Genesis of Medicare* (Columbia, MO: University of Missouri Press, 1979).

9. Erwin Heinz Ackerknecht, *Rudolf Virchow: Doctor, Statesman, Anthropologist* (Madison: University of Wisconsin Press, 1953); Howard Waitzkin, "One and a Half Centuries of Forgetting and Rediscovering: Virchow's Lasting Contributions to Social Medicine," *Social Medicine* 1/1 (2006): 5–10.

10. Jane Pacht Brickman, "Medical McCarthyism and the Punishment of Internationalist Physicians in the United States," in *Comrades in Health: U.S. Health Internationalists, Abroad and at Home*, ed. Anne-Emanuelle Birn and Theodore M. Brown (New Brunswick, NJ: Rutgers University Press, 2013), 82–100; Jane Pacht Brickman, "Minority Politics in the House of Medicine: The Physicians Forum and the New York County Medical Society, 1938–1965," *Journal of Public Health Policy* 20/3 (1999): 282–309.

11. John Dittmer, *The Good Doctors: The Medical Committee for Human Rights and the Struggle for Social Justice in Health Care* (New York: Bloomsbury Press, 2009), 178–204.

12. Walter J. Lear, "American Medical Support for Spanish Democracy, 1936–1938," in *Comrades in Health*, 65–81; Stephen Gloyd, James Pleiffer, and Wendy Johnson, "*Cooperantes*, Solidarity, and the Fight for Health in Mozambique," in *Comrades in Health*, 184–99.

13. As Brown and Birn describe, "health internationalism" stemmed from two main nineteenth-century sources: the social medicine of thinkers like Virchow and "proletarian internationalism" that flowed from the European socialist tradition. Theodore M. Brown and Anne-Emanuelle Birn, "The Making of Health Internationalists," in *Comrades in Health*, 15–26.

14. This paragraph draws throughout from Howard Waitzkin, *Medicine and Public Health at the End of Empire* (Boulder, CO: Paradigm Publishers, 2011), 172–74, quote on 174. The chapter was co-authored by Rebeca Jasso-Aguilar.

15. Aser García Rada, "Spanish Doctors Protest Against Law that Excludes Immigrants from Public Healthcare," *British Medical Journal* 345 (2012): e5716, doi: 10.1136/bmj.e5716.

16. Tom Burridge, "Spain's Indignados Protest Here to Stay," BBC News, May 15, 2012, http://www.bbc.com/news/world-europe-18070246; Vicente Navarro, "Report from Spain: The Political Contexts of the Dismantling of the Spanish Welfare State," *International Journal of Health Services* 45/3 (2015): 411.

17. Helena Legido-Quigley et al., "Will Austerity Cuts Dismantle the Spanish Healthcare System?," *British Medical Journal* 346 (2013): f2363, doi: 10.1136/bmj.f2363.

18. Aser García Rada, "Privatisation in Spain Provokes Protests among Doctors," *British Medical Journal* 345 (2012): e7655, DOI: 10.1136/bmj. e7655.

19. Aser García Rada, "Spain's Largest Healthcare Privatisation Plan Is Halted," *British Medical Journal* 348 (2014): g1240, doi: 10.1136/bmj. g1240.

20. Raymond Tallis, Jacky Davis, and Jacqueline de Romilly, eds., *NHS SOS: How the NHS Was Betrayed—And How We Can Save It* (London: Oneworld, 2013).

21. Nick Triggle, "Junior Doctors' Row: The Dispute Explained," BBC News, February 11, 2016, http://www.bbc.com/news/health-34775980.

22. Adam Gaffney, "Saving the NHS," *Jacobin*, April 26, 2016, https://www. jacobinmag.com/2016/04/nhs-junior-doctors-strike-health-privatiza- tion; Owen Jones, "Junior Doctors Are Striking for Us All to Save the NHS and to Make a Stand," *The Guardian*, January 12, 2016, http:// www.theguardian.com/commentisfree/2016/jan/12/junior-doctor- strike-save-nhs -stand-up-government.

23. Starr, *The Social Transformation of American Medicine*, 79–144.

24. Ibid., 420–49.

25. John B. McKinlay and Joan Arches, "Towards the Proletarianization of Physicians," *International Journal of Health Services* 15/2 (1985): 161–95.

26. Ibid., 191.

27. Starr, *The Social Transformation of American Medicine*, 446.

28. Chris Conover, "Are U.S. Doctors Paid Too Much?," *Forbes*, May 28, 2013, http://www.forbes.com/sites/theapothecary/2013/05/28/are-u-s- doctors -paid-too-much/#6fd2b04a3e5c.

29. Medical historian Henry Sigerist, for instance, favored salaried physi- cians, noting that it "is not by accident that most progress in medicine has been achieved by physicians in salaried positions." Henry E. Sigerist, *Medicine and Human Welfare* (New Haven: Yale University Press, 1941), 140. Additionally, the most recent iteration of the "Physicians Proposal for Single-Payer Health Care" emphasizes the potential benefits of large integrated health systems though asserts that they should be publicly

controlled. Gaffney et al., "Moving Forward from the Affordable Care Act to a Single-Payer System."

30. This paragraph draws on Dario Azzellini, "The Communal State: Communal Councils, Communes, and Workplace Democracy," *NACLA Report on the Americas*, Summer 2013, https://nacla.org/article/communal-state-communal-councils-communes-and-workplace-democracy.

31. John Bellamy Foster, "Chávez and the Communal State: On the Transition to Socialism in Venezuela," *Monthly Review* 66/11 (2015), http://monthlyreview.org/2015/04/01/chavez-and-the-communal-state.

32. International Conference on Primary Health Care, *The Declaration of Alma-Ata*, September 1978, http://www.who.int/publications/almaata_declaration_en.pdf.

33. Harold Osborn, "'To Make a Difference': The Lincoln Collective," *Health PAC Bulletin* 23/2 (1993): 19–20.

34. Richard M. Garfield and Pedro F. Rodriguez, "Health and Health Services in Central America," *Journal of the American Medical Association* 254/7 (1985): 941–42; Tom Frieden and Richard Garfield, "Popular Participation in Health in Nicaragua," *Health Policy and Planning* 2/2 (1987): 162–70.

35. A number of sources describe these changes. The following section on the roots and impact of the health reforms of Chávez and Barrio Adentro relies on Francisco Armada, Carles Muntaner, Haejoo Chung, Leslie Williams-Brennan, and Joan Benach, "Barrio Adentro and the Reduction of Health Inequalities in Venezuela: An Appraisal of the First Years," *International Journal of Health Services* 39/1 (2009): 161–87; Charles L. Briggs and Clara Mantini-Briggs, "Confronting Health Disparities: Latin American Social Medicine in Venezuela," *American Journal of Public Health* 99/3 (2009): 549–55; Steve Brouwer, *Revolutionary Doctors: How Venezuela and Cuba Are Changing the World's Conception of Health Care* (New York: Monthly Review Press, 2011); Carles Muntaner, Joan Benach, María Páez Victor, Edwin Ng, and Haejoo Chung, "Egalitarian Policies and Social Determinants of Health in Bolivarian Venezuela," *International Journal of Health Services* 43/3 (2013): 537–49.

36. The facts about the genesis of the Barrio Adentro in this paragraph are drawn from: Briggs and Briggs, "Confronting Health Disparities: Latin American Social Medicine in Venezuela," 550; Brouwer, *Revolutionary Doctors*, 80–82.

37. Again, the facts in this paragraph rely on both Brouwer as well as Briggs and Briggs, which cover some common ground. The point about reforms in medical education is drawn specifically from Brouwer, who

describes both the origins of the Barrio Adentro and some direct observations of the operations of the system, together with a discussion of the changed system of medical education. The Briggs and Briggs study provides a valuable look at the Barrio Adentro based on extensive on-the-ground interviews and observations in Venezuela. Briggs and Briggs, "Confronting Health Disparities," 550; Brouwer, *Revolutionary Doctors*, 73–128.

38. Gavin H. Mooney, *The Health of Nations: Towards a New Political Economy* (London: Zed Books, 2012), 175.

39. For a discussion of these many factors, see: Gabriel Hetland, "Why Is Venezuela in Crisis?" *The Nation*, August 17, 2016, https://www.the-nation.com/article/why-is-venezuela-in-crisis/.

40. See Nicholas Casey, "Dying Infants and No Medicine: Inside Venezuela's Failing Hospitals," *New York Times*, May 15, 2016, http://www.nytimes.com/2016/05/16/world/americas/dying-infants-and-no-medicine-inside-venezuelas-failing-hospitals.html; Lizzie Wade, "Public Health Money Woes Cripple Venezuela's Health System," *Science* 345/6196 (2014): 499. On the roots of Venezuela's economic crisis, see Hetland, "Why Is Venezuela in Crisis?"

41. Nicholas Casey, "Hard Times in Venezuela Breed Malaria as Desperate Flock to Mines," *New York Times*, August 15, 2016, http://www.nytimes.com/2016/08/15/world/venezuela-malaria-mines.html; Wade, "Public Health. Money Woes Cripple Venezuela's Health System."

42. Oscar A. Cabrera and Fanny Gómez, "Litigating the Right to Health in Venezuela," in *The Right to Health at the Public/Private Divide: A Global Comparative Study*, ed. Colleen M. Flood and Aeyal M. Gross (New York: Cambridge University Press, 2014), 403; Wade, "Public Health Money Woes Cripple Venezuela's Health System."

43. As Jones notes, for instance, "Whatever its failings, however, Barrio Adentro I is providing health care to a sector that previously went largely ignored." Ian Bruce, "Venezuela: 'It's a Battle between 2 Kinds of Health Care," *TeleSUR*, July 29, 2016, http://www.telesurtv.net/english/news/Venezuela-Its-a-Battle-Between-2-Kinds-of-Health-Care-20160729-0027.html; Rachel Jones, "Hugo Chávez's Health-Care Programme Misses Its Goals," *The Lancet* 371/9629 (2008): 1988.

44. Mooney, *The Health of Nations*, 131.

45. Ibid., 139.

46. Ibid., 139–41; Gavin H. Mooney and Scott H. Blackwell, "Whose Health Service Is It Anyway? Community Values in Healthcare," *Medical Journal of Australia* 180/2 (2004): 76–78.

47. Gaffney et al., "Moving Forward from the Affordable Care Act to a Single-Payer System."

48. Howard Waitzkin, *The Second Sickness: Contradictions of Capitalist Health Care*, 2nd ed. (Lanham, MD: Rowman & Littlefield, 2000), chap. 7.

49. This is not a straightforward issue. Some might, for instance, point to the advent of compulsory sickness insurance under the conservative government of Otto von Bismarck. But two points can be made there. First, scholars typically stress that Bismarck, at least in part, was contending with the growing power of the then frankly socialist Social Democratic Party in his move toward a welfare state. But second, Bismarck's system was not universal. In contrast, the Canadian provincial single-payer systems and the British National Health Service historically have been remarkable in their universality and in their provision of free care.

50. See, for instance, Charles Webster, "Conflict and Consensus: Explaining the British Health Service," *Twentieth Century British History* 1/2 (1990): 148–49.

51. Jacob S. Hacker, "The Historical Logic of National Health Insurance: Structure and Sequence in the Development of British, Canadian, and U.S. Medical Policy," *Studies in American Political Development* 12/1 (1998): 68, 99–100.

52. For some policy roots of the ACA, see Jill Quadagno, "Right-Wing Conspiracy? Socialist Plot? The Origins of the Patient Protection and Affordable Care Act," *Journal of Health Politics, Policy, and Law* 39/1 (2014): 35–56.

53. Quoted by: Stephanie Condon, "Hillary Clinton Single-Payer Health Care Will 'Never, Ever' Happen," CBS News, January 29, 2016, http://www.cbsnews.com/news/hillary-clinton-single-payer-health-care-will-never-ever-happen/.

54. For a discussion of one way forward, see Seth Ackerman, "A Blueprint for a New Party," *Jacobin*, November 8, 2016, https://www.jacobinmag.com/2016/11/bernie-sanders-democratic-labor-party-ackerman/.

55. Adam Gaffney, "Is the Path to Racial Health Equity Paved with "Reparations"? The Politics of Health, Part II, Review of *Black Man in a White Coat: A Doctor's Reflections on Race and Medicine* by Damon Tweedy and *Just Medicine: A Cure for Racial Inequality in American Health Care* by Dayna Bowen Matthew," *Los Angeles Review of Books*, March 7, 2016, https://lareviewofbooks.org/review/is-the-path-to-racial-health-equity-paved-with-reparations-the-politics-of-health-part-ii.

56. Some of these are reviewed in Adam Gaffney, "The Politics of Health: Review of *Beyond Obamacare: Life, Death, and Social Policy* by James S. House," *Los Angeles Review of Books*, October 26, 2015, https://lareviewofbooks.org/review/the-politics-of-health. See, for instance:

Nancy Krieger et al., "The Fall and Rise of US Inequities in Premature Mortality: 1960–2002," *PLoS Med* 5/2 (2008): e46; S. Jay Olshansky et al., "Differences in Life Expectancy Due to Race and Educational Differences Are Widening, and Many May Not Catch Up," *Health Affairs* 31/8 (2012): 1803–13; Gregory Pappas et al., "The Increasing Disparity in Mortality between Socioeconomic Groups in the United States, 1960 and 1986," *New England Journal of Medicine* 329/2 (1993): 103–9.

57. Raj Chetty et al., "The Association between Income and Life Expectancy in the United States, 2001–2014," *JAMA* 315/6 (2016): 1750–66.

58. Anne Case and Angus Deaton, "Rising Morbidity and Mortality in Midlife among White Non-Hispanic Americans in the 21st Century," *Proceedings of the National Academy of Sciences* 112/49 (2015): 15078–83.

59. Marta Harnecker, *A World to Build: New Paths toward Twenty-First Century Socialism* (New York: Monthly Review Press, 2015).

Index

CPSIA information can be obtained
at www.ICGtesting.com
Printed in the USA
JSHW021426020720
6463JS00004B/8